YEATS AND ENGLISH RENAISSANCE LITERATURE

Edward Gordon Craig, mask of the Fool in *The Hour-Glass*; woodcut, from *The Mask*, April 1911.

Yeats and English Renaissance Literature

Wayne K. Chapman

St. Martin's Press   New York

© Wayne K. Chapman 1991

All rights reserved. For information, write:
Scholarly and Reference Division,
St. Martin's Press, Inc., 175 Fifth Avenue,
New York, N.Y. 10010

First published in the United States of America in 1991

Printed in Hong Kong

ISBN 0-312-06017-3

Library of Congress Cataloging-in-Publication Data
Chapman, Wayne K.
　Yeats and English Renaissance literature / Wayne K. Chapman
　　p.　　cm.
　Includes bibliographical references and index.
　ISBN 0-312-06017-3
　1. Yeats, W. B. (William Butler), 1865–1939—Knowledge—
Literature.　2. English literature—Early modern, 1500–1700—
History and criticism—Theory, etc.　3. Influence (Literary,
artistic, etc.)　I. Title.
PR5908.L5C4　1991
821'.8—dc20　　　　　　　　　　　　　　　　　90-22923
　　　　　　　　　　　　　　　　　　　　　　　　CIP

To Marilyn, Charis, and Willy

Contents

List of Plates	viii
Preface	xi
Acknowledgements	xv
List of Abbreviations	xvii
1 Tradition, 'Imitation', and the Synthesis of Content and Form	1
2 Proto-Modern Poet, 1885–1910: Summoning the Renaissance Spirit with Arnold, Pater, and John Butler Yeats	31
3 Yeats and Spenser: Form, Philosophy, and Pictorialism, 1881–1902	68
4 Yeats and the School of Jonson: Books, Masques, Epigrams, and Elegies, 1902–19	102
5 Yeats, Donne, and the Metaphysicals: Polemics and Lyrics, 1896–1929	142
6 Conclusion: The Rapprochement with Milton and Spenser, 1918–39	185
Notes	219
Select Bibliography	269
Index	274

List of Plates

Frontispiece Edward Gordon Craig, mask of the Fool in *The Hour-Glass*. Woodcut, from *The Mask*, April 1911

1a W. T. Horton, *Rosa Mystica*, in *A Book of Images*, intro. W. B. Yeats (London: Unicorn, 1898) p. 57. Courtesy of the National Library of Ireland

1b W. T. Horton, *Be Strong* (*A Book of Images*, p. 61). Courtesy of the National Library of Ireland

2a W. T. Horton, *Sancta Dei Genitrix* (*A Book of Images*, p. 51). Courtesy of the National Library of Ireland

2b Jessie M. King, 'And, thinking of those braunches greene to frame', in *Poems of Spenser*, intro. and sel. W. B. Yeats (Edinburgh: Jack, 1906) facing p. 30. Courtesy of the National Library of Ireland and Thomas Nelson and Sons Ltd, London

3a Jessie M. King, 'And in the midst thereof a pillar placed' (*Poems of Spenser*, facing p. 126). Courtesy of the National Library of Ireland and Thomas Nelson and Sons Ltd, London

3b Jessie M. King, 'And therein sate a Lady fresh and fayre' (*Poems of Spenser*, facing p. 186). Courtesy of the National Library of Ireland and Thomas Nelson and Sons Ltd, London

4. Claude Lorrain, *Landscape: The Marriage of Isaac and Rebekah* (or *The Mill*). Courtesy of the National Gallery, London

5 Engraving by John Pye (1828) after J. M. W. Turner's painting *The Temple of Jupiter Panellenius Restored*. Courtesy of Mr Evelyn Joll, Thomas Agnew and Sons Ltd, London

6 Cabbalistic Tree of Life (simplified)

7 Althea Gyles, front cover of *The Secret Rose* (London: Lawrence and Bullen, 1897). Courtesy of Miss Anne B. Yeats

8a Edward Gordon Craig, *Scene for The Hour-Glass*, in *Plays for an Irish Theatre* (London: Bullen, 1911). Courtesy of the Leonard and Virginia Woolf Library, Washington State University

8b Layout from Yeats's sketch of the scene depicted in plate 8a

9 Samuel Palmer's engraving *The Lonely Tower*, in *Shorter Poems of John Milton* (London: Seeley, 1889) facing p. 30, with Palmer's inscription and commentary from p. 30. Photograph courtesy of the British Library, London

10	Verso inscription by Yeats on Thoor Ballylee photograph (plate 11)
11	Thoor Ballylee, from a photograph used as the basis for T. Sturge Moore's cover design for *The Tower*, 1928. Courtesy of the University of London Library and the Yeats Estate
12	W. B. Yeats, two versions of the House of Alma, marginalia from *The Works of Edmund Spenser*, ed. J. Payne Collier (London: Bell and Daldy, 1862) II, 255. Courtesy of Miss Anne B. Yeats and the Yeats Estate

Preface

This book is largely a study of adaptation and development in the craft of poetry. It considers other genres, especially drama and criticism; but it is at heart a book about poetry viewed from various perspectives in order to understand lines and instances of conscious influence. It is therefore a 'study of influence' – though a singularly inductive one, based on rough and polished materials cast and recast into art. It is also a book about W. B. Yeats's response to English Renaissance literature. The primary aim and the secondary disseveration of literature into a manageable focus imply no special claim for the latter in spite of moments when the impression might seem otherwise. Selected both for convenience and to turn old dust from an interesting bit of entablature beneath the Yeats *imago ficta*, the English Renaissance offers salience and stability to the critic who would approach the problem of influence from the side of the process of composition.

The approach is rigorous and, in its way, Platonic: the figure of Yeats emerges from an assembly of viewpoints arranged in the six chapters of the work, assuming contour and colour as projections of his response to numerous 'old masters' and usually more recent mediators. My assumption is that influence can be measured as a function of adaptation (or imitation as it was understood in the Renaissance) and mediation, which now dominates our impression of the way all types of literary influence operate, owing to the popularity of the anxiety theories, 'misprision' and 'eminent domain'. Certainly, Yeats advised younger writers to imitate his distant peers – Milton, Donne, Jonson and others – because he thought their distance assured that the exercise would be therapeutic. Consonant with Yeats's view, the manuscript exhibits in this study are selective, applying only to those instances in which adaptation issues from the example of some Renaissance craftsman. To the exclusion of others, perhaps, the necessity of selecting may exaggerate the relative strength of an influence, yet the fault may be tolerated in the animation of one's subject. In all cases, reconstruction from unpublished work by Yeats is technically diplomatic and meticulous.

The methodology is an innovation, a development in response to the eclectic bent of Yeats himself. I acknowledge, too, the filial relationship between my work and certain precursors. Of course, these include Richard Ellmann (emphatically) and Harold Bloom – but most especially those genetic scholars of 'the Yeats industry', beginning with Curtis Bradford, Jon Stallworthy, and Thomas Parkinson, followed by David Clark, Michael Sidnell, Phillip Marcus, Richard Finneran and others now at work on the Cornell Yeats edition of the manuscripts. While most of the edition is yet in planning, one is fortunate in having the manuscripts themselves to turn to, most of which are available in the large collections cited in the Acknowledgements. Such resources have allowed several remarkable books on Yeats's poetry in the making and have become essential to scholarship which intends not to be undermined by its subject. Bradford's *Yeats at Work*, Stallworthy's *Between the Lines* and *Vision and Revision*, Parkinson's *W. B. Yeats: Self-Critic and the Later Poetry*, and Clark's *Yeats at Songs and Choruses* are convenient examples. Moreover, Parkinson's work, which is interested mainly in Yeats's sense of poetics as revealed in the printed variants of the early poems and in the manuscripts of the post-1917 period, provides a model for the kind of observation pursuant to this study. He suggests how the transitory 'vestiges of creation' are even yet witnessed in the manuscripts, which survive in abundance.

No one suggests, however, that Yeats's sense of poetics and his poetic practice might be studied with respect to the issue of influence or adaptation. Certainly, no one before has proposed to do so by means of a selection of manuscript materials which testify to his interest in English Renaissance literature and to its impact on his stylistic development. This remains the most challenging objective of this project. Probably in the attempt to be accurate, I have sacrificed the virtue of simplicity. Interwoven by association and perpetuated by mental habits which alter over time, lines of influence converge in individual works, cluster at various stages of Yeats's career, and run their course in the canon. The English Renaissance exerted a *powerful* influence on him, yet its authors were often interpreted in relation to the great Romantics (and vice versa). I see no reason to overlook the poets of one age or promote those of another when they converge in the same texts. The 'adaptive complex' and the 'dyad' within it are two of several terms introduced in this study as inductive generalizations – that is, as attempts to describe what one finds in glimpsing Yeats's mind at moments of creation and to understand his complicated, Anglo-Irish intellectual response to the English Renaissance.

The strategy is a deliberate one. I establish on Yeats's terms this study's approach to influence by documenting 'imitation' before I examine his view of the Renaissance in light of several elder 'mediators', principally Arnold, Pater, and J. B. Yeats. After a brief demonstration of Milton's unsuspected presence in one of Yeats's first published poems, the study focuses on the juvenilia and on the progress Yeats made in his early adaptations of Spenser. The later chapters on Jonson and Donne dwell mainly on the developments of Yeats's middle period, during which he read an impressive number of works by English Renaissance writers. The books his daughter inherited from him and the endorsements he made in his lifetime about the vitality of those authors document his reading. The study concludes by examining Yeats's relatively late rapprochment with Milton and Spenser – a development which began, by coincidence, during the modern Irish rebellion and civil war.

Manuscripts can disclose unknown influences; they may also divulge unsuspected sources by which a known influence (say, 'Milton's Platonist' in 'The Phases of the Moon') came to stimulate the imagination of the poet. Perhaps the only thing I regret is that I could not do more with the Renaissance occult writers who helped Yeats with some extravagantly philosophical works. Being an extensive subject in its own right and outside the book's focus, the matter is largely excluded.

Finally, I own that the study has prospered due to the assistance of persons to whom I am very grateful. My thanks to the scholars who extended to me valuable advice and information: Professors Parkinson, Finneran, Clark and Stallworthy (all cited above), George Bornstein, Ronald Schuchard, Roy Foster, Christina Hunt Mahony, James Lovic Allen, Robert Spoo, John Kelly, Elizabeth Loizeaux, Deirdre Toomey and Evelyn Joll. Above all, thanks to my friends at Washington State University, Stanton Linden, Diane Gillespie, John Ehrstine and Virginia Hyde (indefatigable mentor). Thanks to the librarians: Catherine Fahy, Leila Luedeking, Sidney Huttner, Cathy Henderson, Lola Szladits and Linda Matthews. Special thanks to Robert Grindell for the favour of an address (Kansas State University) during several months of revision; and to the English Department, Graduate School and Graduate Studies

Committee of Washington State University for funding my travels and research.

I am much obliged to Michael Yeats for his thoughts on several occasions and to Anne Yeats for her hospitality and aid in assaying select particulars of the W. B. Yeats library in Ireland.

I thank Richard Fallis and Warwick Gould for their service as incisive readers, and Warwick, especially, for the introduction of countless improvements and for making possible one of the larger cuts. To Sarah Roberts-West, Margaret Cannon and the staff of the Macmillan Press I owe thanks for efficiency and care with the manuscript, illustrative materials and advice on permissions. And to my wife, Marilyn Manson, thanks for abetting me during the difficult labour of the production when there was reason for distraction in the delivery of her own first book. Our children will remember, I hope, mainly the buoyancy of these times.

London   W. K. C.

Acknowledgements

Formal acknowledgement is made to the following:

A. P. Watt Ltd, on behalf of Anne Yeats and Michael B. Yeats, for permission to quote unpublished materials by W. B. Yeats, and on behalf of Michael Yeats and Macmillan London Ltd, for permission to quote from the printed works; also, in the United States, the Macmillan Publishing Company for sanction to reprint passages from *The Autobiography* (copyright 1916, 1936 by Macmillan Publishing Company, renewed 1944, 1964 by Bertha Georgie Yeats), *A Vision* (copyright 1937 by W. B. Yeats, renewed 1965 by Bertha Georgie Yeats and Anne Butler Yeats), *Essays and Introductions* (copyright 1961 by Mrs W. B. Yeats), *Explorations* (copyright 1962 by Mrs W. B. Yeats), *Mythologies* (copyright 1959 by Mrs W. B. Yeats), *Letters of W. B. Yeats* (ed. Allan Wade, copyright 1953, 1954, and renewed 1982 by Anne Butler Yeats), and *The Variorum Edition of the Poems of W. B. Yeats* (ed. Peter Allt and Russell K. Alspach, from 1916 copyright, renewed 1944 by Bertha Georgie Yeats); also Oxford University Press for permission to quote from letters destined for or published in *The Collected Letters of W. B. Yeats* (copyright 1985); and John P. Frayne (ed.), for permission to quote from *The Uncollected Prose of W. B. Yeats*, vol. II (copyright 1975).

For permission to use manuscript materials: Council of Trustees of the National Library of Ireland; the Henry W. and Albert A. Berg Collection, New York Public Library (Astor, Lenox, and Tilden Foundations); the Richard Ellmann Collection, Department of Special Collections, McFarlin Library, University of Tulsa; the Department of Manuscripts, British Library; the W. B. Yeats Collection, Special Collections, Woodruff Library, Emory University; the Ezra Pound Literary Property Trust; and the Harry Ransom Humanities Research Center, University of Texas, Austin.

For permission to reproduce pictures and other materials as illustrations: A. P. Watt Ltd, on behalf of Anne Yeats; the University of London Library; the National Gallery, London; Mr Evelyn Joll; Thomas Nelson and Sons Ltd; the National Library of Ireland; and the Leonard and Virginia Woolf Library, Washington State University.

The University of Michigan Press, Warwick Gould and Macmillan London Ltd for permission to reprint my own work and – in permitting quotation from additional texts – the following: Oxford University Press for *Ben Jonson* (ed. C. H. Herford, Percy and Evelyn Simpson, copyright 1954), *Poems of John Donne* (ed. Herbert J. C. Grierson, copyright 1912) and *Poets and Poetry* by John Bailey (copyright 1911); the Macmillan Publishing Company for *John Milton: Complete Poems and Major Prose* (ed. Merritt Hughes, copyright 1957); the University of Michigan Press for *The Complete Works of Matthew Arnold*, vol. v (ed. R. H. Super, copyright 1965); Yale University Press for *Complete Prose Works of John Milton*, vol. II (ed. Ernest Sirluck, copyright 1953); the University of Missouri Press for *Yeats's Interactions with Tradition* by Patrick Keane (copyright 1987); J. M. Dent and Sons Ltd for *The Faerie Queene* (ed. J. W. Hales, copyright 1910 and 1974); and the University of California Press for *The Renaissance: Studies in Art and Poetry – The 1893 Text* by Walter Pater (ed. Donald L. Hill, copyright 1980).

Every effort has been made to trace all the copyright-holders but if any have been inadvertently overlooked the publishers will be pleased to make the necessary arrangement at the first opportunity.

List of Abbreviations

PRIMARY SOURCES AND BIBLIOGRAPHIC WORKS

Au	*Autobiographies* (London: Macmillan, 1955).
AV A	*A Critical Edition of Yeats's 'A Vision' (1925)*, ed. George M. Harper and Walter K. Hood (London: Macmillan, 1978).
AV B	*A Vision* (New York: Macmillan, 1961; London: Macmillan, 1962).
CL1	*The Collected Letters of W. B. Yeats*, vol. I: *1865–1892*, ed. John Kelly and Eric Domville (Oxford: Clarendon Press, 1985).
E&I	*Essays and Introductions* (London and New York: Macmillan, 1961).
Ex	*Explorations* (London: Macmillan, 1962; New York: Macmillan, 1963).
GH	*The Green Helmet and Other Poems* (Dundrum: Cuala Press, 1910).
L	*The Letters of W. B. Yeats*, ed. Allan Wade (London: Rupert Hart-Davis, 1954; New York: Macmillan, 1955).
LDW	*Letters on Poetry from W. B. Yeats to Dorothy Wellesley*, intro. Kathleen Raine (London and New York: Oxford University Press, 1964).
LJBY	*J. B. Yeats: Letters to his Son W. B. Yeats*, ed. Joseph Hone (New York: Dutton, 1946).
LNI	*Letters to the New Island*, ed. Horace Reynolds (Cambridge, Mass.: Harvard University Press, 1934).
LTWBY	*Letters to W. B. Yeats*, ed. Richard J. Finneran, George Mills Harper, and William M. Murphy (London: Macmillan, 1977; New York: Columbia University Press, 1977).
Mem	*Memoirs*, ed. Denis Donoghue (London: Macmillan, 1972; New York: Macmillan, 1973).
Myth	*Mythologies* (London and New York: Macmillan, 1959).
NLI	National Library of Ireland (followed by manuscript number).
OBMV	*The Oxford Book of Modern Verse, 1892–1935*, chosen by W. B. Yeats (Oxford: Clarendon Press, 1936).

P(1895)	*Poems* (London: Unwin, 1895).
PNE	*The Poems: A New Edition*, ed. Richard J. Finneran (New York: Macmillan, 1983; London: Macmillan, 1984).
RPP	*Responsibilities: Poems and a Play* (Dundrum: Cuala Press, 1914).
SS	*The Senate Speeches of W. B. Yeats*, ed. Donald R. Pearce (Bloomington: Indiana University Press, 1960).
TB	*Theatre Business. The Correspondence of the First Abbey Theatre Directors: William Butler Yeats, Lady Gregory and J. M. Synge*, ed. Ann Saddlemyer (University Park and London: Pennsylvania State University Press, 1982).
UP1	*Uncollected Prose by W. B. Yeats*, vol. I, ed. John P. Frayne (London: Macmillan; New York: Columbia University Press, 1970).
UP2	*Uncollected Prose by W. B. Yeats*, vol. II, ed. John P. Frayne and Colton Johnson (London: Macmillan, 1975; New York; Columbia University Press, 1976).
Visions	(Lady) I. A. Gregory, *Visions and Beliefs in the West of Ireland*, with two essays and notes by W. B. Yeats (1920; Gerrards Cross: Colin Smythe, 1979).
VP	*The Variorum Edition of the Poems of W. B. Yeats*, ed. Peter Allt and Russell K. Alspach (New York and London: Macmillan, 1957).
VPl	*The Variorum Edition of the Plays of W. B. Yeats*, ed. Russell K. Alspach (London and New York: Macmillan, 1966).
VSR	*The Secret Rose: Stories by W. B. Yeats: A Variorum Edition*, ed. Phillip L. Marcus, Warwick Gould, and Michael J. Sidnell (Ithaca, NY: Cornell University Press, 1981).
WR	*The Wind Among the Reeds* (London: Elkin Mathews, 1899).
Wade	Allan Wade, *A Bibliography of the Writings of W. B. Yeats*, 3rd edn, rev. Russell K. Alspach (London: Rupert Hart-Davis, 1968).
YL	Edward O'Shea, *A Descriptive Catalog of W. B. Yeats's Library* (New York and London: Garland, 1985). References by catalogue number.
YL1920	Edward O'Shea, 'The 1920s Catalogue of W. B. Yeats's Library', *YA* 4 (1985) 279–90.
YL Notes	Wayne K. Chapman, 'A Descriptive Catalog of W. B.

	Yeats's Library: Notes Supplementary', YA 6 (1987) 234–45. References by YL catalogue number.
YT	Yeats and the Theatre, ed. Robert O'Driscoll and Lorna Reynolds (Toronto and London: Macmillan, 1975).

FREQUENTLY CITED SECONDARY SOURCES

ED	Richard Ellmann, Eminent Domain: Yeats among Wilde, Joyce, Pound, Eliot and Auden (New York: Oxford University Press, 1967).
HonGuest	Denis Donoghue and J. R. Mulryne (eds), An Honoured Guest: New Essays on W. B. Yeats (London: Edward Arnold, 1965).
Identity	Richard Ellmann, The Identity of Yeats (New York: Oxford University Press, 1964).
LT	T. R. Henn, The Lonely Tower: Studies in the Poetry of Yeats (New York and London: Methuen, 1979).
Making AV	George Harper, The Making of Yeats's 'A Vision': A Study of the Automatic Script, 2 vols (London: Macmillan; Carbondale and Edwardsville: Southern Illinois University Press, 1987).
NCom	A. Norman Jeffares, A New Commentary on the Collected Poems of W. B. Yeats (Stanford, Calif.: Stanford University Press, 1984).
RI	Frank Kermode, The Romantic Image (New York: Macmillan, 1957).
SMD	Ronald Bushrui (ed.), 'Sunshine and the Moon's Delight': A Centenary Tribute to John Millington Synge, 1871–1909 (Gerrards Cross: Colin Smythe, 1972).
WBY	Joseph Hone, W. B. Yeats, 1865–1939 (New York: St Martin's Press, 1943).
Y&GI	Donald T. Torchiana, W. B. Yeats and Georgian Ireland, Evanston, Ill.: Northwestern University Press, 1966).
Y&Shel	George Bornstein, Yeats and Shelley (Chicago and London: University of Chicago Press, 1970).
YA	Yeats Annual (followed by number and date).
YAACTS	Yeats: An Annual of Critical and Textual Studies (followed by number and date).
YCP&B	Daniel A. Harris, Yeats: Coole Park and Ballylee (Baltimore and London: Johns Hopkins University Press, 1974).

List of Abbreviations

YM&M	Richard Ellmann, *Yeats: The Man and the Masks* (New York: Dutton, 1948).
YM&P	A. Norman Jeffares, *Yeats: Man and Poet* (London: Routledge and Kegan Paul, 1962).
YS&I	A. Norman Jeffares (ed.), *Yeats, Sligo and Ireland*, Irish Literary Studies 6 (Gerrards Cross: Colin Smythe, 1980).
YSC&LP	Thomas Parkinson, *W. B. Yeats: Self-Critic (A Study of his Early Verse) and The Later Poetry*, 2 vols in one (Berkeley: University of California Press, 1971.
YShak	Rupin Desai, *Yeats's Shakespeare* (Evanston: Northwestern University Press, 1971).
YW	Curtis Bradford, *Yeats at Work* (Carbondale: Southern Illinois University Press, 1965).

1
Tradition, 'Imitation', and the Synthesis of Content and Form

> This *imitatio*, is *dissimilis materei similis tractatio*: and also, *similis materei dissimilis tractatio* . . . .
> (Roger Ascham, *The Scholemaster*, 1570[1])

March 20th 1906   18 Woburn Buildings

Dear Sir,
    I don't know of any book on prosody of the kind you speak of and I don't think that I ever read one. For the most part, all one can do, for anybody who wishes to write it, is to tell them to read as much good poetry as possible, and the older the better; plenty of Elizabethan and Jacobean lyric writers.

Yours Sincerely
W. B. Yeats[2]

I

That Yeats was a poet 'of tradition' is one of the commonplaces of our critical literature. Testaments abound, of course, in his own essays and introductions. But he was also a strikingly original poet, in spite of his tendency to deny it, and what he made was new despite the fact that his materials were often 'received'. He saw himself, perhaps, in an uneasy relationship with the post-war moderns of the generation of Pound, Eliot, C. Day Lewis, Edith Sitwell and W. J. Turner – writers whose lyric work he seldom approved but sometimes preferred to his own. They had 'pulled off the mask', he said, and thus had stood, 'not [as] this or that man[,] but [as] man's naked mind' (*OBMV* xxxvi). Though he too had 'tried to be modern', he was never to doubt the kind of poet he was. Near the end of his career, testifying in the general introduction that he had composed for the 'definitive' but never-realized collected edition of his work, he even seems apologetic – though such posturing is of a most becoming kind considering the importance of the occasion he was preparing to celebrate. 'Because I need a passionate syntax for passionate subject-matter', he wrote,

> I compel myself to accept those traditional metres that have developed with the language. Ezra Pound, Turner, Lawrence wrote admirable free verse, I could not. I would lose myself, become joyless. . . . If I wrote of personal love or sorrow in free verse, or in any rhythm that left it unchanged, amid all its accidence, I would be full of self-contempt because of my egotism and indiscretion, and foresee the boredom of my reader. I must choose a traditional stanza, even what I alter must seem traditional. . . . Talk to me of originality and I will turn on you with rage. I am a crowd, I am a lonely man, I am nothing. Ancient salt is best packing. (*E&I* 522)

Elsewhere, in his posthumous *Pages from a Diary Written in Nineteen Hundred and Thirty* (1944), Yeats is less self-effacing:

> Pound's conception of excellence, like that of all revolutionary schools, is of something so international that it is abstract and outside life. I do not ask myself whether what I find in Elizabethan English, or in that of the early eighteenth century, is better or worse than what I find in some other clime and time. I can only approach that more distant excellence through what I inherit, lest I find it and be stricken dumb. . . . A good poet must, as Henley said of Burns, be the last of a dynasty, and he must see to it that his Court expels the parvenu even though he gather all the riches of the world. (*Ex* 294–5)

In very different moods, then, Yeats speaks his mind about matters that were central to his craft and his individual achievement. Yet form and poetic voice are little more than matters peripheral to his philosophy of poetry, which was rooted in tradition. As he pointed out – and not only on the two occasions cited above – the poet's technique and his language were necessary ingredients of a dynamic process by which poets had long wrought expression for the 'phantasmagoria' that was beyond them until they had written. The poet, a mortal 'bundle of accident and incoherence that sits down to breakfast', is 'reborn as an idea, something intended, complete'; like Shakespeare, he becomes 'a part of his own phantasmagoria' and becomes intelligible to himself as he becomes intelligible to his audience (*E&I* 509). Like the poet, tradition was always in the making, renewing itself; it was something received with deliberate study. Yeats was not a parvenu but a true poet – according to his view, the descendant of an ancient family.

Still, if poets were in several senses 'made', they were also born to their talent. And, if they were not divine, they were adept geniuses at divining truths, 'ideas', which hitherto might not have found expression in the scripture of tradition. In that sense, Yeats is most original, though the act of divination (or the drafting of poems) is, from his point of view, an occult process in which the poet lends his faculties to spiritual forces outside himself. Hence the poet denies his 'originality' because he serves to embody – not as agent of creation, but as crucible or medium – an inspiration made intelligible with the poem. The poem, long held to be a sacred work in which lyric poets in particular reveal extraordinary powers of insight beyond the gifts of most mortals, is the song that is made when tradition collides with new insight.

The poet, in short, is a *vates*, a diviner, or prophet, as he was known among the Romans, or, as Sidney also claims, a natural philosopher like Empedocles, Parmenides, and Pythagoras, 'the philosophers of Greece [who] durst not a long time appear to the world but under the masks of poets'.[3] Certainly Yeats's kinship to such philosopher–poets is well documented in his philosophical labour of many years, *A Vision* (versions of 1925 and 1937), and in his late poetry. However, at an earlier date, as a Celtic revivalist, he had naturally made it a point to acknowledge his native Irish ancestry – the *fili* of Gaelic saga literature, the poet–magi whose powers stemmed from the druidic office of an all-but-lost pagan religion.[4] 'The stars had come so near me that I caught / Their singing', the bard Seanchan chants in Yeats's verse drama *The King's Threshold* (1904, subsequently revised; *VPl* 301, ll. 716–17). The play, virtually Yeats's equivalent to the apologies of Sidney and Shelley, shows very clearly that Yeats's poetic conservatism begins in sympathy with one of poetry's oldest, most universal and enduring traditions: the myth of the poet's ejection from a once-unified prelapsarian society, symbolically his tragic alienation from his audience.[5] In this case, Yeats's attempt to embody tradition, for himself and his own audience, and to make that tradition intelligible as philosophy by seeming to bring mythology to life with dramatic simulation makes ironic his statement that the 'good poet must . . . see to it that his Court expels the parvenu even though he [pronoun with ambiguous reference] gather all the riches of the world'. The opposite occurs in the play.

That Yeats should dramatize the crisis of the poet of tradition shows how vividly the problem appealed to his imagination. That such dramatizations recurred regularly in his work at a time when his poetic method was most in a state of revaluation and change – roughly, between 1900 and 1922 – suggests how vital the issue was to his identity as a poet. Indeed, it demonstrates the interdependence of philosophy and style. No doubt it is significant that the first great achievement of his early career as a poet was a work – a dramatic narrative, *The Wanderings of Oisin* (1889) – which carried its eponymous hero, the legendary poet of the Fenian cycle, from the golden and silver ages of the Irish gods and heroes to confrontation with St Patrick and Christian Ireland in the less illustrious age of bronze. It is also striking that Yeats laboured to make verse drama out of the philosophical, historical, and social crises that fell, according to pastoral tradition, especially hard upon poets as one epoch gave way to another. For example, *The Shadowy Waters* (published 1900; revised 1906 and 1907), *The King's Threshold* (published 1904; revised 1922), *The Hour Glass* (published 1903; revised 1913, 1914, and 1922), and *The Player Queen* (published 1922, with thirty-two drafts between 1908 and the first production of 1919) – arranged here in descending order by historical setting – were plays of such importance to Yeats that his writing and rewriting of them demanded much of his attention for years.[6] In light of such apparent influences on these plays as, respectively, the Irish nautical literature, the Irish folk and bardic traditions, the English Tudor moralities and Jacobean city comedies – let alone the growing impact of Neoplatonism – one is struck by the correspondence between the dramatist's toil to complete these plays as he wished and the lyric poet's simultaneous efforts to develop a new singing voice. Both depended upon Yeats's attempt to express a philosophy, to become 'something intended, complete', to become 'a part of his own phantasmagoria'. His originality, *similis materei dissimilis tractatio*, may be attributed in part to his genius for making novel use of traditional material – or to his magician's knack for synthesis. The sources of his material *are* important. Moreover, after his early career (up to 1899), the literary tradition that mattered most to his technique in poetry was English rather than Irish.

If the poet is a *vates*, a diviner, or magician, he is also a *poietes*, or maker, a craftsman, and he is apprenticed to learn his trade from many masters. The art of poetry is thus 'an Art of imitation', as Jonson teaches in *Timber, or Discoveries*, a work which Yeats knew well and affected to imitate with his own *Discoveries* essays of 1906. This is, however, as Jonson soon adds,[7]

> Not, to imitate servilely, as *Horace* saith, and catch at vices, for vertue: but, to draw forth out of the best, and choisest flowers, with the Bee, and turn all into Honey, worke it into one relish, and savour: make our *Imitation* sweet: observe, how the best writers have imitated, and follow them.

Here, too, Yeats is largely in agreement with tradition, though his views seem to vacillate on the issue of technical imitation. On the one hand, in 'Ego Dominus Tuus', the primary and objective cast of his mind – a cast which is set in dramatic tension against its opposite – affirms that 'style is found by sedentary toil / And by imitation of great masters'. Yet, on the other hand, and a few pages beyond the poem as it appeared in *Per Amica Silentia Lunae* (1917), the poet asserts that imitation becomes a sterilizing agent in certain circumstances (as it had been for five years of his attempt to make tragic allegory of his philosophical drama *The Player Queen*); imitation, in such cases, can lead to a sterility of the imagination which one may only conquer by mocking one's own thought in comedy. 'I was', Yeats confesses, 'always thinking of the element of imitation in style and in life, and of life beyond heroic imitation' (*Myth* 334).

To be sure, in those days Yeats did not hesitate to advocate imitation as a way for young poets to learn their craft. When Thomas MacDonagh, for example, wrote to Yeats for advice and for an opinion on the poems MacDonagh was preparing to publish as his first book, Yeats wrote back to him, on 9 November 1902, and prescribed a remedy for what he thought ailed MacDonagh's verse:

> Now about the verses themselves – They show that you have a thoughtful and imaginative mind – but you have not yet got a precise musical & personal language – Whether you have poetical power or not I could not really say – but I can say that you have not found yourself as a poet – If you are young, & if you feel you/yourself have something you must give expression to, I strongly advise you not to publish for the present – but (1st) to read the great old masters of English, Spenser, Ben Jonson, Sir Thomas Brown[e], perhaps Chaucer – until you have got our feebler modern English out of your head – When we study old writers we imitate nothing but their virtues – for their faults, which were of their time & not ours have no charm for us – If we read modern writers we are likely to imitate their faults for we share their illusions –
>
> (2nd) I will advise you to translate a great deal from the Irish – To translate literally, preserving as much of the idiom as possible – I do[n]t mean that you will stop at this kind of writing, but it will help get rid of the conventionality of language from which we all suffer today . . . .[8]

Yeats, who could translate no Irish himself and who failed to convince MacDonagh not to publish *Through the Ivory Gate* (1903), at least succeeded on the two counts of his prescription. First, MacDonagh went on to make a study of 'the great old masters of English' while at University College, Dublin, publishing his MA thesis, *Thomas Campion and the Art of English Poetry*, in 1913. Finally, translating a number of poems from Irish in his *Songs of Myself* (1910), MacDonagh rejected the conventional mannerisms of his early style and contributed, with his study of Anglo-Irish literature and Gaelic, a significant book about Irish influences on English prosody, *Literature in Ireland* (1916). Yeats owned both of MacDonagh's prosodic studies (see *YL* 1180 and 1182), and especially admired the latter.[9] The admiration was mostly one-sided in 1903, of course, when MacDonagh not only published the poems that Yeats advised him not to, but also dedicated them to him.[10]

Eager to address the same remedy to the national audience, Yeats thought to apply the prescription to raise Ireland's self-consciousness. This involved study of things Irish but required a 'cultivated minority' to contribute a literary ideal not to be recovered from the nearly-lost native tradition. In 'What Is "Popular Poetry"?' (1901), he said that the vigorous journalism that aided the Young Ireland societies did not see 'that its literary ideal belong[ed] more to England than to other countries'. Indeed, he wrote, among the few thousand who had spoken Irish 'from the cradle', perhaps no one had 'enough of the unwritten tradition to know good verses from bad ones, if he [had] enough mother-wit' (*E&I* 11).

A few years later, still intent on raising his homeland's consciousness by embracing the English language and the literature that he was born to, he argued that Ireland was a country which had come to its moment, like 'the moment of Goethe in Germany [or] of the Elizabethan poets in England', when its character was to express itself 'through some group of writers, painters, or musicians' who were to fix 'the finer elements of national character for generations' by using 'the life of their own times' and 'past literature . . . until their revelation is understood' (*Samhain: 1908*, in *Ex* 236–7). Even the songs and ballads of Young Ireland (except for 'a small number which are partly copied from Gaelic models, and a few, almost all by Mangan, that have a personal style') were 'imitations' of English literature (imitations of Burns, Macaulay, and Scott). 'All literature', he wrote, 'is derived from models' – only, its value is determined by the 'presence of a personal element alone that can give it nationality in a fine sense, the nationality of its maker' (*Ex* 233).

Much later, after Yeats had given up hope that Ireland would ever realize the renaissance of which he had dreamed and written, he was to explain, in that apologetic tone of 'A General Introduction for my Work', that he 'owe[d] [his] soul to Shakespeare, to Spenser and to Blake, perhaps to William Morris, and to the English language' in which he thought, spoke, and wrote. Ironically, his country had then achieved her renaissance in literature. 'Everything I love', he said, 'has come to me through English; my hatred tortures me with love, my love with hate' (*E&I* 519). Gaelic, he said, might be his 'national language', but it was not his 'mother tongue'.

Yeats's faith in the use of models could be shaken, certainly, for his endorsement of 'imitation' is often qualified, sceptical – even negative. 'One must not forget that the death of language, . . . a nearly impersonal . . . algebra [of] words and rhythms varying from man to man, is but a part of the tyranny of impersonal things', he warns us (*E&I* 301), by which he meant the putting-on of language like a garment as opposed to the welling-up of passionate speech from beyond the conscious mind. And so he declared that one should not wish to know 'how to imitate the external form' of a piece of literature but wish, instead, to know 'how to express in some equivalent form whatever in the thoughts of [one's] own age seems . . . to press into the future' (*Samhain: 1906*; in *Ex* 209). This is an important qualification, not nearly the pejorative criticism he sometimes cast at the 'literary second-hand', or, borrowing Rossetti's phrase, at the 'soulless self-reflections of man's skill'; one wished to become 'all eye and ear'; one's mind, a 'clear mirror', not a 'smoking lamp' (*Ex* 247–8).

In better humour, his scepticism can be disarming, as it is when, on one occasion in his Diary of 1930, he feigns to write to his son's schoolmaster. In part, the imaginary letter runs as follows:

> Dear Sir,
> My son is now between nine and ten and should begin Greek at once and be taught by the Berlitz method that he may read as soon as possible that most exciting of all stories, the *Odyssey*. . . . Grammar should come when the need comes. As he grows older he will read to me the great lyric poets and I will talk to him about Plato. Do not teach him one word of Latin. The Roman people were the classic decadence, their literature form without matter. They destroyed Milton, the French seventeenth and our own eighteenth century, and our schoolmasters even to-day read Greek with Latin eyes. . . . Do not teach him a word of history. I shall take him to Shakespeare's history plays, if a commercialized theatre permit, and give him all the historical novels of Dumas, and if he cannot pick up the rest he is a fool. . . . If he wants to learn Irish after he is well founded in Greek, let him – it will clear his eyes of the Latin miasma. If you will not do what I say, whether the curriculum or your own will restrain, and my son comes from school a smatterer like his father, may your soul lie chained on the Red Sea bottom. (*Ex* 321)[11]

Yeats was again colliding with tradition. Thus, at Lady Gregory's suggestion (*WBY* 450), it was entirely appropriate that he consider the above piece a prose 'Subject' for a poem. Why he did not then recast it into verse might have had little to do with the merit of the idea or of the poem that might have been the consequence. In fact, he had worked a similar feat with 'Among School Children' (manuscript dated 14 June 1926) – and in *ottava rima* stanzas, no less.[12] Possibly Yeats had no desire to see this more recent exercise altered, because his game of parody depends on an awareness of a very pragmatic tradition of prose literature – a tradition that he would have known from having served six years as senator, with chief responsibilities in cultural and educational affairs. His thought and humour in the letter are informed by such Renaissance humanists as Castiglione (whom Yeats had by Hoby's translation), Erasmus, Elyot, Mulcaster, Daniel, and Milton[13] – along with Ascham, whose second book of *The Scholemaster* (1570), 'teachyng the ready way to the Latin tong', is both a pedagogical handbook for schoolmasters and probably the most extensive sixteenth-century account of imitation in English. Yeats's censure of Latin is most interesting in light of Jonson's strong liking and in light of Yeats's own antiquarian interests and his affinity for Jonson – at least at one point in his career. Even in burlesque, Yeats's objection seems to be only that the Romans had no 'matter' of their own because they were nothing more than great copiers. His views of the poet and of 'imitation' were a commonplace of the Renaissance. Jonson affirmed that the poet is no mere copyist:

> *First*, wee require in our *Poet*, or maker, (for that Title our Language affordes him, elegantly, with the *Greeke*) a goodnes of naturall wit. For, wheras all other Arts consist of Doctrine, and Precepts: the *Poet* must bee able by nature, and instinct, to powre out the Treasure of his mind. . . . But, that, which wee especially require of him is an exactnesse of Studie, and multiplicity of reading, which maketh a full man . . . so to master the matter, and Stile, as to shew, hee knows, how to handle, place, or dispose of either, with *elegancie*, when need shall be. . . . There goes more to his making, then so. For to Nature, Exercise, Imitation, and Studies, *Art* must be added, to make all these perfect.[14]

Yeats would have read similar injunctions in any number of authorities. The apologies of Sidney and Shelley and Arnold's famous Preface to the 1853 edition of *Poems*, for instance, are much too well known to have evaded his attention.[15] A poet might depend upon another poet's testimony and make light of the pedantries of schoolmasters, 'Old, learned, respectful bald heads', who, as Yeats wrote in 'The Scholars',

> Edit and annotate the lines
> That young men, tossing on their beds,
> Rhymed out in love's despair
> To flatter beauty's ignorant ear.
> (*VP* 161, ll. 1–6)

But Yeats's Platonic conception of the imitative act of literature (the poet's imitation of divine 'Ideas') was itself part of the same longstanding and respectable tradition. Since form and matter are the rudiments of creation, matter, in this case, is no less than a prophet's vision, the poet's phantasmagoria, or 'content'. Manner, or form, is that which a craftsman makes to carry that vision to an understanding. The two are joined by instinct and by intelligence in a synthesis that feigns to create what it in fact receives and passes forth with analogies to both natural and divine acts of creation. This imitation, as Ascham put it (in Latin), means dissimilar treatment of similar matter but also similar treatment of dissimilar matter (see epigraph). Just so, one might define Yeats's genius as a special acuity of instinct and intelligence, a seemingly endless capacity for making 'originals' from the artistic mating of received matter and formal technique. The point would not be to stress so much 'the matter what other men wrote . . . and the maner how other men wrote'[16] as it would be to acknowledge his capacity 'to express in some equivalent form whatever . . . the thoughts . . . his own age seem[ed] . . . to press into the future'.

II

For reasons now obvious, the word *adaptation* might be preferred to *imitation* whenever the concept is employed as understood in England in the sixteenth and early seventeenth centuries. Yeats was of two minds about *imitation*, as are most modern readers. As we do, he sometimes associated it with copying. However, he just as often argued for its use, in the older, radical sense of what the word meant, which always involved the transformation and synthesis of one's materials. He was enough of a scholar and draftsman to appreciate the difference and to translate successfully the long tradition of *adaptation* (as it will be called from now on) into some of the most extraordinary poetry written in the post-Romantic era. Yet to demonstrate how adaptation works, particularly in Yeats's case, one must define style in terms of practice. It will not be sufficient to affirm that good poems are harmonious marriages of form and substance, because the finest poems of Yeats's early and later periods bring about such union in different ways. Personality and style, each of which he laboured over a good deal, came increasingly to the same thing. His pursuit of both may be read in the way he made poems.

In practice, Yeats was strongly affected by the Renaissance – and in particular by English Renaissance literature, which contributed substantially to his development of a poetic style and, after 1900, to his conception of personality, which was inextricable from the stylistic departure he inaugurated at that time. He not only wished to renew such an age in contemporary Ireland but, as example, served with conviction the literary movement he helped found – and no less than by adapting, as from other sources, what he thought best from the Renaissance. In cultivating a new style, it has been said, he undertook the momentous task of reshaping his own personality. Indeed, in a letter to George Russell in 1904, Yeats confided that he regarded the issue of personal identity and poetic voice to be so important that his very manhood seemed at stake. '[I]n some of my lyric verse', he reported,

> . . . there is an exaggeration of sentiment and sentimental beauty which I have come to think unmanly. . . . I have been fighting the prevailing decadence for years, and have just got it under foot in my own heart – it is sentiment and sentimental sadness, a womanish introspection. . . . I cannot probably be quite just to any poetry that speaks to me with the sweet insinuating feminine voice of the dwellers in that country of shadows and hollow images. I have dwelt there too long not to dread all that comes out of it. (L 434)

Contemporary culture suffered, he thought, because its 'prevailing decadence' was, in his words, 'feminine', 'passive', and much in need of what the 'old writers' (including Robert Burton, presumably) said men of action had – the 'sanguineous temperament',

> precisely the sanguineous temperament that is fading out of poetry and most obviously out of what is most subtle and living in poetry – its pulse and breath, its rhythm. . . . Every generation has more and more loosened the rhythm, more and more broken

up and disorganized, for the sake of subtlety of detail, those great rhythms which move, as it were, in masses of sound. (*E&I* 379)

In his positive assessment, that is what English literature of the Renaissance came to: a 'sanguineous temperament' embodied by 'great rhythms', 'masses of sound' in motion. That is, the physical tension, or raw nervous energy, of such dynamic personalities, captured perhaps in some dramatic situation, *might* be converted into exemplary poetry.

The English Renaissance, to which he overtly refers in the essay 'Edmund Spenser' (1906) and to which he directs attention in the passage just quoted, influenced Yeats profoundly. Yet, even as the essay itself makes clear (by comparing the technical abilities of Spenser and Shelley as they practised the same stanza), the English Renaissance was far from being the only significant influence on Yeats's poetic style, then or at any other time in his career. In recognition of the heterodox nature of Yeats's intelligence and the complicated way in which adaptation works in the creative process, the present study makes no such claims. Indeed, the opposite is stressed. For an honest study of technical influence must hold, with Yeats, that 'all the machinations of poetry are parts of the conviction of antiquity' (*E&I* 74), that all that unique 'machinery' borne into the genesis of an individual poem is what might reasonably be called its *adaptive complex*. This complex – in effect, what was in Yeats's head as his composition began to take shape on paper – can never be recovered entirely. Yet it *is* possible to capture more than a glimmer of the process and the thinking of the man who brought these compositions into being and who, fortunately, left behind so many of the cast-off relics of his labour that these may now be studied in their own right.

A chronological examination best suits this purpose, since the adaptive complex grows in complexity, and to maturity, with the poet – even in relatively simple forms such as the epigram. Neither Yeats's knack for synthesis nor his celebrated aural genius, in practice, functions as a constant in a formula. If his extraordinary talents were unschooled, as he frequently let on that they were, he observed, nevertheless, at least one rule concerning the fusion of elements which made up his art. The marriage of form and content translated metrically into a rule-of-thumb: 'What moves me and my hearer is a vivid speech that has no laws except that it must not exorcise the ghostly voice' (*E&I* 524).

Theoretically, therefore, the poem was allowed to cut its own figure as the poet conceived it in his imagination, or received it in a state of reverie or in flashes of insight while composing. In practice, though, there was much more dogged physical labour involved than the official position would admit. So, practically speaking, one must convert the terms of the above rule to their utilitarian equivalents. 'Ghostly voice' (or the 'unconscious norm') would become iambic pentameter, ballad measure or any other form established by custom or by nature (the latter granting licence to establish unique forms). However, the term seems to imply more than empty vessels: it implies received 'content' – images, turns of phrase, ideas, associations – transmitted by past poetic voices. In either case, a poet's ability to make poems from such materials requires practice and training. And perhaps there is no better confirmation of this last statement than the poetic fragments that survive from Yeats's own fairly undistinguished apprenticeship.

A single example from the unpublished juvenilia will suffice. In all fairness to Yeats, one must say that the following exhibit is of a very early date and written for personal use, not for posterity. The earliest surviving part of it was written lengthwise on the back of a dislodged sheet, in ink, the rest copied neatly onto one of several still-attached leaves of an old album, beneath the title 'Inscription for a christmas card'. Most, if not all, of the manuscripts in this album (NLI 12,161) were written between, roughly, the poet's sixteenth and nineteenth year.[17] Though he had perhaps not yet entirely given up his father's art, painting, to become a poet by trade, other remnants from this pre-publication period show that he was hard at work training himself to be a writer of verse. In this instance, Edmund Spenser was very evidently his master, the 'ghostly voice' that young Yeats tried to adapt to his own immediate purpose. First, we have the draft from the torn leaf, with its curious cardiographic runs and rests:

May Time be very kind to thee
Through [wreaths?] of purple flowe[r]s
~~Haunts of~~ the honey bee

> ~~there~~
>   by soleta[ry] bowers
>   entered by the hon[e]y bee
> May it lead the[e] to the tree
> Where the white footed charger
> of A[r]thers fairy queen doth prance
> or with he[r] subjects all ro[u]nd her
> mab leeds this stately dance

Then follows the 'Inscription for a christmas card':

> May time be very kind to thee
>   through solitary bowers
> By paths of pur[p]le flow[e]rs
> ~~May it leed thee~~ ∧ ~~the tree~~ (to)
> writers led by the honey bee

The first draft begins, conspicuously, with a finished line, itself anticipated by what is apparently a pre-verbal exercise in which measured stresses are transposed into long periods signifying exaggerated vowel length. Perhaps with the first line already in mind, the young poet applied his initial strokes in an effort to *feel* the line and the rhythm it would later project. It is just as though the first line's kinetic properties – or Yeats's sense of what he wanted even before he had devised the line – were only part-way to their conversion into speech (or 'its pulse and breath, its rhythm', as he subsequently wrote). Indicative of a highly intuitive method, at least, the initial scribble may come as close as anything to illustrating what Yeats later called the 'thinking of the body' (*E&I* 292). Beneath three of his lines, his pen seems to have struck paper only to count syllables. In one case, such counting betrays his use of an artificial metrical convenience, '-èd' (in 'entered'), which pads out the first two measures of iambic tetrameter verse with a technically acceptable trochaic inversion. This and other archaisms, such as 'thee' and 'doth', with the unmistakable allusion to *The Faerie Queene*, make Spenser's presence more than likely though apparently complicated by an early reading of Shelley's *Queen Mab*.[18] Perhaps because the last few lines of the first draft are so self-consciously indebted to Spenser as a 'great old master

Tradition, 'Imitation', Synthesis 15

of English', and perhaps, too, because of the complication, Yeats dropped those lines when he copied over the verse into his notebook. Lines 5 and 10 of the draft were combined ('[3 syllables] . . . by the honey bee' + 'mab leeds . . .') to produce the last line of the inscription: 'writers led by the honey bee'. 'Writers' is the poet's invention – an identity attached to 'thee' (now with plural reference) where none existed before. Once the preliminary draft is set aside, it becomes impossible to detect how thoroughly derivative this work of adaptation was.

Poetic adaptation most often works in this way. Poets prune away what is least their own or what least serves the gesture and intent of the performance that they compose on paper. The poet takes advantage of the accidents that occur as he writes. He shapes, he channels, he articulates, and the old becomes new in the process. He does not *copy* even when he can name the voice that dictates to him, because that voice emanates from his own imagination and memory. (Even when he thought he was quoting, as he sometimes did in verse, Yeats was more often closer to the original in spirit than in actual fact.) In Yeats's case, as the above example suggests most simply, adaptation means metamorphosis and, usually, compression. A day's 'intense unnatural labour', he once confessed to Herbert Grierson, might be reduced to 'four or five lines' (*L* 710), to a quatrain or one well-turned phrase. The unpublished inscription, after all, already given a title, perhaps only needed punctuating:

> May time be very kind to thee [–]
> Through solitary bowers[,]
> By paths of purple flowers [–]
> Writers led by the honey bee[.]

It may not be clear what the poem means. And the poet's voice may be indistinguishable from any other voice bearing best wishes on the same occasion. But the poem has its rhythmic appeal because of some syntactic special effects (chiefly a dislocated appositive), and it *sounds* good. Generally speaking, this was a starting-point for Yeats.

III

In time, Yeats's *matter* would predominate in the struggle with form. Yet, at first, formal achievement seems to have been his foremost preoccupation. One notices, with Bradford, how often Yeats's early poetry, with a little fudging by frequent use of semicolons, manages to bring into agreement the grammatic unit of the sentence and the formal requirements of the stanza (*YW* 40). Consequently, in a short lyric, grammatic period and poem would come to the same thing. Witness such enigmatic, oft-revised incantations as 'The Moods' (1893; *VP* 142) and 'A Poet to his Beloved' (1896; *VP* 157), poems which sustain enchantment to the last syllable. In such works, vowel assonance, alliteration, and repetition predominate, while stylized diction and vaulted syntax demonstrate how far content may be subordinated to form. In MacDonagh's analysis of 'The Lake Isle of Innisfree' (1890; *VP* 117), the metrics of the poem's fifth line – 'And I shall have some peace there, for peace comes dropping slow' – proved sufficiently that the poem existed somewhere between speech and song, defying conventional scansion but affirming the effect of 'Irish chant'.[19] Though 'open to exception', the only reliable means of dividing the poem seemed the caesura. Yet in manuscript (NLI 13,585), such points go without punctuation and phrasal repetition is more pronounced. In fact, before revising, Yeats repeated (as l. 9) the verse MacDonagh chose for exhibit. At second thought, even the revised final half of the line was binary: 'night & day'. Characteristic of Yeats's verse of this time, the first poem that Yeats believed had 'anything in its rhythm of [his] own music' (*Au* 153) is largely incantatory, speaking to the emotions rather than the intellect.

In later years, Yeats would explain that he had desired to capture in a 'powerful and passionate syntax, and a complete coincidence between period and stanza', a 'passionate subject-matter' that compelled him to choose 'those traditional metres that have developed with the language' (*E&I* 522). He would say that this desire came upon him in about 1917. In actuality, he was describing style in 1937 as he had begun to articulate its definition almost forty years before. In practice, his concept of the 'gesture' of poetry, which to him essentially meant a poem's shape and feeling, went back almost to the beginning of his career, before his emphasis on form over matter shifted. An early definition of 'talent' and 'genius' – entered beside the 1886 draft of 'The Wanderings of

Oisin' (in NLI 3726) – illustrates how willing Yeats *had* been, at one time, to allow his meaning to follow wherever his ear led it. Written inside the front cover of an exercise book begun in October 1886, at 10 Ashford Terrace, Harolds Cross, Dublin, the definition is a neat, possibly Johnsonian[20] aphorism of a type Yeats never tired of writing:

> Talent perceives ~~unity~~ Differen[ce]
> <u>Genius</u> ~~unity~~
> Genius ~~perceives~~ unity
> April
> 1887

From this, one surmises the following mental sequence:

(a) Talent perceives unity / Genius [difference] >
(b) Talent perceives differen[ce] / Genius unity >
(c) Talent perceives differen[ce] / Genius perceives unity >
(d) (b) version reinstated.

The contradiction between (a) and (b) shows the plasticity of content. 'Unity' and 'difference', nouns of three syllables receiving about the same stress, differ greatly in vowel quality and in the point and manner of articulation of their consonants. Yeats may have changed his mind about the *sense* of the (a) version, but one guesses that he was more likely following his ear, interchanging the two nouns and settling on the combination that sounded right to him. This conjecture seems confirmed by the trial and rejection of a balanced period – (c) and (d). Metrically, the result is virtually a formula. Its syncope recurs in 'Ego Dominus Tuus', ll. 46–7, for example: 'The rhetorician would deceive his neighbours, / The sentimentalist himself'. Yet by that time, thirty years after defining 'talent' and 'genius', the poet never once contradicted himself in draft or revision.[21] His lyricism no longer dominated the *thought* in his poetry.

What occurred in the interim was a substantial shift in Yeats's style – a shift which had its own reasons but which resembled the celebrated distinction between Elizabethan and Baroque period styles.[22] Moreover, it is tempting to suggest an analogy between the Baroque stylists' affection for *sententiae* and Yeats's fondness for the same. Doubtless, his interest in mystical writers had something to do with their common endeavour to condense intellectual experience into 'golden sayings', as did Pythagoras or, later and in a much different vein, Bacon in his *De Augmentis*.[23] In poetry, the strong-lined tradition of Jonson and Donne, whose strenuous asperity has been faulted for obscurity, was opposed to the 'soft, melting, and diffuse style of the Spenserians', as George Williamson has pointed out,[24] or, indeed, to the dominant style of the Elizabethans. Yeats's shift to a plainer (or, as he saw it, more 'masculine') poetic style is largely a consequence of his reaction to the theatre at the turn of the century and his practical experience writing plays for an Irish audience – hardly the reason for the shift in literary fashion that had anticipated it in England by three hundred years. But, in any case, Yeats's stylistic development, like those literary turns of fashion from the late sixteenth to the mid seventeenth century, was occasioned by a change in emphasis regarding those two rudiments of creation, form and content. The early – one might say, 'Elizabethan' – Yeats was generally preoccupied with the business of making his intellectual matter fit the manner of a highly stylized kind of lyricism. The later Yeats, while naturally opposed to the extreme view held by seventeenth-century men of science, took some trouble to bend his poetic form, if not his prose style, to fit his passionate or philosophical subject matter, which he had made by then into an ambitious programme. With this shift in emphasis from form to content, his method of drafting poems also seems to have altered as he tried to be understood, to be more than incantatory – to develop and inject into his verse a personal language that was also precisely musical, giving it, as he said, 'personality'.

A case in point is the poem 'The Fascination of What's Difficult', drafted in March 1910 but conceived in a Journal entry of September 1909. The poem is *about* the strenuous labour of Yeats's craft, so the use of it here will serve a dual purpose in illustrating the stylistic shift which had occurred. His earliest Journal entry concerning the poem shows, in light both of the drafts and of the final product, that form by then would necessarily give way to the expression of his intellectual freight. Moreover, the poem provides occasion for a further study of adaptation – of a kind at once more complicated and more characteristic of Yeats than the sort that we have observed thus far. In this instance, while the prose 'Subject' seems natural and original, the drafts subsequently entered in the same Journal betray a multiplicity of actual influences. The poem begins with an *idea*, entry 185 in the important daybook that Yeats had begun some ten months before – the first of several such books that he would keep. The *idea* is presented as follows:

> September [1909]. Subject: To complain of the fascination of what's difficult. It spoils spontaneity and pleasure and it wastes time. Repeat the line ending 'difficult' three times, and rhyme on bolt, exult, colt, jolt. One could use the thought of the wild-winged and unbroken colt must drag a cart of stones out of pride because it's difficult, and end by denouncing drama, accounts, public contests – all that's merely difficult. (*Mem* 229)

In execution, however, Yeats greatly simplified the intricate form that he had planned, perhaps either because he had exhausted his content more quickly than he had expected or, more likely, because his content demanded the kind of deliberate, clear-headed compression incident to epigrammatic form if it was to reject the melancholy of its initial lines; it called, in effect, for more of what he had been writing in imitation of Ben Jonson, Pierre de Ronsard, William Blake (as epigrammatist) and others whose example he found useful as he composed the poems of *The Green Helmet* from 1908 to 1911.[25] (At least the first two of these poets, Jonson and Ronsard, have some bearing on the exhibit, and a role in determining the course of this discussion.) The earliest extant draft of the poem was evidently copied into the Journal (*Mem* 242–3) and revised from an even earlier version, now lost. After a short interval, Yeats then wrote two new conclusions, neither of them satisfactory. The early draft, which is dated, shows that most of the trouble came at line 11, with his denunciation of 'drama, accounts, public contests – all that's merely difficult':

March [1910]

> The fascination of what's difficult
> Has dried the sap out of my veins and rent
> Spontaneous joy and natural content
> *Out of my heart. ~~What is it~~ {There is something} ails our colt
> That must, as if it had not holy blood
> Nor on Olympus leaped from cloud to cloud
> *~~Endure~~ {Shiver at} the lash, and strain and sweat and jolt

> As though it dragged road metal. My curse on plays
> That have to be set up in fifty ways
>   knave
> On the day's war with every ~~fool~~ and dolt
> ~~On the day's letters~~
> ~~Theatre business~~
> *On correspondence, management of men.
> I swear before dawn comes round again
> I'll find the stable and pull out the bolt.

(Apart from punctuation, only the three lines designated by asterisks diverge from the printed poem.[26]) The drafting of alternative conclusions occurred on the opposite page and appears as follows:

> ~~On the day's war with every fool and dolt~~
> ~~Content to~~
>   and that
> ~~Arranging this~~
> ~~Arranging this~~
> ~~On plans~~
>   that, to call the tune
> Arranging ~~this~~
> I swear this night, if but there is no moon
> To find etc.

or

>   to right
> Arranging that, and setting this ~~thing~~
> ~~I'll swear I'll~~
>   if
> I swear ~~it that if~~ but there is no moon tonight
>   To
> ~~I'll~~ find the stable and pull out the bolt.
>   planning,
> ~~On settling or setting that thing straight~~

Clearly, Yeats has managed to stay within his script in all but form, even as he attempted the substitution of two different couplets for ll. 11 and 12 of the early draft – the lines which (with the reintroduction of the phrase 'Theatre business' in l. 11) were eventually used when the poem was published. Far from, say, sixteen lines arranged in four quatrain stanzas with treble repetition of 'the line ending "difficult"', we have thirteen lines of a single stanza, no repetition, a rhyme scheme exceedingly tightened from the one planned, plus a discarding of the marvellously Yeatsian 'exult' for the more irascible diction of another voice. In diction and style (now an evident reflection of the poet's own 'passionate personality'), the epigrammatic terseness of this new Yeats is almost certainly indebted to such satires against the 'fools' and 'knaves' of Jacobean England as filled half the volume of Jonson's *Epigrammes*,[27] the other half consisting of slightly longer verses in praise of the social elite – models of poetic decorum which were not lost on Yeats either, at this time, when he wrote 'A Friend's Illness' and 'Upon a House Shaken by the Land Agitation'. Jonson too is humorously self-effacing, but notorious for such indignant rages against the stage as he demonstrates in his 'Ode *to himselfe*' added to the first printed version of *The New Inn* (1631) after the play's failure in 1629:

> COme leaue the lothed stage,
> And the more lothsome age:
> Where pride, and impudence (in faction knit)
> Vsurpe the chaire of wit!
> Indicting, and arraigning euery day
> Something they call a Play.
> Let their fastidious, vaine
> Commission of the braine
> Run on, and rage, sweat, censure, and condemn:
> They were not made for thee, lesse thou for them.
> (ll. 1–10, on the title-page[28])

Conceptually, the 'fastidious, vaine commission of the braine', as Jonson calls the labour, seems very like the slavish workhorse drudgery that takes the place of inspiration, and indeed sounds like it, too:

[Jonson] Run on, and rage, sweat, censure, and condemn

[Yeats] ~~Endure~~ ^Shiver at^ the lash, and strain and sweat and jolt

The immediate historical/biographical context of Yeats's poem is now known in detail. Still, as the best evidence shows – the evidence of his Journal – the poem differs from others of its kind, such as 'Adam's Curse' (c. Nov 1902), in that its history is mostly *literary*. The one intractable problem in Yeats's life of which he speaks in the poem and his Journal was the administrative business of running a theatre. After Synge's death, Lady Gregory's nearly fatal illness, and the withdrawal of the Abbey's most sustaining subsidy – all in 1909 – clearly Yeats's responsibilities compounded his frustration. He can hardly be blamed for resenting the time those responsibilities took from his poetry, of which he wrote little anyway between 1900 and 1910. It is interesting, therefore, that his poetic labour in such cases took so much instruction, if not inspiration, from other poets. His 'thought of the wild-winged and unbroken colt [that] must drag a cart of stones out of pride because it's difficult', for instance, may well have been suggested to him by Ben Jonson's use of the Pegasus myth on other occasions, as for instance in 'A Fit of Rime against Rime', which deftly combines classical allusion with contemporary invective against the theatre:

> All *Parnassus* Greene did wither,
>   And wit vanish'd.
> *Pegasus* did flie away,
> At the Wells no Muse did stay,
>   But bewail'd,
> So to see the Fountaine drie,
> And *Apollo's* Musique die,
>   All light failed!
> Starveling rimes did fill the Stage,
> Not a Poet in an Age,
>   Worth crowning.
>   (*The Under-wood* xxix.17–27[29])

The myth is of course the common property of tradition, and Yeats, whatever his immediate source (if any), has imagined his Pegasus hitched to an Irish cart, 'dragg[ing] road metal' (l. 8) 'out of pride because it's difficult' (prose 'Subject').[30] This is his invention, his original turn with an otherwise conventional device, and his 'wit', which had become a technical matter of style.

Nevertheless, Yeats's notes on 'humour' and 'wit', as he defined them in his Journal before copying in his draft of the epigram, are drawn from Congreve rather than Jonson – which perhaps justifies suspicion of an eighteenth-century association for the word 'dolt' (despite Yeats's purported general dislike for the age of Pope).[31] Congreve's definition of humour – which Yeats gives as 'a singular and unavoidable manner of doing anything, peculiar to one man only, by which speech and actions are distinguished from all other men' (*Mem* 242) – was plainly of interest to him on both dramatic and poetic grounds. His lectures (to be discussed later) show that he was reading Congreve, in March 1910, as part of his technical study of personality in literary style. *Wit*, he surmised from his reading, differs from *humour*, 'being part of its [i.e. humour's] expression', and *humour* is to be distinguished from both 'affectation' and 'habit', the first being 'an imitation' (*Mem* 242). Generally speaking, the point of his study was to discover exactly how subject and style were to be integrated in poetry.

Adaptation, as one concludes from such evidence, is a complicated process. Indeed, if Yeats chose Jonson, from among those epigrammatists whom he read, as a model for venting his irritation in 'The Fascination of What's Difficult', then his most recent reading in Congreve might have primed his creative faculty with the satiric humour of the Restoration comedy of manners. (Congreve's speciality, one recalls, was the unmasking of folly.) Hence 'wit', it seems, is an ever-evolving element of style, as Yeats's Journal confirms again – with more complications.

Commenting on his wit's device in 'The Fascination of What's Difficult', Yeats set down the following note just after entering the alternative couplets:

> When Adam named the beasts, there was one beast that he forgot to name, or else, taking it for some common horse, named wrongly; and so . . . men came to have much knowledge of what lives and moves, [save] the creature whose name they did not know. . . . That creature permits us to call it Pegasus, but it does not answer to that or any name. (*Mem* 243)

More than a year later, Yeats entered a fair copy of 'At the Abbey Theatre', dated 'August 17 [1911]. Poem written in Paris in May' (*Mem* 261), beneath the inscription 'Imitated from Ronsard'. This poem was not the translation that 'When You are Old' (1893) had been but, as Carpenter suggests, amounted to an adaptation of Ronsard's famous sonnet 'A Pontus de Tyard'.[32] Yeats's only copy of the French Renaissance poet (*YL* 1783) did not contain that poem, but he surely had it, since both Synge and Lady Gregory were interested in this subject and were perhaps more content than he to make translations.[33] In any case, Yeats yielded to the original when he declined to employ his Pegasus over Ronsard's Proteus. Compare the Shakespearean ending of Yeats's draft –

>   Proteus
> Is there a bridle for this P̶e̶g̶a̶s̶u̶s̶
> That turns and changes like his draughty seas
> Or is there none, most popular of men
> But when they mock us that we mock again

– with the equivalent ending in Ronsard:

> Dy moy de quels liens, et de quel rang de clous
> Tiendray-je ce Prothé, qui se change a tous coups?
> Tyard, je t'enten bien, il le faut laisser dire,
> Et nous rire de luy, comme il se rit de nous.[34]

(Translation: 'Tell me [*Dis-moi*] with what bonds and with what order of nails would I restrain this Proteus, who changes himself all of a sudden? Tyard, I understand you well – one must be permitted to say so – and we [are] to laugh at him, [even] as he makes sport of us.')

Yeats's confessed imitation of Ronsard – neither translated nor so freely adapted as were some of his poems based on English prototypes – provides further illustration of the process that was at work, earlier, in the conversion of Yeats's poetic style in 'The Fascination of What's Difficult'. The process was almost painfully deliberate, yet the product, a poem written in the language of 'passionate, normal speech' (*E&I* 521), had to '*seem* a moment's thought', as he wrote elsewhere (emphasis added; see *VP* 86, l. 5).

Perhaps, then, what remains to be said about 'The Fascination of What's Difficult' is that its thesis was parcel to a concept lifted from Castiglione in 1903, when Yeats first read the Hoby translation of *The Courtier* under Lady Gregory's eye (see *YL* 351). The concept, *sprezzatura*, prepared for him his rereading of Jonson and Donne, for his first reading of some of the Jacobean dramatists associated with the War of the Theatres, and for his own interpretation of the aristocratic ideal of effortless skill, nonchalance or feigned carelessness which Hoby had misleadingly rendered into English as 'recklessness'.[35] By 1904, in an Abbey circular entitled 'The Play, the Player, and the Scene', Yeats had already anticipated the issue of which he would be making poems in six years. Rhetorically, he asked,

> What is there left for us, that have seen the newly discovered stability of things changed from an enthusiasm to a weariness, but to labour with a high heart . . . to rediscover an art of the theatre that shall be joyful, fantastic, extravagant, whimsical, beautiful, resonant, and altogether reckless? (*Ex* 169)

IV

Despite the denunciations of some of his critics, Yeats's obsession with the 'holy blood' of the divinely inspired poet and with aristocratic heroes was genuine. He was not posturing. Those inventions – the masks, or *personae*, of many of his poems – derided his enemies in a poetry that had become, by the middle of his career, occasional and more frequently addressed to the spectacles of Irish public life. Peerless in its fashion, 'On those that hated "The Playboy of the Western World", 1907' gives us the poet's inspired enmity to one of the most regrettable disturbances suffered by modern theatre in Ireland. The example also brings to light the workings of the adaptive complex.

Not fully understood until recently,[36] Yeats's epigram has none the less been recognized as a satire against mob politics and demagoguery, divisive forces opposed to the aristocratic character concentrated in a mythic figure or in a symbol of 'all creative power', as Yeats confided to his Journal (*Mem* 176) upon the conception of one of his most potent symbols, the 'sinewy thigh' of Don Juan in hell. Technically, the poem has its apparent analogues: (1) formally, in the epigrams of Jonson and others; (2) allusively, in the epic and dramatic satires, respectively, of Byron and Shaw (for instance, *Man and Superman* [1903], Act III, the Dream of Hell); (3) pictorially, in a specific painting Yeats had seen in the studio of his friend Charles Ricketts; and (4), most manifestly, in *The Playboy* itself and in the bitter epigram that Synge had addressed to the same occasion ('The Curse/To a sister of an enemy of the author's who disapproved of "The Playboy"'). Yet, surprisingly, the manuscripts adduce what we do not expect.

Although the *idea* for 'On those that hated "The Playboy . . ."'

was more than a year old before composition began, Yeats did not copy its earliest version into his Journal until 5 April 1910 (*Mem* 244), making it generally the contemporary of the two poems last discussed, 'The Fascination of What's Difficult' and 'At the Abbey Theatre'. In spite of its position in the Journal, more about the poem's birth is told by the unpublished postscript of a letter Yeats wrote to Lady Gregory from London. The postscript, on a separate sheet, was subsequently pasted into Lady Gregory's presentation copy of Yeats's *Collected Works* (1908), on a double sheet at the beginning of volume VII, now in the Berg Collection at the New York Public Library.[37] Undoubtedly inserted for the new poem that it contained, the postscript places Yeats in London early in 1910, when official business had taken him there to raise funds for the Abbey Theatre. Moreover, it shows that considerable time must be allowed after Yeats entered that now well-known note in his Journal, between the entries of 3 and 4 March 1909 (*Mem* 176), and 7 March, when he wrote to Lady Gregory about the idea, reporting that 'Griffith and his like' were like 'the Eunuchs in Ricketts's picture watching Don Juan riding through Hell' (*L* 525).[38] On the occasion of his later interview with the painter, he discovered that he had mistaken the figures in the picture that he had called to mind in his Journal (see plate 4 in *YA* 4 [1985] and J. G. P. Delaney's article on Yeats, Ricketts and Shannon[39]). Hence the idea became Yeats's *property* before he undertook to write the poem. This is the postscript:

PS

Ricketts told me the other day at the ~~Sicilleans~~ last night of the Sicileans (where I came in for Grassos wonderful Othello) that I had invent[e]d that picture of the ~~Eune~~ Eunecs looking at Don Juan – they were old women. On Monday finding I could claim the idea I made this poem.

     'on the attack on "the Play Boy"'

  Once when midnight smote the air
  Eunics ran through Hell, & met
  Rou[n]d about Hells gate, t[o] stare
  At Great Juan riding by;
  And, like these, to rail & sweat

~~Madened~~
Madened at his sinewy thigh.

Yeats's letter to Lady Gregory, extant though unpublished, is dated 'Tuesday' and was posted two days later, in London, on 7 April 1910.[40] In addition, Yeats's account in the postscript makes it clear, once compared with the schedule of theatrical engagements published in the London *Times*, that the earliest draft of the poem (not extant) was made on the day *before* it was copied into the Journal from another surviving manuscript.[41] Obviously, such conclusions are based substantially on references in the postscript – references to the Sicilian players of Giovanni Grassi (spelled 'Grasso' by Yeats and by the press), to the last night of 'Grasso's' performance in the role of Othello, and to the 'Monday' on which the poem was made. Ricketts' picture, it has turned out, long credited with being the source of inspiration for the poem, may not have been its catalyst.

In 'The Theatre', a lecture of 7 March 1910 – the first of three delivered that week at the Adelphi Club to raise money for the Abbey – Yeats began with a comparison which was to become the main one of his speech: a contrast between the modern intellectual 'feat of skill' exemplified by Galsworthy's *Justice* and the play of primitive instinct, the 'joyous spontaneity of ... art' that he witnessed in an unspecified play from the repertory of 'Grasso's' company. 'Last week when I was thinking how I was to arrange my thoughts for this afternoon', he said, 'I saw two plays which may help me to express my meaning – the Sicilians and "Justice".'[42] Yeats agreed with the anonymous *Times* critic who reviewed their opening night and continued to report on them.[43] Of Grassi in particular, the reviewer wrote, he was 'a kind of human volcano, disquieting when on the smoulder and positively terrifying in active eruption. ... When you come away from the theatre you cannot rid your mind of him. He is something more than an actor; he is a physical obsession' (*The Times*, 23 Feb 1910, p. 12f.). Likewise, Yeats confessed to his audience that he thought Grassi 'the greatest actor in the world'; and, as the postscript of his letter to Lady Gregory shows, he thought Grassi's Othello 'wonderful'. Indeed, it is likely that Yeats found Grassi's Othello at the final performance, on Saturday 2 April, quite as awe-inspiring as had the reviewer in *The Times* two weeks before: 'It was an Othello ... glowing with life and passion. ... Grasso, with all his eruptive violence and molten heat, keeps the beauty of the part, the majesty and the pity of it' (*The Times*, 22 Mar 1910, p. 12f.). On Monday 4 April, his mind toying with a picture of Don Juan in hell and obviously still affected by the memory of Grassi's volcanic stage presence, Yeats set down, as the postscript of his letter testifies, the first draft of his *Playboy* epigram.

V

The above example and the others that we have examined demonstrate how adaptation may be documented. To understand Yeats's use of a simple form, that of the epigram – which he began writing after immersing himself in the works of Jonson in 1906 and reflecting on personality and poetry in the following year (in 'Poetry and Tradition' and 'Personality and the Intellectual Essences': *E&I* 246–60 and 265–7) – one considers the literary background, to be sure, yet may not ignore other influences and remain faithful to evidence at hand. These influences might come from the visual arts or theatre. They might even prove unexpected or desultory – like the 'eruptive violence' of a Sicilian actor transplanted to the early-twentieth-century stage in one of the great Shakespearean roles, suggesting to Yeats the concentrated energy of the Elizabethan 'whole man' he wished to convert into poetic voice.

'In the old days, personality was everything', Yeats said in his lecture of 7 March 1910. The Sicilian players were 'full' of 'personal life', as English actors and the English stage were not (*YT* 20). His own art, 'poetical drama', was like a 'fallen king'; like Shakespeare's 'pit', the Irish audience still liked plays in verse. Yeats discoursed, in turn, about comedy, tragedy, and tragi-comedy, with observations on scenery from Shakespeare, on European picture galleries, and on changes introduced by Ricketts and Gordon Craig. He introduced the Congrevian material he had worked up from his Journal and concluded where he began, with a peroration re-emphasizing the distinction between Grassi's Sicilians and the actors in Galsworthy's play: 'These Sicilians [lived] in an age when men delight[ed] in their own personalities and the personalities of others' (*YT* 21–2). The vigorous style of the troop fit with what he had been saying about the 'sanguineous' Renaissance temperament.

All week, from Monday 7 March to Friday 11 March 1910, Yeats spoke in order, as he said, to try 'to define one or two quite simple things, which things one finds in any of the arts'. In his second lecture, he spoke about his friends of the 1890s, 'all the doomed generation', and about his own early style:

> To bring back the arts of personality, the personality of the lyrical poet or the dramatic personalities of plays – that was our thought. . . . But a great deal follows from it. It involves a change from contemplative thought to active, from an impersonal contemplative culture to a culture that could only be attempted in action. That is all involved in one's definition of the art of personality. Personality is not character. . . . [Again, as he proceeds, he seems to recast his notes on 'wit', 'humour' and 'habit'.]
> Personality is greater and finer than character. It differs from character in this, that it [character] . . . is under the control of our will. It is mixed up in style. When a man cultivates a style in literature he is shaping his personality. (YT 38–9)

In the last lecture of that week, entitled 'Contemporary Irish Theatre', he chose mainly to speak about *The Playboy* and about Synge's style – the 'strange thing of his own', his 'shaping joy, mastery, exultation, a complete contradiction betwen the melancholy submissive dreaming soul . . . and what is in the hand . . . , this whimsical strength, . . . a strong man' (YT 48; cf. *Ex* 169, where Yeats used virtually the same language to modify the concept of *sprezzatura*, the ideal artistic personality drawn from the Renaissance). Of course, Yeats was also speaking of the transformation of style he was at that moment attempting to bring about in his own work. In cultivating a new style, he necessarily had to reshape his personality, for these came to the same thing. His thought fell more and more on the Renaissance. Moreover, as he distinguished between characterization in Galsworthy's *Justice* and in the plays performed by Grassi's players, a distinction made between 'things' and 'the heart', he perceived great differences between contemporary 'feminine', 'passive' culture, which sought 'to protect itself with codes of all kinds', and Renaissance culture, which

> was based not on self-realization, on a knowledge of things . . . reflecting themselves in the soul, but upon the deliberate creation

of a great mask. What else was the imitator of Alcibiades? Do you not always feel that mask consciously created when at the death scenes of Plutarch's people? (*YT* 39: allusions to Shakespeare, evidently, and *Timon of Athens*, a work derived from North's translation of Plutarch's *Lives of the Noble Grecians and Romanes*, 1579)

Like Yeats's genius, his response to the Renaissance was complex and not always approving. He was a man very much of his own time as well as a great innovator. Still, the general and particular ways he found to adapt the hearty Renaissance literature of his beloved 'mother tongue', English, should be seen in light of his ambivalent view of that period and in light of his nationalist sympathies, which were antagonistic to the English. Contradiction, as Yeats himself saw in Synge's dramatic style, may be precisely what we find most fascinating and challenging in his work. To a degree, it may even define his modernity. His reading and practical adaptation of a select body of English Renaissance writers helped him – among other sources of influence – to develop a 'modern style'. How we define 'modern' remains an issue which bears on his Aesthetic sensibilities and his response to the contemporary world. However, 'Style' (as Yeats asserted with feigned Jacobean insolence), or 'personality – deliberately adopted and therefore a mask', seemed the 'only escape from the hot-faced bargainers and the money-changers' (*Au* 461; cf. *Mem* 139).

2
Proto-Modern Poet, 1885–1910: Summoning the Renaissance Spirit with Arnold, Pater, and John Butler Yeats

> Supreme art is a traditional statement of certain heroic and religious truths, passed on from age to age, modified by individual genius, but never abandoned. The revolt of individualism came because the tradition had become degraded, or rather because a spurious copy had been accepted in its stead. Classical morality – not quite natural in Christianized Europe – dominated this tradition at the Renaissance, and passed from Milton to Wordsworth and to Arnold, always growing more formal and empty until it became a vulgarity in our time . . . . (*Au* 490)

> The ancients and the Elizabethans abandoned themselves to imagination as a woman abandons herself to love, and created beings who made the people of this world seem but shadows, and great passions which made our loves and hatreds appear but ephemeral and trivial fantasies; but now it is not the great persons or the great passions we imagine which absorb us, for the persons and passions in our poems are mainly reflections our mirror has caught and from older poems or from the life about us, but the wise comments we make upon them, the criticism of life we wring from their fortunes. (*E&I* 196)

I

If style cannot be separated from life, then neither can it be divorced from the forces which manifest themselves in an age. Those forces, as Yeats perceived them, and their manifestations in literature and history were inextricably bound in a coherent process that it was his individual mission to articulate in all its complexity. If that mission was ever accomplished, it was achieved through a series of successive approximations just as his poems went through laborious stages of revision over the years. It was, to a considerable extent, a matter of expropriation and adaptation, a matter of inheritance. His view of history, his regard for the Renaissance and its multi-faceted personalities ('Renaissance men'), his interpretation of the present in light of the past were derived initially and substantially from influential others such as Arnold, Pater, and the elder Yeats. Notwithstanding certain personal tensions, Yeats's gradual development of a philosophy enabled him to become the acknowledged, prototypically modern poet admired by the generation of Pound and Eliot, whose comparatively abrupt revolution also drew a good share of its strength from analogy to the lyric poetry and drama of the English sixteenth and seventeenth centuries. A Platonist and dedicated spiritual alchemist, Yeats fashioned his poetics from more genuinely mystical sources than did they, of course. But the common objective was clear enough: it was simply that the modern poet must try to do again what English poets had presumably been able to do up to the age of Milton. This would not be easy because it seemed to Yeats and the modernists (and to some earlier authors) that in the meantime something mysterious and catastrophic had occurred to frustrate the poet's ability to express himself fully.

The term 'dissociation of sensibility' does not appear in our critical language until Eliot's review, in 1921, of Grierson's edition of *Metaphysical Lyrics and Poems of the Seventeenth Century*.[1] F. W. Bateson asserts that the term was borrowed from Rémy de Gourmont's *Problème du style* (1902), but Kermode demonstrates that the concept was anything but new.[2] Indeed, the notion is reflected again and again in such passages of Yeats's criticism as those submitted above,[3] passages which are not so much anticipations of Eliot's conception (however indebted Eliot may have been to Gourmont) as they are reflections of philosophical judgement cast upon the history of civilization by such eminent

Victorians as Arnold and Pater. The judgement, in fact, was somewhat a Victorian commonplace. Eliot's assertions about 'something which had happened to the mind of England between the time of Donne . . . and the time of Tennyson and Browning' were part of a myth, for him a way of rewriting history to serve the Symbolist poetic.[4] 'Tennyson and Browning are poets, and they think,' he wrote in a now-famous passage; 'but they do not feel their thought as immediately as the odour of a rose.' In contrast, the English Renaissance in the seventeenth century was an end and a beginning. Especially for poetry, it was the last time when 'new wholes' – i.e. poems that reflect the unified sensibilities of the mind that made them – were regularly fashioned from disparate experiences:

> The poets of the seventeenth century, the successors of the dramatists of the sixteenth, possessed a mechanism of sensibility which could devour any kind of experience. . . . [However,] in the seventeenth century a dissociation of sensibility set in, from which we have never recovered; and this dissociation, as is natural, was aggravated by the influence of the two most powerful poets of the century, Milton and Dryden.[5]

The close of the Renaissance in England thus stood at the beginning of a long decline in which language became 'more refined' just as feeling, according to Eliot, became 'more crude'.

Yeats's view of the Renaissance was certainly akin to Eliot's, although the contexts for, the evolution of, and the contradictions inherent in that view make it a difficult subject to arrest. Equally difficult is the problem of assessing Yeats's response to Milton, the pivotal seventeenth-century poet, who generally vexed Eliot and not infrequently teased Yeats, whose ambivalence on the elder poet commands attention both in this chapter and elsewhere. Assuredly, Yeats's view was his own, but it was not entirely original. Rather, his response to the Renaissance was affected by his elders – particularly those Victorians whose prominence established the intellectual climate of the Aesthetic 1880s just as he began his poetic apprenticeship – and by those lesser poets of his generation with whom he kept company up to the turn of the century. His view of history and his particular regard for the English literary Renaissance were themselves *adaptive* developments.

As Bornstein and other recent critics have observed, the practical necessity of dealing with Yeats's affinities to the Victorians affronts the basic premise of modernist poetics, which, as everyone knows, arose out of protest to 'a flaccid Victorian theory and practice of the poetic art'.[6] Yeats's eventual rebellion against his own early practice – a rebellion encouraged by such younger militants as Ezra Pound – befits his Romantic revolutionary commitment to poetic art and imagination. Moreover, like the Protean creature he mocked in 'At the Abbey Theatre', Yeats seems not to have been restrained by any one mythology or poetic theory, however lately received. Rather, evolution is a fortunate principle observed in the poetry that he produced over a career that transversed two centuries, extending to the brink of the Second World War and nearly to the end of the modernist era itself. Yet it all began deep in the crisis-fraught intellectual and political climate of Victorian England and Ireland. Both intellectual and political elements of that climate are demonstrable in the affinity between his views on the Renaissance and those of at least two Victorian writers in relation to whose ideas he hoped to make himself understood to the audiences of his time.

Matthew Arnold, the first to be considered here, responded to the religious and political crises that rocked England in the late 1840s, and did so by articulating in his prose a moral aesthetic which played, beside the theories of Ruskin and Newman, a major role in the development of the modern poetic sensibility. As a poet, the author of *Empedocles on Etna* dramatized for Yeats (and censured) the self-destructive tendencies seemingly inherent to that sensibility.[7] As a theoretician distressed over history, as effected by the undermining of traditional institutional authority by the advance of science and progressive social science, Arnold formulated an influential alternative to the Comtean view of history as progress. He saw history as marked instead by a cultural shifting between two forces which divided the 'empire of the world': Hellenism, which stood for Greek intellectualism and an outward-directed view of nature; and Hebraism, which represented Christian moralism and an inward-looking view of the self. The objective of these forces was the same. Yet, as he explained in *Culture and Anarchy* (1867–8), this 'perfection or salvation' of man was to be achieved by radically differing means. Hence he divided the ages into creative and critical eras.

Arnold's theory of history had the cyclic and alternating features

Yeats subsequently discerned in his sources when he made a synthesis of all that he had received from his late reading of philosophy and from his 'unknown instructors'. This may be pressing too hard on an analogy, of course, but, by adapting Arnold's view of history and by employing that view to the critical disadvantage of his elder – placing Arnold at the end of the line of descent which began with Milton – Yeats said in effect that he regarded Arnold's practice of poetic art as an exemplum of a process that grew 'more formal and empty until it became a vulgarity in our time'. The problem began, Yeats said, when 'Classical morality' resurfaced at the Renaissance though 'not quite natural in Christianized Europe'. Because the 'supreme art [that] is a traditional statement of certain heroic and religious truths' had become degraded in its transmission through the millennia, the 'revolt of individualism' occurred and 'a spurious copy' of real art was accepted instead.

The English, Protestant, Oxford-educated Arnold viewed this crisis in terms of a sequence of developments originating in the Reformation, the 'Hebraising revival' which was a counter-current to the Renaissance. In England, as in Catholic Ireland, where the pendulum swing against the 'uprising and re-instatement of man's intellectual impulses and of Hellenism' was most ruthlessly executed by Cromwell in the mid-seventeenth century, the rise of Puritanism was a revolt against the spirit of the Renaissance and the 'moral weakness' or 'relaxation' that came with it:

> We in England . . . chiefly know the Renascence by its subordinate and secondary side of the Reformation. The Reformation[,] . . . often called a Hebraising revival, . . . was strong, in that it was an earnest return to the Bible and to doing from the heart the will of God as there written. It was weak, in that it never consciously grasped or applied the central idea of the Renascence, – the Hellenic idea of pursuing, in all lines of activity, the law and science, to use Plato's words, of things as they really are. . . .
>
> Puritanism . . . was originally the reaction in the seventeenth century of the conscience and moral sense of our race, against the moral indifference and lax rule of conduct which in the sixteenth century came in with the Renascence. It was a reaction of Hebraism against Hellenism . . . , and [it] has had a great

part in shaping our history for the last two hundred years. Undoubtedly it checked and changed amongst us that movement of the Renascence which we see producing in the reign of Elizabeth such wonderful fruits.[8]

Yeats, a middle-class Irish Protestant by birth rather than by practice, characteristically viewed the English Puritan dilemma of the late sixteenth and seventeenth centuries in terms of class struggle rather than as a justifiable and perhaps necessary moral 'check' on the fruitful Hellenic movement of the Renaissance in England – which was perhaps Arnold's view, though equivocally stated.[9] Yeats strongly opposed the English materialism of his own time, and he naturally regarded the rise of Puritanism in the English Renaissance as the swelling of what he eventually called the 'filthy modern tide' (VP 611, l. 29). The Puritan dilemma, as he saw it – essentially in agreement with Arnold's basic idea – was one with the rise of capitalism, 'individualism', and a petty, democratic-minded class of shopkeepers who had always been the bane of poets. Together, elements of this 'inexplicable movement' had broken up the 'old rhythms of life', the old agreement, for classes of people previously sustained by the 'myths of Christianity and of still older faiths'. Advancing this argument in his 1901 essay on Shakespeare, 'At Stratford-on-Avon', Yeats demonstrates his sympathy with the common Victorian nostalgia for feudal, pre-industrial England:

> The courtly and saintly ideals of the Middle Ages were fading, and the practical ideals of the modern age had begun to threaten the unuseful dome of the sky; Merry England was fading, and yet it was not so faded that the poets could not watch the procession of the world with that untroubled sympathy for men as they are, as apart from all they do and seem, which is the substance of tragic irony. . . .
>
> The Puritanism that drove the theatres into Surrey was but part of an inexplicable movement that was trampling out the minds of all but some few thousands born to cultivated ease. (E&I 106, 110)

Such class distinctions are suggested by Arnold, too, whose division of English society into Barbarians, Philistines, and Populace is least sympathetic to the Philistines, the middle class to which he said he belonged – though we may understand he was properly one of those *'aliens'* who may arise from any class 'led, not by their class spirit, but by a general *humane* spirit, by the love of human perfection'.[10] Presumably poets might rise from any class. Also like Yeats, Arnold sometimes wondered if the charm of a nation resided in its aristocracy. While the English Philistine might be 'stiff-necked and perverse' – a derelict in the pursuit of 'sweetness and light', the intellectual essences of Hellenic culture – the modern Barbarian, or English aristocrat, had about him 'a kind of image or shadow of sweetness'.[11] Indeed, one finds in Arnold a shadow of the racial ideology that became, unfortunately, so much a part of the Yeatsian cult of the hero:

> The stronghold and natural seat of [the Barbarian's 'passion for doing as one likes'] was in the nobles of whom our aristocratic class are the inheritors; and this class, accordingly, have signally manifested it, and have done much . . . to recommend it to the body of the nation, who already, indeed, had it in their blood.[12]

Out of its larger context, of course, this passage ignores Arnold's censure of the aristocracy, whom he dismissed far more than did Carlyle, Tennyson, and some other literary contemporaries. Arnold is *fundamentally* a moderate. Just so, Yeats's anti-bourgeois, anti-utilitarian contempt for the Philistine differs by several degrees from Arnold's qualified, comparatively moderate condescension. After 1900, Yeats made constructive use of his hatred both in poetry and in criticism. Poems such as 'Paudeen' and 'To a Wealthy Man . . .' curse an insolent 'mob' of shopkeepers and merchants for affronting aristocratic generosity. His essays sometimes reveal the anti-English disposition of his loyalty, his enmity in them being all the more discernible when compared with Arnold's appreciation of Celtic genius and his various caveats on the 'Philistinism of [the English] Saxon Nature' in his essay *On the Study of Celtic Literature*. For example, when Yeats wrote in the Introduction to his edition of Spenser's poetry (*Wade* 235) that Spenser had died just as 'Merry England' ended, he asserted that the former event occurred 'in the last days of what we may call the Anglo-French nation, the old feudal nation that had been established when the Norman and the Angevin made French the language of the court and market' (*E&I* 364). This stretches Arnold's well-known argument that English 'powers, shortcomings, and behaviour' derived in part from 'a Celtic, German, or Norman element', of which the Celtic contributed to English poetry much of its style and melancholy and 'nearly all its natural magic'.[13] For Yeats's account seems to deny Englishmen credit for their Renaissance by bestowing at least a good share of that credit on the Latinized Celt:

> I cannot read any Elizabethan poem or romance without feeling the pressure of habits of emotion, and of an order of life, which were conscious, for all their Latin gaiety, of a quarrel to the death with that new Anglo-Saxon nation that was arising amid Puritan sermons and Marprelate pamphlets. This nation had driven out the language of its conquerors, and now it was to overthrow their beautiful haughty imagination and their manners, full of abandon and wilfulness, and to set in their stead earnestness and logic and the timidity and reserve of a counting-house. (*E&I* 365)

Such gratuitous manipulation of history did not go undetected by English readers of the Spenser edition. One of them, deeply offended, took Yeats to task in a long review published in *The Times Literary Supplement* on 2 November 1906. Yeats pasted it onto two pages of an album of news-clippings (NLI 12,146, fos 51–2 headed 'Times Nov 2 06')[14] though he must have found it painful to read. It scolded him for his 'absurdity' in overlooking the 'Teutonic intellectualism and Teutonic seriousness [that] have had at least their full share of influence . . . over the last 250 years' – an unconsciously ironic point that we may now appreciate from our advanced perspective. However, the reviewer did acknowledge the 'originality' of Yeats's conception of English history, which he measured against Arnold's example:

> It has been Mr. Yeats's mission . . . to remind us of an element in poetry too easily forgotten in a critical and self-conscious age, the element of spontaneous mysticism resulting in what Matthew Arnold called 'natural magic'. And he has carried still further Arnold's striking suggestion that this element in English poetry belongs to the Celtic strain in us. He points us back to the half-lost fountain-head of poetry, the 'troubled ecstasy' in the presence of nature which is the most ancient religion of the world. So far we may all go with him. . . . But when these yearnings after the

beautiful infancy of art pass into a denunciation of all ordered action and all ordered thought, . . . then we begin to wish for Matthew Arnold back again, and a little more judgment to control the overflowing exuberance of an original idea. . . . it is a kind of childishness to wish to forget all we have learned in 300 years, to wish to keep the intellect out of poetry, to see the weakness of Puritanism so plainly as to be unable to see its strength. . . . We cannot if we would be Celtic tribesmen again, and we would not if we could be Irish peasants. . . . We shall not wish with Mr. Yeats that Spenser had renounced his Renaissance birthright to model himself exclusively upon Malory and the Minstrels. . . . One would have expected something saner from so fine a poet and critic as Mr. Yeats. But these are the strange places a man gets into when he judges English poets by Irish political prejudice . . . .

As his scrapbooks demonstrate (there were two albums of clippings: the one mentioned above, for 1904–9, and one kept between 1897 and 1904, NLI 12,145), Yeats was well aware of how differently his views played to Irish and English audiences, respectively. The Irish press up to 1904, though it might make fun of the Paterian mannerisms of his prose style, understandably made little fuss over the issue of 'Celtic genius'. With John O'Leary, the venerable Fenian who 'would say things that would have sounded well in some heroic Elizabethan play' (*Au* 95–6), Yeats still believed that politics and literature were profitably allied in the determination of a national revival. In marked contrast, Yeats's English press was more hostile, usually harping on the 'Celtic' or Irish element of his poetry and responding with less interest to its Symbolist and mystical elements, as the following lampoon testifies:

> To Mr. W. B. Yeats
> But, when it comes
> To
> The
> Celtic
> Muse,
> I sneeze:
> There is no such person –
> That is to say,
> The Muse of Mr. Yeats and his following

> Is not Celtic at all,
> But merely the late William Blake
> Done up
> In green petticoats –
> And William Blake
> Was a Cockney.
>
> . . .
> Until you expunge 'Celtic'
> From among the epithets
> Of your Muse,
> Some of us
> Will never feel ourselves
> Really able
> To swallow you.
>
> (Inscribed '*Outlook* June 23 – 1901[?]'
> in NLI 12,145)[15]

The point to make from such evidence is that Arnold was conciliatory to the views of the English audience and Yeats was not. Arnold tried to reconcile the divisive elements of the English character – the forces which threatened to unravel the fabric of English society as it had not been threatened since the seventeenth century. Yeats, on the other hand, was relatively uncompromising, more willing to engage in verbal jousts against adversarial forces. None the less a man of contradictory impulses and independent mind, he raised objection to Arnold's view of the Celtic temperament because he thought Arnold failed to 'underst[an]d that [the Celtic] "natural magic" is but the ancient religion of the world, the ancient worship of Nature' which transcended all races and which is part of all 'folk-song and folk-belief' ('The Celtic Element in Literature', *E&I* 176).[16] Although Yeats never recanted his early opposition to 'the Aesthetic School' (a term which he borrowed from the younger Hallam's essay on Tennyson and which he associated with Arnold's poetry), a diary entry of 1909, later revised and published in the *Autobiographies*, shows that he was generally converted to Arnold's view on the ethical relationship between art and life. 'When I was a boy', Yeats wrote, 'the unimportance of subject was a canon'; but then he saw with Arnold that 'the moral element in poetry' was the 'means' by which poetic art might be 'accepted into the social order and become a part of life and not things of the study' – imagining that poems might rise above the empty substitutes for 'supreme art' which the copyists of the 'Aesthetic School' had passed on 'just as classical forms [had] passed on from Raphael to the Academicians' (*Au* 490).

Yeats's position on Arnold is not easy to comprehend. Perhaps the Irish poet's great productivity should be regarded the more highly in light of his belief that genuine artistic works were no longer possible except in fleeting instants. As he had written about the unusually fertile period of the English Renaissance – in a way reminiscent of the 'age of expansion' that Arnold equated with the age of Shakespeare in 'The Function of Criticism' (1864) but in fact echoing Walter Pater on Coleridge – 'thoughts and qualities sometimes [came] to their perfect expression when they [were] about to pass away' (*E&I* 364).[17] As a rule, the melancholic side of Yeats's Celtic muse is most apparent whenever he seems most Arnoldian. As a figment of consciousness, the 'louring' moral presence of Arnold helped Yeats avoid the fate of the morbidly self-possessed generation of the 1890s. Yet, again in Schuchard's words, if Arnold's culture seemed 'too much a flood of ideas and abstractions that dealt with "exterior law" rather than "interior life"',[18] Yeats could turn to Pater for an anodyne. Consequently, a happier attitude, with excitement over ephemera and magic, spirits his frequent meditations on the *idea* of Renaissance, or on those transitory moments in history during which 'supreme art' materializes.

II

By 1891, Yeats had established himself as a poet of reputable talent. In the six years since his debut, he had earned general critical acclaim for his first book of poetry, *The Wanderings of Oisin and Other Poems* (1889). Most of the poems for his second book, *The Countess Kathleen and Various Legends and Lyrics* (1892), were already in manuscript. His collaboration with Edwin Ellis on his two editions of Blake was at an advanced stage when, in that same year, two closely related events drew his attention to the aesthetic theory of Pater, whose subjectivism strongly appealed to the young English Decadent and Symbolist writers then living in London. First, Yeats gathered with such poets of his acquaintance in a loose circle called the Rhymers' Club, a group which, as he later wrote, 'for some years was to meet every night in an upper room with a sanded floor in an ancient eating-house in the Strand called The Cheshire Cheese' (*Au* 165). If he had wished to resurrect the famous seventeenth-century poetic feasts of Ben Jonson or, perhaps more self-consciously, their eighteenth-century sequels at 'The Cheese',[19] he must have been a little disappointed to find that his group, which seems to have been anything but lively, would revolve around a *philosophy* rather than a presiding poet of magnetic personality. 'We looked consciously to Pater for our philosophy', Yeats wrote; '. . . we shared nothing but the artistic life' (*Au* 302-3). Yeats initially encountered that philosophy as he undertook his first reading of *Marius the Epicurean*, the second of the two events alluded to above. Though none of the other Rhymers were such ardent disciples of Pater as were Yeats's close friends Arthur Symons and Lionel Johnson (who sometimes visited their 'sage' at Oxford), their encouragement undoubtedly led to Yeats's acquaintance with Pater's other works. For the purposes of the present discussion, the most significant of those works were *Studies in the History of the Renaissance* (1873, 1877), probably Pater's single most important book; *Plato and Platonism* (1893); and an essay entitled 'Shakespeare's English Kings' (published in the first edition of *Appreciations*, 1889).[20]

In little time, Yeats became a fair student of Pater, understanding the elder Victorian well enough to define clearly the points over which they differed. Indeed, one critic thinks Yeats's story 'Rosa Alchemica' (1896) 'the first attempt by a major twentieth-century writer to come to terms with Walter Pater'.[21] The retreat of the story's narrator from the pursuit of impossible purities, 'the transmutation of life into art', saves that character from the disaster that falls upon Robartes as ruin fell upon so many of the Rhymer poets. Perhaps not until a later rereading of Pater's novel did Yeats begin 'to wonder if [*Marius*], or the attitude of mind of which it is the noblest expression, had not caused', as he said, 'the disaster of my friends'. The attitude it engendered was like walking a tightrope 'stretched through serene air'; the performers 'were left to keep [their] feet upon a swaying rope in a storm' (*Au* 302). Certainly, Pater had described this situation seductively in the Conclusion to *The Renaissance*, where the idea of flux and primacy of sensuous experience seem to rest dangerously upon the efficacy of science (as his words suggest) – upon a 'whole physical life' which, measured in a moment, was 'but a combination of natural elements . . . present not in the body alone'.[22] Yeats, whose desire for permanence and outspoken belief in the supernatural set him apart from Pater, could not agree that the material world of the senses should be given precedence over the unseen world of the spirit.[23]

But Pater, for whom orthodox belief had crumbled under the pressure of science until a complex new religion of art had arisen in its place, expressed the paradox of human existence for the sensitive intellect and articulated an aesthetic philosophy upon which new artistic works might be founded. Like Arnold, who influenced Pater considerably and whose own collision with science led to a position of tenuous, even ambiguous equilibrium between Hebraism and Hellenism, Pater viewed the historical development of Western culture in terms of a struggle between the sacred and the profane.[24] Yet, as passage after passage from *The Renaissance* confirms, he rated pagan sensuousness much more highly than did Arnold, who generally ignored that Hellenism had a sensuous side. Consequently, in Pater, spirituality or Christian asceticism, influenced by the upsurge of Hellenism at the Renaissance, seems all but lost in, or mixed up with, the expanding moment of 'quickened, multiplied consciousness', or a kind of sensory intellect. Affirming a clear debt to French Romanticism, especially to the doctrine of *l'art pour l'art* of the Parnassians, he seemed to make a direct appeal to the young poets of his audience:

> Well! we are all *condamnés*, as Victor Hugo says: we are all under sentence of death but with a sort of indefinite reprieve . . . : we have an interval, and then our place knows us no more. Some spend this interval in listlessness, some in high passions, the wisest, at least among 'the children of this world', in art and song. For our one chance lies in expanding that interval, in getting as many pulsations as possible into the given time. Great passions may give us this quickened sense of life, ecstasy and sorrow of love, the various forms of enthusiastic activity. . . . Of such wisdom, the poetic passion, the desire of beauty, the love of art for its own sake, has most. For art comes to you proposing frankly to give nothing but the highest quality to your moments as they pass, and simply for those moments' sake.[25]

Yeats, too, insisted that great passions made the best art,

although the 'interval' (or one's *life*, as Pater meant) recurs in his own view of reality. There were motive powers that stood behind passion – 'certain disembodied powers, whose footsteps over our hearts we call emotions' (*E&I* 157). Moreover, 'greater poets' saw that everything is related to 'the national life, and through that to the universal and divine life: nothing is an isolated moment; there is a unity everywhere' (*LNI* 174). Just as a combination of forces had produced the Renaissance in England in the sixteenth century, so another might materialize in Ireland or elsewhere given the appropriate encouragement.[26] Perhaps in assessing how much work was to be done in the way of 'encouragement', the workman, a kind of spiritual alchemist or literary sorcerer, could not help admonishing himself and his contemporaries of the *fin de siècle* in light of what 'the ancients and the Elizabethans' had presumably done – 'abandon[ing] themselves to . . . great passions which made our loves and hatreds appear but ephemeral and trivial fantasies', 'creat[ing] beings who made the people of this world seem but shadows' (*E&I* 196). Although the words 'appear but ephemeral' and 'seem but shadows' mark an essential distinction between Yeats's view of reality and Pater's, that distinction acknowledges similarity as well as difference.

Like Arnold and, later, like Yeats, Pater conceived of the Renaissance as a period in which scholars and artistic men attempted a reconciliation between Christianity and the religion of ancient Greece. The Renaissance 'spirit' in the age of Lorenzo – i.e. 'the intimate alliance with mind' that gave unity to 'the best thoughts which that age produced' – was its struggle 'to attain the Greek spirit'. It was, as Pater said, 'an age productive in personalities, many-sided, centralised, complete'.[27] In essence, he was describing that spirit which Yeats held to be the ideal artistic personality but which occasionally manifested itself imperfectly, as Yeats thought had been the case during the English Renaissance, which did not grow entirely 'out of itself' but had been subject to corrupting foreign influences, chiefly Italian; Shakespeare himself could not 'write perfectly when his web is woven of threads that have been spun in many lands' (*E&I* 109). For the most part, Pater's collection of essays focuses on six fifteenth-century Italian personalities, each portrayed in terms of the struggle to achieve or maintain personal unity, to reconcile within himself the contrary forces of the age of which he was a *physical manifestation*. Pater finds particularly fascinating the first of these personalities – the exceptional philosopher of the group – precisely because the Florentine humanist's 'life is so perfect a parallel to the attempt made in his writings [and to the attempt made by the artists in the book] to reconcile Christianity with the ideas of paganism'; 'the union of contrasts', we are told, 'pervades, in Pico della Mirandola, an actual person'.[28] Without doubt, this fifteenth-century Neoplatonist is one of the earliest keys to unlock the complex, enigmatic nature of Renaissance genius as we find that genius embodied in the succession of artistic personalities inhabiting Pater's work.

Generally, as one of Yeats's commentators observes, 'the Renaissance marches hand in hand with Platonism'.[29] Certainly, Yeats's and Pater's interests in the subject were strikingly complementary. Perhaps it seemed to both writers that, if industrial civilization could destroy a poet's or artist's relationship with nature, that relationship could be restored by renewed contact with the ancient, vital springs of religion – be they (for Yeats) Hellenic, Hebraic, Celtic, or oriental in origin. Eventually, Yeats would rely upon the English Renaissance authorities in his library for his Platonic doctrine and lore, as his unpublished notebooks demonstrate (see below, Ch. 5, section III). But Pater's interest in the subject, given his connection with the Rhymers poets and Yeats's avid reading of Pater in the 1890s, apparently spurred Yeats toward his acquaintance with the works of those Renaissance authorities just mentioned. These were the so-called Cambridge Platonists (More, Glanvil, Cudworth), whom Yeats cites frequently in his essay 'Swedenborg, Mediums, and the Desolate Places' (1914).[30]

Yeats's early reading of *The Renaissance* and *Plato and Platonism* was memorable, and his personal copy of the latter volume – a presentation copy of the first edition – is marked, scored and annotated as few of his books are, outside the occult works themselves and the copytexts created for subsequent editions of his own works.[31] The 'machinery' of Plato, as derived from 'his Pythagorean masters' and as Pater describes it, sounds uncannily like the system Yeats would develop in *A Vision*: 'the mere stargazer may peep into [it] as best he can, with its levers, its spindles and revolving wheels, its spheres'.[32] A couple of pages later, Yeats stroked, scored, and annotated a long passage of which the following is representative:

For in truth we come into the world . . . by the natural course of organic development clothed far more completely than even Pythagoras supposed in a vesture of the past, nay, fatally shrouded . . . in those laws or tricks of heredity which we mistake for our volitions; in the language which is more than one half of our thoughts; in the moral and mental habits, the customs, the literature, the very houses, which we did not make for ourselves; in the vesture of the past, which is (so science would assure us) not ours, but of the race, the species: that *Zeitgeist*, or abstract secular process, in which, as we could have had no direct consciousness of it, so we can pretend to no future personal interest. It is humanity itself now – abstract humanity – that figures as the transmigrating soul, accumulating into its 'colossal manhood' the experience of the ages; making use of, and casting aside in its march, the souls of countless individuals, as Pythagoras supposed the individual soul to cast aside again and again its outworn body.[33]

This curious passage in which modern genetic theory and primitive philosophy are synthesized into a new type of metempsychosis, the latter presented as an ancient concept preserved at the expense of the personal soul, attracted Yeats's attention although it probably suggested to him the opposite of what Pater meant. As in other instances in the chapter called 'Plato and the Doctrine of Number', Yeats noted marginally the extraordinary length of the first of the two sentences quoted above. Then, at the beginning of the second sentence, he underscored the words 'humanity itself' and drew a line into the left margin from the words 'transmigrating soul'. At that point in the margin, he set down the alchemical sigil which represents Saturn (i.e. the scythe). Undoubtedly, Yeats *liked* the idea of the *Zeit-geist* (literally, the 'time-ghost'), which added a dimension to the process of successive incarnations that he allowed for the personal soul as Pater did not. Epochs and eras of history, according to Yeats, were motivated by the same mechanisms and forces as affected the soul's development over time. As a consequence, history and the fortunes of the individual soul down through its many incarnations ran on parallel courses and were thus depicted in the cosmic design of *A Vision*. The spirit of an age, manifested in some representative person, was precisely its *personality*. The Renaissance, however imperfect, struck Yeats as very much the age of the artistic and of the passionate as he read and scored his copy of *Plato and Platonism*, possibly in 1893, and it was ever the most prominent age for the poet whose medium was English. In England, the westward-moving Renaissance had reached its apogee in the age of Shakespeare – an age only much later eclipsed in Yeats's thinking by its eastern complement in sixth-century Byzantium.

Implicitly at issue here is the dynamic process by which personality is made manifest in actual beings who exist in nature at particular junctures; in poets, who are themselves such beings, but who are also the instruments, if not agents, by which Platonic *mimesis* makes art out of nature; and in the fictive creations (albeit imitations of an imitation) borne into existence by the poet or lyric dramatist. The issue was very much on Yeats's mind when he ventured to Stratford-upon-Avon in April 1901, and made perhaps his first thoroughgoing study of Shakespeare since his boyhood, when his father had directed his reading. Yeats's essay 'At Stratford-on-Avon', written in the following month at the conclusion of his term as patron of the Stratford theatre and its library, shows him trying to extrapolate Shakespeare from the *personae* that inhabit several of the history plays. Shakespeare becomes, in a sense, one of Yeats's *creations* as a consequence of this methodology, although Yeats's reading was strongly influenced by Pater's essay 'Shakespeare's English Kings'. While an extensive comparison between the two essays is unnecessary here – since one would need to do no more than chronicle the several accounts provided by Nathan, McGrath, Desai and others[34] – such a comparison would show that Yeats's published views supported adaptation rather than the perceived originality which so much offended his English reviewers.

To be sure, if he had provoked the journalists of England with what they thought a heresy – a gratuitous reinterpretation of Shakespeare – it was because Yeats was honestly upset by much of the criticism that he read in the library of the Shakespeare institute at Stratford. In a letter postmarked 25 April 1901 from his lodgings at the Shakespeare Hotel, he reported to Lady Gregory that he was putting in long days at the library, and, it seems, his patience was almost exhausted with the scholars – a fact which is striking considering how well pleased he was with the nightly productions. 'The more I read', he wrote, 'the worse does the Shakespeare criticism become and Dowden is about the climax of it. I[t] came out [of] the middle class movement and I feel it my legitimate enemy' (*L* 349).

In little time, this thesis had generated the essay published in the *Speaker* on 11 and 18 May. Because of such critics as Dowden, whom he had 'once read carefully' and whom he knew through his father, one received, Yeats said, the mistaken notion 'that Henry V, who . . . had some commonplace vices, was not only the typical Anglo-Saxon, but the model Shakespeare held up before England'. It was plain to Yeats that, quite to the contrary, the Bard's sympathy went out to Richard II, ' "a wild creature" as Pater . . . called him' (*E&I* 105). Exaggerating Pater's position as he defined his own, Yeats's theory about Shakespeare must have seemed to spring from nowhere, or from an overactive imagination, perhaps, although it represented, in fact, his characteristic use of the adaptive complex. Unlike the obvious debt Yeats owed Arnold for the ethno-historical argument propounded in the Introduction to the *Poems of Spenser* (see above, section I), Yeats's debt to Pater went unobserved. At best, the poet's views were suffered, and sometimes (rarely) applauded, for compelling the 'average Saxon' to think in unaccustomed patterns about 'subjects with which he [the average Saxon] is tolerably familiar', as one reviewer noted in the *Pall Mall Gazette* (cutting dated 'July 14 [1903]' in NLI 12,145). 'Intelligent without any particular knowledge of, or sympathy for, the ideas of which Mr. Yeats is the greatest living exponent', the *Gazette*'s readers were nevertheless conditionally recommended 'perhaps the best essay' in the 1903 edition of *Ideas of Good and Evil* (*Wade* 46):

> For the intelligent and cultured Englishman does know something of Shakespeare; he lives, it is true, under the bondage of that conventional criticism which Mr. Yeats takes to task, and he will be as disgusted as astonished at the new way of looking at the great poet to which Mr. Yeats will introduce him. The comparison between Richard II. and Henry V. and the calculation of the values which the author sets on those characters is singularly sure and certain. . . . We recommend this essay . . . because the average Saxon . . . will be compelled . . . , even if it be only in indignation, to read it through; and from it he may proceed to some of the other essays that make up this . . . volume. It is not a book of criticism. It is written for those who have the sixth sense, the spiritual imagination which knows how to distinguish the truths of eternity from their envisagement in

time; and for those who have not that sense, the book must remain closed and sealed; for them it has no message, no beauty, no truth . . . .

In 1906 John Bailey, in his *Times Literary Supplement* review of the Spenser edition, had correctly perceived a connection between Yeats's view of Spenser and the 1901 article on Shakespeare, and he brought this into his rebuttal (quoted in part in section 1). When Yeats, in his 'yearnings after the beautiful infancy of art', attempted to persuade his English audience that

> Shakespeare must have preferred Richard II. to Henry V., and that Henry V. is only the supreme instance of the law 'that the commonplace shall inherit the earth', then we begin to wish for Matthew Arnold back again, and a little more judgment to control the overflowing exuberance of an original idea. He, at least, would not have told us that Henry V. was a smaller man than Richard II. 'in the Divine Hierarchies'. He could love and praise the Celtic side of us, but he knew the other side – and, one may add, the facts. (Clipping in NLI 12,146, fo. 51)

Apparently none of Yeats's English reviewers recognized in the single allusion to Pater the really significant debt that Yeats owed him for so contrary a view. The better part of Pater's essay of 1889 is devoted to Richard, who, according to Pater, does represent something of Shakespeare's personal sentiment, magnificently apparelled in poetry, 'a garden of words!' Pater's prose is infected with excitement as he speaks of Richard and with mild censure for Henry, whose 'speeches . . . are but a kind of flowers, worn for, and effective only as personal embellishment'.[35] However, as seemed to Pater to be true of Shakespeare's kings in general, Richard was not, nor meant to be, a great man. All Shakespeare's kings – Richard II and Henry V included – seemed, 'rather, little or quite ordinary humanity, thrust upon greatness', but 'composed in Shakespeare's embalming pages, with just that touch of nature about them, making the whole world akin'.[36]

In Yeats's essay, on the other hand, the two kings, Richard II and Henry V, are more than 'ordinary humanity, thrust upon greatness'. They are personality types, powerful forces colliding in the age of Shakespeare – the one 'lovable and full of capricious fancy, . . . full of French elegancies'; the other 'so little "too friendly" to his friends that he bundles them out of doors when their time is over' (*E&I* 105, 108). Showing little care for 'the State', Shakespeare's interests in Richard were vested in the 'Divine Hierarchies' (*E&I* 103). (In the next breath, Blake, who 'belonged by right to the ages of Faith, and thought the State of less moment than the Divine Hierarchies', joins Arnold and Pater in this obviously complicated adaptive complex.) Shakespeare, a solitary man, according to Yeats, 'meditated as Solomon'; 'the world was almost as empty in his eyes as it must be in the eyes of God'. Hence the Daimons, the spirits who 'shape our characters and our lives', used him, as they used the Greeks, to create a great mythology. And, though his heart rose to the lyricism that found speech for the fountaining mind of Richard, he had watched Henry V, all the while, 'not . . . as he watched the greater souls in visionary procession, but cheerfully . . . and . . . with tragic irony' (*E&I* 106–7, 109).

Thus Pater's emphasis on the early Renaissance, in his celebrated study of several of its most representative personalities, and his obvious attraction to certain Shakespearean creations such as Richard were not lost on Yeats. Yeats's great affection for the Elizabethan period – for the Renaissance that reached its climax in England before the gradual disintegration of social and cultural order provided substance for satire on the Jacobean stage – seemed confirmed in what Pater wrote. Moreover, Pater gave him an articulated theory of the 'Renaissance man' which Yeats not only found useful as he propounded his own ideas on personality, but found suggestive of how the Renaissance spirit might be translated into modern poetry.

Eventually Yeats concluded that the culture that Pater expressed could 'only create feminine souls', that through such culture 'the soul becomes a mirror not a brazier' (*Mem* 159). Based on the pursuit of self-knowledge, the aestheticism of Pater – as well as of the early Yeats and his circle in the 1890s – could not produce a Shakespeare. And, when Yeats compared it with the culture of the Renaissance, he found it wanting to his taste. Aestheticism (and it is worth remembering that this is Yeats in 1909) led to culture of a kind that 'produces its most perfect flowers in a few high-bred women. It gives to its sons an exquisite delicacy.' In contrast, the culture of the Renaissance was 'founded not on self-knowledge but on knowledge of some other – Christ or Caesar – not on delicate sincerity but on imitative energy' (*Mem* 160). When this shift in Yeats's position occurred, it was decisive and depended on what he then understood to be the mechanics of 'passionate personality', the energy emanating from the whole man – 'blood, imagination, intellect, running together' (*E&I* 266). Taking care to preserve most of the critical apparatus to which the work of twenty-five years committed him, he was perhaps not persuaded suddenly to a position that he seems to have resisted for years. Nevertheless, as he began to change his nineties' Symbolism into a philosophy of life, he was somewhat surprised to discover that he had inherited that philosophy from his father 'in all but its details and applications' (*L* 549).

III

Here, the focus of the present study also shifts. Yeats's counterpoint to his father's point and the poet's ability to reconcile countervailing attitudes in his work (in consonance with the 'union of contrasts' achieved by Pater's Renaissance men) are now much more the issue than is the effort to establish the likeness of mind between Yeats and his fellow literary tradesmen of the Victorian period. Indeed, Yeats's *development* becomes the central issue. And the admission of his father into the study introduces some interesting problems concerning the way influence works – complicated, in this case, precisely because of the father's intimacy, occasional antagonism, and generous assistance with introductions to the host of associates who instructed the fledgling poet whenever the elder Yeats felt unqualified to do so himself.

To be sure, no one made an earlier or more lasting impression upon the poet, or did more to stimulate his interest in the English literary Renaissance, than did J. B. Yeats the painter. Fortunately, a detailed defence of this statement may be waived to avoid merely summarizing the well-known accounts given in several collections of letters, in memoirs (especially in the poet's *Reveries over Childhood and Youth*), and in a number of biographical and critical works.[37] Considering, rather, the nineteenth-century crisis of faith which strongly affected both father and son, one finds that W. B. Yeats's thought, eventually bearing likeness to that of such influential Victorians as Pater and Arnold, sprang first from the exemplary, if somewhat iconoclastic, education that Yeats senior personally administered to his eldest son. Among the most interesting facts are the following. First, J. B. Yeats's own education, taken at Trinity College, Dublin, converted him (despite the fact that he was the son of a deeply orthodox rector of the Church of Ireland) to the positivist views of John Stuart Mill and Auguste Comte. Second, like his friends Edward Dowden and Edwin Ellis, with whom, respectively, his son would quarrel over Shakespeare and collaborate on Blake, the elder Yeats's response to the religious crisis of his time was to substitute a personal philosophy for the faith that had been lost. And finally, unlike the 'carefully upholstered ethicalism' of Matthew Arnold (*YM&M* 14) – or the path followed by Dowden – it was J. B. Yeats's decision, after a false start into law, to strike out in the direction to which Mill had been drawn at the same age – towards art. In committing his personal creed to words, on 31 December 1869, the young art student preached to Dowden perhaps the main lesson that his son, W. B. Yeats, was to receive from him:

It seems to me that the intellect of man *as man*, and therefore of an artist, the most human of all, should obey no voice except that of emotion, but I would have a man know all emotions. Shame, anger, love, pity, contempt, admiration, hatred, and whatever other feelings there be, to have all these roused to their utmost strength, and to have *all* of them roused . . . is the aim, as I take it, of the only right education. A doctrine or idea with Catholicity in it is food to all the feelings, it has been the outcome of some strong and widely developed nature, and every other nature is quickened by it. Art has to do with the sustaining and invigorating of the Personality. To be strong is to be happy. Art by expressing our feelings makes us strong and therefore happy. (*LJBY* 48)

As Ellmann points out (in *YM&M* 15–16), this sceptic's religion of 'Art' and 'Personality' is anti-rational and shows a departure from Mill and Comte. However, the stance allows contradiction, which, befitting the elder Yeats's reputation as a controversialist, may be one with the 'chord' which 'every feeling vibrates' in the emotional man, as the painter said on the same occasion.

Yeats senior was understandably pleased when his fourteen-year-old eldest son proved to have an exceptional aptitude for science, avowing himself 'a complete "evolutionist"', well-read in Huxley, Herbert and Spencer though a great failure as a student of the classics, according to his school chum 'John Eglinton'.[38] Yet the father, supplementing his son's instruction in Latin and directing his reading in narrative poetry and Shakespeare, was *delighted* when the young Darwinist and student of evolutionary botany suddenly threw over his science to write strange, wild epic verses and to become an artist in the father's footsteps. If the change seemed a diametric reversal, it was also fitting, as the elder Yeats commented in his unpublished memoirs,

> because he was living with me among friends and I cared a great deal for poetry and very little for science. . . . I remembered his mother's family and their puritan grimness and, turning to a friend, said, 'If the sea-cliffs had a tongue what a babbling there would be! I have given tongue to the sea cliffs.'[39]

As the poet grew to manhood, he sometimes found himself temperamentally at odds with his flamboyantly contradictory father. Yet in spite of their differences – which were fundamental, for example, on magic – they suffered each other's company for some thirty years in the same household. Assuredly, the relationship accounts for much that ripened, with the poet's later modernity, into that union of contradictory impulses, that complex *personality*, that we read in his poems and criticism and infer to be his own. The poet's interests, though they did not always coincide with his father's, were sometimes whetted by one or another of his father's friends. Dowden, for example, an expert on Shelley, stimulated an important literary interest that J. B. Yeats preferred to arrest in favour of Keats. With Ellis, the religious and esoteric elements in Blake could be explicated without apology or censure. Through O'Leary, Yeats discovered a mission for his poetry by which the sleeping giant of Ireland's heroic past was to be revived simultaneously in a modern cultural renaissance and in nationhood. And by Henley the poet and T. W. Lyster the English Renaissance scholar and Irish curator, his early lessons on poetic craftsmanship were delivered in painful but welcome doses.[40] The circle which revolved around the Bedford Park studio had tangible connections with the Pre-Raphaelites.[41] Moreover, even Maud Gonne, arriving there one day with her letter from O'Leary, was introduced first to Yeats senior. Thus, seeing that his father so strongly and directly influenced his development in various ways, it may seem less surprising to us now than it apparently did to Yeats at mid-life that his poetic theory had grown into a complex hybrid from the root-stock of his father's basic philosophy.

Emphatically, one must stress that both root-stock and hybrid drew their sustenance from the same soil, thriving on the example of the English literary Renaissance – on the period of the Elizabethans and especially on Shakespeare. Nowhere is this more evident than in a particular exchange of letters and in the poet's lectures of early 1910. As a portrait-painter and conversationalist as well as an astute reader of Shakespeare and contemporary writers (particularly dramatists), J. B. Yeats's observations on *personality* were understandably shrewd. Speaking his mind on the subject in an unpublished and perhaps lost letter of February 1910 or earlier, the elder Yeats made himself more than usually clear, for in two letters of response (dated 16 and 23 February), Yeats acknowledges this 'most wonderful' letter which 'clarified [his] thought a great deal' and asks permission to quote from it at the close of his lecture on the Rhymers' Club poets in the following month (*L* 547–9). Both letters use Shakespeare as a touchstone, and the second, at the point where the extant portion breaks off, solicits more of the elder's wisdom. Hence J. B. Yeats's second object lesson was delivered in a letter of 5 March 1910, with a shorter third sent three days later. Judging from the evidence at hand, Yeats seems to have been most excited about the effect of 'will power' on personality.

The following excerpt from the letter of 5 March reveals a comprehensive theory allying art and literature with Elizabethan (i.e. Shakespearean) and native Irish (particularly West of Ireland) character:

> Will represents abstract ideas. The will power is like the police in a city, and sometimes as you know, there are cities like Berlin where everything is in the hands of the police, and then again there are other places like villages in the west of Ireland where one is only aware of the concrete facts of human nature; in the ways, humours, voices and looks of the people; or as in London in the time of Queen Elizabeth. . . . too much will . . . and there is no chance for the poor fine arts or for literature. . . . Wordsworth to my mind was a sort of servile poet enforcing always will power. Browning who was only interested in conduct, much the same, and Shelley suffered also, wasting himself in conflict with the servitude to which Wordsworth complacently

yielded. In England character always means a man in whom the will power is predominant. . . . Such men are valuable for administering empires, provided they are directed and controlled by the people who touch life at many points as do young Irishmen at the present moment, since . . . they have the ancient Elizabethan Englishman's abundance and variety of human nature and therefore their initiative and charm – as the natives could tell you. Had Shakespeare possessed a strong will or *an admiration* for it he would have gone over like Browning and Wordsworth to the side of the authorities and the preceptors. . . . A schoolmaster might know his schoolboys very well, yet he could not . . . get *inside the skin*, as Synge does in his plays. . . . In Ireland we still pursue more or less the simple life and Irish human nature is still a bird uncaged. Personality to my mind is human nature when undergoing a passion for self-expression. (*LJBY* 124–5)

Synge, who, like Shakespeare, had no vigorous life outside an extraordinary imagination, receives the same tribute in the poet's essay 'J. M. Synge and the Ireland of his Time' (dated 14 Sep 1910 in *E&I*). He could 'get *inside the skin*', and he compares with certain great writers (just as J. B. Yeats had suggested with his Elizabethan–Irish model) when the basis of comparison is *personality* – active and passive personal will:

> There are artists like Byron, like Goethe, like Shelley, who have impressive personalities, active wills and all their faculties at the service of the will; but he [i.e. Synge] belonged to those who, like Wordsworth, like Coleridge, like Goldsmith, like Keats, have little personality, so far as the casual eye can see, little personal will, but fiery and brooding imagination. (*E&I* 328–9)

Such passages anticipate what Yeats was later to call the 'primary' and 'antithetical Masks', described in elaborate detail in *A Vision*. 'The *antithetical Mask* and *Will* are *free*', he would observe, 'and the *primary Mask* and *Will enforced*', perhaps translating his father's thought into the tongue of mystic science; 'the *free Mask* and *Will* are personality, while the *enforced Mask* and *Will* are code' (*AV* B 84), like the police in a city. By then Shakespeare and Synge had found quite different places in Phases 20 and 23, respectively, of the great system. However, as in his essay of 1910 and in one of the three lectures delivered 'as a plea for uniting literature once more to personality' (*L* 548), Yeats's interpretation of these two men depends on literary creation viewed as *mimetic* process. Accordingly, Shakespeare's mind was a 'multiplying mirror' while Synge's eavesdropped at 'that hole in the ceiling' and filled 'many notebooks' with vestiges of Elizabethan abundance preserved in Irish syntax and rhythm (*AV B* 152–3 and 166). Indeed, Yeats's view of the 'imitative energy' of the Renaissance (see above, end of section II) and a provisional version of his theory of the masks (see below) form the gravitational centre of the lectures presented in London on 7, 9 and 11 March 1910.

The second of these, about the Rhymers and entitled 'Friends of my Youth' (*YT* 25–41), is a cogent, if at moments paradoxical, assessment of that short-lived group of poets. It was no surprise to anyone that Yeats thought that the movement had been a revolt against mid-Victorian poetry, which he likened to Academic painting. His censure of Tennyson and the reference to what Hallam had called the 'aesthetic school of poetry' (*YT* 28) were reworkings from a Journal entry of only months before (*Mem* 180) and from two book reviews: one on *The Poems of Arthur Henry Hallam, Together with his Essay on the Lyrical Poems of Alfred Tennyson* (1893; *UP1* 276–8), the other entitled 'Mr Lionel Johnson's Poems' (1898; *UP2* 88–91). As we compare these reworkings with the first of those renditions just cited (*Mem* 180) or quoted at the outset of this chapter (*Au* 490), we find that Arnold is now missing from the reproof that still falls hard on Wordsworth, though Milton fares far better than before. The imitative process, degenerating from the Renaissance into 'a formal and cold thing' akin to the taking of measurements 'from classic statues . . . and . . . living men', gave place, Yeats said, to 'the idea of academic morals in poetry', a 'standard of form' which was probably due to the influence of Seneca. Despite this first step toward the depersonalization of verse, the intrusion of academic morals in poetry 'became a noble and wonderful thing . . . in the earnest passionate mind of Milton' (*YT* 27). Certainly, something *had* happened with Milton. He was 'wonderful' but not quite in the same way as were those Elizabethan poets whom Yeats enjoyed reading in the British Library, caring only for 'those wonderful Elizabethan lyrics' when he fancied knowing 'the *imagined* men who sang them, and the incidents in which they arose' (*YT* 30).[42] Remembering his friends – but chiefly Lionel Johnson and Ernest Dowson, who were dead –

Yeats made compensation for their celebrated dissipation with a claim at first perplexing because of his objection to their Paterian pursuit of intellectual purities: their common aim, whether 'consciously or unconsciously', was to 'bring back the arts of personality, the personality of the lyrical poet or the dramatic personalities of plays' (*YT* 38). Their great mistake, as Yeats had not foreseen, was that the personal utterance that took form in their poetry (as in his own) sprang more from contemplative thought than from action. To be sure, 'if you are going to make *yourself* personal', he said somewhat cryptically, 'you will have some kind of a troubled life' (*YT* 31; emphasis added).

Far from abandoning his friends or his early poetics in accommodating himself to his father's point of view, Yeats effected a shift. The shift depended, he argued, on 'one's definition of the art of personality' although he must have been confused then, as he is now puzzling, in his use of various terms constructed on the word *personal*. Most of the details and applications of this shift, in fact, derived from 'The Symbolism of Poetry' (1900) and 'Poetry and Tradition' (1907), theoretical works which explain how the intellectual essences of Pater convert into emotions through speech and how the best language is equal to the reckless, self-consuming yet never exhausted energy of abundant life. However, modern culture, 'the culture of Pater', as he now said (repeating his Journal entry of 3 February 1909), was often shaped

> under an influence that makes us passive men. The end of our culture is a feminine nature, a passive nature, a nature which seeks to protect itself with codes of all kinds. . . . [In contrast,] the culture of the Renaissance was based not on self-realization, . . . but on the deliberate creation of a great mask. (*YT* 39)

The shift of position, according to Yeats, who had already begun an earnest study of several writers of the English Renaissance, 'involves a change from contemplative thought to active, from *impersonal* contemplative culture to a culture that could only be attempted in action' (*YT* 38). For practical reasons – and Yeats was making a concession to a *practical* audience of literary tradesmen and academics – the poet should not be sacrificed in the making of art but must survive the making by offering not himself in an act of 'self-realization', but a *mask* or, as O'Driscoll suggests (*YT* 8), an *objective correlative* of emotion as Eliot defined it – or, better, a *persona* (an identity not co-referential with that of the poet) to which emotions adhere in an *object* of art. Although a remarkable development for the poet who previously put great stock in the self-consuming fire of contemplation, the shift was also *conservative*, maintaining as much as possible of Yeats's existing critical commitments while sustaining his assault against poetry as he found it in England at the turn of the century.

While disagreeing fundamentally on almost all else (because of J. B. Yeats's progressive views on everything save art and literature), the views of father and son had converged, by 1910, in an agreement on the mechanics of passionate personality and in the conviction that modern poets must emulate their precursors of the English Renaissance if 'the concrete facts of human nature', as one might discover them in Ireland, were still to be translated into poetry. As a precept of an earlier conversion, that conviction was accepted almost as a given. However, the agreement on the function of *will power* on personality was not so easily reached by the poet, who, paradoxically, had first to assimilate his father's philosophy into a quasi-religious system of which the elder disapproved.

IV

The dialectical theory of the anti-self, with its personal and historical dimensions, represents at once an attempt to apprehend and arrest contradiction in a rational code (an act of *will* upon *abstract ideas*) and a complex synthesis of viewpoints not always objectively received from J. B. Yeats and/or his associates. Eventually, the theory enabled Yeats to realize how an equilibrium might be achieved between active and contemplative modes of life – a desirable alternative to the disaster that attended either extreme. None the less, a strong dose of the active mode in the early years of the post-Victorian period, Yeats thought, would serve well as a tonic in the convalescence of an anaemic poetic art. Poetry, a mere metaphor for the world-creating process of his great Platonic system, of course upheld the whole theory. And Renaissance English poetry, in particular, seemed the richest of any as a reflection of the fully unified, engaged faculties of its complex poets. Yet it, too, was possessed by contradiction.

The linguistic artifice of the English Renaissance poet transformed chaos into order, and the poetic effect of such artifice – *discordia concors* – remained the aesthetic ideal long after the age of Shakespeare. The countervailing historical forces with which English poets struggled in the sixteenth and seventeenth centuries made good cause for grief. 'Everybody [had been] happy in Shakespeare's time', the elder Yeats held,[43] more or less with his son. Yet the poet prized Shakespeare and the Jacobeans for what he perceived to be their struggle against forces leading to the decline of the arts and the rise of materialism, to social and personal fragmentation, and to the political catastrophe of civil war.

Understandably, Milton seemed to stand at the verge of a great cataclysm for poetry, much as he stood on the 'wrong' side – i.e. on Cromwell's side – as a participant in the policies that went hard against the Irish. Yeats, however, could not deny Milton his deserved recognition as a poet. Indeed, in some respects, Shakespeare and Milton seemed different cuts of the same cloth, since both inspired their contemporaries to action, Yeats thought, because they were able to instill life into great works of imagination. In general, Yeats's ambivalent perspective on Milton is crucial to his view of the English Renaissance as a whole. But in particular, his paradoxical assessment of Milton bears directly on the early stage of his own poetic development – a fact which comes to light in this study and which, in the way of introduction, requires a little more discussion about Shakespeare and about the workings of a poetic psychology which Yeats improvised in order to reconcile poets to the basically tragic circumstances of existence. This reconciliation applies to all poets in all ages, presumably, though some periods provide more conflict than others. Certainly, Yeats saw parallels between the Renaissance and the modern period (even if he contrasted the relative imaginative vigour of the former with the lassitude of the latter). History's drama provided poets with the substance of lyrics, yet did so by means of grave conflicts – the sort of conflicts which give rise to complex poetic angularities, to paradox and irony.

Though he perhaps longed for concord, Yeats conceived of history as a tragic play in which the dread of its most passionate players is transfigured into cathartic gaiety. Hamlet and Lear, Ophelia and Cordelia, those Chinese sages of 'Lapis Lazuli' – transfixed in an object of art but brought to life by an act of imagination – 'are gay'. 'Old Rocky Face', a phrase once self-effacingly employed by Jonson but in Yeats the name of the presiding persona of 'The Gyres',[44] gazes with detachment on the nightmare spectacle of history running to chaos and 'laugh[s] in tragic joy'. 'Tragic joy', a complex emotion, is also, paradoxically, what the artist experiences when, in a 'sudden reckless flash', he achieves his anti-self.[45] Moreover, 'tragic joy', as Yeats's essay 'Poetry and Tradition' makes clear, is equivalent to the Romantic moment of 'reverie', very much a part of the Victorian aesthetic apparatus which Yeats received from Pater, as well as from Tennyson, Ruskin, Rossetti, Swinburne, and others. It is a residual 'strength', a 'still unexpended energy . . . playing' in the work, 'a secret between a craftsman and his craft' which only comes out 'amid overwhelming emotion . . . and in the face of death' (E&I 254). About to be engulfed in their 'last darkness', Shakespeare's *personae*, according to Yeats,

> speak out of an ecstasy that is one-half the surrender of sorrow, and one-half the last playing and mockery of the victorious sword before the defeated world.
> . . . This joy, because it must be always making and mastering, remains in the hands and in the tongue of the artist. . . . Timon of Athens contemplates his own end, and orders his tomb by the beached verge of the salt flood, and Cleopatra sets the asp to her bosom, and their words move us because their sorrow is not their own at tomb or asp, but for all men's fate. *That shaping joy has kept the sorrow pure, . . . for the nobleness of the arts is in the mingling of contraries*, the extremity of sorrow, the extremity of joy, perfection of personality, the perfection of its surrender, overflowing turbulent energy, and marmorean stillness. . . . (E&I 254–5; emphasis added)

By mastering ourselves, freeing ourselves from the bondage of solemn emotions, Yeats said, paraphrasing Blake, 'we are reborn in gaiety' (E&I 252). Generally speaking, however, 'tragic joy' is an emotional complex that derives from the Renaissance concept of *sprezzatura* (defined and illustrated Ch. 1). The writer's freedom to 'take whatever theme he pleases' is analogous to the licence of the aristocrat with whom he is allied. His licence of 'cap and bell' permits him his one 'continual deliberate self-delighting happiness – style, "the only thing that is immortal in literature"', according to Sainte-Beuve (E&I 253–4). In pursuit of *style* – or *personality*, as we have been defining it – Yeats would have us 'go backward to turreted walls, to Courts, to high rocky places, to little walled towns' like Urbino in the time of Castiglione, to the aristocracies which 'made beautiful manners', to the countrymen who 'made beautiful stories', and to the artists who 'made all the rest . . . because Providence has filled them with recklessness' (*E&I* 251–2). In 1907, the extreme conservatism of Yeats's now-outspoken poetic idealism – his aristocratic stance – suddenly emerged from his study of the major Elizabethan and Jacobean writers. That idealism was of course profoundly influenced by his reading and rereading of Castiglione. But *The Courtier*, for all its Platonic wisdom, hardly provided Yeats with practical models for remaking himself in the image of an aristocratic poet. Shakespeare, Spenser, and Jonson could do that, as McAlindon has convincingly argued,[46] though theirs were not the only examples of significance to Yeats at that stage in his development. Moreover, it is demonstrable that Yeats was strongly converted to the Renaissance from the *very beginning* of his career and that Milton's name should appear in the roll of important early influences.

Given Yeats's background, one should not be astonished to observe the adolescent poet struggling precociously with the dialectical forces that, as he later said, accounted for the gradual erosion of the 'supreme art' of poetry from Milton to the Victorians. Evidently of great concern to the young scientist-turned-poet was the head-on collision between modern rationalism and the truth of imagination as told in dreams and preserved in old literature. Perhaps sensing by his twentieth year (or sooner) that his intellectual growth required more consistency than his father's views had to offer, Yeats cast his lot with the ancients and prepared himself for a life-long assault against science by girding his verses with a swaddling of antique diction fresh from his reading in the Leinster House library, T. W. Lyster presiding.[47]

Some evidence of that early contact with sixteenth- and seventeenth-century English authors survives in a draft of the oldest work of the Yeats canon. First appearing as 'An Epilogue. / To "The Island of Statues" and "The Seeker"' in the *Dublin University Review* (Oct 1885), the product of that early labour is more commonly recognized as 'The Song of the Happy Shepherd', the leading work of the 'Crossways' section of the *Collected Poems*. The manuscript (now NLI 3,726, fos 69–71) shows how much Yeats had to learn about *mingling contraries* in order to stir the emotions and to simulate personal reverie in a dramatic monologue. But one passage, a significant expansion of ll. 13–34 (*VP*), demonstrates how he was already making use of the intellectual drama of his own life. The passage runs as follows (*VP* lines are numbered, with '+' indicating lines of the first printed version; the others are variants or unique to the manuscript):[48]

13+ Where are now the old kings hoary
       and
13a ~~Oh~~ they were of no wordy mood
      ~~An mease~~
                      now
14 An idle word is ~~all~~ their glory ~~se~~
                             boy
15 By the stammeri[n]g schools~~by~~ ~~red~~ read
      an[?] the   atic   sayed
In ~~some~~ verse of ~~latinie~~ story
    ~~Chimera on their deads has feed~~
    ~~And words are all   preest~~
        ~~all the heroes works are dead~~
18+ The very world its self may be
     only a flaming sudden word
     ~~In Among~~
20 In a clanging space a moment heard
     ~~From~~
21+ in ~~In~~ the universes revery
     Then worship not/a an Idle dead
23 Nor skeeh [= seek] for this is also sooth –
24 To hunger ~~af~~ fierc[e]ly after truth
    for all   would
    ~~because~~ thy toil ~~shall~~ only breed
26 New Dreams. new dreams Ther[e] is no truth
                        seek then
    Maugre within their heart ~~the sea[r]chers~~
    of science ~~the~~ w[i]sdom of churches
    ~~Shall never ado~~
                           holy
    Shall only dim its ~~shin shiny~~ youth
             orm [= from?]
28 no learning ~~of~~ the starry men
29 f who follow with the optic glass
30 The whily [> whirling] ways of stars that pass
             then
31 seek ~~not~~ – for this is also sooth
    No words of theirs the cold star bane
33+ has torn and rent their heart in twain
34 & dead is all their human truth

This passage represents the poem's *argument* as well as its moment of greatest tension. 'Truth', in l. 4 of the manuscript (or 'Grey truth' in revision), 'is now [the world's] painted ~~troy~~ toy'. Not only is it an elusive object of quest, but, as the 'wisdom' of 'the searchers of science' or 'of churches', it is artificial and thus false – a Trojan horse set out to defeat imagination. Evoking the idea of the *logos*, the speaker (at first a faun, then a 'Satyr' in the first printing, subsequently 'the Last Arcadian' in *The Wanderings of Oisin and Other Poems*, and finally a shepherd in *P(1895)* and later collections) enjoins both the dreamer and the doer of deeds to seek glory in words. When 'dead is all their human truth' (l. 34), 'ruth and joy have brotherhood' (l. 44) due to the transfiguring artifice of the poet, who tells and retells his story 'in melodious guile' (l. 39). This earliest example of tragic joy occurs, conspicuously, in the textual presence of reverie – here 'the universes revery', the context in which the world-as-word becomes the centrepiece of the poem's mechanical *primum mobile*. Also conspicuous is the autobiographical cameo of Yeats in the role of 'the stammering schoolboy', who recites imperfectly the Latin and Greek classics and yet still rejects, after much early interest, both modern science and conventional religion of the type which held his mother, her family, and his paternal grandfather. Indeed, the poem as a whole may be regarded as an early reflection of his father's values – an attitude counterpointed in the companion poem 'The Sad Shepherd' (*VP* 3, ll. 67–9). Art, which expresses our feelings, sustains and invigorates personality, J. B. Yeats said; it 'makes us strong and therefore happy'. A lapsed Christian, a Millite with little interest in science, but above all *an artist*, the elder Yeats had preached to his son the utility of poetry (with an emphasis on narrative poetry since it was the most *concrete*) and little else. A belief which stood on nothing, according to the painter, could not lose its foundations.[49] Hence the poet's affirmation of *words* is founded upon a series of negations which, in early draft at least, offers nothing to the learned 'starry men' who 'hunger fiercely after truth'. Before the revision that produced the commonplace advice '[look] in thine own heart' (possibly from Sidney or Shakespeare),[50] the draft seems abject in its nihilism: 'there is no truth'; 'toil . . . only breed[s] new dreams', and dreams spite the heart and 'dim its holy youth', rending the hearts of scientists and clergymen 'in twain', killing 'all their human truth'.

This passage, obviously difficult for the apprentice poet, is fraught with contraries. But what may have made it more vexing for the author was the problem of concealing his sources. Jeffares and others have attributed to Spenser most of the poem's Arcadian ideas and its archaic diction – attributions well justified considering Yeats's own statements concerning the composition of *The Island of Statues* (*Au* 92).[51] However, the rhetorical mood of the epilogue, besides much of its linguistic landscape, is almost certainly indebted to Milton. The early Yeats was *nothing* if he was not ambitious. Therefore, possibly with some acquaintance with Milton's 'Arcades', he laboured to resurrect in 'The Song of the Happy Shepherd' and 'The Sad Shepherd' (or 'Miserrimus' in the 1886 printing) a tradition which began with the contrapuntal debate between 'L'Allegro' and 'Il Penseroso'.[52] Yeats's little success in this vein was in some measure satisfying, for his two poems remained in the canon, inseparable companions at the head of the poetic corpus. Yet in spite of the poems' apparent kinship with Milton's poetic disquisitions on Mirth and Melancholy, Yeats's manuscript directs us elsewhere – to *Paradise Lost* and, perhaps, to Milton's translation of Psalm 5.

The latter, which castigates 'All workers of iniquity', may have provided Yeats's happy shepherd with a refrain. Rhetorically effective (even 'guileful[ly]' seductive, as Yeats's poem and Milton's psalm assert, respectively, by lauding and condemning those who would substitute words for truth), Milton's 'No word is firm or sooth' is contradicted repeatedly by Yeats's speaker (in the vicinity of refrain lines 23, 31, 44, and 57), just as the truth-seekers' plight in the manuscript seems an inversion of Satan's logic in *Paradise Lost*, IX.119–27:

> and the more I see
> Pleasures about me, so much more I feel
> Torment within me, as from the hateful siege
> Of contraries; all good to me becomes
> Bane, and in Heav'n much worse would be my state.
> But neither here seek I, no nor in Heav'n
> To dwell, unless by maistering Heav'n's Supreme;
> Nor hope to be myself less miserable
> By what I seek . . . .

Evidently Yeats had this passage in mind – or even beside him – as he worked on ll. 18–34. Not far above it, at Satan's entrance, we read how the fiend 'meditated fraud and malice, bent/On Man's destruction, *maugre* what might hap' (*Paraside Lost*, IX.55–6; emphasis added). The intervening sixty-three lines wondrously describe, in biblical and Ptolemaic terms, the *world picture* that Milton's 'Imp of fraud' beheld on his first mercurial flight to Eden. This passage, almost certainly the inspiration for the cosmic machinery of ll. 18–21 in Yeats's poem, suggests its complementary opposite in book I:

> the broad circumference
> Hung on his shoulders like the Moon, whose Orb
> Through Optic Glass the *Tuscan* Artist views
> At Ev'ning from the top of *Fesole*,
> Or in *Valdarno*, to descry new Lands,
> Rivers or Mountains in their spotty Globe.
> (I.286–91)[53]

Seeking truth in the 'whirling ways of stars', Yeats's 'starry men', passively *following* rather than actively pursuing 'with the optic glass' of the new science, find that 'bane' and that 'maugre' (a noun or transitive verb in Yeats's usage) which were Satan's consolation for paradise eternally lost in the 'hateful siege of contraries'.

One concludes, then, that, much more than previously recognized, Milton was a formative influence on the early Yeats. Yet, even in the beginning, that influence is complicated by the fact that Yeats initially used the older poet in order to compose a pair of mutually exclusive arguments to express opposing attitudes on the nature of poetic art and reality. Unlike Milton and unlike the later Yeats, whose craft was the shaping of a mask for the antithetical man of action, the early Yeats upheld in his poems a balance between two poles of argument – the one subjective and happy, the other objective and sad; the one seductive and attractive, the other cold and repulsive. To the poet, who had absorbed much of his father's sceptical temperament into his own personality, the making of poems may be regarded as an attempt to discover which, if either, of the two paths led to the truth. It may have seemed that both or neither did, in some sense; but one without the other, as we read in the early poems and stories, could be cause for alarm. Of course, Yeats was at one point eager to have done with Milton's apparently substantial rhetorical influence. In 1913, for instance, in a letter to Lady Gregory, Yeats boasted that he was then 'writing with a new confidence[,] having gotten Milton off my back'.[54] Milton, one of the fathers of 'modern abstraction' (Yeats's phrase for a condition from which modernist poets recoiled in the attempt to 'get back to the definite and the concrete'), was thus a burdensome influence. Similarly, when Yeats went on the English lecture circuit late in 1910, he spoke (echoing his father, a friend said) 'of the old writers as busy with their own sins and of the new writers as busy with other people's'. He 'had put Shakespeare among the old writers and Milton with the new' (*L* 555; cf. *LJBY* 125). Moreover, at that moment in the Renaissance when speech and music fell apart, it was Milton who was largely responsible for loosening poetic rhythm to support the more important intellectual freight of the scientific-minded seventeenth century (*E&I* 524). Milton stood at that moment in history when 'God . . . took the spinning-jenny / Out of [Locke's] side', as Yeats said in a poem appropriately entitled 'Fragments' (*VP* 439). Yet, with Shakespeare, Milton had 'inspire[d] the active life of England' and had done it by imaginative means, through the creation of 'exceptional' masks (*Mem* 184).

Such praise and censure stand side by side in Yeats's work, both spatially and in time. Fortunately, it is not the purpose here to criticize the poet for inconsistency. Rather, we should praise him for setting off early in the direction of his greatest poetic accomplishments. 'There is a place where Contrarieties are equally true', Blake wrote at the outset of *Milton*, book II. Perhaps it is characteristic that Yeats's father, who judged the English Romantic poet to be interesting though something of a charlatan, first introduced Yeats to Blake's poetry when the youth was at most 'fifteen or sixteen' (*Au* 114). One suspects that Yeats's interest in Milton, in any event, took on new meaning as a consequence, making it all the more fortunate that there were elder *authorities* to consult for advice. Assuredly, it is not easy to reconstruct Yeats's exact progress toward his major (mainly later) achievements, or to trace the development of his mature poetic style as it drew much of its strength, by *imitation*, from English Renaissance example. One may begin at many points. One invariably confirms, however, that Yeats was indebted to such example from the beginning – one of the most important hypotheses of this study. The measure of his indebtedness depends on his use of individual authors – a fact warranting an extension of the theory of the adaptive complex to reflect his generally binary habit of thinking about and remembering the work of other poets.

3
Yeats and Spenser: Form, Philosophy, and Pictorialism, 1881–1902

I am now once more in 'A Vision' busy with that thought the antitheses of day and night, of moon & sun – . . . 'The Rose' . . . was part of my seco[n]d book 'The Counte[ss] Cathlee[n]' a[nd] various lege[n]d[s] & lyrics', & . . . I notice, readi[n]g . . . these poems for the first time for some years that the Rose, diffires from The Intellectua[l] Beauty of Shelley & of Spenser in that I have imagined it has [i.e. 'as'] suff[e]ring with man, as indi[visible?] inseper[a]bl[e] from its human image & symbol. Thoug[h] not identical with its human image & symbol, & so t[o] a yo[u]ng man inevitably an ideal an idea[?] & n[o]t & not as something pursued & seen from afar.   (NLI 13,583; cf. *VP* 842)

[When 'I was but eighteen or nineteen',] I had begun to write poetry in imitation of Shelley and of Edmund Spenser, play after play – for my father exalted dramatic poetry above all other kinds – and I invented fantastic and incoherent plots.   (*Au* 66–7; cf. *E&I* 510)

I

Strictly speaking, the autobiographical accounts of Yeats's conversion from science to poetry are more consistent than absolutely accurate. If he had less than the clearest notion, in 1925, of how his own early aestheticism compared with that of Spenser and Shelley (see above), we know why: he was just then, as he tells us, in the muddle of the first version of *A Vision*. Nevertheless, he also *chose* to promote a myth rather than to reveal more than a few tantalizing details about his earliest, mostly unpublished, poetry. He created the impression (as the second epigraph above illustrates – a composite of two compatible quotations) that his career took wing in 1884, just as his first published work was about to appear. It was as if his career, as auspicious as it became, were born of sudden inspiration and little practice. In fact, as surviving manuscripts prove, the poet's memory served him well in recalling a few details which he did volunteer at last, though he seems consciously misleading about dates. As a consequence, students of this phase of his work – i.e. that part which was most often revised, most scrupulously censured by the poet himself, and generally superseded by the post-1900 phase – have for fifty years groped about in a fog. Spenser's influence, in particular, has been seriously underestimated, while that of Shelley has been overemphasized. Formerly, estimates of Spenser's influence largely depended on two works published in 1885–6 and later suppressed, *The Island of Statues* and, 'The Seeker'. However, it is only when one examines the early manuscript material that the importance of Spenser in Yeats's development becomes apparent. This study seeks to redress the balance by showing that Spenser and Shelley were approximately equal influences on Yeats's early poetry.[1]

As a rule, one finds that Yeats's adaptive use of single poets was complicated by the fact that he seldom thought of their work as isolated examples, divorced from a tradition that drew uncommon strength and substance – i.e. *images* – from the well of the *Anima Mundi*. Since he early developed the habit of thinking in terms of dualities or contraries, those writers who were of greatest interest to him were sometimes remembered in pairs. This tendency is not unprecedented. A long critical tradition has found it equally useful to juxtapose Shakespeare and Jonson, for instance, or Jonson and Donne. Yet the tendency is one of Yeats's most pervasive habits. A few of his pairings, or *dyads* – any two recurrently linked sources of content and/or form in an adaptive complex – played conspicuous roles in the formation of his poetic theory and in his gradual mastery of the poetic craft. Perhaps conveniently located in the same zone of his memory (and for good reasons), such pairings developed by association in the manuscripts and eventually surfaced in the published work, often in modified form. Blake and Milton may have constituted a dyad in this sense.[2] Certainly Spenser and Shelley did, as available evidence now suggests.

Although at sixteen or seventeen Yeats lacked the technical

sophistication to compose, as supposed by Ó hAodha,[3] a sequence of lyrics featuring the octave of Spenser's *Amoretti* stanza and variations of Petrarchan form after Elizabethan precedent, possibly the matter of such study had already been set before him, for he *had* begun to write poetry, prodigious amounts of it, and years before he would later admit having done so. This much is suggested by one of his earliest surviving letters, written at most six months after his family had left London for the first of two lodgings at Howth, County Dublin. Advising its recipient that he had 'very few poem [sic] under a great many hundred lines but of those that [he had] this [see below] is the shortest and most most [sic] intelligible' (*CL1* 5, 7), the letter carried verses requested by Mary Cronin, a former neighbour, who had not long before moved to Cork with her husband. The adolescent poet self-consciously boasts his accomplishments as much as his 'peculearitys', for which, he trusts, his correspondent 'will not much care', though 'they' (the poems presumably) are to 'become classics and [be] set for examinations' one day. Introduced here as a sample of the kind of 'classics' Yeats was writing in late 1881 or 1882, the following verses appear on the verso of Yeats's valuable draft of this letter:

> A flower has blossomed, the world heart core
> The petels and leves were a mo[o]n white flame
> A gathred the flower, the soul colourless lore
> The aboundant meadow of fate and fame
> Many men fathers and few may use
> T[he] sacret oil and the sacret cruse[4]

Under the circumstances, it seems fitting that Yeats sought coaching from two men who could give expert technical instruction based partly on Elizabethan models. Edward Dowden and Thomas William Lyster, who were friends of the family, served as Yeats's mentors in the juvenile phase of his apprenticeship.[5] Dowden often had breakfast with Yeats and his father at the York Street studio or at Dowden's residence, and Yeats was sometimes encouraged to 'read out one of [his] poems' on those occasions (*Au* 85[6]). According to the poet,

> Dowden was wise in his encouragement, never over-praising and never unsympathetic, and he would sometimes lend me

books. [His] orderly, prosperous house[,] where . . . poetry was rightly valued, made Dublin tolerable for a while, and for perhaps a couple of years he was an image of romance. (*Au* 85–6)

On the other hand, we know that Yeats received 'guidance' from Lyster in reading 'Elizabethan literature' and that Lyster also taught him how to correct proof (see *UP2* 471) when the first instalments of *The Island of Statues* were prepared for publication in early 1885.[7] Of the two, possibly Dowden was the greater help, as correspondence seems to imply. Dowden had been given to read the manuscript of 'Time and the Witch Vivien' in its original, longer version (cf. *VP* 720–2); and when J. B. Yeats wrote for its return on 7 January 1884, a spirit of collegiality rather than temper presided. 'Of course I never dreamed of publishing the effort of a youth of eighteen', the elder Yeats confessed to his friend.

> I tell him prose and verse are alike in one thing – the best is that to which went the hardest thoughts. This is also the secret of originality, also the secret of sincerity. So far I have his confidence. That he is a poet I have long believed, where he may reach is another matter.
> . . . His bad metres arise very much from his composing in a loud voice manipulating . . . the quantities to his taste.
> (*LJBY* 52–3)

Later, in a moment of pique, Dowden remarked (with some justice, given his assistance) that the young Yeats hung 'in the balance between genius and (to speak rudely) fool. I shall rejoice if it be the first', Dowden stated, but he added, 'it remains doubtful'.[8]

A young poet standing in hero worship of the enigmatic Dowden (an expert on Shakespeare, to a lesser extent on Spenser and the Elizabethans, and on Shelley) would have received advice in line with the professor's scholarly tastes. One of Dowden's technical interests, the effect of hypermetric variation, was discussed in his reply to a complimentary letter from Edmund Gosse, who had praised him for his 'scholarly volume' of *Poems* (1876).[9] Dowden, who was delighted to receive such praise from a fellow contributor to Grosart's *The Complete Works in Verse and Prose of Edmund Spenser* (1882–4),[10] recommended two books on French prosody and volunteered the following note on Ebenezer Elliott, the nineteenth-century Elizabethan revivalist, whom Dowden, in his reply of 12 February 1877, claimed to have 'just read for an *Academy* article':

He is particularly fond of five lines (in his long narrative poems) rhyming a b a b b. . . . He dislikes the stop at line 8 of the Sonnet, and writes 'Preceded by five lines linked to it in melody, and concluding occasionally with an Alexandrine, or . . . by four lines only if concluding with a triplet – the far-famed measure of Spenser is the best which the English Sonneteer can employ.'[11]

One is reminded of Yeats's general disclaimer about understanding what 'poetry societies' understood: 'books of prosody' (*E&I* xi). His professed ignorance contrasts sharply with the metrical competence of Dowden's brand of conventionally learned poetry. Notwithstanding the fact, Yeats was soon busy with similar experiments.

As far as one can tell, the surviving fragments of an early epic poem in Spenserian stanzas date from Yeats's enrolment as a student at the Erasmus Smith High School (formerly the Harcourt Street mansion of Dean Swift) between late autumn 1881 and December 1883 (*CL1* xii). Since his closest friend at that time, Charles Johnston, has said that Yeats's local reputation as a Darwinist preceded his conversion as a poet, it is probably safe to assume that the poet's earliest experiments with verse did not occur before 1882.[12] Yet, once his conversion had begun, its momentum increased with the proliferation of such long, fantastic poems as he much later admitted writing – without much sense of their value:

> In the Irish school my chief friend was Charles Johnston. . . . Some instinct drew us together, it was to him I used to read my poems. They were all plays – except one long poem in Spenserian stanzas, which some woman of whom I remember nothing, not even if she was pretty, borrowed and lost out of her carriage when shopping. I recall three plays, not of any merit, one vaguely Elizabethan, its scene a German forest, one an imitation of Shelley, its scene a crater in the moon, one of somebody's translations from the Sanskrit, its scene an Indian temple. Charles Johnston admired these poems so much that I doubt if he ever thought I had fulfilled their promise. ('I Became an Author', *The Listener*, 4 Aug 1939; *UP2* 506–7)

Johnston, in fact, deeply appreciated Yeats's earliest poems, recalling how he had heard them first in Yeats's room and sometimes during the pair's 'interminable rambles' over Howth peninsula. To Johnston, those verses seemed borne 'out of a vast murmurous gloom of dreams'.[13] In light of his friend's 'later days of precise enameling' (an interesting choice of words for 1906), Johnston said that he regretted the loss of what he called the poet's 'largeness', the 'epic sweep of the earliest work'. And he recalled with pleasure the lines

> Dwelt the princess great Wiagin
> Fairest child of Sweden old,
> In her castle by the Baltic
> In her towers calm and cold . . .[14]

This fragment may have a slight bearing on one of the most interesting cases of formal transmutation to arise from the study of Yeats's manuscripts. Something like it metrically was cast in a lyric entitled 'Sansloy – sansfoy – sansjoy', a poem twice recast and embedded in an epic which featured a knight errant by the name of 'Roland', a second knight called 'Olaf the Hero dane', a Nordic maiden 'Ingeborg', three paynim knights extracted from book I of *The Faerie Queene*, and an indeterminate landscape with proximity to both mountains and sea. Partial reconstruction of this literary pot-pourri confirms Yeats's later criticism: the 'fantastic and incoherent plots' were one with a diversity of particulars either invented or summoned from exotic places.[15] ('There were also "a timid folk who dwelt among the pines" ', Johnston recalls, 'and a majestic Sintram, "a great twin brother", who revealed himself a shining form, in the gold and crimson of sunset, and who was bound by mysterious destiny with his earthly counterpart'.[16]) The metamorphoses of *The Faerie Queene* were inspirational, but Yeats obviously felt himself at liberty to adapt as he liked. Hence the Redcrosse Knight's adversaries became Romantic fallen heroes in Yeats's poem. Elegiacally, their change bestows on them the immortality of the restless wind (Sansloy), the wild wave (Sansfoy), and the 'drooping' lily (Sansjoy):

> Tis of a vision heard and seen
> In a garden by the sea
> on a day of graceous mein
> once when oer a lily spotted
> Broken all and pale and blotted

oer the lawn with daisies dotted
came the wind along the green
cried the ever roving wind
  'Sansloy my name is – joy I seek
  never chain my way shall bind'
Cried the wave – 'full many a one
now a wave worn skeleton
Knew my name, sans foy, and on
Seeking joy I ever wind –

Sighed the lily 'white as snow
once my g[l–] curving petals were,
Now drooping on my stem a low
And my name it is sansjoy
selfsame as the paynim boy –
Nothing's holy saving joy
This much only do I know –
                    (NLI 30,440)

This lyric poem should not be regarded as finished. Still, neither is it a prose sketch in which the poem's rhymes have been set out in the manner of Yeats's occasional practice in later years. Here, the poet has evidently been guided by the ear, not the eye – perhaps 'swaying his head from side to side . . . [and] filling the air with murmured verses', as his father noted.[17] Metrically fitful, many of the poem's lines allow four stresses only if one imagines 'a loud voice manipulating . . . the quantities to [one's] taste' (for example, 'In a gárden by the séa' > 'Ín a gárden bý the séa'). Moreover, the most decisive effect of the poem is aural: the lachrymose effect of the latently positioned triplet in each stanza (*à la* Poe's 'The Raven' or one or two stanzas of 'Israfel' or 'Bridal Ballad'). Probably, if he had a model (as the visual arrangement of lines in the first stanza suggests), it derived from Shelley, several of whose miscellaneous shorter poems (for instance, 'Marianne's Dream', ix–xiii and xxii–xxiii; 'Two Laments'; 'To Night'; 'A Winter's Day'; and 'The Flower That Shines Today') were written variously in heterometric seven-line stanzas, sometimes clustering a rhyme into triplet formation. With the single exception of the *rime royal* stanza, however, the septet is an unusual form in English poetry, and Yeats's particular rendition, in this instance, appears to be unique.

Naturally enough, when Yeats next selected a stanza for what must have been the first version of the epic described above, he wanted a more traditional and suitable form to carry the burden of his exotic narrative. Two surviving stanzas from this version show a vast improvement in their formal translation and expansion of the first stanza of the 'Sansloy' lyric. The tetrameter septet has been converted into nearly conventional *rime royal* stanzas, the utility of which Yeats probably learned from Spenser's pastorals *The Ruines of Time* and *Daphnaida* and from the Platonic *Fowre Hymnes*, even though the form originated with Chaucer (possibly as an adaptation from the French) and was common throughout the English Renaissance. The form provided Yeats with an opportunity to develop the details of his picture. And, surprisingly, as the 'garden by the sea' became a more Irish and Spenserian shadowy wood, his later and perhaps most famous icon of the rising spiral assumed the shape of rings of smoke and the sound of wings beating toward cavern-light – both metaphors for the ghostly utterance of the wind, the spirit of Sansloy:

28 –
Low hums the wind and as the smoky rings
Fall ring on ring from kindling watch fires heart
And light where-with dumb nature speaks and sings
pours forth – so humming from the winds soul start
Sound rings on rings and withering depart
Unto the cavern high with fluttering flight
The
~~This~~ word arose – yea speach is natures spoken light

29 –
'Sansloy my name is and all chains I hurl
Afar for fain would I free pinioned seek
Joys footing on the sea or where the merle
Goes through the shadowy woods with flootings week
And I have asked all things that shine or speak
The glow worms and the old owls in the trees
Where dwelleth joy by mere or mountain peak or sea burd
(NLI 30,440)

The odd thing about Yeats's use of the *rime royal* stanza here is the

Alexandrine with which he closed each – a modification anticipating the final transformation of his pastoral romance into the conventional Spenserian stanzas of *The Faerie Queene*. In revising, Yeats also brightened the picture as he compressed his material again into a single stanza:

27

The weeping wind seemed ever singingly
Unto the vale that heard insasiate
To whisper some forlorn old history
of some once fair now star be baffled fate
At last these words did grow articulate
'Sansloy may name is joy I ever seek
O surely she doth somewhere hidden wait
             or
By mere or mountain of by shady creek –
Hath thou seen joy' and dying then the voice grew weak
                                                     (NLI 30,440)

Three more stanzas (numbered 28–30) complete the translation of 'Sansloy – sansfoy – sansjoy'. Moreover, those stanzas would appear to complete the longer poem itself, or at least a canto of the poem (since Yeats, by his own admission, wrote but 'one long poem in Spenserian stanzas'). Stanza 30 thus marks the '– END –' just as seven stanzas (numbered 1–6, with substantial cancellations and revisions) appear to mark the beginning of an apparently earlier, provisional stage of the poem, now preserved in NLI 30,830. The narrative, then, ran for at least thirty stanzas – and possibly more, if the exercise was redoubled with additional cantos. Truly, the scope of Yeats's early exercise of Spenserian form *is* impressive.

But, with the specimen stanza just quoted, one detects a further influence not out of keeping with Yeats's attempt to imitate his Renaissance master. The other influence is Shelley's, and it is expressed in the allusion to the 'star be[-]baffled fate' of the prostrate, expiring *Alastor* poet at the end of his frustrating quest for, in Yeats's words, a woman who 'doth somewhere hidden wait'. Yeats's own search for supreme beauty is usually associated with his poems of the 1890s, though Bornstein has traced the same (as well as the Shelleyan star motif) through *The Island of Statues* and 'The Seeker',[18] works long associated with the poet's reading of Spenser and Shelley. The present study holds that the poet's quest in fact began before he had developed a coherent itinerary, and that coherence itself came after much mimicry and rehearsal of parts. Indeed, we may best understand how such convergent influences as Spenser and Shelley came to occupy an important place in Yeats's imagination (i.e. as a dyadic cluster in an adaptive complex) by recalling that his poetic conversion occurred late in his boyhood – as he said, 'among the rhododendrons and rocks in the wilder part of the grounds of Howth Castle' when he 'still carried [his] green net but . . . began to play at being a sage, a magician or a poet':

> I had many idols, and as I climbed along the narrow ledge I was now Manfred on his glacier, and now Prince Athanase with his solitary lamp, but I soon chose Alastor for my chief of men and longed to share his melancholy, and maybe at last to disappear from everybody's sight as he disappeared drifting in a boat along some slow-moving river between great trees. When I thought of women they were modelled on those in my favourite poets and loved in brief tragedy, or like the girl in *The Revolt of Islam*, accompanied their lovers through all manner of wild places, lawless women without homes and without children.
>
> (*Au* 63–4)

Clearly, Yeats was conscious of the fact that Shelley, too, had elected to use the Spenserian stanza of *The Faerie Queene* on various occasions, most notably in the narrative poem *Laon and Cythna, or The Revolution of the Golden City* (usually known as *The Revolt of Islam*) and *Adonais*. In twenty years, Yeats would cite both of these poems by Shelley and would quote a stanza from the first of these in the Introduction to his selected edition of the *Poems of Spenser* (1906; the Introduction, entitled 'Edmund Spenser' in *Discoveries* [Bullen, 1908] and in *E&I*, is dated 'October 1902' in reprint). Of the two practitioners of the form, Yeats preferred the father to the poetic son, for in Shelley he found the rhythm 'varied and troubled, and the lines, which are in Spenser like bars of gold thrown ringing one upon another, . . . broken capriciously' (*E&I* 379). Poetry, he thought, using Shelley again as an example, had become 'more spiritual' but had 'lost in weight and measure and in its power of telling long stories and of dealing with great and complicated events', missing, as had *The Earthly Paradise* of William Morris, *The Faerie Queene*'s 'old happy-go-lucky tune that had kept the story marching' (E&I 380). These were observations which sprang from Yeats's own experience with the epic genre and from his early drilling in a prosodic form which Spenser and Shelley both employed extensively. In short, like Shelley, Yeats had attempted a direct adaptation of Spenser. Nevertheless, his attempt to *imitate* Spenser was complicated by the *mediation* of Shelley.[19]

II

After this experiment and until 1918, when 'Astrophel' and the pastoral dialogues of *The Shepheardes Calender* became the principal models for the first of Yeats's elegies to Robert Gregory, Spenser's work does not seem to have much influenced the actual cast, or *form*, of Yeats's poetry, although it remained a presence for a number of years. Eventually, with Shelley, Spenser moved to the background as Yeats promoted a new set of idols shortly after the turn of the century. Such circumstances limit the case which can be made for *imitation*, yet, while Spenser prevailed as one of Yeats's chief gods, he contributed *materially* to Yeats's poetry and philosophy. At first, when that philosophy was perhaps no more than a vague feeling in search of expression – something like a juvenile poet's enraptured suffering for reasons most of all mysterious to himself – Spenser's work contributed much more than the obvious archaisms of Yeats's early diction. The most important contribution, apart from Spenser's fabulous inventions, was the quest motif, which Yeats adopted to serve the quenchless intellectual curiosity of his characteristic heroes – Oisin, Fergus, Forgael, and Cuchulain – and such of his spiritual journeymen as Aedh, Hanrahan, Robartes, and Aherne.

Before he learned how to make such creations his own, Yeats was happy to borrow from Spenser. What seems to have impressed Yeats above all with the quest were the failures *en route*, as opposed to the eventual victories, of *The Faerie Queene*'s several male protagonists – that, and the symbolic fact that the overall mission of Spenser's great hero, Arthur, is incomplete and permanently unsatisfied. In point of fact, the archaic diction of Yeats's nowfragmentary epic in imitation of Spenser is not the only dated feature in those literary remnants. Its hero, too, passing upon the 'unfruit ful sand', is 'An old man . . . with visage worn and wan' and with a time-seamed brow and eyes that but 'dimly' beam from within (or 'at that thing or at this/Of memory [he] would smile'). This 'Sir Roland' old, who wears 'a pilgrim's face' and 'A temples cross of red sown upon/His shoulders thin', might easily pass for Spenser's Redcrosse Knight years after the episodes of *The Faerie Queene*, book I. Mixing his hero's and his narrator's voices, the young poet intones, 'O lon[e]ly is/The way – His comrads are mainly [']mong the dead[,] I wiss' (NLI 30,830, L1v). In similar vein, the Old Knight of 'The Seeker' (*VP* 681–5 – a short dramatic poem composed not long after this) calls to mind Spenser's knight of Temperance, as one unsympathetic to Sir Guyon's righteousness might have imagined him in old age, come at last to a certain '*ruined palace in the forest*' and to the '*motionless* Figure' of 'Infamy'. Like the Poet of Shelley's *Alastor*, Yeats's Old Knight has been wandering about the world 'dream-led . . . on the star-trod seas' (*VP* 682, l.17–18). However, unlike Shelley's Poet, Yeats's errant knight confronts a very *real* agent of deception – an agent a good deal more real than imagined because it exists outside his imagination. The Old Knight's quest of 'fourscore years' (II.46) has been in fact, as he learns, his seduction by Infamy, 'A bearded witch, her sluggish head low bent/On her broad breast!' (II.72–3). This 'lover' is not the false 'Virgin Rose' of *The Faerie Queene* (II.xii.74–8), the 'faire Enchauntresse' Acrasia, now aged like the knight. But we are reminded that the false temple and false paradise of Acrasia's Bower of Bliss were laid to ruin by Guyon, assisted by the Palmer. And the coincidence adds a dimension to Yeats's allegory which the poem would not have had were the protagonist only another *Alastor* poet.[20]

More complicated than either of the cases cited thus far – and in the same vein – is Spenser's role in *The Island of Statues* (*c.* June 1884–1885; published April–July 1885), Yeats's better-known 'Arcadian play in imitation of Edmund Spenser' (*Au* 92). The range of Yeats's early reading (much of it directed by Lyster and focused upon the Elizabethans) is apparent in manuscript. Bornstein discusses it in his Introduction to *W. B. Yeats: The Early Poetry*, volume I. Such reading included Ben Jonson's pastoral drama *The Sad Shepherd*, which lent its name, eventually, to one of Yeats's poems (*VP* 67–9), and the mood of its title character, 'AEGLAMOUR, the SAD', to a brief speech by Almintor in *The Island of Statues* (I.ii.8–16). (See *UP2* 508, where Jonson's influence is joined with that of Keats and Shelley.) Yeats's reading included Beaumont and Fletcher's *The Maid's Tragedy*, the lovers of which, Evadne and

Amintor, suggested Yeats's characters Evadne (later Naschina) and Almintor – but with *Evadne; or, The Statue*, an early-nineteenth-century Irish play by Richard Sheil, also in the background.[21] There are resonances of Shelley's *Alastor*, too, but this time in no pervasive or overt way.[22] Yeats obviously did recall the shallop of *Alastor* and the enchanted craft of *The Witch of Atlas* in 1902, when he reread *The Faerie Queene* for his edition of Spenser. The notation 'Shelley's boats' is jotted in Yeats's personal copy of Spenser's *Works* (YL 1978A) beside the following description of Phaedria's 'little skippet':

>   Eftsoones her shallow ship did slide,
>   More swift then swallow sheres the liquide skye,
>   Withouten oare or Pilot it to guide,
>   Or winged canvas with the wind to fly:
>   Onely she turned a pin, and by and by
>   It cut away upon the yielding wave,
>   Ne cared she her course for to apply;
>   For it was taught the way which she would have . . .
>   (*The Faerie Queene*, II.vi.5)

Nevertheless, the above passage shows that Yeats followed Spenser (in keeping with his claim that *The Island of Statues* was for the most part an adaptation of Spenser, not Shelley) and that, if anything, he tried to exceed Spenser's inventiveness – to 'out-Spenser' Spenser. Quite unlike the leaky craft of *Alastor*, the boat that ferries Almintor to the 'lake-embosomed isle' is 'Living, wide winged, . . . The winged wonder of all Faery Land' (*The Island of Statues*, I.iii.54–7). Its sides are adorned with 'Strange draperies' (like Spenser's 'little Gondelay, bedecked trim/With boughs and arbours woven cunningly' – *The Faerie Queene*, II.vi.2). The waves bow 'like mown corn' before Yeats's craft (*The Island of Statues*, I.iii.56) just as Phaedria's vessel 'cut away upon the yielding wave'. And Yeats's invention *flies* without pilot (whereas Spenser's only *seemed* to do so) across the Echo-haunted 'dolorous lake' (cf. Spenser's 'Idle lake'):

>   between each wing
>   He sat, and then I heard the white lake sing,
>   Curving beneath the prow; as some wild drake

> Half lit, so flapt the wings across the lake –
> (*The Island of Statues*, ii.i.14–17)

Moreover, Almintor the hunter, Naschina's beloved, is set upon a quest very different from that of Shelley's *Alastor* poet. More Spenserian in conception, the Arcadian hero receives his marching-orders in a speech characteristic of Spenser's brand of allegorical romance. Asserting that the Arcadian hunter must genuinely prove himself worthy of her love (since 'Joy's brother, Fear, dwells ever in each [Arcadian] breast'), Naschina, one of the first of a long line of Yeatsian women to prefer action over *mere* words, complains,

> I weary of your songs and hunter's toys.
> To prove his love a knight with a lance in rest
> Will circle round the world upon a quest,
> Until afar appear the gleaming dragon-scales:
> From morn the twain until the evening pales
> Will struggle. Or he'll seek enchanter old,
> Who sits in lonely splendour, mail'd in gold,
> And they will war, 'mid wondrous elfin-sights:
> Such may I love. The shuddering forest lights
> Of green Arcadia do not hide, I trow,
> Such men, such hearts . . .
> (*The Island of Statues*, i.i.157–67)

This complaint, which establishes the purpose of Almintor's quest, comes at the end of a pastoral singing-match between the shepherds Colin and Thernot (or occasionally 'Thenot' in manuscript, after a character in the 'February', 'April', and 'November' eclogues of *The Shepheardes Calender*) and follows a serio-comic exchange between Almintor and Antonio, his page. Interestingly enough, 'Perigot', the identity assumed by Naschina in the first draft of Act ii, scene i, is also the name of the singing shepherd who competes with 'Willy' in Spenser's 'August' eclogue. Spenser's Rosalind, to be sure, must have invoked the memory of Shakespeare's heroine of *As You Like It*, since one of the unexpected consequences of Yeats's adaptation of Spenser at this point is a comic turn of relief in which Antonio plays Touchstone to Naschina's Rosalind. Indeed, disguised as a 'youth' in 'shepherd garments', Naschina ventures after her beloved into the enchanted wilderness of Faery Land. And, once there, she discovers that he (like Orlando and company, or like Jonson's melancholic shepherd) has 'carved [her name] on trees, and with a sundry weed . . . [written] it on the sands' (*The Island of Statues*, II.i.8–9). Thus 'the owls may read / And ponder it if they will', Antonio quips, clownishly (ll. 9–10).

With epigrammatic succinctness, the problem of the play could hardly be summed up more tersely. Owls, too, brood over the depraved, mere semblance of paradise in book II, canto xii of *The Faerie Queene*. Ominously and symbolically, the 'ill-faste Owle, deaths dreadful messengere' – along with the raven, the bat, and the 'hellish Harpyes' of night (II.xii.36) – betokens the terrible price that can be exacted in the quest. Similarly, the fateful end of an era is signalled in *The Island of Statues* by a hundred-year-old owl, hooting above the Irish 'wolf, and boar, and steer' although 'his wings were plumeless stumps, / And all his veins had near run dry' (II.iii.122, 118–19). While Yeats's play is by definition a comedy and must end happily, the consequences of failure in it are, paradoxically, just as great as in Spenser's poem without seeming as severe. In failing to pluck the 'goblin fruit of joy', Almintor falls under a spell and assumes the form of a 'moon-pale' statue, becoming a lifeless but also undying figure of art. He may be rescued from his fate, but not entirely returned to happiness. His beloved shepherdess, victorious by a turn of fortune, supplants the Enchantress, awakens Almintor and the 'Sleepers' in the garden of petrified lovers, and becomes immortal (i.e. 'shadowless') and hence unattainable.

Drawing upon Spenser's example (but without Spenser's Christian ethics), Yeats dramatized the contradictions of reality which make happiness ultimately impossible for the artist, a being who desires to arrest absolute beauty in a lasting work yet seeks communion with the object of his desire. 'One would have thought', wrote Spenser, pointing out to the 'sober eye' the excessive 'sweet diversity' of the fraudulent Eden of Acrasia, ' . . . That nature had for wantonesse ensude / Art, and that Art at nature did repine; / So striving each th' other to undermine' (*The Faerie Queene*, II.i.59). In *The Island of Statues*, the conflict between art and nature is inherently the collision between the materially static but supernaturally animated world of Faery Land and the materially animated but spiritually static world of Arcadia. As in *The Faerie Queene*, these two worlds exist side by side – the one timeless, the other in time. Yet each world penetrates the other at points – and never so well as when mortal lovers, in an attempt to confer on their loved ones a gesture of immortal love (or 'elvish wisdom'), counterfeit themselves all too humanly in a quest which dispels delusion. In spite of this antagonism, both worlds, until the epochal change of Act II, scene iii, are essentially pagan and untouched by the notion of *sin*, indicative of Yeats's rejection of the Christian vision upon which his main device (borrowed from Spenser) was once conceived. The island itself, with its garden of spellbound lovers knee-deep in fairy flowers, is the product of synthesis. In it, Yeats made one what Spenser held apart. Thus, Phaedria's floating 'Island waste and voyd' (*The Faerie Queene*, II.vi.11) and Acrasia's island bower of 'painted flowers', 'most daintie Paradise on ground' (II.xii.58), are combined with the Garden of Adonis, which appears at the heart of *The Faerie Queene* (III.vi). Quite likely, the 'naked babes' (or souls of 'living wights') which fructify and grow like flowers in the 'beds' of the latter paradise – and are harvested by 'wicked Tyme', whose scythe 'Does mow the flowring herbes and goodly things' (III.vi.39) – suggested Yeats's 'immovable figures[,] . . . those who have failed in their quest' (*VP* 655), 'some . . . bending, with their hands among the flowers[,] others . . . holding withered flowers' (*VP* 667). Moreover, situated 'in fruitfull soyle of old, / And girt with two walls on either side; / The one of yron, the other of bright gold' (*The Faerie Queene*, III.vi.31), the Garden of Adonis is cinctured like the 'brazen-gated glade' of *The Island of Statues* (II.iii.43). Similarly, the unseemly metamorphosis, in the garden of Acrasia, of men into bestial forms kindred to their appetites gives place, in Yeats's play, to a strange but pleasant metamorphosis based upon the figured Garden of Adonis – save for the fact that the lovers are finally liberated from their enchantment, just as they are, though hideously, at the close of book II of *The Faerie Queene*.

Before Act II, Yeats's Faery Land and his green Arcadia have somehow been held in suspension, preserved despite the unsympathetic rule of a 'new god'. 'Oh! gracious Pan', the votive Almintor prays to the ancient deity of the woods, 'take now thy servant's part', though the hunter must 'speak low, / And not too clear' so that 'the new god' (Christ) will think himself called on (*VP* 657–8). Ambiguously, the magic of Yeats's island in the lake is associated with the 'green paradise' of 'Eden-sod' as well as with Satan's 'winning' of Eve and man's Fall (see above, last extract in Ch. 2). Seductively, the fairy Voice sings to Almintor 'but as some dead maiden's singing in a dream' (*The Island of Statues*, I.ii.59):

> When the tree was o'er-appled
> For mother Eve's winning
> I was at her sinning.
> O'er the grass light-endappled
> I wandered and trod,
> O'er the green Eden-sod;
> And I sang round the tree:
> Arise from the hollow,
> And follow, and follow!
> (I.ii.60–9)

Again, the ambiguous identity occurs because of Yeats's synthesis of the false and true kinds of paradise found, respectively, in books II and III of *The Faerie Queene*. By negative and positive example, Spenser's gardens of sensual excess and sanctified generation served ethical themes (temperance and chastity) which failed to interest Yeats.

Nevertheless, the young poet, then beginning to break away from his father's influence by developing an interest in esoteric subjects,[23] paid attention to the way Spenser had recurrently interwoven the mysteries of the Rose and of Venus. The 'Virgin Rose' Acrasia, neither an Eve nor a Venus except by dissemblance, is plucked and deflowered by her 'Paramowre' in 'wastfull luxuree' – and 'So passeth', we are told (with consummate art), 'Of mortal life the leafe, the bud, the flowre'; 'Upon a bed of Roses she was layd, . . . And was arayd, or rather disarayd' (*The Faerie Queene*, II.xii.75, 77). The rose and flower motif is borne to greater heights, of course, in the description of the Garden of Adonis, where Venus and Adonis reap their pleasure honestly in 'thickest covert' beneath 'a pleasaunt Arber, not by art / But of the trees owne inclination made' of 'wanton yvie' and eglantine entwined (III.vi.44). Indeed, the whole episode of book III, canto vi, is a long parenthesis on the miraculous conception and rearing of Belphoebe, whose flower, the rose, adorns the 'girlond of her honour' – an 'ensample' of God's heavenly grace sown in Paradise and a priceless token of her 'fresh flowring Maydenhead' (This token she guards against 'poysnous Envy' at the close of canto v and refuses to use as a restorative to heal the smitten Timias.) In contrast, the indeterminate Voice of Yeats's Faery Land sings in puns and tropes (seemingly) about the island's elixir flower – shortly afterwards referred to as a 'scarlet bloom', 'that famed flower of wizardry' (*VP* 673):

> I rose, I rose
> Where in white exultation
> The long lily blows,
> And the wan wave that lingers
> From flood-time encloses
> With infantine fingers
> The roots of the roses.
> Thence have I come winging;
> I there had been keeping
> A mouse from his sleeping,
> With shouting and singing.
>
> (*The Island of Statutes*,
> II.iii.163–73)

Bearing portentous news of the deaths of Colin and Thernot, Yeats's fairy Voice calls to mind Time's harvest of infant souls where all is 'subject to mortalitie, / Yet is eterne in mutabilitie, / And by succesion made perpetuall' (*The Faerie Queene*, III.vi.48). The island's long tranquillity is broken, the guardian spirit of the rose announces, when 'A wriggling thing on the white lake moved, / As the canker-worm on a milk-white rose' (*The Island of Statues*, II.iii.176–7; cf. *The Shepheardes Calender*, 'February', ll. 179–80, where Thenot claims to be his Lord's own 'primrose', the 'branches' of which 'oft he lets his canker-wormes light / Upon . . . to work me more spite' – but also Milton, 'Lycidas', ll. 45–9: 'As killing as the Canker to the Rose, / Or Taint-worm to the weanling Herds that graze, . . . When first the White-thorn blows; / Such, *Lycidas*, thy loss to Shepherd's ear').

Although in three years Yeats chose to reprint only the last scene of *The Island of Statues* when preparing copy for his first book of poems, *The Wanderings of Oisin and Other Poems* (1889), he fully recognized the significant poetic progress which followed from his adaptation of Spenser. As he confessed to Katharine Tynan, everything written up to that point had been 'harmonious[,] narrow, calm'. His thinking had never been 'out of . . . depth'. Everything had been 'passionless' and yet one with 'a quite harmonious poetic life' – a life that abruptly changed at the end of that work. 'Since I have left the "Island" ', he said,

I have been going about on shoreless seas. Nothing anywhere has clear outline. Everywhere is cloud and foam. . . . The early poems I know to be quite choherent [sic] and at no time are there clouds in my details for I hate the soft modern manner. The clouds began about 4 years ago. I was finishing the Island. They came and robbed Nachina of her Shaddow [sic] as you will see, the rest is cloudless narrow and calm. (CL1 98)

Added late (apparently at the proof-stage of the last instalment), Yeats's concluding stage-direction touched off the disturbance to which he alluded in 1888: 'The rising moon casts the shadows of Almintor and the Sleepers across the grass. Close by Almintor's side, Naschina is standing, shadowless.' Up to this point in the manuscripts, Bornstein notes, 'the lovers' final success symbolized the resolution of the antinomies like nature and art, time and eternity, and real and ideal which the play presents'.[24] With the stage-direction, however, a 'new philosophy' subverts the play's meaning by contradicting the affirmation of Naschina and the others, as Bornstein says, 'implicitly anticipating the poet's later contention that man can embody truth but he cannot know it'.

Yeats, of course, would have one believe that obscure 'clouds' had fallen over him (like Spenser's 'grosse fog', the 'dull vapour' which 'heavens chearefull face enveloped' in *The Faerie Queene*, II.xii.34) when in fact he had worked his play toward a most logical conclusion (perhaps without realizing it until late) while maintaining his un-Spenserian neutrality toward *The Faerie Queene*'s false and true paradises, Venuses, and roses. Fairyland may never have appealed to Spenser in quite the way that it did to Yeats – or so Yeats asserted (*E&I* 372) – for Spenser knew Ireland only as an outsider and, hence, may not have come as near as Yeats did to being engulfed by its druidic fog. Yet, if that is what happened to Yeats, the early mystification of his verse was intentional and was related to the studied ambiguity of his fairies and his only partly wicked enchantress. He was certainly conscious of his ambivalent sympathies when he toned down the assault on the 'goblin queen' of *The Island of Statues* (fourth version) by discarding the line 'Thou dealer with foul Phantoms and black art' in favour of the much more flattering 'For faded now is all thy fa wondrous art' (*VP* 673, l. 194).[25] In essence, his final stage direction (in which his heroine loses her shadow) turns the table on nature in deference to art – a fact which should not seem surprising, given Yeats's background and his desire to make a good impression with his first substantial publication. The *philosophical* consequence of that reversal was a life-long quest to restore coherence to his work while remaining faithful to the subversive metaphysics to which he had just committed himself in print.[26] The most striking *poetic* consequence of that departure was probably the group of short lyrics called 'The Rose' (in P(1895)), which he thought of in terms of the intellectualized beauty one finds in select works of Spenser and Shelley.

III

After *The Island of Statues*, Yeats's quest for truth turned for metaphors to Irish and occult sources. Versions of the Spenserian enchanted isle recur throughout the early poems – for instance, in the 'leafy island/Where flapping herons wake' in 'The Stolen Child' (1886), in 'To an Isle in the Water' (*c.* 1889), in 'The Lake Isle of Innisfree' (1890), in the 'woven world-forgotten isle' of 'The Man who Dreamed of Faeryland' (1891), and in the Danaan islands of 'The White Birds' (1892) and 'The Wanderings of Oisin' (1889, revised 1895). Yet by the 1890s the topography as well as the figures in his landscapes were either locally inspired or drawn from native sources such as Standish O'Grady, Samuel Ferguson (over whom Yeats quarrelled with Dowden[27]), and the seventeenth-century historian Geoffrey Keating.[28] The figure of the Rose itself, as Yeats explained in his notes to *The Countess Kathleen and Various Legends and Lyrics* (1892) and *P(1895)*, was part of a tradition which had long Irish roots in both love poems and religious lyrics (see VP 842) but which had universal significance as the symbol of 'divine nature', 'the symbolic heart of things' (both affiliated with the sun), 'spiritual love', 'supreme beauty' (also called the Eastern 'lotus of beauty'), 'the western Flower of Life' growing upon 'the Tree of Life', as well as the Pilot-star hanging upon the 'axle-tree' of the heavens (*VP* 811–12). Such complex symbolism was incident to the Neoplatonic tradition that confronted Yeats in his initial reading of *The Faerie Queene* and, soon after that, in his study of Rosicrucian symbolism for the rituals he helped prepare for the Golden Dawn.[29] Indeed, such symbolism must have seemed essential to him if abstractions were to be given a sense of reality and were to be represented artistically.

As an ineffable abstraction, the 'Intellectual Beauty of Shelley and of Spenser' and Yeats (*VP* 842) can only be understood in terms of the seemingly palpable forms which they used to represent it. Though a poem differs from a painting as time differs from space, a poet's attempt to pictorialize an abstraction received from a supernatural source may be regarded as an attempt both to confer reality upon that abstraction (i.e. by producing the appearance of evidence to confirm its existence) and to make the abstraction intelligible to himself and to his correspondent, or audience. Spenser argues, in a similar vein, that Platonic love (a complex abstraction applied to a female love-object in Neoplatonic tradition) exists when a lover beholds and fashions 'An heavenly beauty to his fancies will, / And it embracing in his mind entyre, / The mirrour of his owne thought doth admyre' ('An Hymne in Honour of Beautie', ll. 222–4). That 'heavenly beauty' (or 'goodly Paterne') the lover may suppose to be a reality with pre-existence in his own 'forms first sourse' in the celestial picture (ll. 190–203). But heavenly beauty and Platonic love, for the faithful as well as the faithless, are abstract concepts with reality conferred upon them by concrete images or symbols. The poet's ability to portray (and hence embody) abstract essences with natural objects is simultaneously a magical and, implicitly, a polemical skill. Tokens are offered in place of intangibles, and the offering may be taken for an argument. Given his devotion to magic, his training as an artist, and his vacillation between unorthodox faith and scepticism (the stamp of his father), Yeats's image-making and myth-making are rhetorically intertwined and driven by a strong sense of mission. How one distinguishes between *his* conception of Intellectual Beauty and the analogous conceptions of Spenser and Shelley depends partly on differences in visual representation.

The Intellectual Beauty of which Yeats speaks in the essay 'The Philosophy of Shelley's Poetry' is a composite derived from the sum of Shelley's work. On the whole, then, Yeats considers Shelley to be, like Spenser, a 'good' Platonist who associates Intellectual Beauty with light – albeit the 'faint and fleeting light' of the Morning and Evening Stars – but a mystic, by and large, for whom the 'central power of the world' often assumes a woman's form. This last was a departure from Platonic tradition but in line with the fifteenth-century Neoplatonism of Ficino's influential *De Amore* and Castiglione's *Il Cortegiano*, book IV, which combined Platonic theory with medieval courtly love.[30] Such depiction is illustrated by the incomplete apotheosis which occurs in Shelley's 'Hymn to Intellectual Beauty', ll. 37–41:

> Love, Hope, and Self-esteem, like clouds depart
> And come, for some uncertain moments lent.
> Man were immortal, and omnipotent,
> Didst thou, unknown and awful as thou art,
> Keep with thy glorious train firm state within his heart.

This is the only point in the hymn at which Intellectual Beauty comes near personification. Nevertheless, *she* (Yeats does not hesitate to use the feminine pronoun, though it may be hard to justify in this poem) is with certainty only a *regal* figure towing a 'glorious train'. If Spenser's *Fowre Hymnes* affected his poem (and it evidently did), Shelley may have deliberately compounded Spenser's Venus and Cupid (also the offspring of Penury and Plenty, which give love both his hunger and his rich taste), for Shelley soon refers to this regal, gender-indeterminate Intellectual Beauty as the 'messenger of sympathies, / That wax and wane in lovers' eyes – / Thou that to human thought art nourishment' (ll. 42–4). In this poem, clearly, Shelley's Intellectual Beauty is a formless, substanceless essence or 'unseen Power'. Names given to it, such as 'Demon, Ghost, and Heaven' (l. 27), are abstractions, 'Frail spells, whose uttered charm might not avail to sever, / From all we hear and all we see, / Doubt, chance, and mutability' (ll. 29–31). Yet it is a beauty made comprehensible by association with natural but transitory phenomena: summer winds, moonbeams, hues and harmonies in evening clouds, sunlight which makes rainbows, wind driven through the strings of an instrument, a shadow frightening one into an ecstasy. Words at last fail to portray the 'awful Loveliness', the 'Spirit fair' who engages, as do Spenser's Venuses, the 'phantoms of a thousand hours' in 'visioned bowers' – gardens not merely of sensual bliss, but 'Of studious zeal or love's delight' (ll. 64–6).[31]

Ultimately, Spenser's Intellectual Beauty (though he never called it that) also exceeds man's ability to conceive a likeness for it. This is significant, for as we have seen, Spenser's Neoplatonic conception of love depends on the lover's apprehension of 'heavenly beauty' by analogy to the faculty of sight (i.e. by *insight*, 'embracing in his mind entyre, / The mirrour of his . . . thought', etc.) and on his ability to draw 'out of the object of [his] eyes'

A more refynéd forme, which [he] present[s]
Unto [his] mind, voide of all blemishment;
Which it reducing to her first perfection,
Beholdeth free from fleshes frayle infection.
('Hymne in Honour of Beautie', ll. 213–17)

Beauty is personified repeatedly in the hymn to earthly beauty – a point Yeats noticed in this most-annotated of the *Fowre Hymnes* in his personal library (see YL 1978D).[32] His reading-copy is dotted with the symbols of Venus and the sun and with other marginalia. In one place, he compares the 'Queen of Beauty, / Mother of love' in stanza 3 with the version of her in the Garden of Adonis (cf. *E&I* 366); in another, he notes, apropos of stanza vii (cf. *E&I* 366–7), the qualities of an ideal knight – qualities which simultaneously made Spenser an ambivalent Puritan and commended him to the ladies of his dedication. At another point (just below the preceding note in YL 1978D and beneath Spenser's 'Doing away the drosse which dims the light / Of that fair beame, which therein is empight'), Yeats comments that 'Beauty is the hidden Pattern' while light emanates from 'the star' (i.e. Venus; cf. Spenser's 'goodly Patterne', l. 32).[33] This comment confirms Yeats's awareness of the twofold nature of Venus as Spenser and Ficino conceived of her. On the one hand, she stands for 'that intelligence which . . . was in the Angelic Mind' as a form; on the other, she represents 'the power of generation with which the soul is endowed', 'the World-Soul which moves the heavens', the Venus which 'translates sparks . . . into earthly matter'.[34]

If Yeats's notes are any indication, he seems to have taken little interest in the orthodox Christianity of Spenser's third hymn, the first of the redactive hymns devoted to Christ as Heavenly Love. The symbol of Venus is entered, however, beside references to the well, flower, star, and lamp of ll. 169–70 – a note in the poem complemented, in the final hymn, by a notice of Sapience, who sits as 'The soveraine dearling of the Deity, / Clad like a Queene in royall robes' (ll. 184–5). Thus Christ, the second person of the Trinity, is both masculine (a 'Son') and feminine (a peerless Venus the likeness of which no painter or poet can hope to portray). By earthly analogy, this Sapience (or *wisdom*, as in the Wisdom of Solomon 6–10) is beyond compare. Yet, while the 'Hymne of Heavenly Beautie' asserts that 'the fairenesse of her face no tongue can tell' and that 'it doth farre exceed all humane thought, / Ne on earth compared be to ought' (ll. 204, 209–10), Spenser must necessarily make analogies in order to make poetry and therefore must draw them 'compared be to [aught – i.e. anything or nothing]' as best he can. The result is a figure of hyperbole (stanzas 31–2) based on an ancient artistic wonder – the picture of Aphrodite Anadyomene (or floating Venus) by Apelles of Ephesus – and on the lyric account of it by Anacreon.[35]

There is a tendency, then, for professed word-painters such as Spenser to find Intellectual Beauty too profoundly abstract or intellectual for words:

> How wondrously would [Anacreon] her face commend
> Above that Idole of his fayning thought
> . . .
>
> How then dare I, the novice of his Art,
> Presume to picture so divine a wight,
> Or hope t' expresse her least perfections part,
> Whose beautie filles the heavens with her light,
> And darkes the earth with shadow of her sight?
> Ah, gentle Muse! thou art too weake and faint
> The pourtraict of so heavenly hew to paint.
> ('Hymne of Heavenly Beautie', ll. 222–31)

Though perhaps not a pictorial poet. Shelley exhibited this tendency; and Yeats, who reduced Spenser and Shelley to a single dyadic cluster in an adaptive complex, attempted to give poetic embodiment to conflicts between nature and art. In keeping with the binary custom of his thinking, part of Yeats sought 'the transmutation of life into art, . . . a world made wholly of essences', while another part feared that intellect might be deceived by subtlety and that one's heart might be flattered with beauty (*Myth* 267, 292). Perhaps it was this other part of his mind that held that 'Beauty is . . . but bodily life in some ideal condition' or that images, symbols, and personifications were 'living and vivid' and had 'minds' behind them (*Myth* 349, 346). Possibly these are allusions to Plato's Ideas, which were (accordingly to the notes to Yeats's *Poems of Spenser*, p. 265) 'both archetypes or originals, and copies or "real existences" '.[36] Beauty had the power to deceive but might be copied (hence revealed) by the artist. (Yeats hated 'clouds', we remember, and loved what was concrete.)

During his apprenticeship, the early Yeats professed 'small interest in people but [was] most ardently moved by the more minute kinds of natural beauty' (*CL1* 98). Though he put away his naturalist's net to write epic verse in imitation of Spenser, he almost as soon declared that 'a song should be/a painted and be[-]pictured argosy' (in stanza 1, NLI 30,830). Loizeaux calls this declaration a 'corrective to abstraction', citing it as the earliest example of Yeats's 'attempt to reconcile the narrative and pictorial'.[37] Since he had studied to be a painter, it was natural that he should try to paint pictures with words. Indeed, the pictorial medium seemed so natural to him that, when he tried to distinguish his treatment of Intellectual Beauty in 'The Rose' from that of Spenser and Shelley, he found it useful to illustrate the distinction by means of the following anecdote:

> the quality symbolised as The Rose differs from the Intellectual Beauty of Shelley and of Spenser [NB: Yeats attributes congruity to 'the Intellectual Beauty of Shelley and of Spenser'] in that I have imagined it as suffering with man and not as something pursued and seen from afar. It must have been a thought of my generation, for I remember the mystical painter Horton, whose work had little of his personal charm and real strangeness, writing me these words, 'I met your beloved in Russell Square, and she was weeping', by which he meant that he had seen a vision of my neglected soul. – 1925   (*VP* 842)

W. T. Horton is perhaps best known for his collection of drawings *A Book of Images* (London: Unicorn, 1898; *Wade* 255), a publication lent distinction by Yeats's Introduction (only the first two parts of which were reprinted, in *E&I*, as 'Symbolism in Painting'). Several of Horton's designs (for example, *Mammon, St George, Temptation, Chateau Ultimate, Be Strong*) demonstrate the sway over the imagination that *The Faerie Queene* and *Pilgrim's Progress* still exercised for some (see *E&I* 146). Horton's 'visionary Symbolist' art was immature but attracted Yeats because of the 'kind of humorous piety like that of the medieval miracle-plays and moralities' which found expression in his work. The 'principal symbols' of these productions were the woman of *Rosa Mystica*, the knight of *Be Strong*, and the magi of *Sancta Dei Genitrix*. According to Yeats, these were Horton's symbols, respectively, for 'the Divine womanhood', 'the Divine manhood', and 'the wisdom of the world, uplifting their thuribles before the Christ, who is the union of the Divine manhood and the Divine womanhood' (*Book of Images*, p. 14; see plates 1a–2a). Similarly duplex, Yeats's Rose was both universal and personal, differing from the Intellectual Beauty of Spenser and Shelley in that his symbol stood for 'suffering with man' rather than 'something pursued and seen from afar'. More importantly (and we read this only in manuscript), Yeats's abstraction, 'suffering with man', was either 'indivisible/inseparable from its human image and symbol' (i.e. as it may be embodied by human form) or '*not* identical with [though very close to] its human image and symbol', so that a young man might suppose it to be an ideal or only an idea. (See the first epigraph to this chapter.) The difference between options is not decided in the poet's revision. But Yeats has made his point. Like Horton, Yeats is 'content to copy common life' (*Images*, p. 15); his spiritual and artistic purposes coalesce in the figure of his beloved, the reflection of his soul in the looking-glass. The abstract conception behind the Rose, like divine womanhood in Horton's *Rosa Mystica*, is more substantial, personal, and mundane, less ethereal than are its cousins in Spenser and Shelley.

Of course, some of the elaborate abstractions which Yeats received and fleshed with images from common life are themselves most uncommon. For example, a rose attached to the centre of a symbolic cross – a ceremonial construction fashioned by each member of the Rosicrucian order to which Yeats belonged – became the central icon of the poem 'To the Rose upon the Rood of Time' (*VP* 100–1).[38] According to Rosicrucian lore, this icon is a most abstruse, mystical affair; most simply put, as Jeffares writes, 'a conjunction of rose (with four leaves) and cross forms a fifth element – a mystic marriage – the rose possessing feminine sexual elements, the cross masculine' (*NCom* 21). Emphatically, Yeats's success in making poetic use of such recondite matter depends on his ability to confer reality upon it by calling up sensual images of life. A good illustration of this appears in a purely visual comparison between the Sephiroth of the Christian Cabbala and the device Yeats chose to adorn the front cover of his book of stories *The Secret Rose* (1897; *Wade* 21). Suggesting his wish to restore 'natural form' to the severely abstract geometry of the Cabbalistic Tree of Life ('a geometrical figure made up of ten circles or spheres called Sephiroth joined by straight lines'), Yeats opined that men had once imagined this figure to be 'as like some great tree covered with its fruit and foliage' before it had, 'in the thirteenth century perhaps, touched by the mathematical genius of Arabia in all likelihood, . . . lost its natural form' (*Au* 375). The geometrical figure that Yeats received (see plate 6) was therefore converted into the fantastically imaginative, serpentine yet tree-like rose-bush of Althea Gyles's conception (see plate 7), a visual interpretation of the literary works folded within the boards of the book.[39] The cover-design, based on the biblical Tree of Jesse but thematically conjunctive with Yeats's story 'Out of the Rose' (with its knight templar of the 'Divine Rose of Intellectual Flame', a fictional resurrection of the Spenserian Old Knight of 'The Seeker'), receives inspiration from the poem 'The Secret Rose' (originally 'O'Sullivan Rua to the Secret Rose'), the first work in the volume:[40]

> Far-off, most secret, and inviolate Rose,
> Enfold me in my hour of hours; where those
> Who sought thee in the Holy Sepulchre,
> Or in the wine-vat, dwell beyond the stir
> And tumult of defeated dreams . . .
> (*VP* 169, ll. 1–5)

In the leaves of the tree, opposites are reconciled, lovers are joined, seekers find what they have sought, the wisdom of the world is met with divine intelligence in 'the sleep/Men have named beauty' (ll. 6–7). The rose-vines, as the artist drew them, are reminiscent of the path of the serpent around the Tipareth (Beauty), the centre of the Cabbalistic Tree of Life.[41] At the centre, a rose of four leaves hangs at the junction of the upright and transverse members of the Rosy Cross, and a symbolic mystic marriage is made graphic with the union of male and female figures 'enfolded' in a thorny embrace at the top of the tree. The artist is true to Yeats in interpretation (see again plate 7), preferring to depict essentials rather than a catalogue of details (such as the 'ancient beards' and 'helms of ruby and gold/Of the crowned Magi' and trappings of Conchubar, Cuchulain, Fergus, and a couple of synthetic creations based on Larminie and O'Grady) which would have cluttered the tree. The main difference between Gyles's design and Yeats's iconographic poem is that the former presents to the viewer a static, vegetable life while in the latter that life is animated by the serial allusions cited above – allusions that open up little narrative picture-windows in the poem.

Such distinctions are worth making because of the curious way in which Yeats made pictorialism an issue in the *Poems of Spenser*. There, the issue is perhaps easily missed because the book's selections may seem overshadowed by the complicated position Yeats articulated in the introductory essay. The work is, perhaps, 'a hazardous edition for the student first coming to Yeats', as O'Shea has commented;[42] however, it was not out of keeping with the poet's taste. Quite to the contrary, we have Yeats's testimony that the edition included 'only those passages from Spenser that I wanted to remember and carry about with me'. He assiduously tried to avoid making 'a dull book' filled with 'what people call characteristic passages'. Instead, he justified his editorial choices with the following rationale:

> One never really knows anybody's taste but one's own, and if one likes anything sincerely one may be certain that there are other people made out of the same earth to like it too. I have taken out of *The Shepheards Calender* only those parts which are about love or about old age, and I have taken out of the *Faerie Queene* passages about shepherds and lovers, and fauns and satyrs, and a few allegorical processions. (*E&I* 381–2)

Yeats was, of course, severe with Spenser on politics (see above, Ch. 2), although he understood the elder poet's 'Puritan thoughts' to be the consequence of his being born at a 'moment of change'. Probably it was not Yeats's purpose, conscious or otherwise, either to condemn or to reject his great precursor, as some critics suggest.[43] Rather, his commission to do a select edition of Spenser permitted the Irish poet an opportunity to make a showcase of precisely that part of Spenser's work which he held in highest esteem. Both Yeats's selections and his essay uphold the sanguineous side of Spenser – 'the beautiful and sensuous life' that Spenser 'called before our eyes' (*E&I* 368) – emphatically rejecting the new, cold-blooded, bourgeois, Puritanical, allegorically inclined Saxon side, which sought vainly to barter poetry for official recognition and for social advantage. Given his predilections, Yeats put together a book to demonstrate that Spenser's 'genius was pictorial', that 'pictures of happiness were more natural to it than any personal pride, or joy, or sorrow', that he 'seemed always to feel through the eyes, imagining everything in pictures' (*E&I* 362, 383).[44]

In fact, in the way of illustration, Yeats likened *The Faerie Queene* to an engraving of Claude Lorrain's *The Mill*, which he found hanging in a friend's house beneath an engraving of J. M. W. Turner's *The Temple of Jupiter* (see plates 4 and 5).[45] Like Spenser's generally happy work, 'those dancing country people [in *The Mill*], those cowherds . . . and that quiet mill-race made one think of Merry England with its glad Latin heart' (*E&I* 377). Conversely, the 'stately goddesses [of Turner's picture], moving in slow procession towards that marble architrave among mysterious trees', reminded Yeats of Shelley's mode of thought – Shelley's 'religion of the wilderness' (*E&I* 377–8). The juxtaposition of Spenser and Shelley (an example of the dyadic phenomenon defined briefly at the beginning of this chapter) was a way of throwing into relief the inconsolably wandering Alastor against 'Colin Clout, the companionable shepherd, and Calidore, the courtly man-at-arms' (*E&I* 378). The literary reconstruction of Spenser in Yeats's edition is consistent with this distinction, and the art nouveau illustrations made for the same (apparently neither to Yeats's blame nor to his credit) reinforce the impression established by Yeats's idiosyncratic selections.[46] (See, for example, plates 2b–3b, which show how vignette titles drawn from Spenser – from passages which accompanied the illustrations on facing pages – were used to integrate the artist's very stylized visual interpretations with Yeats's selections.)

In spite of some unfortunate setbacks,[47] the book's illustrator, Jessie M. King, managed to capture something of the charm and sensuality which drew Yeats's attention to the accompanying passages. Depictions included a ring of nymphs bearing a 'gay girland' of lilies and roses for the bride of the *Epithalamion* (ll. 37–44); the lover Fradubio, as an enchanted tree, bleeding from his torn bough (see plate 2b); the sea-nymph escort of an expiring Marinell (*The Faerie Queene*, III.iv.43); a 'glistering', would-be-hanged, 'Despair-stricken knight' (I.ix.21–32), the first of the 'Emblems or Qualities' in the section so called by Yeats; Scudamore kneeling before the Temple of Venus and before Love's shield (together, another 'emblem or quality'; see plate 3a); 'rich arrayed' August in the procession of months at the bar of Nature's court (*The Faerie Queene*, VII.vii.37); the magic skippet of Phaedria, by which the artist commemorated the islands of Phaedria and Acrasia (see plate 3b), as had Yeats once; and an opulently cloaked Una among Beardsleyesque fauns and satyrs (*The Faerie Queene*, I.vi.11–13).

Assembled in five sections – 'Happy and Unhappy Love', 'Courtiers and Great Men', 'Emblems and Qualities', 'Gardens of Delight' (a rubric combining the bad and good gardens of books II and III of *The Faerie Queene*), and 'Fauns and Satyrs and Shepherds' – the selections themselves are free-standing pictures or 'regions', just as Yeats deemed *The Island of Statues* to be a 'region', or sequence of pastoral pictures, as opposed to an 'incident or series of incidents', of which 'Oisin' has been constructed (*L* 106). As Loizeaux explains, Yeats's landscapes in his early pastoral dramas were directly indebted to Spenser but in the context of a genre of poetic landscape-painting derived from Virgil and running parallel to the idealized landscapes of Claude Lorrain, Blake, Palmer, Calvert, and Turner in the visual arts.[48] Thus, Yeats consciously imitated Spenser, Loizeaux claims, while regarding the result as a pastoral 'region' akin to Turner's *The Golden Bough* – a definite but generalized location inhabited by pastoral characters – but also akin to the idea of poetic 'Region' that Leigh Hunt advocated to his friend John Keats.[49]

One might supplement this account by pointing out that Yeats's *Poems of Spenser* fairly recalls Leigh Hunt's presentation of the Elizabethan as the 'Poet of the Painters'. Hunt's 'Gallery of Pictures from Spenser', in *Imagination and Fancy; or Selections from the English Poets* (1844),[50] attempts, like Yeats, to show that Spenser 'is never more free from superfluousness than when painting a picture', that 'when he gets into a moral, or intellectual, or narrative vein, we might often spare him a good deal of the flow of it; but on occasions of sheer poetry and painting, he is too happy to wander so much from his point'.[51]

Spenser's pictorialism, much as Yeats perceived it, now seems confirmed in the focusing-, framing-, and scanning-techniques investigated by Bender and in Dundas's meticulous study of Spenser's visual art.[52] None the less, like Hunt, Yeats did not everywhere approve of Spenser's pictures, and he clearly did exercise his editor's licence to withhold passages which he felt were drawn without passion. These were allegorical passages which, he thought, 'disappointed' and 'interrupted' the reader's 'preoccupation with the beautiful and sensuous life' depicted everywhere else in Spenser's poetry (*E&I* 368). Unlike Dante, Langland, and Bunyan, Spenser could not – or so Yeats believed – turn his hand to allegory except by cold-blooded ingenuity. Though dissonant with his nature, it was something he wanted to do (like

Sidney) 'to justify himself to his new masters' (*E&I* 367).

The most striking example of Yeats's censorship by editorial recision is the conspicuous absence of Spenser's 'house of Temperance, in which/Doth sober Alma dwell' (*The Faerie Queene*, II.ix) among the four 'houses' represented in the section 'Emblems and Qualities' of *Poems of Spenser*. Not surprisingly, as we might surmise from its occult strangeness and the heavy textual gloss beneath the passage in Yeats's reading-edition (*YL* 1978A), the House of Alma very much attracted Yeats's attention. It held him longer, in fact, than did the kindred passages eventually selected.[53] Beside the famous twenty-second stanza (the so-called 'Arithmetical stanza'), Yeats began an attempt at visualization which culminated, fourteen stanzas later, in the weirdly anthropomorphic figure that he drew in the margin beside stanzas 47 and 48 (see plate 12). This began with a simple vertical construction of circle, rectangle, and triangle –

$$\underset{\triangle}{\overset{\bigcirc}{\square}}$$

– pencilled in the margin at the close of stanza 22 and based on the faulty instruction of a long footnote which began,

> We cannot do better than quote, regarding this Stanza, the note inserted by Professor Child, in his edit. of 'Spenser', Boston, 1855. 'This verse [stanza] describes the plan and proportions of Alma's castle, the human body. The circular part is the head, the triangular the legs, the base of the triangle being wanting. The quadrate or parallelogram, which forms the base of both, is the trunk.' (*YL* 1978A, p. 246)

Most of the note is scored in the margin, but trebly scored was the note's conclusion (also in the words of Child, with editorial incisions): 'All parts of this edifice fitly joined together made "a goodly Diapase", or concord. The mystical interpretation of this verse by Sir Kenelm Digby [in his "Letter to Sir Edward Esterling", first printed in 1644] and Upton, is, to say the least, quite unnecessary.'

Yeats was possibly in sympathy with the editor's opinion and was apparently put off by the ingenious explications that Digby,

Upton and others (including Dowden) contributed on the subject.[54] After 1918, Yeats would not be averse to teasing his audience with occultly inspired geometric or figurative riddles of his own in such poems as 'The Phases of the Moon' (*VP* 372–7) and, particularly relevant to this study, 'Shepherd and Goatherd' (*VP* 338–43), a pastoral dialogue in which (see Ch. 4) the poet returned to the regions of Spenser in order to provide appropriate form for his exposition on the genesis of the soul. It is significant, therefore, that Yeats chose not to print any part of *The Faerie Queene*, book II, canto ix, in his selected Spenser – despite the very great attention it commanded in his reading. Finally, the emblematic passages on the House of Alma must have seemed perplexing to him,[55] and perhaps forced and unnatural, like the fearsome-looking mechanical creature to which he gave expression, at last, in the margins of his reading-copy.

In sum, the *Poems of Spenser* celebrates that part of his mentor's work which mattered most to Yeats as a poet. The religious and political aspects of Spenser's life are addressed in Yeats's Introduction, which runs contrary to the more pietistic, if more learned, view of another mentor, Edward Dowden, whose 'Spenser, the Poet and Teacher' shows more understanding for Spenser's allegory though it regrets the Elizabethan's 'emphatic approval of the terrible policy of Lord Grey'.[56] Those aspects of the life, to be sure, were excised from the work and were no part of Yeats's selections, for the pictorial – the visionary – and the sensual side of Spenser is what Yeats chose to celebrate:

> the processions . . . like the House of Mammon, that have enough ancient mythology, always an implicit symbolism, or, like the Cave of Despair, enough sheer passion to make one forget or forgive their allegory, or else . . . like that vision of Scudamour [Spenser's 'finest invention'], so visionary, so full of a sort of ghostly midnight animation, that one is persuaded that they had some strange purpose and did truly appear in just that way to some mind worn out with war and trouble.   (*E&I* 382)

'Despite a temperament that delighted in sensuous beauty alone', Spenser contributed to poetic tradition 'that worship of Intellectual Beauty which Shelley carried to a greater subtlety and applied to the whole of life' (*E&I* 366), Yeats said as he was beginning to move away from the intellectual aesthetics of both Spenser and

Shelley, developing what Bornstein refers to as the 'aesthetics of antinomy', in which 'mundane reality held sway with ideal visions' (Y&Shel 114). This shift coincided with Yeats's study of the relationship between personality and style (discussed at some length in Chs 1 and 2) and his new-found belief that poetry might once again express the whole man – body, soul, and intellect. He loved those 'good gardens of Adonis and [those] bad gardens of Phaedria and Acrasia' (and 'more particularly those bad islands') which exhibit 'Spenser's power of describing bodily happiness and bodily beauty at its greatest'. Limited to the faculty of sight, however, that power necessarily fell short of its potential, Yeats thought. Marlowe's *Hero and Leander*, for instance, had more energy and sensuality, was 'more complicated in its intellectual energy' (E&I 383). Moreover, in those 'Gardens of Delight', Spenser had distilled 'certain qualities of beauty, certain forms of sensuous loveliness . . . from all the general purposes of life'. This was an historic event for European literature, as Yeats later wrote in *The Tragic Generation* (Au 313), for it led, with mixed results, to the poetry of Keats and Shelley and to the thought of his own generation – a poetry and a thought which 'so separated certain images and regions of the mind . . . that [those] images gr[e]w in beauty as they gr[e]w in sterility'. Only Shakespeare and the playwrights of the English Renaissance were spared this fault of sterility, because, reproached and persecuted, they celebrated the soul's 'heroical, passionate will going its own path'. They prospered in a 'disorderly world' because their imagination, 'driven hither and thither by beauty and sympathy, put on something of the nature of eternity' (E&I 370).

Thus, the spirit of the ideal poet, as Yeats conceived of that abstraction in 1902, came to be exemplified by such professional men of the Renaissance stage as Shakespeare, Marlowe, Jonson, and Chapman – writers whose works became objects of intense study for Yeats as he began his apprenticeship as a playwright and a director of the Abbey Theatre. The masters of his first apprenticeship (Spenser and Shelley) necessarily made way for the mentors of his second. In the long run, the pictorial aspect of his early poetry graduated to take its place in an ampler range of expression. In the course of this second apprenticeship (occurring roughly between 1900 and 1919), his poetry became more *kinetic* – a fundamentally dramatic quality transferred to poetry because of increased attention given to action and character (to 'passionate personality'). Just how Yeats managed to transfer energy from modern life to modern art – to make action of words and to make words eternal in the marriage of 'beauty' and 'sympathy' – is certainly a tale worth telling. The story, as developed in the next chapter, demonstrates again how, in technique and in deed, he consciously strove to adapt the poetic voice and manners of the English Renaissance.

4
Yeats and the School of Jonson: Books, Masques, Epigrams, and Elegies, 1902–19

Sept 21 [1906]   Coole Park

My dear Bullen,
    I am groaning over the task of copying the next installment of 'Thoughts and Second Thoughts'. . . .
    I am deep in Ben Jonson, and have tried to buy your Marston in vain. I have a great desire upon me to read the *Satiromastix* of Dekker, and got the *Mermaid* Dekker, but it is not in that. Can you tell me where I can get it, or can you lend it me? I am thinking of writing something on Ben Jonson, or . . . the ideal of life that flitted before the imagination of Jonson and the others when they thought of the Court. The thought grows out of my Spenser essay. . . .
    Is there any possibility that Jonson meant Shakespeare not Chapman by the character of Virgil in *The Poetaster*? . . . I haven't read the Elizabethans for fifteen years, except Shakespeare and Spenser, and find myself drifting about a good deal.
    Is there any book that would tell me about the various people the plays are dedicated to, and the various ladies one lights upon in Ben Jonson's Masques? I have been dipping into Clarendon. Yours

W B Yeats[1]

I

With implications for both his poetry and his poetic drama, Yeats's ambitious study of Ben Jonson and the principal combatants of the 1601 War of the Theatres succeeded his investigations at the Shakespeare Institute, Stratford-upon-Avon, and at the British Library, London, respectively, in 1901 and 1902. In the four years after concluding his research for the select *Poems of Spenser*, Yeats had become almost exclusively committed to play-writing and to the affairs of the Irish National Theatre Society, co-founding the Abbey Theatre, in 1904, under a restrictive Crown patent which forbade the acting of 'English' plays.[2] The patent specifically allowed his theatre to 'exhibit plays in the Irish and English languages, written by Irish writers on Irish subjects, or such dramatic works of foreign authors as would tend to interest the public in the higher works of dramatic art'.[3] The exclusion of English masterpieces, as Yeats later said, was basically an unnecessary imposition requested by rival theatres whose interests were vested in the plays of Goldsmith and Sheridan (*UP2* 365–6; cf. *L* 437–9 and *TB* 50–5). Although the Abbey directors were pleased to operate much as they had hoped under such a covenant, they regretted that they could not exhibit Elizabethan and Jacobean works via an arrangement with the Elizabethan Stage Society (*Ex* 130). The practical consequence of the British Solicitor-General's ruling was that foreign dramatists such as Goldoni and Molière could be presented directly (in Lady Gregory's translations) while such English Renaissance masters as Shakespeare and Ben Jonson had to be *adapted*, or indirectly translated, into works 'on Irish subjects'.[4]

Such adaptation was necessarily more difficult than producing literally translated works: it required more art, more study. Adaptation, or *imitation* as it was understood during the Renaissance (see Ch. 1), meant probing beneath linguistic surfaces to apprehend the personality – the network of emotion and intellect – which conferred life to the words of a master verse-*maker*, the Jonsonian poetic dramatist. In reality, the adaptive artist (Yeats) was never bound to one model, or voice, but constructed as freely as he liked a *simulacrum*, an 'original' artistic work, from a manifold *complex* of images or voices. Though practice often accompanied the instruction Yeats took from his reading, his probing beneath the surface, like many another traditional poet's, generally preceded his verse-making. No doubt, his study of Ben Jonson in 1906 was as 'deep' as Yeats said it was in the letter to Bullen quoted above. Yet his interest did not particularly lie with individual works. Rather, most of the reading suggested in this letter indicates an acute attraction to a single species of personality, Jonson's, which must have seemed strong, pertinacious, exultant where Spenser's had seemed weary, set to contradictory purposes, and driven to bitterness by a 'tumult of events' he could not understand (E&I 360). Yeats's opinion of Jonson, moreover, seems not much founded on the variety of testimony implied by Yeats's reading-list. Only Jonson's works were flattering to the self-assertive author of *Cynthia's Revels* and *The Poetaster*.

The opposition view was depicted in the specific works Yeats mentioned to Bullen. Evidently, since Yeats had been unable to purchase Bullen's three-volume scholarly edition of *The Works of John Marston* (1887), the publisher presented him with a set, now YL 1238. Given his primary interest in Jonson, the poet bothered to cut only the first volume (up to p. 120) and a little of the second (up to p. 57). *The Histriomastix* was not even included in the edition, because Bullen thought Marston's share in the play 'slight' (I, lii n. 1), most notably consisting of those parts of the revision which ridiculed Jonson. Yeats apparently found volume I of the *Works* sufficient for his use, which depended on the authority of Bullen's informative Introduction, sustained by his own reading of *Antonio and Mellida, Part 1*, a work concluding with the 'armed Epilogue' Jonson parodied in the prologue of *The Poetaster*. If Yeats began further readings, they were aborted, getting no further than Act I of *Antonio and Mellida, Part 2* and Act II, scene ii, of *The Dutch Cortezan*. He may never have got to the point of reading Dekker's *The Satiromastix*, which contains much contemporary information on Jonson. The Mermaid Dekker (YL 503), edited by one of the co-founders of the Rhymers' Club, Ernest Rhys (see Au 164–5), did indeed leave out the play, as Yeats noticed. The pages devoted to it in Rhys's introduction find it interesting only as 'a young poet's retort upon an unsparing antagonist of Ben Jonson's autocratic position' (pp. xxiv–xxv).[5] Rhys's discussion may have been what stimulated Yeats's interest in the play ('I have a great desire upon me to read the *Satiromastix*'). However, the difficulty of obtaining the play for himself (in light of Rhys's dismissal of it) may have terminated the project Yeats contemplated. Certainly, his study intensified on the works of Jonson himself and on Jonson's 'autocratic position'.

Above all, it is important to note that Yeats's study of Jonson in 1906 was accompanied by a formidable 'dipping into Clarendon', a reference to Edward Hyde's eight-volume *History of the Civil Wars in England Begun in the Year 1641* (1826), and perhaps also the three-volume *Life of Edward, Earl of Clarendon* (1827), which continued the Earl's history of the rebellion. Clearly, the convulsive English Civil War (or more likely the Puritan dilemma which contributed to it) was the greater of two issues attracting Yeats to Jonson. It was an event which seemed to cast on English literary history a pall which Jonson anticipated intuitively and combated, in contrast to Spenser (that 'theoretical mind'), who was incapable of doing such in time to avoid the personal catastrophe reported in Jonson's *Conversations with Drummond* (see *E&I* 363). The forces which eventually coalesced in an English democratic revolution – the rise of individualism, materialism, and a 'Philistine' middle class; the Puritan revolt against the spirit of the Renaissance, as discussed in Chapter 2 – still seemed to grip the collective spirit of the Western world. Without causing great alarm, Yeats found opportunity to defend his position against science (the 'hated name' that his friends of the 1890s, associated with materialism) by citing Jonson's name and deeds as though he stood in high rank among the Romantics or Yeats's 'tragic generation', opposed to 'physical objectivity . . . in the historical process':

> we might have argued something after this fashion: 'Science through much ridicule and some persecution has won its right to explore whatever passes before its corporeal eye, and merely because it passes, to set as it were upon an equality the beetle and the whale, though Ben Jonson could find no justification for the entomologist in *The New Inn*, but that he had been crossed in love. Literature now demands the same right of exploration of all that passes before the mind's eye, and merely because it passes.' (*Au* 325–6)

Hence, if Jonson supplied Yeats's rebuttal to Huxley and Victorian men of science, Yeats's antagonism to Locke and Bacon was also demonstrated.

After Shakespeare, Jonson comes next to mind when Yeats tells us that Spenser should have had sense enough to be satisfied with being 'a master of ceremony to the world' (*E&I* 360).[6] Jonson was, of course, long-reigning master of revels to James I and Charles I. As Yeats said, the project he proposed to Bullen – to write an essay on Jonson and/or on 'the ideal of life that flitted before the imagination of Jonson and the others when they thought of the Court' – grew out of his Spenser essay of 1902. In writing that essay, he renewed an old and hitherto casual acquaintance with Jonson's work – an early acquaintance which included with certainty *The Sad Shepherd* (*E&I* 510; *UP2* 508), some (perhaps not all) of the masques (*LNI* 216), and a little of the poetry (*E&I* 7; *Ex* 81) – probably much less than he let on.[7]

Yeats's interest in Jonson was surely encouraged, just as his study was assisted, by various friends and respected contemporaries. Jonson particularly affected Synge, as Duncan points out.[8] Swinburne and J. A. Symonds both wrote full-length critical assessments of Jonson, either of which might have contributed, in time, the phrase 'passionate intensity' (applied to Volpone), which surfaced in 'The Second Coming' (*VP* 402, l. 8) – although Yeats did not own a copy of Swinburne's book as he did of Symonds's (*YL* 2049).[9] Yeats's earliest apprenticeship had been assisted by the Elizabethan literature and scholarship that he read at the suggestion (and sometimes at the direction) of Lyster and Dowden. Hence it will not do to regard Yeats's later turning to Jonson and Jacobean literature as unprecedented, unmotivated, or untutored. The Rhymers poets had been deeply interested in the Renaissance, as they could not fail to be and still admire Pater. Rhys, for example, translated his interest into producing a stock of inexpensive editions (including a two-volume Jonson) for the Everyman's Library series published by the firm J. M. Dent; Arthur Symons edited a two-volume Massinger (*YL* 1286) for Unwin's Mermaid series. Moreover, Yeats's first real contact with Jonson's 'passionate[ly] intense', if inexorably judicious, satire was prompted by the Irish poet's practical observations as a dramaturge (see *E&I* 261–4) and by the shift in his poetics to that 'intensity of personal life' (*E&I* 265) which held the centre ground for J. B. Yeats and Synge.[10]

Yeats's new philosophy of art and poetry sought its first expression in the tentative and loosely associated 'My Thoughts and Second Thoughts', which Bullen serialized and which Yeats's sisters brought out in the following year as *Discoveries: A Volume of Essays* (*Wade* 72) in imitation of Jonson's *Discoveries*, or *Explorata*, as Jonson also called them.[11] Certainly, if Yeats didn't already know that there was a tradition that both he and Jonson followed with the forays of their *Discoveries*, he might have been told by Bullen, whose vast knowledge of Elizabethan literature seems to have stimulated the poet's appetite.[12] The tradition included the *Essais* of Montaigne (a set of which, YL 1343, Yeats purchased but refrained from cutting extensively), the *Table Talk* of Selden (YL 1920 288), and *The Essayes or Counsels Civill and Morall* of Bacon.[13] The anti-Ciceronian terseness of Jonson's prose style must have seemed harsh beside the mannerisms of Drummond's *A Cypress Grove* (YL 558, a product of Bullen's press) and Browne's *Religio Medici* and *Urn Burial* (YL 289–91).[14] Also, Bullen might have encouraged Yeats's Shakespeare studies at Stratford, the home of the Shakespeare Head Press. After concluding this study, Yeats acquired the Press's ten-volume *Works* of Shakespeare (YL 1881; see L 659) plus its booklets (YL 1876 and 1878). To be sure, he began consulting Jonson's *Discoveries* for 'At Stratford-on-Avon' (1901), although readers generally failed to notice its impact until the appearance of Bullen's *Collected Works of William Butler Yeats*, volume VIII: *Discoveries, Edmund Spenser, Poetry and Tradition, and Other Essays* (1908; Wade 82). This selection of Yeats's (at that time) latest thoughts about his craft shows how decidedly he had elected to abandon the aesthetics of Spenser and Shelley.

At the heart of this emergent philosophy was another dyadic cluster – Jonson and Shakespeare. The two were closely related in Yeats's mind, partly because his understanding of Shakespeare was based largely on Jonson's biographical details (those given in *Discoveries*, in the *Conversations*, and in the 1623 epistle affixed to Shakespeare's *Works*). To some extent, therefore, Jonson *mediated* Shakespeare's influence just as Shelley mediated Spenser's. Obviously, a major difference here is that Jonson, unlike Shelley, was not the Romantic that Yeats made him out to be. As 'Renaissance men', both Jonson and Shakespeare embodied the profuse spirit that dominated England in their lifetime. Yet, of the two, Jonson had the more dominant personality, was the more combative defender of courtly values, and was more inclined to stand up to ridicule for the polemical battles he waged in his comedies. In similar circumstances, Yeats consciously identified with Jonson's bravura, as he did in 1923, when in lecturing the Swedish court he recited a compliment from *Cynthia's Revels* (end of the dedication to the Induction):

I had repeated to myself what I could remember of Ben Jonson's address to the court of his time, 'Thou art a beautiful and brave spring and waterest all the noble plants of this Island. In thee the whole Kingdom dresseth itself and is ambitious to use thee as her glass. Beware then thou render men's figures truly and teach them no less to hate their deformities, than to love their forms. . . . Thy servant but not slave, Ben Jonson.' (*Au* 545–6)

What is more, Jonson and Shakespeare appeared to be opposites, as J. J. Jusserand wrote in 'Ben Jonson's Views on Shakespeare's Art' (printed in Bullen's Shakespeare, YL 1881).[15] Yeats was sure to have noticed this himself and, in 1922, said much the same thing:

> Shakespeare . . . was – if we may judge by the few biographical facts, and by such adjectives as 'sweet' and 'gentle' applied to him by his contemporaries – a man whose actual personality seemed faint and passionless. Unlike Ben Jonson he fought no duels; he kept out of quarrels in a quarrelsome age; not even complaining when somebody pirated his sonnets; he dominated no Mermaid Tavern, but – through *Mask* and Image, reflected in a multiplying mirror – he created the most passionate art that exists. (*AV B* 153)

It is unclear precisely what standing Jonson would have had in Yeats's *A Vision* in relation to Shakespeare's Phase 20. This problem is similar to the one regarding Spenser's uncertain relation to Shelley's Phase 17. Yeats's statement quoted above specifically applies only to Shakespeare, and it seems unwise to speculate where Yeats would have placed Jonson on the wheel of incarnations. Certainly, he saw the two friends as discrete personalities despite his tendency to use Jonson as a reflective agent – a use that blurs rather than sharpens the distinction between the two English dramatists.

A case in point is the series of approximate quotations that Yeats derived from *The Poetaster* (v.i.14–16, 136–8). These all assert that those who lack imagination, or 'Promethean fire', are 'but a hollow statue' (*E&I* 278; *Mem* 51) and that others – such as Shakespeare, Edward Evans (Dublin Arts Club member), and 'the passionate dead' – are 'so rammed with life they can but grow in life with being' (*Au* 480; *Mem* 165; *Myth* 360). Originally, these words were spoken by 'Caesar' and 'Horace', the thinly disguised *personae* of Jonson as he defended himself against his critics 'Crispinus' (Marston) and 'Demetrius' (Dekker). However, once Yeats appropriated the words, they became *his* property: they could be turned to or on anyone he wished – including Jonson (for example, '*The Silent Woman* rammed a century of laughter into two hours' traffic' – *E&I* 280). Shakespeare became a part of the adaptive complex because Yeats convinced himself that 'Horace's' commendation of 'Virgil' was intended not for Chapman but for Shakespeare ('His learning labours not the schoole-like glosse' – *The Poetaster*, v.i.129). Yeats consulted Bullen to see if his opinion might agree with an expert's, though probably the publisher could not have persuaded him to change his mind.[16] Yeats introduced this argument just after his query: 'I find it hard to believe that the few not too lively plays written by Chapman before that date could have made Jonson say as he does that whatever event of life came upon one, one could find appropriate words for it in the writings of "Virgil"' (*L* 479).

Yeats's authority for this opinion dates from his reading of Chapman before the fifteen-year neglect of the Elizabethans mentioned in the same letter. His substantial reading of around 1890 (see *LNI* 216) was positive, indicating his susceptibility to autocratic rhetoric. His attraction to *The Revenge of Bussy D'Ambois*, in particular – to the passionate 'Umbra' of the title character and to Clermont's noble but sometimes indignant oratory ('jesters, parasites, / Servile observers'!)[17] – is in keeping with the pleasure that he took in Jonson's instructive satires. Soon after, Yeats registered a similar response to such works as Beaumont and Fletcher's *The Elder Brother*, as may be judged from Eustace's speech (marked in *YL* 136): 'you make the Court, that is the abstract of all Academies, to teach and practice noble undertakings'.[18]

In short, an adaptive complex may become a 'school', in some sense, when the members are dedicated to the same ethic or are dominated by a single personality. It may happen that the characteristics which define each member of the complex will seem 'generalized and shared' – Ure's phrase where he indicts Yeats for interpreting 'life' in a way that Jonson could not have intended – as the kind of primordial 'purified passion' with which, he believed, 'Virgil's' (or Shakespeare's) poetry was 'rammed'.[19] Such a life seemed confirmed by the works of Jonson, Shakespeare, Chapman, Beaumont and Fletcher (if not Jacobean dramatists generally), not to mention Herrick and the poets of the fabled 'Tribe of Ben'. Yeats persistently mistook Jonsonian humour for Shakespearean character (his study of Congreve – see Ch. 1 – is indicative of this); and he likewise created the impression that great writers, whose immortality was their place in the memory of the living, formed a collective presence felt as a single body. Such an amalgamation seems to have been realized in a loose 'school of Jonson' as that presence began to exert a powerful influence on the mind and art of Yeats at the turn of the century. Its contradictions were one in the poet's mind with the quarrelsome writers that he had to reconcile as a group. In practice, its influence was tempered by numerous literary and theatrical developments, all of which contributed to that aristocratic, if not courtly, theatre of rarefied passion which was Yeats's gift to Ireland's literary renaissance.

II

In 1914 Yeats was introduced to the drama of Japan's courts and shrines via the manuscript translations that Pound received from Mrs Ernest Fenollosa. Yeats's almost immediate attempt to adapt the Noh in *At the Hawk's Well*, though, relied significantly on a line of old and new European theatrical conventions which he had for years studied to implement in his 'theatre of beauty', a non-realistic poet's theatre in which art was to reign supreme in a reconciliation of poetry, gesture, and scene. This reconciliation was to be historic because, as Yeats said, 'the two great energies of the world that in Shakespeare's day penetrated each other' had since fallen apart. Hence the modern theatre had to prepare for the eventual fusion of 'those energies that would free the arts from imitation' (here signifying *representation* or *realism*) and 'ally acting to decoration and to the dance' (*Ex* 258). Since it was 'at the Renaissance' that these 'energies' had ceased to penetrate each other (that is, just as 'speech and music fell apart'), Yeats looked first and most often to the Renaissance, and to its masked entertainments, for clues to how he might bring to the stage 'an art that is close to pure music'.

The Paterian echo within this pronouncement is entirely apt given Yeats's claim that the Rhymers had, at the *fin de siècle*, tried to bring back 'the personality of the lyrical poet or the dramatic personalities of plays' (*YT* 38). Poetic drama, as Yeats said of the Renaissance, must be based on 'the deliberate creation of a great mask' (a concept derived in part from Wilde),[20] not on the passive nature of contemporary culture or on self-realization, which proved disastrous for so many of Yeats's friends of that period. His eventual use of masks as stage properties had a direct bearing on his rather surprising belief that Renaissance culture, Renaissance men, and Romantic poets such as Shelley and Byron were able to project images of themselves because of a 'theatrical quality' inherent in passionate life. (The presence of Shelley and Byron in the adaptive complex demonstrates Yeats's habit of reading the Renaissance through Romantic glasses.) Before making this discovery about *personae*, Yeats did exactly what his friends were doing: he emulated England's Renaissance masters and strove to bring back poetic drama in a literary climate increasingly friendly to such a revival. His first published play, *The Island of Statues*, written in imitation of Spenser and Shelley, drew on the dramatic example of Ben Jonson's nostalgic pastoral romance *The Sad Shepherd*. *Mosada* (*VPl* 1263–78) and the truncated published version of *Time and the Witch Vivien* (*VPl* 1279–81) show fugitive resemblances to John Todhunter's neo-Elizabethan *The Poison Flower*, which Yeats reviewed in 1891 and slighted only in the comparison with the same author's *A Sicilian Idyll*, which he had praised so highly the previous year.[21] *A Sicilian Idyll*, with Todhunter's *Helena in Troas* and a revival of Fletcher's *The Faithful Shepherdess*, suggested how poetic drama, when presented in the open air, might lift an audience 'out of what Shelley called "the trance of real life" by beautiful and strange surroundings' (*LNI* 133; *UP2* 191). Yeats expressed excitement over the way Todhunter's plays had been brought into 'a little club theatre in Bedford Park' and presented to 'really distinguished audiences' in a 'long room with . . . black panels and gilt Cupids'. The choral arrangements and the acting of Mrs Edward Emery (Florence Farr), whom Yeats later employed on the psaltery to mark the distinction between excellent speech and music, were singled out for special commendation: 'When the curtain fell, one heard on all sides, "How pretty!" "How beautiful!" "I would not have missed it for the world." It was not merely the play itself that gave one this feeling, for acting, scenery and verse were all a perfect unity' (*LNI* 117). Translated into an exotic drama of exquisite, startling effects, the union of these variables became the poet's main objective in the succession of theatrical experiments that he conducted, over the next twenty-five years, on a combination of Irish, English, and eventually also Japanese materials.

In the Todhunter reviews, Yeats's point of reference – his understanding of how the Elizabethans regarded theatre – was clearly established by his reading, of which he cited Jonson's masques – probably from the Henry Morley edition of *Masques and Entertainments* (London: Routledge, 1890; YL 1032); Chapman's *Bussy D'Ambois* (from YL 368 or 369); and the love scenes of Dekker's *Old Fortunatus* (see 'A Poetic Drama', LNI 216). Yeats's early contact with Jonson's masques was stimulated (to quote the elder Yeats) by the young poet's 'almost breathless interest in [Todhunter's] career as a dramatic poet' (CL1 515). Edward Dowden wrote on the masque, while Arthur Symons critiqued its modern adaptations and performed, under Walter Crane's direction, in the Art Workers' Guild production of *Beauty's Awakening: A Masque of Winter and Spring* (1899).[22] The Rhymers can only have served to increase Yeats's interest during the 1890s. Ernest Dowson published one masque, *The Pierrot of the Minute*, and was at work collating editions of *Volpone* when the death of Beardsley in 1898 scotched the joint project.[23] In general, John Davidson's numerous attempts at poetic drama, including a pseudo-Elizabethan *Scaramouch in Naxos: A Pantomime* (1889), bear witness to the attention that the old forms received within Yeats's circle.[24] But, in particular, the Hermetic Students of the Golden Dawn provided Yeats with an early opportunity to rehearse the fundamentals of these forms in little ritual dialogues composed for its services, the 'Vault' ceremony of which he deployed in the climax of 'Rosa Alchemica' (first published in *The Savoy*, 1896; see Myth 287–90).[25] When Florence Farr, a student of the Order, later went on stage to demonstrate his notion of musical recitation, he prepared for her such a ceremony, called 'The Players ask for a Blessing on the Psalteries and on Themselves' (VP 212–13) – a work conceived in June 1902, in rather occult fashion, as a 'Prayer to the Seven Archangels to bless the Seven Notes' (L 373).[26]

By 1900, certainly, Yeats had a sufficient grasp of the rudiments of masked entertainment to make counterpoint based on a metaphor of Greek and Elizabethan traditions. As editor of *Beltaine*, he observed that the plays of the Irish Literary Theatre for that year had 'a half deliberate unity':

Mr. Martyn's *Maive*, which I understand to symbolise Ireland's choice between English materialism and her own natural idealism, as well as the choice of every individual soul, will be followed, as Greek tragedies were followed by satires and Elizabethan masques by anti-masques, by Mr. George Moore's *The Bending of the Bough*, which tells of a like choice and of a contrary decision.[27]

The following year, after Martyn and Moore had both quit the movement, Yeats regretted the fact that Shakespeare was 'the only great dramatist known to Irish writers' – a fact which 'made them cast their work too much on the English model' (*Ex* 78). 'Let us learn construction from the masters, and dialogue from ourselves', he said, noting how 'a relation' had called to mind a passage in Jonson when claiming for contemporary Ireland a 'reckless abandonment and naturalness' which had declined in England since Shakespeare's day (*Ex* 81).

Early the same year, in London and in Stratford, Yeats's interest in Elizabethan theatrical conventions discharged in great excitement as he met the revolution that William Poel had sparked, in 1894, with the formation of the Elizabethan Stage Society. In his Shakespeare essay for *The Speaker* (*UP2* 247–52), Yeats praised F. R. Benson's productions of Shakespeare on the basis of the company's acting and speaking, faulting them only for the shape of the stage and suggesting the remedy he had just discovered in the decorative scenes of Edward Gordon Craig. A disciple of Poel and the designer–director of Henry Purcell's *Dido and Aeneas* and *The Masque of Love* (that is, the masque from Purcell's opera *Diocletian*), Craig soon became the subject of Yeats's campaign for 'the only admirable stage scenery of our time' (*L* 366).[28] Yeats quickly proposed a scheme to enlist Benson as director of a touring company of Irish players (*Ex* 75, 77), and Craig to design a new set for *The Countess Cathleen*, which had not been well received by audiences or critics (*L* 394; *YT* 86).

On 2 April 1901, Yeats asked Craig to dinner in order to discuss an article the poet wished to do on the 'new art' exemplified by *Dido and Aeneas*.[29] Evidently, the article was displaced by other projects until it developed into a lecture piece, 'The Theatre of Beauty' (*UP2* 397–401); into an essay, 'The Tragic Theatre', originally published in Craig's journal *The Mask* (*UP2* 384–92); and, with little revision, into the Preface of Yeats's *Plays for an Irish Theatre, with Designs by Gordon Craig* (1911; *Wade* 92). The thesis of each, however, arose in Yeats's Shakespeare essay, the first work to occupy the poet after his meeting with Craig in 1901. There,

Yeats complained about naturalistic scene-painting and about the shortcomings of Stratford's semi-Gothic Shakespeare Memorial Theatre, which needed an Elizabethan half-round design akin to the arrangement of Wagner's theatre at Bayreuth and like the one Craig had put to exemplary use at the Coronet Theatre, London. Realistic scenery, a tradesman's 'attempt to copy the more obvious effects of nature by methods of the ordinary landscape painter', coarsens, Yeats said, and 'lowers the taste it appeals to' (*UP2* 250). Put in historical terms, he later wrote, the modern theatre of 1911 had become 'a meretricious easel painting, a bad academy picture,' a 'stage landscape' framed with 'ugly borders'; and it needed liberating in just the way that he and Craig were trying to liberate it at the Abbey, by converting the theatre to the use of Craig's monochromatic folding screens. 'Easel painting', Yeats asserted,

is no part of the theatre. It was imposed upon it at the end of the Renaissance by the graphic genius of Italy. Up to that moment the theatre had used its real perspective and its real light almost wholly. For a time all art dwindled before painting, but now that the proportions have returned, we have restored the theatre to its normal state. This . . . will bring about a change in the shape of the building, for our theatrical architecture is at present arranged for effects of painting and does not admit of free play of light. (*UP2* 399–400)

For the sake of later developments, it is worth stressing here that Yeats compared this re-engineered theatre to the Elizabethan platform stage and to the Japanese theatre, which might represent an interior in detail but which only *suggested* an exterior scene by means of a symbolic pattern. He wanted no artificial perspective, no 'painted light and shade, . . . no objects represented in mass'. Conscious of the quarrel that had driven apart Jonson and the designer Inigo Jones, Yeats said that he wished to create a theatre to please 'the poet and the player and the painter'; he envisioned 'an old quarrel . . . ended, the stage . . . beautifully decorated, [and] every change . . . full of meaning and [without] . . . competing interest, or . . . bounds to the suggestions of speech and motion' (*Plays for an Irish Theatre*, p. xii).

Obviously, the directors of the Abbey Theatre could not afford the extravagance of 'competing interests'. Hence it was fortunate that Yeats's aesthetic call for simplicity – for the *beautiful effect* wrought in a harmonious conjunction of verse, player, and scene – justified the economy necessary on financial grounds. Thanks to her son's painting, Augusta Gregory's *Kincora* had been made 'beautiful, with a high, grave dignity and that strangeness which Ben Jonson thought to be a part of all excellent beauty'; and Yeats added, 'the expense of scenery, dresses, and all was hardly above thirty pounds' (*Ex* 181; see also *UP2* 429–30). This boast, made in 1905 (well before the installation of Craig's movable screens), seems the composite of several voices cemented together in Yeats's memory. The most general of these was Pater's frequent call for 'strange' music in *The Renaissance* – music as a condition to which art aspires. The more apparent sources were Bacon's 'there is no excellent beauty that hath not some strangeness in the proportion', from the essay 'Of Beauty' (cf. *UP1* 237; *UP2* 412; and Pater's adaptive 'Postscript' to *Appreciations*, in addition to Jonson's stage-directions to *Hymenaei* (or *The Masque of Hymen*, ll. 568–86):[30]

Such was the exquisit performance, as . . . that alone . . . was of power to surprize with delight, and steale away the *spectators* from themselues. Nor was there wanting whatsoeuer might giue to the *furniture*, or *complement*; eyther in *riches*, or stangenesse of the *habites*, delicacie of *daunces*, magnificence of the *scene*, or diuine rapture of *musique*. . . . [The *Attyres*], of the Lords, had part of it . . . taken from the *antique Greeke* statue; mixed with some *moderne* additions: which made it both gracefull, and strange.

Jonson's view of poetry as a talking picture and of masques as '*Hieroglyphickes, Emblemes*, or *Impreses* . . . peculiarly apted to . . . magnificent Inuentions' (ll. 254–7)[31] would have appealed to Yeats in principle, although he obviously would not have endorsed the showy Italianate devices engineered by Jones to upstage the poet. 'The conceits of the mind are Pictures of things, and the tongue is the Interpreter of those Pictures', Jonson wrote in *Discoveries*.[32] Platonic Ideas, depicted symbolically, might be arrested and understood – indeed, carried to an audience momentarily by a combination of fine pictorial poetry and ingenious poetic pictures (or 'mute Poesie'). Yeats would have had good reason in 1903 to try his own hand at Jonson's craft. Certainly, the literary atmosphere favoured such experiments. Todhunter was very likely busy with his masque (in the manner of *Cynthia's Revels*) for the unpublished play *Queen o' Scots*, a verse drama performed by amateurs two years later.[33] Also in 1903, Craig began working on a series of 'shows and motions' which culminated, in the next several years, in *The Masque of Hunger, The Masque of Lunatics, The Masque of London,* and *The Dance of Death.*[34] Moreover, between 28 March and 12 November 1903, Yeats was an active member of a short-lived society called 'The Masquers', in company with Craig, Craig's sister Edith, Sturge Moore, Arthur Symons, Pamela Coleman Smith, a reluctant Gilbert Murray, and Walter Crane (chairman).[35] The Masquers' Society was dedicated to fulfilling Yeats's dream of a 'Theatre of Beauty', which in fact he thought a fitting name for the organization[36] – although the dream was more of an aggregate experience informed by the group's interest in masques. Yeats endeavoured to raise money for the Society, at one point collecting £22 for it at a hall at Clifford's Inn prior to a performance of beautiful speaking by Florence Farr (*WBY* 202). Previously, he had expected the formation of 'some Order naming itself from the Golden Violet of the Troubadours' – a society which would be composed of 'none but well-taught and well-mannered speakers who will keep the new art from disrepute' (*E&I* 19). Possibly the Craigs' and his own considerable interest in the highly stylized, ceremonial theatre of the Jacobean court masque shifted that objective slightly when such a society was finally formed. According to its Prospectus,[37] the Masquers intended

> to give performances of plays, masques, ballets, and ceremonies; and to produce only those works which convey a sentiment of beauty. One of its objectives [was] to bring the stage back again to that beauty of appropriate simplicity in the presentation of a play which will liberate the attention of an audience for the words of a writer and the movements of an actor.

According to Schuchard, the Society produced a tentative list of plays it wished to sponsor, beginning with Yeats's *The King's Threshold* (which the poet set about revising) but including Marlowe's *Doctor Faustus* (see *YL* 1234), Euripides' *Hippolytus* (Murray's translation, *YL* 646), Robert Bridges' *Return of Ulysses*, an unspecified play by Congreve, and 'some ballets and masques'.[38]

Given this initiative and such an agenda, Yeats devised (though probably not before September 1903 – see *L* 711) a simple ceremony which both affirms the values it celebrates and *simulates* the inventive Jonsonian court masque. ('Simulates' is here preferable to 'imitates' because Yeats tended to associate 'imitation' with 'realism' – i.e. the imitation of nature. He had no objection to the imitation of art.) Apparently the product of dictation, a typescript scenario bearing his initials is all that remains of this effort and may be all it ever came to.[39] Entitled 'Opening Ceremony for The Masquers', this two-page document survives among the Lady Gregory papers in the Berg Collection and suggests her involvement as a correspondent if not as a typist. In the piece, Beauty or Truth, a veiled woman heralded by one who opens the ceremony with a blast of his horn, is gradually revealed to the audience by the conceit of the looking-glass, a device adapted from Jonson (from *Cynthia's Revels* and *Hymenaei*) but with Yeats's usual innovative touch: the mirror in this case belongs to the artist, not to the abstraction Beauty which he studies to arrest in a work of art. The mirror is the artist's instrument, his medium, and symbolizes the mimetic process itself. Yeats was still thinking about this device in his essay 'The Looking-Glass' when he said that 'a wise theatre might make [the fashion] a training in strong and beautiful life, . . . the heroic discipline of the looking-glass', concluding rhetorically with the query, 'for is not beauty, even as lasting love, one of the most difficult of the arts?' (*E&I* 270). The mirror, one of the most conventional metaphors in Renaissance literature, is central to *Cynthia's Revels*, in which Jonson instructed the court to behave as though it were the kingdom's 'glass' (see *Au* 545–6). Similarly, in *The Masque of Hymen*, Truth wears 'A christall mirror . . . By which mens consciences are search'd, and drest' (ll. 899–900).[40] In the 'Opening Ceremony for The Masquers', Yeats blends Beauty, Truth, and Love into a single persona. She is veiled, like Eros in the 'Vault' ceremony of 'Rosa Alchemica' (*Myth* 289), but allows 'all who are worthy' a glimpse of her face. We learn that she will reveal herself only to her 'servants the artists', who have, unfortunately, 'wandered away from her' and 'have been blindfolded by her enemies' in the world. Once these servants are returned to their mistress and have had their 'hoodwinks' removed (that is, have seen the end of their 'enchantment'), they may behold her as the audience may not. As she has turned her back on the audience to remove her veil, her image is reflected and multiplied in the mirrors of the artists, who attempt to project what they see. The device is intentionally imperfect, a demonstration of the fractional impression of beauty glimpsed from many angles;

but, more important, it is central to the communal service of which Yeats's ceremony consists. The Society (the Masquers) itself drew praise in this revival of a type of theatre which chiefly existed to affirm the common values of its participants – audience and performers alike. With Craig, Yeats believed the masque to be part of a living tradition, one in which mere spectacle could be transcended because communal values were celebrated.[41] In the absence of a court and courtiers, Yeats substituted his 'Theatre of Beauty' and its artists – the poets, players, and painters.

When the Masquers dissolved, however, Yeats lost this particular court. In a few months, the Abbey Theatre was founded, and Yeats made himself busy producing, according to its patent, plays 'on Irish subjects'. In 1908, he began *The Player Queen*, his only play not set in Ireland and his one play conceived almost entirely for presentation in the mode of Craig's so-called 'new theatre'. Yet, since the play was not completed until 1917 nor produced until 1919 (with revisions thereafter) – making it roughly contemporary with his early dance plays and with the Noh influence – Yeats's traditional morality play *The Hour-Glass*, in its production of 1910, became the first of his plays to employ sets and props derived from Craig. In that instance, Craig not only collaborated with Yeats at the Abbey, permitting advance use of the mobile scenes he had invented for a Shakespearean performance, but also designed the costumes for Yeats's play, rendering its Shakespearean wise Fool in masked attire to make him seem 'less a human being than a principle of the mind' (*VPl* 645; see the frontispiece and Plates 8a–b). Craig also designed a mask for the Blind Man in *On Baile's Strand*, and his emphasis on the artificiality of drama, furthermore, attracted Yeats to mime and puppet theatre, both of which were much discussed in Craig's journals *The Mask* (1908–29) and *The Marionette* (1918–19).[42] Craig's theory of acting by symbolic movement, propounded in such essays as 'The Actor and the Ueber-Marionette',[43] continued to influence Yeats as he described the gestures he desired in his *Four Plays for Dancers* (1921): 'the players must move a little stiffly and gravely like marionettes' (*VPl* 1304). To be sure, Yeats's letters, essays, and press notices between 1909 and 1913 speak of his great excitement over Craig's scenes – even if he had expressed, as early as 1904, a doubt that the designer was not interested enough in actors and that Craig's 'wonderful' effects were only 'a new externality' (*Ex* 179).[44] In 1916, when Yeats's city-comedy-*cum*-masque, *The Player Queen*, looked as though it might be staged at the Aldwych Theatre in London 'to impress Dublin', the playwright elected to work with Charles Ricketts and Edmund Dulac, rather than Craig, despite the admission that 'both the tragedy [Yeats] first planned, and the farce [he] wrote, were intended to be played in front of Craig's screens' (*VPl* 761). The ultimate objective (with revision of the Abbey patent, presumably) was to be 'absolute control', 'no compromise – romance, fine scenery, the whole *Hamlet, Volpone* and some Molière plays staged strangely and beautifully' (*L* 612). This desire to produce beautiful, if uncustomary, effects once again echoes the prescription that Yeats assembled from Jonson, Bacon, and Pater. Nevertheless, Yeats's aim also reflects the bizarre experiments he was just then attempting in London, without Craig, as his adaptive use of early-seventeenth-century courtly drama shifted globally from West to East. As his letter implies, the change in venue was motivated, in part, by practical matters.

Although he was himself most famous for his productions of *Hamlet*, Craig believed Shakespeare an 'untheatrical . . . aberration', a poet of ideas which required not words but physical images appealing to an audience's senses.[45] Though a student of Jonson's masques, Craig was in greater sympathy with the non-verbal art of Jonson's partner and arch-rival, Jones. Conversely, Yeats, who thought Shakespeare a greater writer than Jonson because he held tragic art in higher esteem than comic art, and rated tragi-comedy highest of all (see *Ex* 225; *E&I* 240), studiously endorsed Jonson's positions on the supremacy of poetry over mere stagecraft and on natural extravagance enhanced by painstaking craftsmanship. Yeats was not above playing Jonson to Craig's Jones, although this analogy much oversimplifies their relationship, undercuts the liberating effect that the artist had on Yeats's perception of modern theatre, and deflates those oriental influences to which each responded at an early date.[46] Craig's difficulty as a collaborator, his jealousy of his invention, and his late struggle with Yeats over artistic autonomy are acknowledged facts.[47] Hence, it is interesting that Yeats should have turned to *other* designers as he negotiated with management for 'absolute control' of production (and sought 'strangely' beautiful effects, after those recorded in Jonson's masques) when a plan had just miscarried to unite Craig and Yeats in a new poetic theatre in London – one producing 'not only plays in the ordinary sense, but mime dramas, etc.'[48]

In retrospect, the particular adaptive complex which converted

Yeats's study of Renaissance entertainment into an exotic species of modern poetic drama involved the mediation of Craig and others – 'great improvisators', as Craig dubbed Shakespeare's many supposed compositors.[49] *Adaptation*, the essence of artistic creation for Jonson as well as for Yeats, is in reality a *process*, the complicated nature of which is affirmed by Yeats's creation of plays for dancers. Like Jonson, he made novel simulations by compounding existing conventions. By 1916, in his Introduction to the Japanese plays translated by Fenollosa and completed by Pound, Yeats was stressing the importance of his experiments of 1903–12 in 'simplified scenery' for *The Hour-Glass*, the revision of which evolved to satisfaction with the aid of 'those admirable ivory-coloured screens invented by Gordon Craig' (*E&I* 222). Obviously, Yeats still had in mind the general theatrical reform he had tried to implement a decade earlier, when he initially linked the speaking-technique of Italian marionettes, the impulsive mannerisms of a company of Japanese players, and the simplicity of Elizabethan scenery (*Samhain*, Sep 1903, p. 35). Indeed, as he projected writing new 'half-Asiatic' Cuchulain plays, he placed this 'invention', as he called it, of 'aristocratic form' in the context of the gradual decline of English drama since around 1600, the apogee of the Renaissance in England. 'For nearly three centuries', he said, 'invention [had] been making the human voice and the movements of the body seem always less expressive' (cf. *UP2* 355). In actuality, his 'invention' was no less than a *counter-invention* in his own theory, since he saw parallels between the adaptation of the Noh and the sort of theatre once performed at the English court. An equation is implicit in Yeats's thought that *Hamlet* had just opened in London as the princes of Kyoto were for the first time being 'encouraged to witness and to perform in spectacles where speech, music, song, and dance created an image of nobility and strange beauty' (*E&I* 229). As Yeats understood it, this was precisely the aesthetic objective of the English court masque in the age of Jonson and Shakespeare.

III

With the exception of the earlier works of Shakespeare, Yeats's acquaintance with English Renaissance drama seems to have been concentrated on the Jacobeans. His library holdings now suggest that his study at mid-career of 'Jonson and the others' was just marginally supplemented by readings in Tudor pageants, moralities, and interludes (*YL* 649), by Gascoigne's Italianate adaptations (*YL* 734), by Kyd's *Spanish Tragedy* (*YL 1920* 285), and by Fletcher's (and Shakespeare's) *Two Noble Kinsmen* (*YL 1920* 283).[50] Of Marlowe's works, oddly enough, Yeats owned only Masefield's edition of *Doctor Faustus* (illustrated by Charles Ricketts, 1903; *YL* 1234) although he had drawn upon the Faustus myth for *The Hour Glass*, written in 1902, and was well acquainted with *Hero and Leander* (Chapman's 'Second Sestiad' included), praising its 'energetic . . . sensuality' and 'complicated . . . intellectual energy' (*E&I* 383). Indeed, soon after he began displacing his early idealism with the irony and realism of *In the Seven Woods* (1903), he drew as consciously from Marlowe as from the Jacobeans Beaumont and Fletcher, from whose play Yeats derived both title and idea for his poem 'King and No King' (*VP* 258).[51] 'A Woman Homer Sung', 'No Second Troy', and 'Peace' (*VP* 254, 256, 258) collectively recall a passage in *Doctor Faustus*: 'Was this the face that launched a thousand ships, / And burnt the topless towers of Ilium?' (v.i.94–5). These lines are later echoed in the 'topless towers' of 'When Helen Lived' (*VP* 293, l. 8) and 'Long-legged Fly' (*VP* 617, l. 11) and in the 'broken wall, the burning roof and tower / And Agamemnon dead' of 'Leda and the Swan' (*VP* 441, ll. 10–11).[52]

Yet the most pervasive Renaissance voice in Yeats's embittered poetry of 1908–14 is Ben Jonson's. Yeats's new Jonsonian histrionics coincide with his recasting of *The Golden Helmet* (acting version of 1908) into the Jonsonian heroic couplets of *The Green Helmet: An Heroic Farce* (1910), and with the commencement of his long ordeal drafting and revising *The Player Queen*. Palpably Jonsonian are the 'knave and dolt', the mob which, once aroused by the 'strangeness' of Maud Gonne's beauty in 'Against Unworthy Praise' (*VP* 259–60), gives the Abbey director his 'day's war' in 'The Fascination of What's Difficult' (*VP* 270). With *The Green Helmet and Other Poems* (1910), Yeats proved himself to be a poet of generous, if fastidious, praise and of severe invective – a virtual 'son' of the antinomian epigrammatist Jonson.

At best indifferent to the Christian ethicalism of Spenser, Yeats would not have responded as favourably as he did to the 'ripest' of Jonson's studies, the intentionally instructive *Epigrammes*, if the irascible seventeenth-century poet had not presented his lessons on virtue and vice according to a view of poetry similar to Yeats's own. Of the many poetic forms and genres that Jonson imitated from his Latin masters, only two types much affected the Irish poet. Both of these may be traced to the *Epigrammes*, the verse '*pictures*' Jonson made either to remember 'with posteritie' the 'good and great names [his] verses mention on the better part', or to 'publish [the] faces' of the 'Mountebanke, or Iester', so that 'truth' may be disclosed in the exposure.[53] To adopt such a twofold agenda amounted to an innovation on Yeats's part. The precept on pictures underlying this scheme, however – that 'Poetry, and Picture, are Arts of a like nature; and [that] both are busie about imitation', as Jonson wrote in *Discoveries* (ll. 1509–10)[54] – was hardly news to Yeats, who must have enjoyed seeing his own views confirmed by England's first Poet Laureate. Quite likely, though, Jonson's outspoken convictions were inspirational, for Yeats now turned to the precept itself for poetic subjects. This is most evident in an unpublished poem entitled 'Art without imitation' (NLI 30,510),[55] a work self-consciously written in imitation of such Jonsonian epigrams as 'To Old-End Gatherer' and 'To Provle the Plagiary' (*Epigrammes*, LIII and LXXXI). As a prelude to Yeats's poem, one should note once again that Jonson thought poetry superior to painting: in *Discoveries* he asserts, '*Picture* tooke her faining from *Poetry* from *Geometry* her rule, compasse, lines, proportion, and the whole *Symmetry*' (ll. 1549–50).[56] Possibly with this passage in mind, Yeats coined a Jonsonian epithet for the vice figure in 'Art without imitation':

> Old Mathe matics plied the shears
> He has the ~~remnants~~ fragments in his bag
> And tumbles it about & swears
> Nature may fling off every rag
> And hardly find a single painter
> To beg her picture for his book
> Or who is billed for the quainter
> ~~Occupation~~ opperation of sweet love.
> How could he answer look for look
> And after clip being clipped enough

Like 'Long-gathering OLD-END', who 'pill'd a booke, which no man

Yeats and the School of Jonson 123

buyes' and passed it for his own (*Epigrammes*, LIII.1–2), 'Old Mathematics' is a con-artist, a man of science plying the instrument of a tailor to collect fabric for 'his book'. As he snips and tumbles the fragments of Dame Nature's cloth into his ragbag, he obscenely regards her loss as his profit. Indeed, the poem turns emphatically pornographic as Mathematics fancies Nature stark naked and without so much as a painter willing to do her picture or a customer for 'the quainter/ Occupation opperation of sweet love'. The racy sexual and commercial *double entendre* cheapens Nature (and 'sweet love', perhaps not as Yeats intended), and it cheapens the poem. Such effects may have been, at once, the lyric's object lesson on 'art without imitation' as well as Yeats's motive for suppressing it. The poem is too exacting an imitation of one type of Jonsonian epigram, being 'bold, licentious, full of gall,/Wormewood, and sulphure, sharpe, and tooth'd withall; . . . a petulant thing' (*Epigrammes*, II.3–5). Preferring alternating rhymes to rhymed couplets and tetrameter to pentameter rhythm, Yeats's poem otherwise resembles Epigram 53 in, for example, its length and the rhetorical query of the final couplet. His poem is a *simulacrum* – neither a plagiarism nor a wholly original work, but an intentionally derivative exercise like his early epic in Spenserian stanzas. Its *wit* is that it seems to quarrel with the concept of imitation even as it contradicts that quarrel *as* imitation.

If compelled to assist with the explication of such a poem, Yeats might have cited a passage in his *Discoveries* essay 'The Thinking of the Body', wherein Blake would seem another source and 'Old Mathematics' would stand among 'all those butts of traditional humour', the 'learned men who are a terror to children and an ignominious sight in lovers' eyes' – 'mathematicians, theologians, lawyers, men of science' who seek

> some abstract reverie . . . and have therefore stood before the looking-glass without pleasure and never known those thoughts that shape the lines of the body for beauty or animation, and wake a desire for praise or for display.
> . . . Art bids us touch and taste and hear and see the world, and shrinks from what Blake calls mathematic form, from every abstract thing, from all that is of the brain only. (*E&I* 292)

Moreover, Yeats's seemingly ambiguous quarrel with imitation goes back to a distinction he made at another point in *Discoveries* (see *E&I* 285), where he extolled Renaissance imitation for being 'conscious or all but conscious', its 'originality . . . so much the more a part of the man himself', whereas, he said, 'it is our imitation that is unconscious and that waits the uncertainties of time'.[57] In introducing the Jonsonian view of creative energy as 'Promethean fire' (*E&I* 279), Yeats discussed the principle of the universal mind (that of Shakespeare, Tintoretto, 'nearly all the great men of the Renaissance'), disavowing the disorder which arose as a once-unified college of faculties succumbed to logic. Renaissance men did not *see* as a naturalist sees:

> Their minds were never quiescent, never . . . in a mood for scientific observations, always in exaltation, never . . . founded upon an elimination of the personal factor; and their attention . . . dwelt constantly with what is present to the mind in exaltation.

Yeats's anti-materialistic and, in that sense, anti-naturalistic imitative art found expression at that time in several smart four-line epigrams, poems such as 'To a Poet, who would have me Praise certain Bad Poets, Imitators of His and Mine' (*VP* 262), which is directed against *bad imitators* rather than against imitation itself, and has been worked hard to achieve its *seemingly* spontaneous canine bite at the close.[58] Like Jonson, Yeats employed terse forms to assail or lecture those with whom he disagreed. To be sure, he made show of his disagreements with George Russell in 'To a Poet . . .'; with Douglas Hyde in 'At the Abbey Theatre' (*VP* 264–5); with Lord Ardilaun in 'To a Wealthy Man . . .' (*VP* 287–8); with the 'fumbling wits' of an inferior audience in 'Paudeen' (*VP* 292) and 'On those that hated "The Playboy of the Western World", 1907' (*VP* 294); with advocates of censorship in 'On hearing that the Students of our New University have joined the Agitation against Immoral Literature' (*VP* 262); with certain unnamed government administrators in 'An Appointment' (*VP* 317); and with George Moore, the 'brazen throat' of 'To a Friend whose Work has come to Nothing' (*VP* 290–1) and the 'dull ass's hoof' of the epilogue of *Responsibilities* (*VP* 320–1).[59]

Something between a sonnet and an epigram, the poem last cited shows how Yeats's adaptation of Jonson eventually produced a hybrid, a cross between the celebration of 'good and great names' and the invective necessary to publish to the world the face of a

1a. W. T. Horton, *Rosa Mystica*

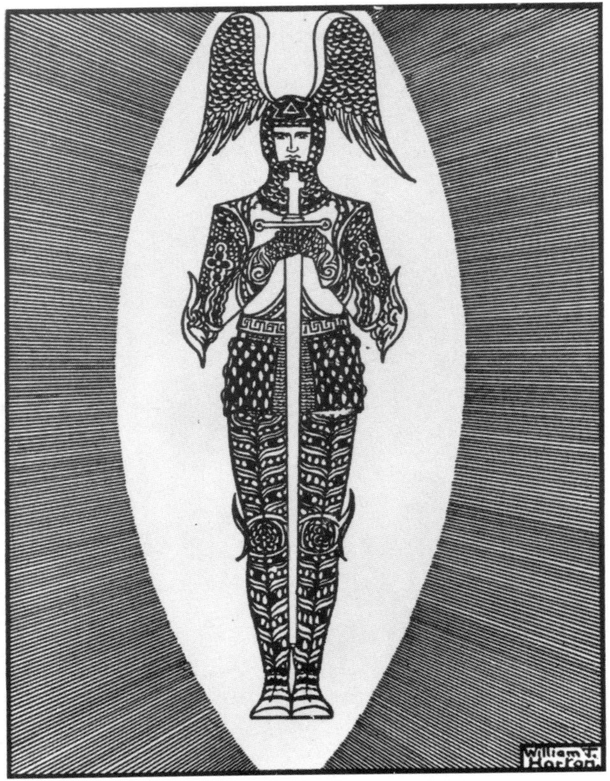

1b. W. T. Horton, *Be Strong*

2a. W. T. Horton, *Sancta Dei Genitrix*

2b. Jessie M. King, *'And, thinking of those braunches greene . . .'*

3a. Jessie M. King, 'And in the midst thereof a pillar'

3b. Jessie M. King, 'And therein sate a Lady fresh and fayre'

4. Claude Lorrain, *Landscape: The Marriage of Isaac and Rebekah* (or *The Mill*)

5. Engraving by John Pye (1828) after J. M. W. Turner's *The Temple of Jupiter Panellenius Restored*

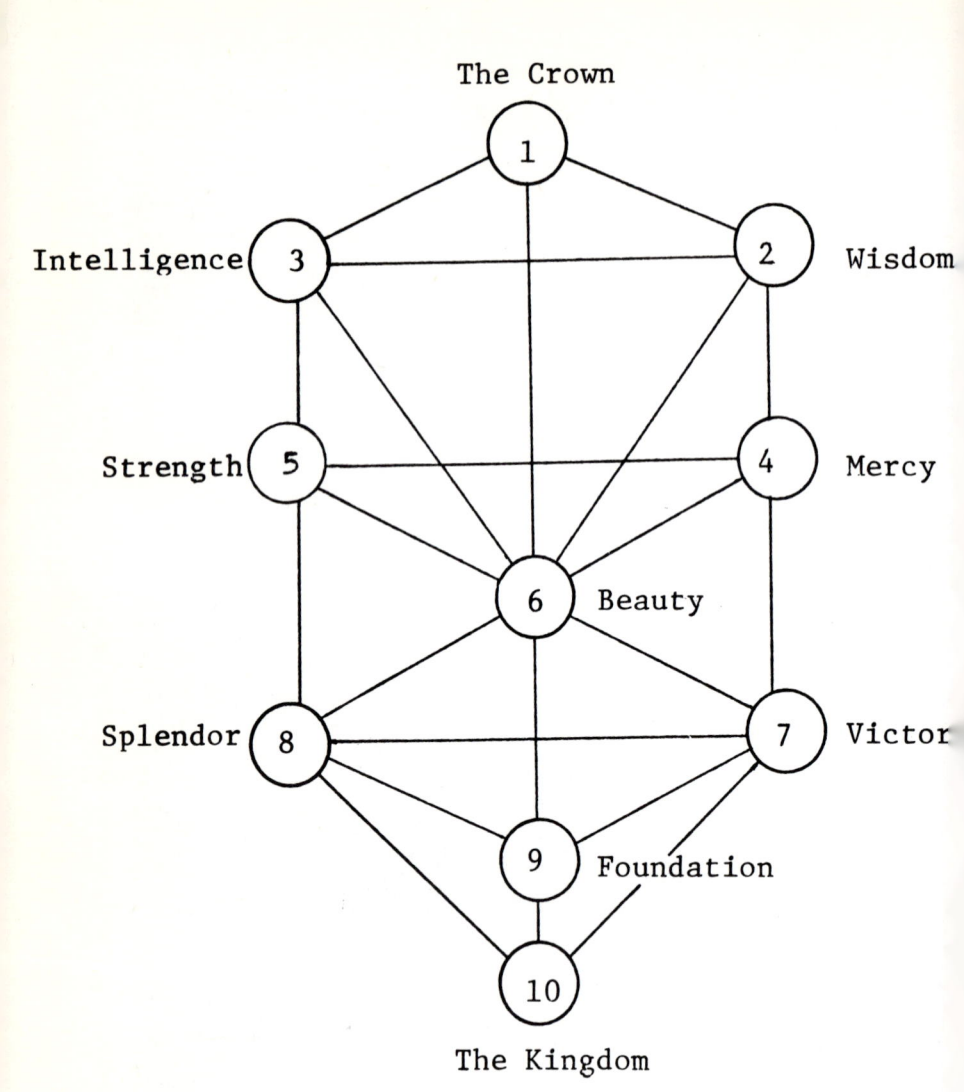

6. Cabbalistic Tree of Life (simplified)

7. Althea Gyles, front cover of *The Secret Rose* (London, 1897)

8a. Edward Gordon Craig, woodcut of *Scene for The Hour-Glass*

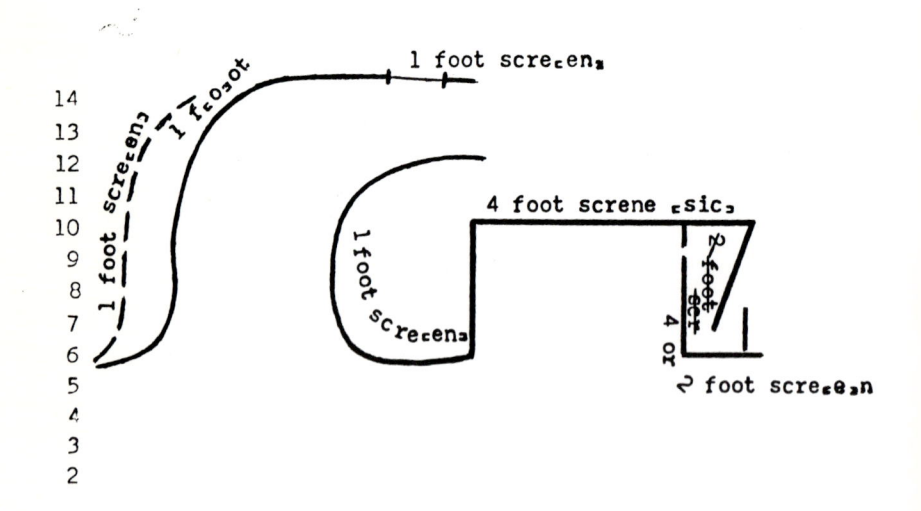

8b. Layout from Yeats's sketch of the scene depicted in Plate 8a

THE LONELY TOWER.

"Or let my lamp at midnight hour,
Be seen in some high lonely tow'r,
Where I may oft out-watch the Bear,
With thrice-great Hermes . . . ."

"Here poetic loneliness has been attempted; not the loneliness of a desert, but a secluded spot in a genial, pastoral country, enriched also by antique relics, such as those *so-called* 'Druidic' stones upon the distant hill. The constellation of the 'Bear' may help to explain that the building is the tower of 'Il Penseroso.' Two shepherds, watching their flocks, speak together of the mysterious light above them."

9. Samuel Palmer, *The Lonely Tower* in *Shorter Poems of John Milton*

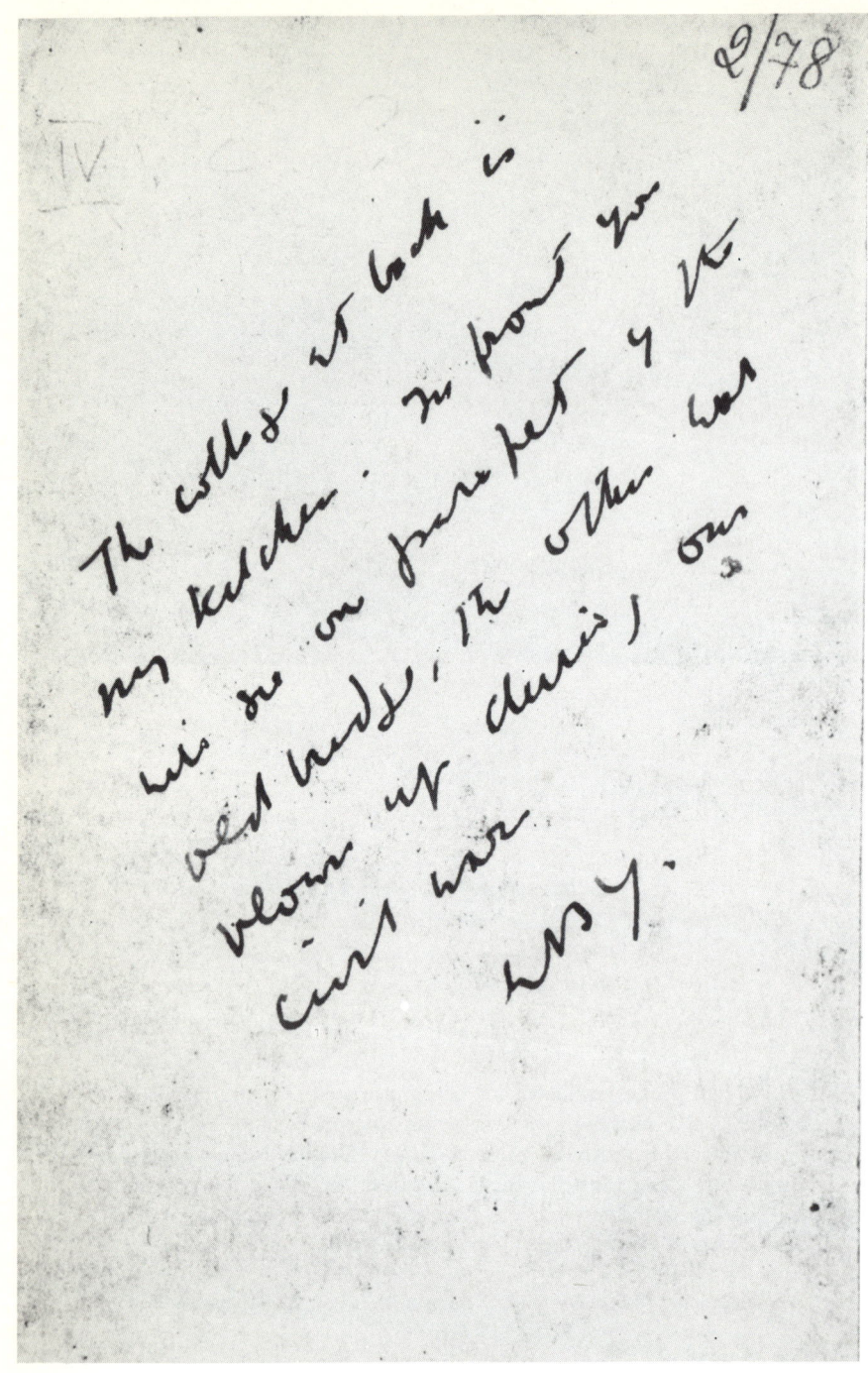

10. Verso inscription by Yeats on Thoor Ballylee photograph (see Plate 11)

11. Thoor Ballylee, from a photograph used as the basis for Sturge Moore's cover design for *The Tower* (1928)

C. 9. *THE FAERIE QUEENE.* 255

46.

The roofe hereof was arched over head,
  And deckt with flowers and herbars daintily:
  Two goodly Beacons, set in watches stead,
  Therein gave light, and flamd continually;
  For they of living fire most subtilly
  Were made, and set in silver sockets bright,
  Cover'd with lids deviz'd of substance sly,
  That readily they shut and open might.
O! who can tell the prayses of that makers might?

47.

Ne can I tell, ne can I stay to tell,
  This parts great workemanship and wondrous powre,
  That all this other worldes worke doth excell,^g
  And likest is unto that heavenly towre
  That God hath built for his owne blessed bowre.
  Therein were divers rowmes, and divers stages;
  But three the chiefest and of greatest powre,
  In which there dwelt three honorable sages,
The wisest men, I weene, that lived in their ages.

48.

Not he, whom Greece, the Nourse of all good arts,
  By Phœbus doome the wisest thought alive,
  Might be compar'd to these by many parts:
  Nor that sage Pylian syre, which did survive
  Three ages, such as mortall men contrive,^h

---

^g *That all this other worldes worke doth excell.*] We ought not to pass over the fact that in this line Drayton read *neather* for "other;" on what authority does not appear. It seems in some degree supported by what follows; but all impressions, 4to. and folio, ancient and modern, concur in reading "other." Drayton wrote *neather* in the margin of his copy of the folio 1611. C.

^h *such as mortall men contrive.*] Jortin and Upton have each remarked upon the Latinism of " contrive," from *contero*, to *wear away*, or *spend*; and they refer to Shakespeare's "Taming of the Shrew," A. i. Sc. 2, where " contrive" occurs in the same sense. Our great dramatist, as they might not be aware, found the word in this sense in the story of

---

12. W. B. Yeats, two versions of the House of Alma (marginalia)

'Mountebanke'. Imitation – indeed, the whole creative process, as one infers from this poem – is part of the Renaissance value system that Yeats redeemed at that time and used to defend himself against his accusers:

> While I, from that reed-throated whisperer
> Who comes at need, although not now as once
> A clear articulation in the air,
> But inwardly, surmise companions
> Beyond the fling of the dull ass's hoof
> – Ben Jonson's phrase – and find when June is come
> At Kyle-na-no under that ancient roof
> A sterner conscience and a friendlier home,
> I can forgive even that wrong of wrongs,
> Those undreamt accidents that have made me
> Seeing that Fame has perished this long while,
> Being but a part of ancient ceremony –
> Notorious, till all my priceless things
> Are but a post the passing dogs defile.

Jonson's phrase occurs on two occasions in his writings: (1) in the 'apologeticall' epilogue of *The Poetaster* (ll. 238–9),[60] and (2) in 'An Ode. To himselfe' in *The Under-wood* (ll. 35–6).[61] Yeats may have known both versions, undoubtedly being impressed by the way Jonson affected remoteness yet hurled insult at his enemies in an image too fittingly contemptuous to compel Yeats to attempt a better one when he had the occasion: 's[i]ng, high, and aloofe, / Safe from the wolves black [j]aw, and the dull asses hoofe'. Yeats's adaptation is an interesting case because of his deliberate effort to publicize the poem's relationship to one of its models. The citation within the poem (i.e. ' – Ben Jonson's phrase – ') acknowledges the public's growing awareness of Jonson owing to the critical interest of Swinburne, Symonds, and others.[62] It also reflects Yeats's fanciful vision of Jonson as a Romantic hero[63] and his own recent and current use of Jonson as a brickbat to cast at *The Playboy* audience (*Freeman's Journal*, 30 Jan 1907, p. 7) and at George Moore (*Mem* 269–70). That last instance, which amounted to a private venting of anger in his Journal, occurred in January 1914 at Stone Cottage, Coleman's Hatch, Sussex, in company with Ezra Pound. In the following month Yeats wrote the epilogue, rather more elaborately prescribing for himself the advice he had given Lady

Gregory – 'Be secret and exult' (see *VP* 291, l. 14) – for dealing with insults levelled at both of them in the serialized printings of *Vale*, Moore's autobiography. In private, Yeats expressed his indignation forthrightly, as he had done in March 1909 in an epigram on Moore written, as he said, to 'amuse' himself at a 'moment of exasperation with that artless man':

> Moore once had visits from the Muse
> But fearing that she would refuse
> An ancient lecher took to geese
> He now gets novels at his ease.
>   (*Mem* 182; *VPl* 1170)

In public, however, the poet was elliptical, withholding the offender's name and delaying his chief insult until the conclusion of a long parenthesis celebrating the Muse's sanctuary at Coole Park.

Under the circumstances, Yeats very likely borrowed Jonson's phrase from *The Poetaster* epilogue, rather than from the ode; indeed, the example of *The Poetaster*, Jonson's single decisive contribution to the famous war of the theatres, might even have given Yeats the idea that a militantly *un*apologetic prologue and epilogue should be written for *Responsibilities*, his only collection of lyrics to be so distinguished. Moreover, 'Fame', which 'has perished this long while, / Being but a part of ancient ceremony', is also the subject addressed by Horace and Caesar in Jonson's play (v.i.14–16 and 136–8) in passages that Yeats regularly cited as if they upheld his view of the imagination as pyrogenic intensity (see above, section I). Leading the first of those passages is the line 'To shew, your titles are not writ on posts' – an image that ostensibly combined with an Erasmian metaphor of urination to form Yeats's concluding riposte.[64] At that moment, as his toughest critic advised him, Yeats became a modern poet; 'an image of urination', Ellmann writes, 'had . . . brought Pound to his knees' (*ED* 67).[65] Assuming no such posture of worship, we may be certain, Moore wisely chose to rewrite some of the offending portions of his book.

Finally, the epilogue to *Responsibilities* succeeds in converting action into words and in developing the public voice that Yeats had been rehearsing for more than a dozen years. With this work of adaptation (and others), he surpassed the mere simulacra of his second apprenticeship to produce something incomparable. The poem forecasts the muscular-but-subtle, complex voice of his maturity. But it also looks back to what Pound called the 'old Yeats', to Miltonic rhetoric, and to the 'just moulting eagle' of 'Elizifbeefan' imitation.[66] In 1911 Yeats is said to have been in the habit of 'reading a little of Milton's prose every morning before he began to work' (*WBY* 252).[67] Without mentioning the epilogue, Kenner associates Jonson and Milton with Yeats's art of the long sentence.[68] Jochum observes that Yeats's mixture of Shakespearean and Italian form is 'disturbed by . . . the unrelenting drive of . . . complicated . . . syntax', that his 'models are only used to be called into question'.[69] Yet, if the intricacies of the epilogue were not simply reflections of the Paterian prose style Yeats so much admired,[70] neither did they parody his Renaissance masters. At Pound's recommendation, the credit line was altered in proof, as were ll. 6–8 generally – seemingly more to amend bad rhyme and flaccid rhythm than in objection to the erudite tag. Line 7 was least changed in the revision, although most reflecting Pound's office as secretary.[71] In recasting ll. 6 and 8 (from ' – Ben Jonson's phrase – and still may turn my feet . . . By the wood's edge where only equals meet,' to 'And still can find where equals come, . . . A sterner conscience and a second home,'), Yeats suppressed the credit before reconsidering the theft which appeared, technically, the consequence.

Hence a third stage of polishing occurred (unfortunately lost on the proofs), which brought to lustre Jonson's premium on friendship and on highly principled noble patronage. A ray of 'To Penshurst' is perceptible overall, a foreshadowing of full light in 'Coole Park, 1929' (*VP* 488–9) and 'Coole Park and Ballylee, 1931' (*VP* 490–2). The phrase 'ancient ceremony' (l. 12) anticipates both 'A Prayer for my Daughter' (*VP* 403–6) and its opposite, 'The Second Coming' (*VP* 401–2).[72] Clearly, by February 1914 Yeats had learned, by synthesizing extremes he found in Jonson's work, to exaggerate the internal tensions of poetry (in the epilogue, those arising from two sharply contrasted perspectives brought to focus within a single system of ethics). He had learned to curse very ably. Yet his praise, unlike Jonson's in the *Epigrammes* and in the verse epistles of *The Forrest* and *The Under-wood*, was elegiac. In the dream of life, the Yeatsian persona could 'But inwardly . . . surmise companions', imagining himself part of a vanishing tradition, prophesying, as the poet did most ceremoniously in 'The Tower' (*VP* 409–27), the desecration of everything he valued.

IV

Yeats's mythologizing about the Coole Park estate of Lady Gregory began, in 1900 and 1902, with 'I walked the seven woods of Coole' (*VP* 217–19: introductory verses to *The Shadowy Waters*) and with the title poem of *In the Seven Woods* (*VP* 198). While those poems were largely tributes to the Edenic serenity of the demesne, they admitted elements of external reality that Yeats eventually learned how to attack in poetry written on occasional topics. Coole was originally portrayed as a half-wild place where the weary poet could 'put away/The unavailing outcries and the old bitterness/That empty the heart' and temporarily forget 'Tara uprooted, and new commonness/Upon the throne and crying about the streets' (*VP* 198, ll. 4–7). But, as his Journal testifies (*Mem* 225), Yeats soon discovered that successful contemporary poems could be written on issues of public concern, that the quotidian and the real inevitably intruded upon the landscapes of poets who were also men of action:

> August 7 [1909] Subject for a poem. 'A Shaken House'. How should the world gain if this house failed, even though a hundred little houses were the better for it, for here power [has] gone forth or lingered, giving energy, precision; it gave to a far people beneficent rule, and still under its roof living intellect is sweetened by old memories of its descent from far off? How should the world be better if the wren's nest flourish and the eagle's house is scattered?

The poem, written at Coole and inspired by a court order for the reduction of rents on Irish tenanted estates, followed on the same day, at least in part drafted beneath this prose 'Subject' (see *Mem* 226). Jonson's role is suggested by the titles the poem bore into print. These were 'To a Certain Country House in Time of Change', 'Upon a Threatened House', and 'Upon a House shaken by the Land Agitation' (*VP* 264). Tending toward severity with Yeats for his unpopular anti-democratic sympathies, some Irish scholars have recently objected to the distortion of reality which was incident to the poet's revival of an English genre initiated by Jonson and perpetuated by Carew, Herrick, Marvell, Cotton, Waller, Pope, and others.[73] The country-house poem in its native English context is quite a different matter from Yeats's panegyrics on the Anglo-Irish 'Big House'.[74] Coleman[75] correctly distinguishes between Yeats's divisiveness and Jonson's theme of community, his ideal of 'mutuality between magister and minister', ruler and ruled – an ideal which did not stand to be contradicted, as Yeats's was, by the brutal reality of the Penal Laws in Ireland. Yeats may have made a mistake in generalizing from the particular when fear of a breach in Victorian manners prevented him from praising his patroness outright, as was the Renaissance custom. Yeats needs no apology here, however, since his myth-making, which was essential to his hyperbole, simply reflected what he believed.[76] Of greater interest is the peculiar way in which he made use of Renaissance material.

In the first place, 'Upon a House . . .' stands among a number of epigrams gathered under one title, 'Momentary Thoughts', in the Cuala Press edition of *The Green Helmet and Other Poems* (1910; Wade 84). As a country-house poem of only twelve lines, it lacks the scope of virtually all other poems of the genre, turning its whole weight on a single figure, that of the eagle's nest:

> How should the world be luckier if this house,
> Where passion and precision have been one
> Time out of mind, became too ruinous
> To breed the lidless eye that loves the sun?
> And the sweet laughing eagle thoughts that grow
> Where wings have memory of wings, and all
> That comes of the best knit to the best? Although
> Mean roof-trees were the sturdier for its fall,
> How should their luck run high enough to reach
> The gifts that govern men, and after these
> To gradual Time's last gift, a written speech
> Wrought of high laughter, loveliness and ease?

The poem's 'eagle thoughts' (l. 5) *may* have arisen as a consequence of several references to eagles in Yeats's selected edition of Blake (including one occurrence in the poem 'An Imitation of Spenser').[77] More likely, however, the phrase and its attendant imagery derived from the adaptive complex, that general 'school' of 'Jonson and the others', as Yeats had referred to it. The prose draft seems to recall Shakespeare's 'Wrens make prey where eagles dare not perch' (*Richard III*, I.iii.70). Yet more compelling is the following note in Yeats's *Poems of Spenser* (p. 265):

It was a common tradition in medieval natural history that the eagle strengthened its eyesight by gazing at the noonday sun. Cf. Milton's *Areopagitica*: 'A noble and puissant nation . . . as an eagle mewing with her mighty youth and kindling her undazzled eyes at the full midday beam.'

The gloss is to 'An Hymne of Heavenly Beautie', ll. 134–40:

> Thence gathering plumes of perfect speculation,
> To impe the wings of thy high flying mynd,
> Mount up aloft through heavenly contemplation,
> From this darke world, whose damps the soule do blynd,
> And like the native brood of Eagles kynd,
> On that bright Sunne of glorie fixe thine eyes,
> Cleared from grosse mists of fraile infirmities.

Yeats repeated part of the image cluster *eagle + nest (or brood) + fixed eye + 'Sunne of glorie'* (or *majesty*) in another twelve-line epigram, 'These are the Clouds' (*VP* 265) – a poem also addressed to Lady Gregory and her heirs – and injected all of it into 'To a Wealthy Man who promised a Second Subscription to the Dublin Municipal Gallery if it were proved the People wanted Pictures' (*VP* 287–8). Given its long, flattering argument and its roll of the great patrons of Renaissance Florence and Urbino, the latter poem is the closest approximation in Yeats's work to Jonson's hortatory verse epistles written to English nobility. Its concluding lines, however, are epigrammatic:

> Let Paudeens play at pitch and toss,
> Look up in the sun's eye and give
> What the exultant heart calls good
> That some new day may breed the best
> Because you gave, not what they would,
> But the right twigs for an eagle's nest!

In other words, as the correspondent (Lord Ardilaun) proves with generosity that he is as noble as his title, he helps bring about a 'new age', or a higher Renaissance (see *E&I* 526) – a suggestion, as it is phrased, reminiscent of the poet's later Platonically motivated eugenic call for the cradles of Europe to be filled aright. By imagery and by point of reference, certainly, these poems are entitled to be called 'neo-Elizabethan' but are 'Jonsonian' in spirit more than in technique. The bicameral division of epigrams into satiric and panegyric types in *The Green Helmet* (1910) is emphatically Jonsonian, of course. Nevertheless, the rubric Yeats devised for these types as a whole, 'Momentary Thoughts', implies that he compounded his genres, regarding his 'public' epigrams as *pensées* (the prose model employed in *Discoveries*) to distinguish them from those painfully 'private' lyrics which masqueraded under the title 'Raymond Lully and his Wife Pernella', some eight poems commemorating Yeats's relationship with Maud Gonne.

A further observation worth emphasizing (for epigrams and epistolary verses alike) is that the prevalent attitude of Yeats's poetic celebration of Coole Park and the Gregorys was *elegiac*. Almost without exception, his praise seems to have depended on the conviction that its subject, the finer-but-diminished agent of a dialectical struggle for mastery and power, was teetering on the brink of extinction. Yeats *can* be blamed for dubiously exaggerating conditions for the sake of poetry. To be sure, 'The New Faces' (*VP* 435), a panegyric epigram sometimes cited as a forerunner of the country-house poems 'Coole Park, 1929' and 'Coole Park and Ballylee, 1931', is so funereal, with its exaggeration of Lady Gregory's age and its transformation of her into a restless ghost, that she took offence at it and Yeats was obliged to suppress the poem for many years.[78] Prophetically, on the other hand, he correctly anticipated the natural force (not an earthquake but a democratic 'land agitation') that was destined to bring down the Gregory mansion, symbolically defiling all it represented to those who forged Ireland's literary renaissance. The Gregory house, in effect, was a *locus* and Lady Gregory its *genius loci*. To the poet, it was a sacred place 'Where passion and precision have been one/Time out of mind' – an eagle's nest that Platonically bred high-flying intelligence (that is, 'the lidless eye that loves the sun', 'sweet laughing eagle thoughts') and moved those living beneath its gables to reach 'To gradual Time's last gift, a written speech/Wrought of high laughter, loveliness and ease'. (See also 'The New Faces', l. 4: 'Where we wrought that shall break the teeth of Time'.) Elegies are, in one sense, expressions of mourning set in time (i.e. metre) protesting what becomes of the best of us in time. Time provides but also reaps. An artist feigns to arrest ('Time out of mind') what he may only imitate in effigy: a quality of perception bred over a long time. Thus a painter, as Jonson wrote in 'The Mind', the fourth segment of his remarkable elegy to Lady Digby, 'Eupheme', may

> make shift to paint an Eye,
> An Eagle towring in the skye,
> The Sunne, a Sea, or soundlesse Pit;
> But these are *like* a Mind, not it.
>
> No, to expresse a Mind to sense,
> Would aske a Heavens Intelligence;
> Since nothing can report that flame,
> But what's of kinne to whence it came.
> (ll. 9–16; emphasis added)[79]

By such accounts, the estimate of one's value is measured in generations and appreciated only by those of like mind, the friends and companions who are so often celebrated in the poetry of Jonson – his lyric 'Sons' – and Yeats.

Between January 1912 and July 1914, Yeats penned his first successful elegy, 'Upon a Dying Lady' (*VP* 362–7). Like Jonson's 'Eupheme', Yeats's elegy paid tribute to the memory of a friend, Mabel Beardsley, by means of a verse medley arranged in progression; the metaphysical, social, and (to use Yeats's word) 'radical' themes of the melange were improvised upon the conceit of a death-bed portrait.[80] By late January 1918, the death in Italy of Robert Gregory had given Yeats occasion to consult another Renaissance elegist, Edmund Spenser, and to adapt the pastoral form employed in 'Astrophel' to mourn the death of Sidney. Yeats's experiment ('Shepherd and Goatherd', *VP* 338–43) was not entirely successful, though he worked extraordinarily hard at it, as we now know. As a consequence, he seems to have turned to Jonson's Cary–Morison ode[81] and in due course produced the modern elegiac masterpiece 'In Memory of Major Robert Gregory' (*VP* 323–8). The two cases are worth comparing for what they reveal about Yeats's use of English Renaissance models in his maturity and about the poetic lessons he drew from such exercises.

The first thing that seems remarkable about Yeats's adaptation of the pastoral elegy is that he should attempt it at all after chastising Spenser for faults which herein became Yeats's own: namely, the imposition of distractingly prolix, recondite matter on relatively unassuming forms. Yeats exercised Spenser's licence with pastoral dialogue but threw out Christian allegory because it intruded upon the 'paganism that is natural to proud and happy people' (E&I 366). In essence, he allowed that Spenser *could* distract the reader with strange disquisitions that drew upon Neoplatonic philosophy. Accordingly, Yeats's 'Shepherd and Goatherd' is, of his mature poems, the most Spenserian and, given the subject matter explored in the poem, appropriately so. Yeats's initial attraction to 'Astrophel', however, probably occurred simply because he thought Robert Gregory a 'Renaissance man', like Sidney. Yeats remembered young Gregory, in an obituary 'note of appreciation' in *The Observer*, as the most 'accomplished' man he had ever known – 'painter, classical scholar, scholar in painting and in modern literature, boxer, horseman, airman' (*UP2* 429); and Yeats's Sidney was the 'Astrophel' of the poems (see *YL* 1916–17). Certainly, when Yeats first wrote to Lady Gregory about 'Shepherd and Goatherd', on 22 February 1918, he presented it as an experiment with perhaps not much promise: 'I am trying a poem in manner like one that Spenser wrote for Sir Philip Sidney. It may come to nothing' (*L* 646). But on 19 March he wrote with greater assurance about this work – although leaning on his wife's judgement and complicating our view of the adaptive complex, which may also have included Shelley's 'Adonais', a work quoted and alluded to, with Spenser and Henry More, in *Per Amica Silentia Lunae* (1917). 'I have to-day finished my poem about Robert', he informed Lady Gregory,

> a pastoral, modelled on what Virgil wrote for some friend of his and on what Spenser wrote of Sidney. My wife thinks it good. A goatherd and a shepherd are talking in some vague place, perhaps the Burren Hills, in some remote period of the world. It is a new form for me and I think for modern poetry. I hope it may please Margaret [Mrs Robert Gregory] also.   (*L* 647–8)

Virgil's *Eclogues*, translated and illustrated by Samuel Palmer (*YL* 2202), supplemented by the prose translation of C. Davidson and Theodore Buckley (*YL* 2203), was one of Yeats's reference books. His own edition of Spenser (*Wade* 235) omitted 'Astrophel' (which is not a dialogue and therefore formally at variance with Yeats's poem), since he apparently had preferred in 1902 the elegiac vignette on the Earl of Leicester in *The Ruines of Time*.[82] Possibly, with Virgil's fifth Eclogue ('Daphnis'), Yeats also consulted

Theocritus – as Spenser had done in writing *The Shepheardes Calender* – especially such dialogues between herdsmen as 'Thyrsis' and 'The Shepherd and the Goatherd' (*Idylls* I and v, respectively).[83] Such reading could easily have taken place at the Bodleian Library (Oxford), near which Yeats lived at the time. The eclogues of Sidney's *Arcadia* might have been consulted as well, although it is doubtful that it would have been necessary.

Yeats's renewed interest in pastoral poetry for this occasion might also have led to some brief reading in the Spenserians Nicholas Breton, George Wither, and William Browne of Tavistock (*YL* 272). But, if anything, Yeats's researches were more of a spiritual kind, as we know from Harper's study of the experiments in automatic script undertaken by Yeats and his wife within days of their marriage late in 1917.[84] The chief way in which the poem offers condolences for the death of Robert Gregory (in 'Shepherd and Goatherd', ll. 16–17, 'He that was best in every country sport / And every country craft'; see 'Astrophel', ll. 89–96) has long been suspected. Wilson traced it to the heart of Platonic theology with the conjecture that the poet

> probably made early acquaintance with the tradition that the soul, after death, lives backwards through time, for he will have read of it in the section on Dionysus in Taylor's *Dissertation*:
> According to the Orphic theology, souls, while under the government of Saturn, . . . instead of progressing, as now, from youth to age, advance in retrograde progression from age to youth.[85]

Such speculation seems confirmed by other discursive lyrics on supernatural subjects in *The Wild Swans at Coole* (for example, by 'The Phases of the Moon', *VP* 372-7, ll. 58–71). It arises from the yarn, pern, and cradle imagery at the end of 'Shepherd and Goatherd', in the Goatherd's song:

> Jaunting, journeying
> To his own dayspring,
> He unpacks the loaded pern
> Of all 'twas pain or joy to learn,
> Of all that he had made.
> The outrageous war shall fade.
> . . .

> Knowledge he shall unwind
> Through victories of the mind,
> Till clambering at the cradle-side
> He dreams himself his mother's pride . . . .
> (ll. 95–100, 107–10)

The riddle of this condolence, so obviously intended for the dead swain's mother (see 'Astrophel', ll. 31–36), was explained in draft, as the following version of the conclusion testifies (NLI 13,587[6]; asterisked lines anticipate ll. 113–15 in *VP*):[86]

[L1v]
                  Shephe[r]d
                  ~~Goathe[r]d~~
I have hea[r]d my mother say that whe[n] we die
we dwindle or increase t[o] thos[e] years
A[n]d stay so

                  Goatherd
                      That is[?] how [(noun)] has[?] it
A[n]d yet I think that the wind has quickened as
would neve[r] be conte[n]t to stay as lo[n]g as ma[?]d
~~But must unwind it all until he come~~
~~To his first stat[e]~~
How could h[e] rest till hed un wou[n]d it all
~~And come t[o] his first state~~
And come by some strange circles of thought
To his first stat[e]

                  Sheph[erd]
*   we ll t[o] the hous[e]

                      yews
*whe[n] I have shut up these eye & then
                      ewes

---

                              at its height
But how ca[n] p[(noun)] maste[re]d[?] ~~bring conte[n]t~~
Leave us content – no we must un wind it all
   and come, as by a
By some ~~que~~ stra[n]ge circling in the mind
A[n]d come t[o] our first state

                    Sheph.
          *   Wh[en] I ha[ve] shut
   *Thes[e]∧ ra̶ & this old ram a[n]d its fold
                 ewes
   *we ll car[v]e our rhymes on st[r]ip[s] of [t]he t[?] bush

[L2v]   *   Whe[n] I ha[ve] drive[n] home
   *Thes[e] ewes & this ol[d] ram, we['ll] car[v]e our rhymes
   *on strips of bark, & leave them at his door

        [a series of geometrical marks and
        vertical strokes follow, apparently
        made to clean the tip of the pen]

   By some stra[n]ge [?(noun)] & thus
   T̶o̶ h̶i̶s̶ f̶i̶r̶s̶t̶ i̶n̶n̶o̶c̶e̶n̶s̶e̶   knowled[ge]
   To his first stat[e] agai[n] – [?] exchange[d]
   F̶o̶r̶ i̶n̶n̶o̶c̶e̶n̶c̶e̶ –
   For something that we see as he[a]rt & child
   To his first state, & his knowl[e]d[ge] all exchang[ed]
   For something that we see as he[a]rt & chi[l]d

The point is that Yeats withheld the explanation that he contemplated – indeed, wrote – preferring the shorter, elliptical conclusion that we know. One recognizes the problem that his partially surgical revision addressed, even if it failed to correct it: the poem's *form* is overwhelmed by its *matter*. Hitherto, scholars have taken the view that Yeats's adaptation of Spenser and Virgil failed as poetry because of the artificiality of the form.[87] The truth is that his subsequent and most admired elegy to Robert Gregory was far more prescriptive in that regard.

It seems, too, that Yeats realized that his effort to console Gregory's mother lacked feeling, although it had been forged from deep convictions about the soul's voyage in life and death. Hence his next attempt to remember the airman in elegy concentrated on his own response to the young man's death, rather than condolence. The poetic artefact was to be a song about 'the natural life', as the old Goatherd observed on listening to the Shepherd's lament, and about the poet's grief over 'that young man [Gregory] / And certain lost companions of my own' ('Shepherd and Goatherd', ll. 77–8). Rather than posting anonymous rhymes

'Cut out . . . on strips of new-torn bark' (l. 115) in 'some vague place . . . in some remote period of the world', he prepared to sing in his own voice, at his own hearth, and about his own moment of mourning.

By no accident did Yeats again turn to Jonson and his poetic circle. The social mode of Jonson (or what Miner has called the 'radical feature of Cavalier poetry'[88]) was ready and working in Yeats's verse by 1910 in those epigrams that honour Augusta and Robert Gregory in *The Green Helmet* (for instance, in 'These are the Clouds', l. 9: 'Have you made greatness your companion'; and 'At Galway Races', l. 7: 'Aye, horsemen for companions'). *Responsibilities* opened with a Jonsonian salutation: 'Poets with whom I learned my trade, / Companions of the Cheshire Cheese' ('The Grey Rock', ll. 1-2). Moreover, as records of the Yeats library now suggest, the poet was well-read in Herrick (*Hesperides* seemingly without *Noble Numbers*; see YL 886-9) and possessed copies of the collected poems of Suckling (YL 2031, decorated by Ricketts) and of Waller (YL 1920 289). His knowledge of seventeenth-century English poetry was extensive, centring on the 'schools' of Jonson and Donne (which overlapped to some extent, as the next chapter argues). He read well beyond the books that he owned, and developed, among other things, almost a penchant for borrowing stanzas from Cowley, who first turned Yeats's head with the much-anthologized 5a-5a-5b-4b-5c-4d-4d-5c stanzas of 'Ode on the Death of Mr William Harvey'.[89] Notwithstanding serious reservations about this rambling, 'uneven, over-long and over-witty' Pindaric ode, Kermode points to a number of features likely to have recommended it to Yeats as a model for 'In Memory of Major Robert Gregory':

> It has balance and variety, and in the long concluding line Cowley began an experiment in the elegiac possibilities of slow, heavily retarded monosyllabic movement, which Yeats was happy to continue. . . . Yeats here practices a poet's not a critic's imitation. William Harvey was not a Sidney, but he was, according to Cowley, a many-sided genius who died young, and the poem which commemorates him struck certain chords that interested Yeats; he therefore imitated it. (*RI* 39, 40)

Yeats's preceding attempt at elegy is also marked by metrical experimentation, which led him into some significant difficulties.

As an effort to *simulate* rustic literary dialect, his imitation of Spenser and Virgil is fraught with initial trochaic and medial ionic inversions; with hypermetric, broken, and enjambed lines; and with caesuras that migrate in approximation to natural speech. The Shepherd's haphazard rhyming and metrical irregularity ('maybe "I am sorry" in plain prose/Had sounded better' – ll. 61–2) is counterpointed by the Goatherd's dozen elaborately stressed couplets (by pairs, 4–3–4–2–4–3–4–3–4–3–4–3). Jonson's own conspicuously derivative choral strophes in *The Under-wood*, LXX (with its rhymed couplets metrically distributed 4–5–3–4–5 in stanzas labelled 'The Turne', 'The Counter-turne', and 'The Stand'), would have appealed little to Yeats, although he might have taken instruction from the way Jonson boldly injected his own persona into an elegy honouring a 'Souldier', 'most a vertuous Sonne', 'Perfect Patriot, and . . . noble friend'. To be sure, Jonson personally celebrates the full delight of his Sidneyan hero – a delight which prefigures Gregory's escape into action and death:

> Hee leap'd the present age,
> Possest with holy rage,
> To see that bright eternall Day:
> Of which we *Priests*, and *Poets* say
> Such truths as we expect for happy men,
> And there he lives with memorie; and *Ben*
>
> *The Stand*
> *Johnson*, who sung this of him, e're he went
> Himselfe to rest,
> Or taste a part of that full joy he meant
> To have exprest . . . .
> (ll. 79–88)[90]

McAlindon first put forward the hypothesis that Yeats's second elegy to Robert Gregory owes more to Jonson's ode 'To the Immortall Memorie, and Friendship of that Noble Paire, Sir Lucius Cary, and S. H. Morison' than to Cowley's poem.[91] The hypothesis is a compelling one, suggesting, in short, that Yeats's search through English literature for elegiac models led to his formal adaptation of Cowley and material adaptation of Jonson. The fact that the poems of Jonson and Yeats celebrate their subjects (i.e. Morison and Gregory) in terms of friendship (that between Cary and the deceased Morison, and that between Yeats and 'the friends that cannot sup with us' – 'In Memory of Major Robert Gregory', l. 2) more convincingly argues the hypothesis than does such merely conventional hyperbole as Yeats's

> Soldier, scholar, horseman, he
> As 'twere all life's epitome.
> What made us dream that he could comb grey hair?
> (ll. 86–8)

Compare Jonson's fifth stanza:

> Alas, but *Morison* fell young:
> Hee never fell, thou fall'st, my tongue.
> Hee stood, a Souldier to the last right end,
> A perfect Patriot, and a noble friend,
> But most, a vertuous Sonne.
> All Offices were done
> By him, so ample, full, and round,
> In weight, in measure, number, sound,
> As though his age imperfect might appeare,
> His life was of Humanitie the Spheare.

Yeats's compliment, however, originated in a familiar Jonsonian image cluster. The 'passionate dead' have their deserved immortality in the memories and imaginations of the living:

> Soldier, scholar, horseman, he,
> And yet he had that intensity
> To have published all to be a world's delight.
> ('In Memory of Major Robert Gregory', ll. 71–3)

This recalls Jonson's 'passionate intensity' (Symonds's and Swinburne's phrase), to which Yeats alluded in the following year ('The Second Coming', l. 8) and which he misapplied, in May 1917, in the 'Anima Mundi' section of *Per Amica Silentia Lunae*: 'Surely of the passionate dead we can but cry in words Ben Jonson meant for none but Shakespeare: "So rammed" are they "with life they can but grow in life with being"' (*Myth* 360). As one of the 'passionate dead', Gregory joins Lionel Johnson, John Synge, and George Pollexfen – 'Discoverers of forgotten truth / Or mere companions of my youth' ('In Memory of Major Robert Gregory', ll. 6–7) – who enter the troubled poet's thoughts 'being dead' (l. 8). By implication, the airman is now one with the disembodied 'burning eye' of the majestic 'fallen sun' ('These are the Clouds', ll. 1–2) and the 'Delight [that] makes all of the one mind' ('At Galway Races', l. 2). Having entered the poet's mind by occultation, 'Our Sidney and our perfect man' ('In Memory of Major Robert Gregory', l. 47) calls up images of the world in which he has become an *absence*:

> For all things the delighted eye now sees
> Were loved by him: the old storm-broken trees
> That cast their shadows upon road and bridge;
> The tower set on the stream's edge;
> The ford where drinking cattle make a stir . . . .
> (ll. 49–53)

And we are startled by the memories he raises of intense being in a world once flushed with his spirit:

> When with the Galway foxhounds he would ride
> From Castle Taylor to the Roxborough side
> Or Esserkelly plain, few kept his pace;
> At Mooneen he had leaped a place
> So perilous that half the astonished meet
> Had shut their eyes; and where was it
> He rode a race without a bit?
> And yet his mind outran the horses' feet.
> (ll. 57–64)

In short, the elegy gains from such pointedly personal and specific references to the world of actuality. Yeats *learned* this, as it now appears, in the course of his two adaptive exercises in the minor elegiac tradition that gave honour to the Sidneyan hero, and he *stressed* that lesson by adding the eighth stanza (quoted fully just above) in a very late stage of revision.[92] In short, as Martin writes, 'What in "Shepherd and Goatherd" exists as esoteric theory, "In Memory" converts into exoteric poetic structure, one of art's "monuments of unaging intellect".'[93] Certainly, by 14 June 1918 (see *L* 650), Yeats had learned that elegiac form requires cognizable matter, that it is a public ritual demanding the subordination of its supermediary mysteries to worldly points of reference. By this time, the Spenserian idealized landscape had given place to the Jonsonian *locus* (Harris's 'myths of place'). The simulacrum had given place to liberal, sophisticated adaptation. The poet *in absentia* had given place to the poet *praesidium*. Yeats was prepared at this point for some of his greatest work – for those half-elegiac, half-meditative country-house poems of *The Tower* and *The Winding Stair* collections. It would be a mistake to underestimate the significant progress he made as a poet simply because he had, in a sense, apprenticed himself to Jonson and the poets of his circle. Still, it would be wrong to exaggerate the importance of the lessons he took under their influence and to proceed directly to the major works of his maturity. Donne and the Metaphysical poets, for example, were equally important influences. To proceed, one must go back a step to the dichotomy inherent in *The Green Helmet* (1910) and its division between the epigrams of 'Momentary Thoughts' and the love poems of 'Raymond Lully and his Wife Pernella'.

5
Yeats, Donne, and the Metaphysicals: Polemics and Lyrics, 1896–1929

I have felt in certain early works of my own which I have long abandoned, and here and there in the work of others of my generation, a slight, sentimental sensuality which is disagreeable, and does not exist in the work of Donne, let us say, because he, being permitted to say what he pleased, was never tempted to linger, or rather to pretend that we can linger, between spirit and sense. How often had I heard men of my time talk of the meeting of spirit and sense, yet there is no meeting but only change upon the instant, and it is by the perception of a change, like the sudden 'blacking out' of the lights of the stage, that passion creates its most violent sensation. (*Au* 326)

I

Throughout his career, Yeats remained steadfast in his belief that a polarity of forces emanating from body and soul gave rise to instants of supraliminal insight which poets were empowered to translate into poetry. By the turn of the century, he saw the need for a significant mid-course adjustment in the stylistic tack his work was taking; but it would be a misreading of his later poetry and criticism to equate his election to become a man of action with rejection of his commitment to the concept of spiritual progress as it figured largely in the love poems and sequences of his early works. The so-called 'manly' voice he began cultivating at middle age, on Jonsonian models (among others), perfectly suited certain occasions. It was public and exoteric rather than private and esoteric, arising from antagonism between the poet and the world. Still, as he quickly understood, poetry originates in the antagonism between the poet and himself (*Myth* 331). In opting for a more vigorous style, Yeats indeed rejected as 'exaggeration of sentiment and sentimental beauty' what he called 'the sweet insinuating feminine voice of the dwellers in that [spiritual] country of shadows and hollow images' (*L* 434). He did not reject, however, the spirit for the world as he strove to recast himself by throwing himself into public affairs and into literary scrimmages with his enemies. Rather, he tried to wed the two, despite their determined resistance not to be joined, into a condition he called 'unity of being'. Naturally enough, John Donne's influence in this endeavour, also twofold, gradually translated into a poetic idiom after 1912. This idiom, in fact – linked by various scholars to the modernist revival of metaphysical poetry[1] – arose from an extremely idiosyncratic synthesis of Yeatsian philosophy and certain 'Metaphysical', or Baroque, mannerisms associated with the passionate intellectuality of Donne's supposed 'unified sensibility' (Eliot's phrase). It arose from a synthesis that made rigid Yeats's antagonism to Donne's eighteenth-century detractors, despite his tacit acceptance of at least one of their observations.

When Samuel Johnson defined 'wit' in *The Life of Cowley* (1779), he described a disposition of mind which he thought characteristic of certain seventeenth-century 'metaphysical poets', a term he derived from Dryden's famous observation that Donne had 'too much affect[ed] the metaphysics'. By this, Dryden meant, in his *Discourse concerning the Original and Progress of Satire* (1693), that most of Donne's poetry was confounding to women (the audience of his amorous verse) because of its philosophical matter, its heat of the mind rather than the heart. Johnson surmised from this remark – and from his reading-acquaintance with the 'race' of metaphysical writers with which he associated both Donne and Cowley – a *dialectical* manner of expression, 'a kind of *discordia concors*; a combination of dissimilar images, or discovery of occult resemblances in things apparently unlike. . . . The most heterogeneous ideas are yoked by violence together.'[2]

As a heterodox dialectician, Yeats rose to the peak of his powers, a century and a half later, making deliberate adaptations of Donne and, to some extent, other Metaphysical poets. Diametrically opposed to the pejorative attitude of Donne's Augustan critics, Yeats demonstrated once again that poetry could be written with naturalness and 'wit', feeling and philosophical substance, without neglecting the Platonic prescriptions which, as he believed, define its imitative relationship to 'life' as broadly interpreted. To a great extent, his adaptations were something new to English poetry, because, mirroring the distinctions between Dryden's and Johnson's terms, they sprang from the synthesis of Yeats's own eclectically acquired metaphysics and some of the more attractive mannerisms of Donne and his poetic following.

At present, it seems taxonomically convenient, but not altogether accurate, to divide the corpus of pre-Restoration seventeenth-century poetry into 'schools' of Jonson and Donne. Yeats's early mentor Edward Dowden, who also lent his voice to the nineteenth-century Donne revival, frankly disavowed the existence of a 'metaphysical school' founded by the enigmatic Dean of St Paul's, and instead associated the older poet's characteristic poetry with 'the flood-tide hour of Elizabethan literature'.[3] More recently, Warnke has similarly argued that Metaphysical poetry is no less than 'a great and fully typical manifestation of the Baroque style in literature'.[4] Such perspectives may blur distinctions we care to maintain for pedagogical reasons, but they are worth noting because of Yeats's tendency to view Donne and Jonson as opposite sides of the same coin. His adaptation of Donne's predominantly private and Jonson's predominantly public poetic modes was one factor tending to set them apart. In such a light, the multiplying mirror of Shakespeare, who stands in dialectical relation to Jonson the dramatist in *AV B* 152–3, seems to be the central conceit of 'To a Young Beauty' (*VP* 335–6; cf. *Myth* 344), a poem which pays Jonsonian tribute to Yeats's imaginary companions Landor (possibly to be correlated with Jonson) and Donne.[5] But, as different sides of the same coin in 'The Tragic Generation', Donne and Jonson are opposed while simultaneously allied in opposition to Shelley, much as the Romantic poet and Spenser had been paired in an earlier phase of Yeats's poetry (see Ch. 3). Clearly, the equiponderate dyad must admit another dimension, a vertical as well as a horizontal index. For just as Jonson, as we learn in the *Autobiographies*, 'could find no justification for the entomologist . . . but that he had been crossed in love', so Yeats and the poets of his generation took delight 'in writing with an unscientific partiality for subjects long forbidden' and discovered in Donne a poet who 'could be as metaphysical as he pleased, and yet never seemed unhuman and hysterical as Shelley often does, because he could be as physical as he pleased' (*Au* 325–6, the passage concluding with the paragraph cited as the epigraph to this chapter).

Although the works of Jonson and Donne might be distinguished by their respective public and private manners, Yeats owned (recalling Blake) that both poets beheld a 'Vision of Evil'. Nevertheless, of the two poets it was Donne who seemed more clearly to represent the balance between the spiritual and the physical in poetry, and to counter, in this particularly complicated adaptive complex, Shelley's 'thirst for the metaphysical', Shelley's 'parched tongue'.[6]

Should we wish to consider the case for Donne and Jonson as distinct influences on Yeats, a good place to begin would be with the partitioning of *The Green Helmet and Other Poems* (1910; *Wade* 84), although that story is anticipated by circumstances of a much earlier date. Should we prefer to study the way in which these influences eventually coalesced, it is still best to begin with the half-hermetic, lyric monologues and the bipartite group of epigrams in *The Green Helmet*. One's attention would necessarily shift to later works – especially to Yeats's meditative and conversational poems, works which speak in the registers of both Renaissance poets. Hence, to complement the preceding treatment of Yeats and Jonson, this chapter's devotion to Donne and the Metaphysical poets distinguishes its subject as a discrete influence and shows how that influence, within the first dozen years of Yeats's marriage, contributed to the development of a lyric style which was itself a marriage of diverse modes.[7] Of these modes, the most compatible were the verse epistles, panegyric epigrams and elegies of Donne and Jonson, some few of which have been claimed for both writers.[8] Although it appears that most formal aspects of Donne's work failed to attract Yeats's attention until comparatively late, the Irish poet was long an admirer of Donne's natural-sounding poetic voice and his racy contrapuntal image-making ability. In particular, Donne's lyric mixing of the erotic and the philosophic struck a nerve in Yeats as early as the 1890s, when the younger poet's private life, albeit thinly veiled, went on public display in his art. Those admired characteristics of Donne's poetry remained, largely, outside Yeats's register until he initiated a series of imitative exercises after his marriage in 1917. However, until he made them his property, he was indebted to Donne for an ambience, or guise, which he could exploit in verse without having quite to bare his soul to the general public.

II

In 1891, after Yeats gave Maud Gonne a vellum notebook which he entitled *The Flame of the Spirit* and into which he entered early versions of a number of poems he had written to her,[9] he persuaded her to join him as a member of the Hermetic Students of the Golden Dawn. This order, to which he had belonged for little more than a year himself, brought him into touch with occult traditions that had attracted such Renaissance men of learning as John Dee, Jacob Boehme, Henry More, Ralph Cudworth, Joseph Glanvil, and others whose books Yeats eventually owned and studied (see YL 234–9, 453–4, 501, 750, and 1377–80). The simultaneous founding of the Rhymers' Club promoted, as much as anything at the time, a more advanced and practical phase of the poet's literary education than he had hitherto received as an adolescent, under the tutelage of various elders. His collaboration at that moment with Edwin Ellis on a selected edition of Blake's poetry certainly effected a conjunction of the young poet's occult and poetic interests. However, the Rhymers reinforced his affection for Elizabethan writers (particularly those with a philosophical bent, such as Donne) and encouraged through Pater his interest in Platonic philosophy (see Ch. 2). In the 'expandible talisman' – the manuscript grimoire that Yeats gave to Maud Gonne, 'summoning [his] beloved to occult service as well as to love'[10] – the poet introduced the first of a host of short dramatic monologues later arranged in sequence in the manner of countless Elizabethan prototypes, but most especially suggesting kinship with the 'songs and sonnets' and elegies of Donne.

To be sure, Yeats's failed progress in his love affair with this woman and his signal but temporary contentment, in 1896, with Olivia Shakespear (to whom he also wrote poems) complicates one's view of the poetic sequence Yeats made to dramatize the conflicts produced in his personal life.[11] The poet could not originally have intended those lyrics to be read as an homogeneous collection of biographical documents, given the range of speakers to whom he attributed them when he wrote them. Yet for the 1906 *Poetical Works* Yeats revised the titles of these poems (*VP* nos 44, 52, 53, 54, 55, 56, 57, 58, 59, 62, 63, 64, 65, 66, 69, 71, 72, 73, 74, 75, 76), suppressing the various imaginary personae of *The Wind Among the Reeds* (1899; *Wade* 27) in favour of a single voice. That is, collectively and permanently, Aedh, Mongan, Michael Robartes, and Red Hanrahan gave way to more transparent and evidently co-referential identities: 'He', 'The Poet', 'The Lover' (Aedh, for example, became all three: 'Aedh wishes his Beloved were dead' was retitled 'He wishes . . .'; 'Aedh pleads with the Elemental Powers' became 'The Poet pleads . . .'; and 'Aedh tells of the Rose in his Heart' was retitled 'The Lover tells . . .').

As originally published between 1893 and 1899, these poems mythologized the poet and his beloved. As Dectora, Mary Lavell, or a more vaguely generalized ideal, Maud Gonne received much of Yeats's tribute as the love object of some half-dozen fictionalized manifestations of himself – although an object, for 'several . . . elaborate' lyrics, supplanted by Mrs Shakespear (see *Mem* 86). If he had yet to develop the stylistic mannerisms of Metaphysical poetry, he was already committed to the lover's quest for the 'hidden mysterie' of 'rich and long delight', the elixir of Donne's 'Loves Alchimie', 'The Extasie', and other poems. Yeats's hermetic studies prepared him for a life-long career as a spiritual alchemist devoted to the transmutation of life into art, although he remained an inconstant believer in spiritual perfection.[12] The chemical marriage of male and female, of body and soul, of heaven and earth (or vice versa), was frustrated, though it stood squarely behind the polemic these poems provided. The argumentative aspect of the sequence was brought into sharper focus when Yeats restricted the number of referents to two – the poet/lover and his beloved – by renaming the poems. As he sharpened the focus, he redefined the sequence; and therein we witness the birth of a Yeatsian prototype: a sequence of lyric poems featuring polemic tensions between the poet and his lady and between the poet and himself – notably repeated in *The Green Helmet* (1910) and, quite differently, in the supernatural songs appended to *The Tower* (1928) and *The Winding Stair* (1933). Although a marriage of mind and heart had not yet given issue in Yeats's poetry to wit in the Metaphysical sense, circumstances point to the suggestive (if then minor) role that Donne played in shaping the type of sequence that his work increasingly inspired in Yeats.

It is clear that in the 1890s Yeats took up reading a number of Renaissance writers whose works were then the projects of his friends or who received their admiration. His acquaintance with Jonson's masques, with Herrick's poetry, and with several Jacobean playwrights was made in this way, as Chapter 4 has shown. Similarly, evidence from Yeats's library and his works points to a concatenation of English Renaissance influences that arose in this way to assist him with the handling of recondite material. The hermetic stories of *The Secret Rose* (1897), within which were embedded early versions of several of the poems listed above, testify that he was no idle reader of Thomas Browne (see *Myth* 267; *UP1* 407–8; *YL* 289–91), whose *Religio Medici* and *Urn Burial* the poet owned in more than one copy. While Yeats's knowledge of the alchemists Basilius Valentinus, Avicenna, Morienus, Alfarabi, Flamel, and Lully was second-hand – all cited in 'Rosa Alchemica' but derived from thumbnail sketches in A. E. Waite's *Lives of Alchemystical Philosophers* (1888; *YL* 2210) – Browne's influence was direct. Likewise, between 1896 and 1899 (when most of the lyric monologues for *The Wind Among the Reeds* were written), Yeats would have been directed to Donne. In 1896, for example, Lionel Johnson – who shared Yeats's Irish preoccupation with the Elizabethan and Stuart periods (see *Poetry and Ireland*, 1908; *Wade* 242) – published three essays of note on the Donne circle.[13] The first of these, 'Father Izaak', was a tribute to Walton as 'eulogist' of Donne, Wotton, Hooker, Herbert, and Sanderson – and, most especially, to Walton's *Lives* itself, a used copy of which Yeats may have obtained by then (with or without its marginal scorings in the life of Donne).[14] A month later, Johnson's 'The Soul of Sacred Poetry' drew on Walton's biographical authority as he made a measuring-rod of the 'mystical' and/or devotional works of Donne, Vaughan, Crashaw, and Herbert. Towards the end of the year, 'Henry Vaughan, Silurist', Johnson's review of the E. K. Chambers edition of Vaughan's *Poems* (London: Lawrence and Bullen, 1896), betrayed its author's own inclination toward 'philosophical conceptions, . . . Christian Platonism, [and] theological mysticism' set nobly, rather than rapturously, to poetry.[15] Though Donne is nowhere mentioned in the review, several of Yeats's enthusiasms do surface: Walton again, the Herberts, Browne, and (of later significance) Henry More. This shortcoming, however, was redressed by Yeats's purchase of the two-volume Chambers edition of Donne's *Poems* (London: Routledge, 1896; *YL 1920* 282). Masefield's gift of the Le Gallienne edition of *The Compleat Angler*, by Walton and Cotton (1897; *YL* 2223), and Yeats's acquisition of the Adolphus Ward biography of Wotton (1898; *YL* 2224) testify to an awakening interest in Donne and his associates – an interest which would have been encouraged by Yeats's close friend Arthur Symons.

Symons, who had once shared rooms with Yeats – and who

mediated the Symbolist phase of Yeats's development by translating the arcane writings of Mallarmé, Calderón, and St John of the Cross (see *Au* 320) – published a long disquisition in the *Fortnightly Review* that barely masqueraded as a critique of Edmund Gosse's *Life and Letters of John Donne, Dean of St Paul's* (1899).[16] Beyond the first paragraph of this essay (and some three references made simply to acknowledge his text), Symons left Gosse in order to muse on Donne, the paradoxical subject of the professor's valuable 'piece of history'.[17] While faulting Donne for apparent weaknesses – among which were the unwelcome introduction of scientific and technical words in poetry; a morbid preoccupation with death; and a too-speculative, casuistical frame of mind – Symons's 6000-word analysis of the Paterian 'many-sided activity of [Donne's] mind and temperament'[18] was the most cogent of any Yeats was likely to have read up to that time. Citing the same weaknesses, Saintsbury (in his Introduction to Chambers' *Poems of John Donne*) and Dowden both argued less convincingly that Donne was an 'inspired poetical creator' despite his eccentricities.[19] Although Symons concluded characteristically with a preference for Herrick over Donne, he forgave Donne his indiscretions against form (the 'heres[ies] of the realist') because 'almost every poem that he wrote [was] written on a genuine . . . personal inspiration'.[20] Just as he took no time or care to weed from his poetry words which had no association with beauty (or a correspondence with 'a diviner world'), so Donne put 'his "naked thinking heart" into verse as if he were setting forth an argument'. Because Symons felt that poetry should be the perfect interfusion of 'personal or human reality' and 'imagination or divine reality', he observed in Donne, as had Dryden, a 'fatal division of two forces' – 'intellect and the poetical spirit' – which, pulling apart rather than together, produced a result not 'wholly splendid'. Still, Symons said, Donne was a 'great lover', a lover of women and a lover of God. As a poet, moreover, 'he had the passions and the passionate adventures, in body and mind, which make the material for poetry'.[21]

Years later, in light of such 'talk of the meeting of spirit and sense', Symons's censure of Donne may have partly inspired Yeats's unsympathetic repudiation of 'certain early works' of his own and some unspecified works of 'others' of his generation (*Au* 326). In view of Yeats's unqualified embrace of Donne, Symons's ideal of the interfusion of the personal and the imaginative yielded to the complex anatomy of the world outlined in *A*

Vision. By then, the individual realization of 'unity of being', or the reconciliation of human and divine reality, seemed all but impossible. Yet several of Symons's observations would have been attractive to Yeats, who by 1899 had already tired of the 'sentimental sensuality' of his work up to that point. First, according to Symons, Donne spoke with 'unparalleled directness' and remained, in spite of the neglect of almost two centuries, 'the model in English of masculine sensual sobriety'.[22] Second, Donne's faults and virtues were products of dialectical divisions which Yeats himself had struggled to reconcile in his private life and in his art. Third, the 'powerful individuality' of Donne's personal life had been transmuted into the passionate art of 'the greatest poets'.[23] He spoke 'with an exalted simplicity which seem[ed] to make a new language for love'; and his dialectician's mind, finally, with its 'ecstatic' reasoning justified by passion, seemed 'to anticipate a metaphysical Blake'[24] – and what is more, as Yeats eventually argued on behalf of the Rhymers (see YT 38), all subsequent poets who tried to write 'personal verse'. On this final point, Symons was both memorable and emphatic:

> It may be, though I doubt it, that other poets who have written personal verse in English, have known as much of women's hearts and the senses of men, and the interchanges of passionate intercourse between man and woman; but, partly by reason of this very method of saying things, no one has ever rendered so exactly, and with such elaborate subtlety, every mood of the actual passion. . . . Donne, making a new thing certainly, if not always a thing of beauty, tells us exactly what a man really feels. . . . A woman cares most for the lover who understands her best, and is least taken in by what it is the method of her tradition to feign.[25]

Sir Herbert Grierson, who made Yeats's acquaintance in 1906, has said that 'to Yeats Donne had always been a source of interest'.[26] The dramatic lyrics of *The Wind Among the Reeds*, furthermore, represent only Yeats's first attempt to set in a poetic sequence 'the interchanges of passionate intercourse between man and woman – an attempt which became clearer with the adoption of archaic titles reminiscent of Donne's anti-Petrarchan love poetry.[27] The fantastic conceits and hyperboles of Yeats's early sequence, as revised in the *Poetical Works* of 1906, confirm his kinship to the Tudor sonneteers Sidney, Wyatt, Surrey, Spenser and Shakespeare.

However, these writers did not share with Yeats, as Donne did, a preoccupation with the arcana. Indeed, the sensational morbidity of Yeats's misshapen sonnet 'He wishes his Beloved were Dead' (*VP* 175–6) is Donnean, though it most recalls the necrophilia of Swinburne and Rossetti, whose *House of Life: A Sonnet-Sequence* (1870, 1881), with the imitative verses of Edward Dowden, almost certainly had a place in the background of Yeats's poem.[28] To the adaptive complex of Renaissance and nineteenth-century poets, one would then add both Thomas Nashe, whose lyric 'Adieu, farewell Earth's Bliss' contributed a title to one of Yeats's essays ('Dust Hath Closed Helen's Eye'), and Walter Savage Landor, whose epigrams to 'Iantha' similarly use the abducted Homeric queen to exaggerate the difference between 'the immortal beauty of the poet's eye' and 'the realities of mortality'.[29] Both writers (with the help of Marlowe, Chapman, and others) contributed to the *Maud Gonne = Helen of Troy* equation that Yeats formulated and strikingly employed in the elegiac love poems of *The Green Helmet*.[30] Even *The Autobiography of Edward, Lord Herbert of Cherbury* (London: Routledge, 1906; see *YL Notes* 878) seems most to have attracted the modern poet by its rare notice of the eternal feminine and by its wealth of information on the Herbert family and the Herbert circle. (Between 1885 and about 1913, Yeats acquired three volumes of poetry, *YL* 879–80 and *YL 1920* 284, by Edward's younger brother, George.) The coincidence of three events in 1906 – the onset of the most ambitious phase of Yeats's life-long study of Renaissance literature, his apparent shift of interest from sixteenth- to seventeenth-century English authors (see Ch. 4), and his introduction to Grierson on the occasion of delivering his lecture 'Literature and the Living Voice' (*Ex* 202–22)[31] – precipitated yet another sequence of discursive love poems on metaphysical topics.

Yeats knew himself to be at one of the 'crossways' of his career – a term of mystical significance in the diction of one of his characters, Michael Robartes (*VSR* 132), and known to Burton, as Yeats later discovered.[32] In 1906, fearing that his poetry had become unintelligible, he offered his friends an explanation (in effect, an apology) on the allure of play-writing. In doing so, he could hardly suppress the metaphor of the *quintessence*, which continued to be central to his poetic philosophy and his craft as a dramatic lyricist. Clearly, he sought a 'deliberate change in style' by inverting (with Blakean overtones) the hitherto sacrosanct Paterian precept of life-into-art:

drama . . . has been the search for more manful energy. . . . All art is in the last analysis an endeavour to condense as out of the flying vapour of the world an image of human perfection, and for its own and not the art's sake, and that is why the labour of the alchemists, who were called artists in their day, is a befitting comparison for all deliberate change of style. We live with images, that is our renunciation, for only the silent sage or saint can make himself into that perfection, turning the life inward at the tongue as though it heard the cry *Secretum meum mihi*; choosing not, as we do, to say all and know nothing, but to know all and to say nothing.

(*Poems, 1899–1905*, pp. xii–xiii; *Wade* 64)

At Grierson's invitation Yeats visited the Students' Literary Society at the University of Aberdeen, where he gave an address which repeated these sentiments. Modern poetry, he said, had become 'monotonous in its structure and effeminate in its continual insistence upon certain moments of strained lyricism' (*Ex* 220). A poet was not to trouble himself about 'the complexity that was outside his craft', but only about that 'within' it (*Ex* 208); he was cautioned about 'imitat[ing] . . . the external form' but encouraged to find 'in some equivalent form' expression for that which 'his own age . . . presse[d] into the future' (*Ex* 209). Such Platonizing was hardly new to Yeats or his poetry. For instance, in 'Adam's Curse' he had dramatized, rather ambiguously, the comparison between the poet's mean labour to fashion beautiful art and the apparent ease by which his love object (Maud Gonne) 'labour[s] to be beautiful'. Those 'beautiful old books' which the poet so much admired (partly to his detriment in the poem) were most probably British – of all great literatures the one 'completely shaped . . . in the printing-press', Yeats said (*Ex* 206). As a consequence, when medieval culture passed – that is, the 'old culture' in which a man's work 'was not at the expense of life, but the exaltation of life itself' (*Ex* 207) – the imaginative life lingered on in the oral tradition of Raftery and illiterate street singers and sailors. Significantly, Grierson's history *The First Half of the Seventeenth Century* (1906; *YL 1920* 284) linked Donne to 'the medieval or scholastic reaction'[33] – a designation which might have indicated to the Irish poet a sympathy between Donne's contradictory

Renaissance personality and Chaucer's 'many-sided nature' (*Ex* 221). Grierson's counsel, to be sure, was such a stimulus to Yeats that the poet conceded (perhaps with exaggeration) that his trip to Italy the following year with Lady Gregory and her retinue resulted from a sequence of reading the professor had recommended.[34]

One can imagine how Grierson reinforced Yeats's budding interest in Castiglione and the Platonic idealism of Duke Frederick's court.[35] However, Grierson's expertise in seventeenth-century English literature primarily furnished Yeats with a serviceable alembic in which to attempt the distillation of philosophically diverse poetic substances. Remarkably for the criticism of the period, Grierson's essay on English poetry claimed pre-eminence for Donne and Jonson in 'two discordant streams of tendency in the first half of the seventeenth century'. Donne's poetry revived 'all that was most subtle and metaphysical in the thought and fancy of the Middle Ages', while Jonson's represented 'the movement towards the rationalism and classicism of the closing century'.[36] Of the two, Jonson seemed the less pedantic, the more humanistic, restrained, and obsessed with form; but Donne – as Yeats read – 'blended in the strangest way' the so-called 'emancipated spirit of the Renaissance' and the 'scholastic pedantry and subtlety of the controversial court of James'.[37] Donne's love poetry had the 'sting of real feeling' – but, much as Symons noted, passion had 'quicken[ed] the intellect to intense and rapid trains of thought, and [had found] utterance in images, bizarre sometimes and even repellent, often of penetrating vividness and power'.[38] As Yeats reformulated his philosophy of art and life in *Discoveries* (1906–7), he naturally infused his Jonsonian model (that of the *Discoveries* or *Explorata*) with the metaphysical matter of Donne, as exemplified by the following passage from 'The Second Anniversary' (the main part of the epicedium 'Of the Progresse of the Soule'):

> She, of whose soule, if wee may say, 'twas Gold,
> Her body was th'Electrum, and did hold
> Many degrees of that; wee understood
> Her by her sight; her pure, and eloquent blood
> Spoke in her cheekes, and so distinctly wrought,
> That one might almost say, her body thought ....
> (ll. 241–6)[39]

The connection between Donne's praise of Elizabeth Drury ('her body thought') and the title of Yeats's essay 'The Thinking of the Body' (*E&I* 292–3) has not been missed by critics.[40] The famous passage was in fact quoted by Saintsbury in the only copy of Donne's poems that Yeats owned in 1906.[41] As Yeats immersed himself in Jonson, he probably read those 'profane . . . blasphemies' on 'the Idea of a Woman' (Donne's *Anniversaries*) to which Jonson objected.[42] Donne's transposition of body and intellect *was* something more than figurative ('her . . . eloquent blood/Spoke in her cheekes'), and Yeats followed suit: 'Neither painting could move us . . . if our thought did not rush to the edges of our flesh.' Although occult resonances of this idea occur elsewhere in *Discoveries*, here a poetic flight on imitation eventually summons 'those that talked or wrestled or tilted under the walls of [Castiglione's] Urbino, or sat in those great window-seats discussing all things, with love ever in their thought'. Thus, unwittingly perhaps, Grierson served as catalyst and mediator as the adaptive complex Donne–Jonson–Castiglione, later to find expression in the poems of *The Green Helmet* and *Responsibilities*, assembled itself in this essay.

By autumn 1908, it seemed possible that Yeats and Maud Gonne MacBride would be reconciled (see *VP* 257). The progress of their second courtship was recorded in Yeats's Journal, where were born the poems soon after gathered under the title 'Raymond Lully and his Wife Pernella' (an erratum slip in *Wade* 84 substituted for Lully the correct alchemist, Nicholas Flamel, possibly after the poet checked his Waite's *Lives*). The intended invocation of the duo Yeats and his beloved once aspired to emulate was a private gesture that harked back to the Irish couple's 'spiritual marriage' between 1898 and Gonne's actual marriage to the intemperate John MacBride in 1903.[43] For the public, the poet's resort to an archetype, Helen, elevated to monumental stature an ostensible examination of the quintessential feminine (the antithetic agent of the hermetic process, Donne's 'Idea of a Woman'). Privately, however, his subject was not then so abstract, thanks to the complication of Olivia Shakespear; hence his miniature sequel to the dramatic lyrics of *The Wind Among the Reeds* (as revised in 1906) succeeds mainly because of its sense of the *actual* woman (a 'Platonic' spouse) who presides over the poet's courtly jousts with himself and with the offending public. In *The Green Helmet and Other Poems* (1910), those tournaments were generally conducted according to standards derived from either Donne or Jonson, although the division of the book is imperfect. The pivotal poem 'Against Unworthy Praise', for instance, is surcharged with Jonsonian invective as well as strange scholastic imagery: the sphinx-like beloved perplexed by the riddle of her own nature. Conversely, the poem 'A Friend's Illness' (in 'Momentary Thoughts') extols the Cavalier virtue of friendship (here, the poet's regard for Lady Gregory) with a Metaphysical conceit compounded, apparently, from poems by Donne ('A Feaver') and Herbert ('Virtue'):[44]

[Yeats] Why should I be dismayed
Though flame had burned the whole
World, as it were a coal,
Now I have seen it weighed
Against a soul?

[Donne] O wrangling worlds, that search what fire
Shall burn this world, had none the wit
Unto this knowledge to aspire,
That this her feaver might be it?

[Herbert] Only a sweet and vertuous soul
Like seasoned timber never gives;
But though the whole world turn to coal
Then chiefly lives.

The following construct may help explain the lack of stylistic differentiation in such places and why Donne soon after emerges as a major deity in Yeats's pantheon of poets:

Realism ───────────────── Idealism
(Jonson)   (Donne)   (Castiglione, *The Courtier*)

One of the most obvious aspects of Yeats's 'deliberate change of style' during this period is the pervasive irony which undercuts his old idealism, the metaphysical current of his early poetry. Though Jonson was not a 'realist', he dealt with actuality; as a man of the world and a writer of personality, he epitomized for Yeats the poet of courtesy and scorn. Castiglione, on the other hand – or, rather, Hoby's *The Courtyer of Count Baldessar Castilio* (1561), which Yeats specifically commended in his unfinished second series of *Discoveries*[45] – stood for an ideal world, a world at one with itself; his Urbino was steeped in Neoplatonic tradition and seldom, if ever, condescended to parry with the slanderous mob, as Yeats did for the sake of his beloved (see *VP* 257, 259–60). Perhaps without Donne, we might still have had those oxymoronic crabbed-courteous lyrics Yeats wrote to his idea of a woman (mainly to Maud Gonne) in 1908–9. Yet Donne's work was noted for its 'sting of real feeling', its fusion of quotidian (personal) and Platonic (imaginative) realities in passionate poetry. His personal verse spanned the range suggested by the figure above; and because he was, like Yeats, a metaphysical artist or poet–alchemist, he would become, as circumstances already indicated, *central* among those English Renaissance writers whom the younger poet adapted.

Yeats's craving for physical congress with the woman he loved was at once a personal fact ('dear, cling close to me; since you were gone,/My barren thoughts have chilled me to the bone' – *VP* 257, 'Reconciliation', ll. 11–12) and a symptom, as Donne argued in 'The Extasie', of 'interanimated' souls which must 'repair' to the body if love is not to be arrested in its growth:

> So must pure lovers soules descend
> T'affections, and to faculties,
> Which sense may reach and apprehend . . . .
> (ll. 65–8)[46]

The pun on Mrs MacBride's maiden name in the lines from 'Reconciliation' quoted above may have been summoned up by the memorable close of Donne's poem:

> To'our bodies turne wee then, that so
> Weake men on love reveal'd may looke;
> . . . .
> And if some lover, such as wee,
> Have heard this dialogue of one,
> Let him still marke us, he shall see
> Small change, when we'are to bodies gone.

Yeats's punning is rarely recognized; but, when it is, the name Donne invariably surfaces.[47] In 'King and No King' (*VP* 258) – under the influence of the Beaumont and Fletcher comedy of like title, but denied a happy ending (see *NCom* 89) – the Irish poet mimicked Donne's closing invitation in 'The Extasie', although the psychology and conceit of Yeats's appeal also recall Donne's poems 'The Funerall' and 'The Relique'.[48] Words become speech ('so good a thing as that'), but 'No King's' (Yeats's) discourse with Panthea (Maud Gonne MacBride) involves no fruitful intercourse, since 'neither soul nor body has been crossed'. Under the circumstances, he questions her 'faith' that 'in the blinding light beyond the grave / We'll find so good a thing as that we have lost'.

Yeats's 'dialogue of one' in the mistitled sequence 'Raymond Lully and his Wife Pernella' is accompanied by a number of soliloquies. 'His Dream' (*VP* 253–4), which gives a name to Death, may stand without precedent. (Still, see Donne's 'The Dreame'.[49]) His three poems on Helen ('A Woman Homer Sung', 'No Second Troy', and 'Peace' – *VP* 254–9) in fact dramatize the poet's mimetic struggle to arrest life in art – just as Homer had 'shadowed in a glass / What thing her body was' (*VP* 255, ll. 10–11). In lieu of a marriage of body and soul, these poems were made to 'apprehend' (to use Donne's word) the spirit Yeats's beloved 'brought / To such a pitch in his thought' (ll. 13–14). Mrs MacBride's well-known remark that he would be just as happy without her because he made 'beautiful poetry out of . . . [his] unhappiness' and that he was 'happy in that'[50] seems apt given the admirable verses he crafted on that very thought. As ever, he was disturbed and fascinated by her nature, a blend of grace and contradiction worthy of Donne: 'such noble lines, . . . Such a delicate high head, / All that sternness amid charm, / All that sweetness amid strength' (*VP* 259, ll. 6–9). Her high-strung beauty, 'Being . . . solitary and most stern', Yeats noted in his first Journal entry (dated 'December 1908'), could hardly be blamed for his misery: it was 'not natural in an age like this' –

> Why[,] what could she have done[,] being what she is?
> Was there another Troy for her to burn?
> (*Mem* 137; cf. *VP* 257, ll. 10–12)

In the next month, the magician Yeats/Flamel ('Demon Est Deus Inversus', or 'D.E.D.I.', as he signed himself in the Order of the Golden Dawn) took charge of his Pernella's astute observation and began fulfilling its prophecy:

Today the thought came to me that PIAL ['Per Ignem Ad Lucem', Maud Gonne's motto] never really understands my plans, or nature, or ideas. Then came the thought, what matter? How much of the best I have done and still do is but the attempt to explain myself to her? If she understood, I should lack reason for writing, and one never can have too many reasons for doing what is so laborious. (*Mem* 141–2)

This thought, as it happens, became the prose 'Subject' of a poem entitled 'The Consolation' (later, 'Words' in *VP* 255–6), worked out two entries later in Yeats's Journal and dated 'January 22 [1909]' (*Mem* 143). In the poem, as in its prose draft and in the penultimate line of 'No Second Troy' (quoted above), Yeats toyed with a device which bears the very stamp of Donne's influence: the play on the Elizabethan poet's name. Yeats knew of Donne's 'unblushing' affection for this particular gambit, for it was pointed out in Saintsbury's essay.[51] Moreover, Yeats would have noticed it himself in such passages as the following:

> I wonder by my troth, what thou, and I
> Did, till we lov'd?
> ('The good-morrow', ll. 1–2)

> I have done one braver thing
> Then all the *Worthies* did,
> And yet a braver thence doth spring,
> Which is, to keepe that hid.

. . .

> If, as I have, you also doe
> Vertue'attir'd in woman see,
> And dare love that, and say so too,
> And forget the Hee and Shee;

. . .

> Then you have done a braver thing
> Then all the *Worthies* did; . . . .
> ('The undertaking', ll. 1–4, 17–20, 25–6)

> Thou sunne art halfe as happy'as wee,
> In that the world's contracted thus;
> Thine age askes ease, and since thy duties bee
> To warme the world, that's done in warming us.
> ('The Sunne Rising', ll. 25–8)[52]

One doubts that Yeats wished specifically to pun on 'Donne'. More likely, he was attracted to the phonological effects of such wordplay and to its vernacular sexual connotation. The sentence 'My darling cannot understand / What I have done, or what would do' is a plaint, not a confession. Yet as the poet struggled with the poem's only other noteworthy device, a real Platonic-seeming mystery, the double meaning of the infinitive 'to do' becomes clearer. In draft, the trouble began at the midway point, just as Yeats seized upon the conceit of the sieve (a leaky *vas* or Platonic *frustra*, perhaps, but also an instrument of refinement in a physical process of creation):[53] his poetic translation of the idea that his failure with Maud Gonne motivated his 'doing what is so laborious'. In his labour to manufacture poetry from this idea, he made three radically different conclusions to the poem (the first two of which were discarded):[54]

[1] But/And had she done so He can say
   Who shook me from his sieve
   If I'd have thrown poor words away
   And been content to live.

[2] But/And/How/That had she done so He/who can say
   Who/But he that shook me from his sieve
   Whether/If I'd have thrown poor words away
   And been content to live.

[3] That had she done so – who can say
   What would have shaken from the sieve –
   I might then/have thrown poor words away
   And been content to live.

Quite likely, Yeats had been reading Waite's life of Flamel when he first conceived the thought he eventually fleshed with the third version above.[55] The first two were off the mark, but they do address Gonne's understanding of his 'nature', as he called it in prose draft. Yeats himself is shaken from the sieve of the Heavenly Chef – rather than the images, ideas, or words which obey the call of the mage in the third version. The collaboration of Flamel and his wife in the production of the *prima materia*, and most especially Pernella's understanding of the process, is very relevant to the poem, although the manufacture of the elixir in furnaces differs decidedly from the function of Yeats's vessel. In short, the latter resembles the Metaphysical conceits which Saintsbury and Symons had complained about in Donne's verse. The mastery of words which Yeats then contemplated ('for the word's sake, or for a woman's praise') put him on a par with the quintessential poet he envisioned on a windy road near Urbino (*E&I* 291). Yet that idealism combined with a kind of intellectual realism that Yeats found perplexing until Grierson once again stepped forward to mediate the poet's education with a gift copy of his edition of *The Poems of John Donne* (2 vols, Oxford: Clarendon Press, 1912; *YL* 531).

III

Surely no scholarly work drew higher praise from a poet than did Grierson's edition when Yeats posted from Coole his somewhat belated letter of appreciation on 14 November 1912: 'I do not like . . . to delay longer about thanking you for work that has given me and shall give me I think more pleasure than any other book I can imagine. . . . I shall fish for pike and plan out poems' (*L* 570). Unusual for the rich detail it offers on Yeats's response to a gift of this kind (there were many in his lifetime), the letter shows how Grierson's scholarship suddenly laid open an aspect of Donne's work previously closed to the Irish poet. The edition elicited his immediate and continuing excitement:

> I have been using it constantly and find that at last I can understand Donne. Your notes tell me exactly what I want to know. Poems that I could not understand or could but understand are now clear and I notice that the more precise and learned the thought the greater the beauty, the passion; the intricacy and subtleties of his imagination are the length and depths of the furrow made by his passion. His obscenity – the rock and loam of his Eden – but make me the more certain that one who is but a man like us all has seen God.

Just what poems Yeats had been rereading and to which of these his thoughts apply may be inferred from the volumes themselves. Entirely or substantially cut, according to YL, are the sections 'Songs and Sonets', 'Elegies', 'Satyres', and 'Of the Progresses of the Soule', complemented in the second volume by corresponding cut sections in the commentaries (referred to in Yeats's letter). Although Donne's verse epistles, or 'Letters to Severall Personages', was evidently left uncut (and thus unread), Yeats did examine the notes on them (in vol. II) in keeping with his biographical interest in the Donne–Herbert–Walton–Wotton circle. Since he already knew Donne's work from the Chambers edition of 1896, it is not surprising he should have abridged his study in this way. The fact that he discarded (or sold off) his copy of the 1896 edition and retained the one that Grierson presented to the post-Victorian world supports Yeats's implicit claim that Grierson's was, to him, the nonpareil version. Yeats's apparent neglect of Donne's obsequies, 'Holy Sonnets', hymns, odes, and litanies is also consistent with his lack of interest in the devotional poetry of Herrick. Beyond the passionate secular poetry of Donne and the commentaries which revealed how his 'beauty' and 'passion' depended on the 'learned' 'subtleties of his imagination', Yeats also cut and read the Introduction to volume II, Grierson's lengthy reassessment of Donne's poetry.

In fact, Grierson would have recognized that Yeats had shared with him observations which concurred, generally, with the views published in the Introduction. They were gratulatory. In the professor's view, Donne's worst traits seemed to roost in his religious writings, while the love songs and elegies (with the 'Holy Sonnets') teemed with subtleties enough to plague the critics of two centuries. 'Donne's peculiarity', as De Quincey had pointed out, was due to 'the combination of dialectical subtlety with the weight and force of passion'; his Metaphysical wit raised objections 'from those who [were] indisposed to admit that passion, and especially the passion of love, can ever speak so ingeniously' (eighteenth-century critics), and from 'more modern' (or nineteenth-century) critics who denied Donne's greatness because, as they thought, 'his songs and elegies lack beauty'.[56] However, just as Yeats said and Grierson himself went on to argue, the beauty of Donne's poetry was proportional to the degree of interchange between subtle thinking and intense feeling. Largely, Grierson's essay and Yeats's letter agree in the affirmative response both made to the question posed to Donne's modern readers: 'Can poetry be at once passionate and ingenious, sincere in feeling and witty, – packed with thought, and that subtle and abstract, Scholastic dialectic?' Grierson answered this query by extending the framework not long before laid down in his history *The First Half of the Seventeenth Century*. Yeats, on the other hand, vouched for his correspondent's reading of Donne as only a poet could, having tested it on the drafting-table.

With publication of *The Green Helmet and Other Poems* (London: Macmillan, 1912; *Wade* 101), three lyrics (among six) were added which suggest Donne's influence. These lyrics ('Friends', 'The Cold Heaven', and 'That the Night Come' – each wholly or partly about Maud Gonne) were later shifted as a group to *Responsibilities* (Dublin: Cuala Press, 1914; *Wade* 113), where they found their station in the canon (*VP* 315–17). In proximity to such kindred poems as 'When Helen Lived,' 'The Mountain Tomb', 'To a Child Dancing in the Wind', 'Two Years Later', 'A Memory of Youth' and 'Fallen Majesty' – poems also written about Maud Gonne, about her daughter Iseult, or composed in their house in Colville, France, in the autumn of 1912 – the shifted lyrics partly obviated the need for the section titles used in *The Green Helmet* and helped constitute a movement, if not an actual sequence, in the last quarter of *Responsibilities*. Yeats's renewed excitement over Donne's love songs and elegies thus advanced a mode of poetry that he had already been developing with Donne as one of its models. Grierson's case that 'A nocturnall upon S. Lucies day'[57] should be read as beautiful love poetry 'not less passionate because that passion finds expression in abstract and subtle thought'[58] won Yeats over to the poem, as his letters indicate ever after (see *L* 571, 710, and 902); but it also sent the Irish poet to the commentaries on the verse epistles so that he might learn more about Donne's alleged affair with the Countess of Bedford. 'No courtly compliment could go so far, no courtly beauty accept such compliments', Yeats felt certain, unless they were lovers (*L* 571). His poetic mixing of the spiritual and the sensual (or outwardly sexual) in 1912 became, for the first time, recognizably Metaphysical and unmistakably Donnean in manner. In view of his characteristic affinity for imagery forged from contrarieties, such imagery became more fully developed, concentrated, and conspicuous under Donne's influence.

In *Responsibilities*, the poems 'Fallen Majesty' and 'The Cold

Heaven' yoked together opposites (fire and water, heat and cold) and created sensational images: respectively, 'burning cloud' and 'ice burned'.[59] 'The Cold Heaven' is the one lyric, moreover, that Henn (*LT* 92) associated with Donne by way of Yeats's reading of the Grierson edition. The poem is the virtual re-enactment of a spiritual exercise (or 'meditation', as Martz has made us understand) on the subject of the 'cold and rook-delighting' sky in winter and features the same galvanic paroxysm as appears in its companion poem, 'Friends', when the poet's thought turns to Maud Gonne's cold and pitiless demeanour: a sexual – neurological reflex which wells up from the poet's 'heart's root' at the poem's climax. In 'The Cold Heaven', the fully integrated faculties of the poet reach such a peak of intensity 'every casual thought' dissolves, leaving only memories of 'love crossed long ago' and a metaphysical conundrum:

> I took all the blame out of all sense and reason,
> Until I cried and trembled and rocked to and fro,
> Riddled with light. Ah! when the ghost begins to quicken,
> Confusion of the death-bed over, is it sent
> Out naked on the roads, as the books say, and stricken
> By the injustice of the skies for punishment?
>
> (ll. 7–12)

The ambiguity of the phrase 'out of all sense' – meaning both 'to an extent far beyond what common-sense could justify' and 'beyond the reach of sensation' (*LT* 93) – is sustained by the ambiguous 'it' of l. 10 (accepting as antecedents the 'blame' of l. 7 and the 'ghost' of l. 9, the latter of which 'quickens' within the dying body just as life stirs within a spore). The ghost in Yeats's poem might have been suggested by Donne's 'The Apparition'. Certainly, memories of 'love crossed', according to Yeats's speaker, 'should be' (and probably would have been) 'out of season / With the hot blood of youth' save for Donne's thought that 'our blood labours to beget / Spirits, as like soules as it can' ('The Extasie', ll. 61–2), an idea compressed in the later Yeatsian phase 'blood-begotten spirits' (*VP* 498, l. 28; see *LT* 221). Improbably, to be sure, 'The Cold Heaven' translates Grierson's observation that in Donne's poetry, 'one feels the quickening of the brain, the vision extending its range'.[60] Yet, in a moment of vision, Yeats's equivocal escape from blame resembles Donne's characteristic 'escape from courtly or ascetic idealism', those fatal antinomies of the Renaissance doctrine of love, by making poems which did 'justice to love as a passion in which body and soul alike have their part, and of which there is no reason to repent'.[61]

The significance of this poem to the development of Yeats's later metaphysical lyrics should be stressed, but not exaggerated. Yeats was himself a dialectical poet, and his tribulations as a lover were genuine. He observed many masters and discovered, only relatively late, that he might take instruction from Donne and the Metaphysical poets. Yet, like Donne especially, Yeats cultivated in his love poetry 'a very complex phenomenon' (to quote Grierson again), the by-product of two opposing strains: 'The strain of dialectic, subtle play of argument and wit, erudite and fantastic; and the strain of vivid realism, the record of a passion which is not ideal nor conventional, . . . but love as an actual, immediate experience in all its moods . . . .'[62] Grierson's assertion that Donne had fashioned in his verse 'a new philosophy of love' – one 'less transcendental' but 'juster' than Dante's 'because less dualistic and ascetic' – would have appealed to Yeats, whose lyric dialogues soon after proclaimed a similar philosophy by drawing on models of the conventional, idealized passion of books and on the lessons of actuality. One of Yeats's most famous dialogues on metaphysical themes, 'Ego Dominus Tuus' (VP 367–71), even makes a point of opposing the ascetic Dante and the more sensuous Keats, literary precursors of the divided casts of Yeats's mind before 1917, the year of his marriage to fellow mystic Georgie Hyde-Lees.[63]

The Wild Swans at Coole (London: Macmillan, 1919; Wade 124), the first significant collection of Yeats's poetry to appear after his marriage, merged two strikingly different bodies of verse: one morose and terse, the other ebullient and voluble; one the lyric poetry of a dejectedly aging man (wholly drawn from the Cuala Press *Wild Swans* of 1917; Wade 118), the other the love poetry of a well-pleased groom (in part drawn from the unauthorized *Nine Poems* of 1918; Wade 122). The latest poems, in fact, belonged to neither group but derived from a common philosophical background that Yeats mined most notably in the treatise *Per Amica Silentia Lunae* (1918; Wade 120) and from a related, but somewhat more disparate, poetic tradition. The connection between these two fields of discourse, the philosophic and the poetic, set him earnestly in pursuit of his seventeenth-century English masters, as the Irish poet Austin Clarke casually noted in an obituary years later.[64]

Yeats's interest in spiritualism and the supernatural seems to have been on the upswing in 1912, and it soon led to the notes and essays he contributed to Augusta Gregory's *Visions and Beliefs in the West of Ireland* (1920).[65] His essays 'Witches and Wizards and Irish Lore' and 'Swedenborg, Mediums, and the Desolate Places' are dated, respectively, '1914' and '14th October, 1914', and, like the 'Notes', provided an impressive, completely respectable background for the vernacular materials compiled by Lady Gregory. A collaborative effort, the book was to verify the connection between the spiritual realm and the physical world: to find 'a clue, a thread, leading through the maze to that mountain top where things visible and invisible meet' (*Visions* 15). Yeats's scholarly performance, as he acknowledged in the book, was particularly indebted so such English seventeenth-century authorities as Henry More, Joseph Glanvil, Ralph Cudworth, John Beaumont, Robert Kirk, and Sir Thomas Browne – 'all magical or Platonic writers of the time' (*Visions* 303; see *YL*). The second-hand nature of Yeats's knowledge of Platonic philosophy at that time[66] is evident in his rough draft (NLI 13,575) for part XI of 'Swedenborg, Mediums, and the Desolate Places', with its references to ancient works that he scarcely knew except by the intervening agency of interpreters: 'the seventeenth-century Platonists who are the handier for my purpose' (*Visions* 330–1).

By May 1917, 'More and the Platonists' – with Agrippa, Boehme, Swedenborg, Madame Blavatsky and others – had given Yeats sufficient smatterings of philosophy to allow him to undertake the important synthesis of *Per Amica Silentia Lunae* (see *Myth* 348), the most thorough declaration of his mystic beliefs before his marriage and the collaborative invention of *A Vision* (1925, 1937). In particular, More confirmed Yeats's belief that beauty was none other than 'bodily life in some ideal condition' (*Myth* 349); that existence was of two worlds, 'the terrestrial and the condition of fire' (*Myth* 356); and that the conjunction of the two might be achieved in poetry, a 'rhythmic body' by which one could 'pass into the Condition of Fire', a moment of music and rest. Like Donne's, Yeats's interest in systems of correspondence between the physical and the spiritual worlds had motivated a wide reading in 'philosophical and pseudo-philosophical writings';[67] and, as a poet, he had begun translating that reading into verse. His thoughts on Dante, Keats, and Landor (*Myth* 328–31) looked back to the introspective 'Ego Dominus Tuus' and ahead to the banquet 'at journey's end / With Landor and with Donne' ('To a Young Beauty', *VP* 336) and to the poetic alloy soon after forged from diversely related literary materials.

Setting Donne aside for a moment – although not without suggesting that his histrionic 'dialogues of one' possibly combined in Yeats's imagination with the exchanges featured in Landor's *Imaginary Conversations* and several poems[68] – the sudden emergence of the lyric dialogue in *The Wild Swans at Coole* (1919) might be associated with various seventeenth-century models that Yeats encountered in his reading at that time. His interest in the Spenserians seems not very great, despite his affection for pastoral forms and his appropriation of the Spenserian eclogue and 'Astrophel' in 1918 (see Ch. 4). His copy of the pastoral poems of Nicholas Breton, George Wither, and William Browne of Tavistock (*YL* 272) is minuscule; and his Phineas Fletcher (*YL* 684), acquired after 1926, is virtually uncut. Still, he had Henry More 'in his verse and in his prose' (*Visions* 331, a reference to *YL* 2226, Richard Ward's life of More, containing 'divers philosophical poems and hymns') and thought well enough of the 'Psychozoia' and the minor lyrics to acquire Geoffrey Bullough's edition of the *Philosophical Poems* (1931; *YL* 1379). Beyond More, Yeats's chief influences among the 'verse talkers' of the English Renaissance, as Grierson called them,[69] were the Metaphysical poets.

Of these, Crashaw was perhaps least admired because the most precious; yet even the 'most impersonal of ecstasies' in 'A Hymn to . . . Saint Teresa' (pp. 130–6 in *The Poems of Richard Crashaw*, ed. J. R. Tutin, 1905; *YL 1920* 282) seemed to Yeats the work of 'no sedentary man out of reach of common sympathy, no disembodied mind', although 'in his day the life that appeared most rich and stirring was already half forgotten with Villon and Dante' (*E&I* 348). The Irish renaissance that Yeats attempted to nurture with frequent journalistic works in *United Ireland* and other dailies in the 1890s would irradiate the streets with the same 'mild light of imagination' as shined when a Herbert, Crashaw, or Herrick (the Rhymers' Club idol) 'lived and laboured' (*UP1* 211). Yeats's knowledge of Henry Vaughan, 'Silurist', in 1894 (see *UP1* 341) reflected Lionel Johnson's influence, on the one hand, but on the other, Yeats's own basic commitment to spiritual alchemy and (with Vaughan's brother Thomas) to hermetic philosophy of all kinds.[70] Although indicative of an apparent lapse of interest over time,[71] Yeats's personal set of Vaughan's works (*YL* 2192) is thus misleadingly uncut (Yeats's meddling with Vaughan's 'The Retreate' has already been noted,[72] and a sampling of the Welsh poet's wares was available in facsimile in YL 816). Vaughan, Herbert, and Donne have each been associated with the imagery of the Byzantium poems,[73] and the title of Yeats's book *The Winding Stair* has recalled Herbert's line 'Is all true doctrine in a winding stair' (*LT* 12). Indeed, Yeats seems to have attached to Herbert the rather dubious distinction of being the most characteristic Metaphysical poet – an inhabitant of the twenty-fifth crescent beside the mystic George Russell (with whom Yeats quarrelled) and those poets who must 'always [be] stirred to an imaginative intensity by some form of propaganda', their work neither 'consciously aesthetic nor consciously speculative but imitative of a central Being' (*AV B* 175–6). In occult experiments conducted (*à la* Flamel and Pernella) by Yeats and his wife between December 1917 and October 1918, the poet repeatedly pressed the 'Communicators' in automatic script about Herbert's standing on the Great Wheel of Incarnations.[74] Conversely, Yeats may have felt that Donne belonged in company with Dante, Landor, Shelley, and himself, among the 'lyrical poets . . . [of] the fantastic Phase 17' (*AV B* 108).[75]

Contrary to Samuel Johnson's indictment of the so-called unmusical school of the Metaphysical poets, England's 'verse talkers' since the seventeenth century have not all 'stood the trial of the [metrical] finger better than the ear'.[76] Conveniently, Professor Grierson listed such poets in pairs – 'Butler and Dryden, Pope and Swift, Cowper and Burns, Byron and Shelley, Browning and Landor' – and argued their descent from Ben Jonson and Donne.[77] The imaginative convergence of the two Renaissance poets is, moreover, implicit in Yeats's elegy 'In Memory of Major Robert Gregory', a master-piece which drew formally, if in part, on Jonson's example (see Ch. 4) but also bestowed upon Coole Park's daring heir Donne's thinking of the body and the lovers' self-consuming intensity of Donne's 'The Feaver', 'The Sunne Rising', and 'The Canonization'.[78] Possibly, too, 'Upon a Dying Lady' (*VP* 362–7), which Yeats wrote for Mabel Beardsley between January 1912 and July 1914, drew upon the example of Jonson's memorial to Venetia Digby (*The Under-wood*, LXXXIV) and Donne's better elegies to Ann More, Elizabeth Drury, and the Countess of Bedford.[79]

In a few years, Grierson would provide two new stimuli which, more of less, jointly affected Yeats's poetic development because of their bearing on his artistic quest to unify the exoteric and esoteric elements of his poetry. Probably the first of these, his adaptation of the *ottava rima* stanza in part I of 'Nineteen Hundred and Nineteen' (1921; *VP* 428–33), was suggested by an Academy paper Yeats may have heard, or at least learned about, while he resided in Oxford.[80] The second stimulus can be documented because he dropped a line to Grierson about it on his way to lecture at Sheffield on 20 November 1922: 'I have your Metaphysical Poets with me for my train book.'[81]

The book in question was Grierson's influential anthology *Metaphysical Lyrics and Poems of the Seventeenth Century, Donne to Butler* (Oxford: Clarendon Press, 1921; *YL* 816), which, for all the trials and distractions of the poet's travel and business, introduced him to a range and variety of good verse by poets not all of whom, apparently, were well known to him at the time.[82] It presented him with several verse dialogues, the most important of which were Marvell's 'A Dialogue between the Resolved Soul and Created Pleasure' and 'A Dialogue between the Soul and Body' (poems which bear directly on the next chapter's discussion of the Marvellian and the Miltonic inspiration behind Yeats's 'A Dialogue of Self and Soul');[83] it provided a large enough sampling to suggest a literary movement but then declined to quite define one as such;[84] it created, rather, a showcase for Donne's 'complex harmonies', his 'acute and subtle intellect', the 'unruly servant' of 'a strangely blended temperament, an intense emotion, a vivid imagination'.[85] When the Introduction was reprinted in *The Background of English Literature* (1925), sandwiched between two essays on Byron ('Lord Byron: Arnold and Swinburne' and 'Byron and the English Society'), the new context for Donne was intended to spur his devotees to the reassessment of another neglected, an allegedly 'fleshly', poet:

Byron was a lover, masculine and passionate, as Donne and Burns had been. . . .

[Southey's 'Satanic' poet], like Donne or Marlowe, Byron or the Swinburne of the first *Poems and Ballads*, shocks and startles and also enchants his age by the challenge which his poetry offers to the accepted moral conventions. . . .

The accents of poetry which appeals to audiences . . . are those of the orator and those of the talker. Byron began in the one; he ended in the other. His greatest success was achieved when he found a measure . . . the *ottava rima*, in which he could write poetry as he talked or as he wrote racy letters to his friends.[86]

The argument was not lost on Yeats, who had recently adapted for one of his works Donne's stanza in 'A Nocturnall' (see below, section IV) and who went on to become a master of the *ottava rima* stanza, as many of his subsequent poems bear witness.[87] Indeed, Yeats accepted Grierson's case for Byron, though with reservations that reflected the Romantic poet's Metaphysical company in Grierson's book:

I have had your book at my bed side for weeks and have read it very constantly. I am particularly indebted to you for your essay on Byron. . . . The over childish or over pretty or feminine element in . . . much poetry up to our date comes from the lack of natural momentum in the syntax. This momentum underlies almost every Elizabethan and Jacobean lyric and is far more important than simplicity of vocabulary. . . . Byron, unlike the Elizabethans though he always tries for it, constantly allows it to die out in some mind-created construction, but is I think the one great English poet – though one can hardly call him great except in purpose and manhood – who sought it constantly. (L 709–10)

In actuality, the student of Jonson and Donne had discovered a stanzaic vessel within which the classicist's regard for form might be reconciled with the impulsive locutions of the scholastic dialectician. He went on to join the two in such decorous, meditative verses as 'Ancestral Houses' (part I of 'Meditations in Time of Civil War'), 'Among School Children', 'Coole Park, 1929', 'Coole Park and Ballylee, 1931', and 'The Municipal Gallery Re-visited', and in such visionary poems as 'Sailing to Byzantium', 'Her Vision in the Wood', 'The Gyres', and 'The Circus Animals' Desertion'. In another direction, he developed a more consciously Metaphysical line of poetry – a joyful one originating in the lyrics about Solomon and Sheba (or Mr and Mrs Yeats in late 1917) and extending through his later sequences.

IV

In the context of both stair and tower, auspiciously, the first poetic celebration of Yeats's marriage came with 'Under the Round Tower', a poem probably written in March 1918 and featuring the hermetic union of 'golden king and silver lady' – apparitions arising from 'the image of shuttle spiral & funnell [sic]' which emerged from the newlyweds' nocturnal experiments at the Royal Hotel at Glendalough (see *Making AV* I, 240-3). In proximity to this poem in *VP* are several lyrics by which Donne's role in the adaptive complex can be detected. His invocation in the exultant 'To a Young Beauty', a poem about Iseult Gonne which uses Donne's name to 'praise the winters gone' and to renounce the folly of labouring for the 'wages beauty gives', acknowledges the debt Yeats owed in its sister poems 'The Living Beauty', 'A Song', and 'To a Young Girl' – all written for Maud Gonne as much as for her daughter. Like the 'body thought' of Donne's Lady Drury, it is the mother's 'wild thought' – 'Set[ting] all her blood astir/And glitter[ing] in her eyes' – that broke the poet's heart (*VP* 336, ll. 7, 10–11). Now a wiser if older man, he returns to the riddle of 'The Cold Heaven':

> I have not lost desire
> But the heart that I had;
> I thought 'twould burn my body
> Laid on the death-bed . . . .
> (*VP* 335, 13–16)

The poet's recognition 'That the heart grows old' recurs in the elegy to his 'discontented heart', 'The Living Beauty' ('O heart, we are old;/The living beauty is for younger men:/We cannot pay its tribute of wild tears – *VP* 334, ll. 8–10). But in manuscript this poem proves literally to be a turning-point in the Yeats canon.

In this lyric, the self-consuming lovers of Donne's 'The Canonization' ('We'are Tapers too, and at our owne cost die' – l. 21[88]) seem the basis of Yeats's conceit of wick and oil, a metaphor which took shape immediately on L13v of NLI 13,587(21):

> Let me imagin[e] that I drew [content]
> And that the oil & wick is
> youth spent

> The wick & oil of yout[h] bur[ne]d out & spe[n]t
> appears, makes eyes drop[,] is gone ag[a]in
>   O heart we ar[e] old

Such a device seems nowhere anticipated except in Donne and, interestingly enough, in Browning, whose 'Cleon' ('Increase our power, supply fresh oil to life' – l. 247) Yeats parodied when writing his nuptial song 'The Gift of Harun Al-Rashid' (*VP* 460–70).[89] The remainder of the original draft of 'The Living Beauty', found in NLI 13,587(4), bears on the verso fragment written in the middle distance between the sadly renunciatory poems of 1915–17 and the rejuvenating personal mythology born into verse in 'Solomon to Sheba'. The fragment, unpublished until recently,[90] dramatizes the moment of decision excised from the buoyantly sexual latter poem (if indeed the fragment were ever part of it). The speaker, worrying and cautious, has yet to reach Solomon's Donnean conclusion ('There's not a thing but love can make/The world a narrow pound' – *VP* 333, ll. 23–4). Rather, beginning and ending with queries for an unnamed auditor (presumably a counterpart of Sheba), he seems arrested in this moment, locked out of her supposed labyrinthine mind:

> Am I a fool or a wise man?
> And if a fool what other can
> Keep clear of folly ~~when~~ if he look
> Upon your devils pec[u]liar book
> Made up of ivory flat or slope?
> King Solomon could he but hope
> By wagering her wizard crown
> To run his finger up and down
> . . .
> Would murmer 'now my proverbs stop
> Between the [w]rist & finger top';
> . . .
> O never did King Solomon find
> A secret b[u]t in Sheba's mind.
> Shall I be the better
> ~~And what any can I be~~ proved
> O beauty in your labyrinth closed
> A perfect scholour in the school
> If I turn wise or but a fool

We might remind ourselves that wages and wagers are part of the 'unpoetic' jargon that Donne was faulted for dragging into poetry. Moreover, the notion of a 'school' of beauty, with Platonic doctrine drawn from 'old books' (here 'your deveils pec[u]liar book'), goes back to 'Adam's Curse' but advances, dialectically, toward the dialogues 'Michael Robartes and the Dancer' and 'Solomon and the Witch' (*VP* 385–9). In the collaborative search for wisdom and 'unity of being', the invention or discovery of 'metaphors for poety' (*AV B* 8) depended, as did such poetry, upon a more dramatic and radical play of argument than Donne allowed in his secular verse.

Yeats's monologue 'On Woman' (*VP* 345–6), possibly related to the fragment quoted above and bearing general kinship to 'The Expostulation' of Donne (or Jonson), makes wit and draws a lesson from the so-called war of the sexes. Yet the polemical pitch of the confrontation between male and female dramatically sharpened when Yeats shifted from single-sided, male-dominated exposition to the seeming give-and-take of two-sided engagement. Granted, the Dancer (in 'Michael Robartes and the Dancer') is a woman given few words and equally guarded about 'great danger in the body', but her sceptical response to Robartes' argument, a rhetorical calling to love for the body's sake, questions the apparent sexism of her suitor's 'principles' and the authority of his 'Latin text'. The *wit* arising from this confrontation is double-edged, for Robartes may be right (in Yeats's view)

> That blest souls are not composite,
> And that all beautiful women may
> Live in uncomposite blessedness,
> And lead us to the like – if they
> Will banish every thought . . . .
> (*VP* 387, ll. 44–8)

This is orthodox Donne if unconventional wooing – or, again, 'interanimated' souls repairing to the body. Still, unlike Donne, Yeats gives womankind a voice and, what is more, the last word: 'They say such different things at school.'

In 'Solomon and the Witch', the school has moved to the 'forbidden sacred grove' where Solomon and Sheba attempt to restore the world to paradise with their love-making. With paradox and humour – as Frye observes, citing Donne's 'The Extasie' and Shakespeare's 'The Phoenix and the Turtle' as analogous examples[91] – the poem argues that in perfect sexual congress 'the world ends' in 'a single light, / When oil and wick are burned in one' (ll. 29–30).[92] (See Donne's 'The Canonization', third stanza.) This hermetic union of the sexes in a mutually consuming act of bodily passion, so figured, represents an affirmative reversal of the poet's conceit of youth's burnt-out taper in 'The Living Beauty'. Vaughan's cock herald[93] and Donne's 'spider love' ('Twicknam Garden', l. 6[94]) converge, moreover, in Solomon's wry, learned assessment of the preceding night's ecstasy:

>   A cockerel
>   Crew from a blossoming apple bough
>   . . . .
>   He that crowed out eternity
>   Thought to have crowed it in again.
>   For love has a spider's eye
>   To find out some appropriate pain
>   . . .
>   For every nerve, and tests a lover
>   With cruelties of Choice and Chance . . . .
>   (*VP* 387–8, ll. 9–10, 18–20, 22–3)

In counterpoint to the fundamental disagreement dramatized in 'Michael Robartes and the Dancer', the liaison between Solomon and 'that Arab lady' is positive even though they commit themselves to an impossible task. Like the Dancer, Sheba delivers the closing line (but in a very different vein): 'O! Solomon! let us try again.'

As Clark shows, Yeats's view that 'the world ends' when Choice and Chance become 'a single light' – the main point of 'Solomon and the Witch' – has a direct bearing on the later sequence 'Words for Music Perhaps' and particularly on the dialogue 'Crazy Jane on the Day of Judgement'.[95] One must accept human failure in the perfection of life, since only in failure, brought about by the mundane 'cruelties of Choice and Chance', may Solomon and Sheba 'try again' and may the poet profit from Donne's mixed success at forging poetry from the audacious union of pedantry and obscenity, 'the rock and loam of his Eden'. The acceptance of failure comes at frightful cost, however, as the poet complained in 'The Choice', a poem once conceived as the penultimate, *ottava rima* stanza of 'Coole Park and Ballylee, 1931':

> The intellect of man is forced to choose
> Perfection of the life, or of the work,
> And if it take the second must refuse
> A heavenly mansion, raging in the dark.
> (*VP* 495, ll. 1–4)

The connection between the poems just discussed – or the line of descent perpetuated by each one of them with respect to Donne and the Metaphysical influence – may be extended to the latest phase of Yeats's career as a poet. Nevertheless, that line of development is nowhere better illustrated than in his sequences on 'the tragic cycle of human love in the mortal world',[96] the eleven-part lyric histories 'A Man Young and Old' and 'A Woman Young and Old', which appeared in *The Tower* (1928; Wade 158) and *The Winding Stair* (1929; Wade 164) respectively. Since the poet reported to Grierson, in 1926, that 'for two years now I have written meditative poems, which are arranged in serieses [*sic*], and nothing I had at that time could have been taken from its context',[97] it should come as no surprise that the roots of many of these lyrics are tangled in the same manuscripts. This condition poses real difficulty for anyone attempting to trace the genesis of individual poems, but it also makes possible the representation of both series by selection.[98] The contiguity of these poems, moreover, proves essential in demonstrating how Yeats brought the adaptation of Donne and the Metaphysical poets to its climax in these series.

The first of three exhibits selected for examination relates to 'The Empty Cup', the epitome of the sequence 'A Man Young and Old', according to Somer, because it stands at the point of 'transition from a young man's problems to those of an old man'.[99] Entitled 'Youth over' in early draft, the furtive beginnings of the poem may be found, *inter alia*, among twenty-seven leaves containing remnants of contemporary lyrics in similar states. Not surprisingly, the tentative jottings under 'Youth over' (in NLI 13,589[25]) show that the eventual poem is the development of an icon. The poet's false starts in draft (simplified below) testify that the figure of the empty chalice ('healing wine . . . wet it once'), a veritable Metaphysical conceit, presages the poem:

> [a] I saw a standing empty cup
> [b] That sun & air had dried
> >

> [c] Thinking of my empty cup
> [d] ~~Has made me hollow~~ eyed
> [b]
>   >
> [e] I call t[o] mind an empty ~~glas[s]~~ cup
> [b]

The image precedes the poem, which, as we witness, begins in mimicry of 'All Souls' Night' ('I call to mind . . .') and develops (in NLI 13,589[24]) into the variant transmitted first to Olivia Shakespear on 6 December 1926:

> One looks back to one's youth as to [a] cup that a mad man dying of thirst left half tasted. I wonder if you feel like that. . . .
>
> > A mad man found a cup of wine
> > And half dead of thirst
> > Hardly dared to wet his mouth,
> > Imagining, moon accurst,
> > That another mouthful
> > And his beating heart would burst.
> >
> > But my discovery of the change
> > For it cannot be denied
> > That all is ancient metal now
> > The four winds have dried –
> > Has kept me waking half the night
> > And made me hollow-eyed.
> >
> > (L 721–2)

Recalling the ceremonial image of 'All Souls' Night' ('two long glasses brimmed with muscatel / Bubble upon the table'), the empty chalice, here, functions rather like the Donnean conceit of the taper employed in 'The Living Beauty' (in manuscript, 'the oil & wick is youth spent / The wick & oil of yout[h] bur[ne]d out & spe[n]t'). The cup's iconographic significance, however, stems from the Tarot and the Romaunt emblems of the Grail (illustrated in Harold Bayley's study of arcana, *A New Light on the Renaissance*, YL 132) and from the poem's main source, the 'Tale of the Steward' from the *Arabian Nights*.[100] Thoughts set before the poem in Yeats's letter of 6 December allude to a quatrain addressed to the tale's youthful protagonist: 'A year or two I waited / And then I drank it up, /

Love which is love, a cup/You never tasked.' In revision, Yeats compressed his dozen lines into one ten-line stanza, enhanced his conceit's affiliation with the water symbol of the Tarot by excising the eucharistic/festal reference to wine, and increased the personal connotations of the poem while posing as the 'Man Young and Old' featured in the verse sequence overall (see *L* 725). In a new ending (devised, probably, after a copy of the first version had been sent to Mrs Shakespear),[101] he planted allusions which could refer to most of the important loves of his life to that point:

> October last I found it too
> But found it dry as bone,
> And for that reason am I crazed
> And my sleep is gone.
> (*VP* 454, ll. 7–10)

Yeats hopes to meet with Olivia Shakespear (and apparently did) in October 1926 (see *L* 718–20); but the suggested comic background of the *Nights* story 'The Sleeper Wakened' (*YL* 251, pp. 323–74), with its alternating banj-induced cycles of magnificent and mad 'dreaming' (a 'gift' of Harun al-Rashid introduced at the feasting cup), follows from sources notably mined for the celebration of his marriage, in October 1917. Perhaps reflexively, the new ending also re-employed a convergence of image and pun (ll. 8, 10) not seen since the poems 'Reconciliation' (*VP* 257, ll. 11–12) and 'The Living Beauty' (*VP* 334, l. 6). The yoking of disparate identities in conceited poetry is a labour of 'Metaphysical wit'. Yeats's verbal parody of Donne, rehearsed in earlier poetry, naturally facilitated the compounding of particular women into a generalized feminine principle, an 'Idea of a Woman', a 'profane . . . blasphem[y]', an antithesis to the barren rationalism of the modern, Western, male-dominated world.

'From "Oedipus at Colonus"', a work of adaptation and the last lyric of the male sequence, concludes in 'very bad Grecian but very good Elizabethan' (*L* 723): 'a gay goodnight and quickly turn away'. The first poem in the complementary series 'A Woman Young and Old' begins by combining the outcry of Herbert – 'I struck the board, and cry'd, No more' ('The Collar', l. 1) – and the domestic life of the Yeatses as recorded by their amused head of household in one of his daybooks (in NLI 13,576, under the date 'March 1926'):

George has just told me that yesterday she said to Anne 'I dont like so & so' so & so being a little boy of Anne's age 'he is a very nasty child' Anne replied 'Yes but he has such lovely hair & his eyes are as cold as a march wind.' I should put this int[o] verse for it is the Cry of every woman who loves a blac[k]guard.[102]

Parkinson's reduction of the draft that soon followed on the facing page fails to show just how or where the Herbert echo got planted in the first place – or, indeed, that a Herbert influence ever existed.[103] The transcript below shows that the echo (in l. 1 of 'Father and Child') occurred late in the draft, first as an afterthought and alternate beginning and then as a substitution:

> It is but waste of breath t[o] say
> That she is under ban
> of all good men & women,
> Being mentioned with a [m?]an
> That [h?]as the worst of all bad nam[e?]s
> And thereupon
> If thereon she replies
> That his hair is beautiful
> And Cold as the march wind his eyes.
> or
> the
> She hears me stri[k]e board [&] say
> Ete
> And there upon replies
> Etc.

In this way, Herbert becomes a sounding-board, amplifying rather than muting Yeats's amusement over his seven-year-old daughter's wit. Mock exasperation over the child's defiance of conventional moral 'bans' gives way to ironic play which uses Herbert's call for submission to authority ('I heard one calling *Child*! / And I replied, *My Lord*') as a standard against which the Yeatsian doting father covertly registers his approval of his child's unsubmissiveness. The poem does not, as Keane claims,[104] alter its precursor, but uses it ironically as a stable point of reference. By making parody of a conventional patriarchal posture, the poet subverts his literal meaning in favour of the opposite one intended – in this case, from the original draft.

Yeats's embrace of female liberty, if one cannot quite call it feminism, was nevertheless one with his rejection of Herbert's Christian submissiveness; and that rejection, as Keane finds in the other poems of the sequence,[105] was accompanied by 'a genital concentering . . . reminiscent of John Donne at his most blasphemous', an unorthodox turning of Christian theology 'on its head by making original sin serve the ends of sexuality (rather as Byron had, his guilt-ridden Calvinism sweetening the forbidden fruit)'. One of those poems mentioned, 'Consolation' (*VP* 534), with 'A First Confession' (*VP* 532–3), gained perhaps its first audience when sent to Olivia Shakespear (on 23 June 1927) as 'one of the first [of] my woman series to balance that of "The Young and Old Countryman" [or "A Man Young and Old"]' (*L* 725). Clearly, the evidence provided by the manuscripts of these two poems, due to their relation to the complicated genesis reported by Stallworthy,[106] confirms a connection with Donne.

At present, the remains of three series in-the-making – 'A Man Young and Old', 'A Woman Young and Old', and 'Words for Music Perhaps' – are dispersed about files arranged for *The Tower* (NLI 13,589[1]–[32]) and *The Winding Stair* (NLI 13,590[1]–[23]; 13,591[1]–[25]; 13,592[1]–[12], as well as several manuscript-books used for *A Vision* (NLI 13,576, 13,580, 13,581), including the famous Great Vellum Notebook, recently sold. The confusion that such dispersal engenders is, however, compensated for by the fact that the manuscript arrangements are frequently diachronic and natural, rather than a matter of authorial 'choice' or mere happenstance.[107] Because of this fact, one can see how clusters of the Crazy Jane poems, for example, developed their suggestive hair and thorn imagery – or how such leitmotivs in 'Her Dream', 'His Bargain', and 'Love's Loneliness' (via Rapallo Notebook C, NLI 13,580) exactly parallel the same in 'A First Confession' (NLI 13,589[29]; 13,592[4]) and 'Veronica's Napkin' (Rapallo Notebook D, NLI 13,581).[108] Yeats's use of hair in the lyrics of 1926–7 follows more from Donne's example than from the Pre-Raphaelite fetishism of the early Yeats. Duncan first noted Yeats's fascination with the Elizabethan's sensational, if disturbing, precedent in 'The Funerall' and 'The Relique':

> Donne thought that [the lock of hair that he imagined buried with himself and his mistress] might lead the lovers' souls to meet after death. In Yeats's 'Crazy Jane and Jack the Journeyman' love is a skein that will bind the lovers 'ghost to ghost'. In 'Her

Dream' the speaker thinks she has shorn her locks away and 'laid them on Love's lettered tomb', only to see 'nailed upon the night/Berenice's burning hair'. The image is striking the same way as Donne's 'bracelet of bright haire about the bone'. In Yeats's 'His Bargain', as in 'The Relique', the hair is the means to a union that transcends the grave.[109]

Henn (*LT* 245) suggests that the astrological apotheosis of the speaker's 'locks' in 'Her Dream' ('And after nailed upon the night/Berenice's burning hair') may derive from a reference to the 'lampe of Berenice's hayre' in Ben Jonson's epistle to Elizabeth, Countess of Rutland (*The Forrest* XII.61).[110] To be sure, a long adaptation of Donne which Yeats abandoned in all but two of its segments, 'Chosen' and 'Parting', further demonstrates the convergence of Donne and Jonson in the mature Yeats.[111]

The phrase 'household spies' in 'Parting', l. 3 (*VP* 535–6; or L5r in Yeats's notebook), also occurs in Jonson's *Volpone* (III.ii.177) and 'Song. To Celia' (*The Forrest*, v.12; see *LT* 245). However, the principal analogues must be Donne's twelfth Elegy, 'His parting from her' (l. 40)[112] and 'Breake of day', one of his rare works in the voice of a female persona.[113] As executed in exercise book NLI 13,589(31), 'Parting' (there untitled) was the first of four movements of a poem written in the form of a dialogue. Entitled 'Two Voices' (then 'Morning' in the exercise book), the longer poem developed by compounding image, diction, and scene in more or less conscious imitation of some of the poet's favourite Renaissance authors. One of the nearest analogies to the scene, as set in part 1 of the dialogue (i.e. 'Parting'), might be *Romeo and Juliet* (II.v), as Stallworthy points out, because of 'the lover's . . . uncertainty over lark or nightingale'. Part 2 (on L6r of the exercise book), like part 4 (or 'Chosen', eventually), gives the woman's view, opposed to that of her lover, in the kind of exotic diction and imagery common to Elizabethan drama:

> Love's morning is its setting
> All night its memories burn
> But day is foul forgetting
> And if night's noon return
> That is a great defiance,
> For Turks & blackamores,
> Abbysinian lions,
> Indian warriors,

> A dragons winding gullet
> That has sucked in the moon,
> Rage tooth turk & bullet
> To drive it from its noon

The 'genital concentering' at the end of 'Parting' ('I offer to love's play/My dark declivities'; in manuscript, 'Between these breasts maternal dark lies hid') and at the end of part 3 of 'Morning' ('O heart lie close where all thats done/Is idleness') is Donnean, although the inverse of Donne's

> Since she must go, and I must mourn, come Night,
> Environ me with darkness, whilst I write:
> . . . .
> Was't not enough, that thou didst hazard us
> To paths in love so dark, so dangerous:
> And those so ambush'd round with household
>   spies . . . .
>   (Elegy xii, ll. 1–2, 39–41)[114]

By coincidence, Yeats's *New Poems* (1938) are ushered in by echoes of Jonson[115] and Donne ('Or dark betwixt the polecat and the owl,/Or any rich, dark nothing' – *VP* 565, ll. 21–2). Possibly a distortion of Donne's 'witty discussion of different degrees of nothingness' in 'A Nocturnall',[116] the apocalyptic figures of 'The Gyres' were, in fact, anticipated by the more affirmative metaphysics Yeats cast into poetry in response to the work he referred to as 'that intoxicating "St. Lucies Day"' (*L* 710), which by 21 February 1926 had already lent its stanza to 'a poem of my own, just finished'.[117]

The poem 'Chosen' (originally called 'The Choice') has been credited with being something more than a five-finger exercise of form. Wilson and Melchiori cite its ingenuity as a philosophical counterpoint to Donne's 'Nocturnall' – as intentional 'counter-truth to [Donne's] catalogue of love's "privations"'[118] and as Yeats's affirmation that 'sexual consummation could be the most effective expression of the achievement . . . of final unity . . . on the human and on the cosmic plane'.[119] In emphasizing the similarity between Yeats and his Renaissance precursor, Keane stresses the Irish poet's Donnean 'laicizing' of the spiritual world, Yeats's reversal of the Neoplatonic theory of transcendence by 'identifying occult perfection with the post-coital stillness of very human lovers'.[120] In this respect, 'Chosen' extends in series (although it predates in manuscript) the impenitent attitude of 'A First Confession' and the obscenity of 'Consolation', an old woman's reply to 'what the sages said' (*VP* 534, l. 2). A draft note prepared for *The Winding Stair* (New York: Fountain, 1929; see *VP* 830) testifies further to a strategic link between lyrics III, VI, and VII of Yeats's 'woman series':

> In 'A First Confession', 'The Choice' and 'The Parting' I have made use of that symbolic marriage of the Sun and Light with the Earth and Darkness, current in literature since the Renaissance. The sun's northern (not northward) way is his passage under the earth, his sojourn in the bed of love. Earth would bar his way and so prevent the dawn.[121]

This seems preliminary to Yeats's note of March 1928: 'I have symbolised a woman's love as the struggle of the darkness to keep the sun from rising from its earthly bed. In the last stanza of The Choice I change the symbol to that of the souls of man and woman ascending through the Zodiac' (*VP* 830).[122] The astrological matrices of that particular stanza, drawn from 'some Neoplatonist or Hermatist' – later identified as Macrobius in his comment on 'Scipio's Dream' (*VP* 830) – have attracted much of the attention scholars have paid up to now to the subject of Yeats's poetic response to Donne's 'poem of great passion' (*L* 902). Wilson and Melchiori speculate that the model for 'zodiacal' imagery originated with Donne himself. Melchiori makes the better case,[123] but neither argued from evidence now at hand.

Several pages of manuscript (particularly L1v–3v, 7v–9r, and 14r) show that Yeats's labour over the 'Nocturnall' stanza was accompanied by a liberal compounding of Donne-like locutions from various sources, most of them already mentioned in this chapter. The first stanza of 'Chosen' begins part 4 of 'Morning' with an image of eclipse ('I knew th[a]t he would change or meet his death –/. . . Befor[e] my shadow could be filled again'), which permutated, with revision, into the mechanism Yeats later described in his note (see above) and into a case of expropriation:

[Donne] Where can we finde two better hemispheares
Without sharpe North, without declining West?
Whatever dyes, was not mixt equally . . . .
('The good-morrow', ll. 17–19)

But as all severall soules containe
  Mixture of things, they know not what,
Love, these mixt soules, doth mixe againe,
  And makes both one . . . .
('The Extasie', ll. 33–6)

Aske for those Kings whom thou saw'st yesterday,
And thou shalt heare, All here in one bed lay.
('The Sunne Rising', ll. 19–20)

[Yeats]
Love sets at dawn, but will dawn again
Never never will he come again
For he will change or somewhere meet his death
Scarce had breath been mixed with breath
Scarce had one with tother lain
That he might find his rest   west
And sink in subterranean rest
Among the ivory shadows of breast
                        northern
Before Id marched him on his southern way
And stood stock still though in one bed we lay.
(NLI 13,589[31], L8r)

An intermediate stage of revision on L7v provides a gloss for the new first and second lines: 'Passion has its dawn as the sun set[s] / And sets again defeated at the dawn.' For the second stanza, the poet at first copied in (and revised as he did so) the profit of five pages of drafting (L1v–4r) in which the speaker imagines herself as 'an old crouching hag with speckled shin'. Donne's use of 'midnight' in l. 1 of the 'Nocturnall' attaches itself initially to her thought that life's 'flood' might be caught in 'night's deep overflowing cup', 'one deep night's hollow cup . . . Being too full of its own sweet to spill' (on L2r–4r). But in the revision executed in L8r and 9r, the conceit 'midnight's hollow cup' (recalling 'The Empty Cup', discussed earlier) fuses with a Donnean symbol of sexual consummation and spiritual unity:

[Donne]   one little roome, an every where.
. . .
Let us possesse one world, each hath one, and is one,
('The good-morrow', ll. 11, 14)

Shine here to us, and thou art every where;
This bed thy centre is, these walls, thy spheare.
('The Sunne Rising', ll. 29–30)

So thy love may be my loves spheare . . . .
('Aire and Angels', l. 25)

[Yeats]   ~~When on my death bed I have reckoned up~~
~~What ever I have known of the worlds good~~
                always starry
For all ~~starry~~ nature would not stop
~~For yet when grown Old~~
Yet when an old hag measuring all her ~~years~~ long
I shall declare it flowed
Into one midnight's hollow cup
And did that cup so fill
It seemed as though all life stood still
Being too full of its own sweet to spill
And that I played in starry waters where
The zodiac is changed into a sphere
(NLI 13,589[31], L8r and 9r)

Melchiori[124] cites passages in which Donne uses the words 'Zodiake' and 'Sphericall' in 'An Anatomie of the World', a poem apparently left uncut in YL 531. Revision of ll. 1–5 of the first stanza followed the above draft on L9r, contributing, finally, only the significant phrase 'the whirling zodiac'. After that, the wild jottings of L9v–13r bear witness to the rapid breakdown of the poet's relatively orderly exercise in adaptation as he began to integrate material from Macrobius.

Once finished, Yeats's hymn to 'the lot of love' in the mortal world was more recondite[125] than were the lyrics of 1896 and even the model it imitated. The poem achieves distinction, moreover, as a benchmark, an index of Yeats's progress as a 'Metaphysical poet'. As the central poem of its sequence, it is also the one 'Metaphysical' poem in the Yeats canon virtually assured of its station by patent. (Intention may be read in the act of simulation.) The wild activity of L9r–13r corresponds in the creative process to that point at which the poem began to distinguish itself as an unequal entity in the dialogue it was supposed to serve. The simulacrum (as observed in the preceding chapter) gives place to sophisticated adaptation – with inspiration suddenly taking charge and modifying the best-laid plans of the poet. The rejected parts 2 and 3 of the poem originally conceived under the influence of various Renaissance writers were not rejected so much for dialectical reasons – 'the lovers talk almost at cross-purposes'[126] – as because the poet, possessed by an 'intoxicating' model, had shifted attention almost entirely to the final movement. The frame might stand in separable units ('Parting' and 'Chosen'), but the body of the dialogue could not – although its reprise was eventually worked out under a different set of prescriptions and other Renaissance models. Not a specially great poem, 'Chosen' is, at least, a good poem rising from the peculiar metaphysics of Yeats and the poetic know-how summoned from thirty years' interest in Donne and the Metaphysical poets. As the last chapter of this study shows, some of the later, greater poems of Yeats appear to rise from other Renaissance influences – influences which were not entirely new to Yeats but which were reintroduced, experimentally (as we have seen), soon after his marriage. The renewal of latent influences such as Milton and Spenser, however, occurred at no cost to the Metaphysical influence. Indeed, Yeats made these various influences compatible and compounded them, as we have come to expect.

6
Conclusion: The Rapprochement with Milton and Spenser, 1918–39

> The gyre ebbs out in order and reason, the Jacobean poets succeed the Elizabethan, Cowley and Dryden the Jacobean as belief dies out. Elsewhere Christendom keeps a kind of spectral unity for a while, now with one, now with the other element of the synthesis dominant; a declamatory holiness defaces old churches, innumerable Tritons and Neptunes pour water from their mouths. What had been a beauty like the burning sun fades out . . . , [converted] to certain recognised forms of the picturesque constantly repeated, chance travellers at the inn door, men about a fire, men skating, the same pose or grouping, where the subject is different, passing from picture or picture. (*AV B* 295)

I

Yeats's 'spectral' procession of the ages in book v of *A Vision* ('Written at Capri, February 1925') might start up a shiver of recognition like that recounted in his *Poems of Spenser*. Such 'ghostly midnight animation', perceived as if by 'watching ghostly kings and queens setting out upon their unearthly business' (*E&I* 382–3), was the forte of the elder poet, as the modern poet readily acknowledged and featured in a group of selections entitled 'Emblems and Qualities'.[1] Both 'Mutabilitie' cantos were part of this group and seem especially compatible with Yeats's later occult treatise. Yet it surprises one that a Renaissance poet whose influence Yeats outgrew in many ways by 1902 – or about whom he expressed so many reservations – should be resurrected, in 1937, as an inspiration for so good a poem as 'The Municipal Gallery Re-visited'. Spenser was a precursor whom the Irish poet found incomplete and politically repugnant, a man whose life and art ended bitterly in sight of 'the ever-whirling wheele, / Of Change' (*The Faerie Queene*, VII.vi.1), a verbal genius who felt only 'through the eyes, imagining everything in pictures' (*E&I* 383). Living in the last days of 'Merry England', he had nevertheless 'many Puritan thoughts' (*E&I* 367) – thoughts from a loathsome religion, as Yeats said, which 'denied the sacredness of an earth that commerce . . . corrupt[ed] and ravish[ed]' (*E&I* 365). At best the robust master of Keats and Shelley, Spenser had given 'his heart to the State', to 'unconscious hypocrisy', or 'undelighted obedience' to the censorious *bête noir* of poets, Lord Burleigh (*E&I* 373, 369). A man of his time, like Milton in the last generation of the English Renaissance, Spenser had been both agent and victim of 'Choice and Chance' (or Will and Fortune). 'The gyre ebbs out in order and reason . . .'

Interestingly enough, for all of Yeats's effort to get 'Milton off my back', or permanently rid himself of 'Miltonic rhetoric' (see above, pp. 66, 127), Milton succeeded exceptionally well in retaining his place beside the esteemed Jacobeans, in Yeats's view, when he might have been excluded, as Pound and Eliot preferred.[2] Although in Milton 'God and the Angels . . . seemed artificial', the poet could be admired for attempting to renew the violence of a sinking gyre – for trying to effect an artistic 'return to the synthesis of the Camera della Segnatura and the Sistine Chapel' (*AV B* 295) in spite of the fact that it was, by that time, too late to do so. His 'unreality' and his 'cold rhetoric' were products of an experiment for which he might be praised, since he had attempted the impossible: a Phase 18 re-creation of 'all the music and magnificence of the still violent gyre' of Phase 16. To be sure, Yeats hoped that something like Milton's effort might succeed in the twentieth century. 'We are completing in this age', Yeats wrote as early as 1908, 'a work begun in the Renaissance; we are reuniting the mind and soul and body of man to the living world outside us'.[3] A like thought virtually concludes *A Vision*, suggesting that the work of fully integrated individuals was possible, and only possible, at such moments (as seemed imminent) when the birth of a gyre stimulates the 'psychological contagion' of a new Renaissance:

I too think of famous works where synthesis has been carried to
the utmost limit possible, . . . and I notice that . . . when the
new gyre begins to stir, I am filled with excitement. . . . I can
recognise that the limit itself has become a new dimension, that
this ever-hidden thing which makes us fold our hands has begun
to press down upon multitudes. Having bruised their hands
upon th[e] limit [of the objective world of the Newtonian Phase
19], men, for the first time since the seventeenth century, see
the world as an object of contemplation, not as something to be
remade. . . . (*AV B* 300)

To Yeats, correspondences existed between the historic Renaissance and the modern literary revival he had worked to bring about in Ireland. And the heterogeneous philosophical disposition of such writers as Milton and Spenser, whose works were invested with the 'old science' of their day, seemed to anticipate the later contemplative genius of Yeats himself, who wished to restore to wholeness a soul and world brought to disruption by the materialism of Bacon, Locke, Hobbes, and Newton.[4] Yeats's relatively late warming to Swift, Berkeley, Goldsmith, Grattan, and Burke – figures central to that tradition which revisionists now argue was largely a Yeatsian myth[5] – perhaps helped soften the poet's objections to the militant Spenser and Milton. Clearly, if the Introduction to Yeats's edition of Spenser airs differences which led to a sixteen-year censure (broken finally with the adaptation of 'Astrophel' in 'Shepherd and Goatherd'), Yeats's quarrel with Milton over Puritan self-righteousness (*L* 555), rhetoric (*Au* 145, *UP1* 307 and 420), and the Latinization of letters (*AV B* 297; *Y&GI* 114) was of longer standing but caused no rift between Yeats and the elder poet. Indeed, as a reactionary Irish senator, Yeats had upheld Milton's position in *The Doctrine and Discipline of Divorce* (1643) as if Milton had stood with the Anglo-Irish figures mentioned above and had contributed 'a famous part of the history of the Protestant people' (*SS* 92; see also pp. 99 and 100–2). However, the one factor that probably most encouraged Yeats's rapprochement with Milton and Spenser was their philosophical kinship to one another and to the poetry on metaphysical subjects that Yeats was writing in 1918.

When Yeats returned to the poetic regions of Spenser, Virgil, and

Theocritus in the first months of his marriage, he followed the Renaissance poet's example in imposing upon the pastoral dialogue the exposition of an occult tableau. Spenser's well-known Neoplatonic prolixity, as Yeats noticed particularly in *The Faerie Queene*'s Garden of Adonis and in the geometric riddle of stanza II.ix.22 (see Ch. 3), established a precedent for Yeats's application of Platonic theology derived from Thomas Taylor (see Ch. 4) and Henry More (see Ch. 5). The automatic script of early 1918 was turned into literary capital in the fashion of Spenser's tribute to Sir Philip Sidney (see *L* 646–8 and 650).[6] By June, apparently after a period in which Mrs Yeats had been away, such efforts had produced a fictional prose dialogue with a connection in manuscript to the poem 'The Phases of the Moon'.[7] The poem, in its prose context, seems formally more directly inspired by Landor than by Plato. (Yeats then owned copies of *The Dialogues* and *The Republic*, but seems not really to have encountered the Graeco-Roman Platonists until slightly later.[8] The poem also acknowledges a few honest debts of Yeats's past. The clustering of Milton, Shelley, Palmer, Blake, and Pater in orbit around a didactic corpus (*VP* 373–7, ll. 31–123) is characteristic of the poet's attempt to make 'real' and thus intelligible the abstractions of his psychic research.[9] In embryonic state, the poem and prose dialogue of which it was part promised 'simple' wisdom which could not have fully anticipated, as a prolusion, the philosophical toil of the next two decades.

Yeats's conception of the poem changed radically in the course of its writing, although its scene was always pastoral and possibly always stationed at Yeats's own Thoor Ballylee castle. One's view of the adaptive complex must now shift, however, as unpublished evidence dictates, to make room for company not previously considered. The first revelation the manuscripts have in store for us (in NLI 13,587[21]) is that the poem's initial relations were Yeats's own early poems 'The Harp of Aengus' (*VP* 219, l. 2: 'young Aengus in his tower of glass') and 'Under the Moon' (*VP* 209, l. 8: 'Land-of-the-tower, where Aengus has thrown the gates apart').[10] Instead of a Robartes–Aherne dialogue, we find an Aengus/Cuchulain-arbitrated vision, which dissolves supernaturally with the apparent metamorphosis of the Irish god of love and poetry (a 'crude' [possibly 'wide'] 'ragged man') into an object of nature which, at the end of an early fragment, 'Slid slowly down, & dropped into the stream'. Indeed, 'a rat or water-hen ... or an otter' in 'The Phases of the Moon', ll. 8–9 (*VP* 372), recalls 'Niamh

Conclusion

and Laban and Fand, who could change to an otter or fawn' in 'Under the Moon', l. 12. Although the draft ends where the poem begins, Yeats's 'system', as delivered in ll.31–123 of 'The Phases of the Moon' (*VP*) seems already in place. The mystical Robartes had only to take possession of it from Aengus. Hence, the shift from Aengus–Cuchulain to Robartes–Aherne transferred ostensible authority for the visionary content of the poem from suprahuman sources such as the *Tuatha De Danaan* to a mediator (or even medium), in keeping with actual circumstances. This shift occurred with Yeats's attempt to transplant the verse exposition of the first draft into the two approximately forty-page prose dialogues cited, and antedates the revision of the poem, in two stages (*c*. June 1918), based on an English – especially Miltonic – literary venue and a Platonic doctrine long undetected in the finished poem.

In revision, the narrative preface of ll. 1–7 (set in italic in the next stage) began to take shape around the 'rocks & briars', an 'uneven road', and 'that lat[e] scarce r[i]sen dwindl[in]g c[r]escent' of the moon – all very much in tune with the actual scene at the Yeats tower, but also (and as frequently recognized) in keeping with Samuel Palmer's illustration in *The Shorter Poems of John Milton* (London: Seeley, 1889), *The Lonely Tower*.[11] Palmer's illustration for 'Il Penseroso', ll. 85–7 (quoted opposite the illustration; see plate 9), features 'two shepherds' who 'speak together of the mysterious light above them'. Giving this scene the local accent of the region near Gort, County Galway, Yeats made Aherne and Robartes 'old men' in 'conne mar [*sic*] cloth worn out of shape'. The beginnings of their talk rises from the concluding scene of the Aengus–Cuchulain fragments (as related above) and quickly introduces most of the analogues recognizable in *VP*:

[L4r]   ~~Ahern Robartes~~
                Rob[art]es Aherne
~~Th~~
What m[a]d[e] tha[t] sound

                Roba[r]t[es]
                      a rat or wat[e]r hen
spla[sh]ed   slid int[o]
~~perhaps~~ or ott[e]r ~~slipping in~~ the strea[m]

Aherne

~~ahern~~
~~Once [~~   ] th[i]s ~~comes~~ we ca[n] ~~see his~~ lamp
we hav[e] cleared[?] in vision & can [see?] his lamp
~~From t[he] towe[r] window~~
~~or candle shining~~ fro[m]
      gl[eaming?]
or [   ] his candle glimme[ring] in t[he] tower

Robartes

He has found after the manne[r] of hi[s] kind
  mere   chose this place t[o] live in
~~The outward~~ images, & chose t[he] tower[?]
       shin[ing?]
Because it may be, of th[e] lamp ~~li[t] skies~~
~~From the old tower~~
       th[at] Mil[t]on
Saw throug[h] th[e] night, & that mor[e] ne[ar] our time
     en
Samu[e]l Palmer ∧ graver, & Shell[e]y['s] prince,
Yo[un]g A[t]henean li[gh]t aga[i]n, an image
of some my[s]ter[io]us wisdo[m] won by toil
or chose it from the river bub[b]l[in]g up
From th[e] hard [poss. 'hollow'] rock: an image th[a]t
of natural insti[n]ct which is a bond[?]

   choose   after his kind
[L4v] And ~~choos~~ th[at] h[e] shall liv[e] ~~as liv[e] by~~ kind
  Distu[r]bed
Ousted by thos[e] he speak[s] th[rough?] [his] lines
And ~~hesitat[e] & stumbl[e]~~
        stare
stu[m]ble & hesitate – the e[a]gl[e] look
Belo[n]gs t[o] thos[e] who have dar[e]d t[o] tred thes[e]
          roads

Aherne

     of the moon
Sing me the changes ∧ once more
~~[not?] sung because~~
True song for it ecchoes th[e] tho[u]ght
 True
~~Truegh~~ song tho[u]gh b[u]t ~~spoke[n]~~ speech
~~True song tho[u]g[h] spoken~~
      "Mine Author sung it me"

Yeats himself presides over this creation, as we read here and in the finished poem. Iconographically, his tower is the same one as Milton imagined (or in Yeats's words, 'saw through the night') with his midnight lamp set

> in some high lonely Tow'r
> Where I may oft outwatch the *Bear*,
> With thrice great *Hermes*, or unsphere
> The spirit of *Plato* to unfold
> What Worlds, or what vast Regions hold
> The immortal mind that hath forsook
> Her mansion in this fleshly nook:
> And of those *Daemons* that are found
> In fire, air, flood, or underground,
> Whose power hath a true consent
> With Planet, or with Element.
> ('Il Penseroso', ll. 86–96)[12]

By the second draft, the person of Milton had been displaced by the persona of his poem. After some difficulty with Shelley and Athena (the latter subsequently shifted to *VP* 374, l. 45),[13] Yeats delivered the lines

> From the far tower where Milton's Platonist
> Sat late, or Shelley's visionary prince:
> The lonely light that Samuel Palmer engraved . . .
> (*VP* 373, ll. 15–17)

Beyond this stage, the poet discarded Milton's oily lamp for the Donnean self-consuming taper ('The Canonization', l. 21) as a sheet of manuscript from 'The Living Beauty' (see Ch. 5, section IV) joined the poem-in-progress, producing 'candle-light' in l. 14. This incident recalls two of Yeats's agonizing courtships of 1917 and the equally relevant fact that the designated light beams from his bedroom (see, for example, *VP* 324, l. 5: 'Climb up the narrow winding stair to bed'). After a few verses, Yeats permitted his creations to ridicule the 'elaborate style / He had learnt from Pater', suggestive of his own marginalia in *Plato and Platonism*.[14] But even before that, at the close of the first-draft exchange quoted above, the poet had left an important clue to the poem's meaning – a clue just as impressive, despite its private nature, as are the obvious references to various iconographic models. We should be mindful of correspondences with the Tarot Hermit and Tower, as Raine is,[15] and suspect links with the 'Masters' of MacGregor Mathers, the 'Instructors' (later the 'singing masters') of Yeats, and the 'Eternals' of Blake ('I dare not pretend to be any other than the Secretary[;] the Authors are in Eternity').[16] Yet one's attention might profitably focus on Aherne's peculiar use of quotation in l. 30, crucially placed before the important poem-within-the-poem:

> *Aherne.* Sing me the changes of the moon once more;
> True song, though speech: 'mine author sung it me'.

Gould and Smith[17] each argue that the phrase approximates Chaucer's 'For as myn auctor seyde, so seye I' (*Troilus and Criseyde*, II.18), following the valid assumption that in conceiving the heart of the poem Yeats remembered the Franklin's use of a hearsay book of 'magik naturel' which 'spak muchel of the operaciouns, / Touchinge the eighte and twenty mansiouns / That longen to the mone, and swich folye' (*Canterbury Tales*, F.1125ff.).[18] In fact, the quotation which Yeats uncharacteristically in a draft put between quotation marks, with its implication that Robartes's discourse ought to be regarded as song, derived from Milton's tractate *The Doctrine and Discipline and Divorce*, 1644 edition, I.vi: 'The Fourth Reason of this Law, that God regards Love and Peace in the family, more than a compulsive performance of mariage . . .'. Appropriately, Milton's 'author' – unlike Chaucer's – is Plato, and his song a dialectic of love with direct appeal to Yeats's theory of the self and anti-self:

> Love, if he be not twin-born, yet hath a brother wondrous like him, call'd *Anteros*: whom while he seeks all about, his chance is to meet with many fals and faining Desires that wander singly up and down in his likenes. . . . But after a while, as his manner is, when soaring up into the high Towr of his *Apogaeum*, above the shadow of the earth, he darts out the direct rayes of his then most piercing eyesight upon the impostures, and trim disguises that were us'd with him, and discerns that this is not his genuin brother, as he imagin'd, he has no longer the power to hold fellowship with such a personated mate. For strait his arrows loose their golden heads, and shed their purple feathers, his

silk'n breades untwine, and slip their knots and that original and firie vertue giv'n him by Fate, all on a sudden goes out and leaves him undeifi'd, and despoil'd of all his force: till finding *Anteros* at last, he kindles and repairs that almost faded ammunition of his Deity by the reflection of a coequal and *homogeneal* fire. *Thus mine author sung it to me* . . . .

(Emphasis added at close)[19]

The 'Towr of [Love's] *Apogaeum*' seems one attraction the passage held for Yeats. He would not have found it in the *Phaedrus* he possessed, if indeed *Phaedrus* was one of the only 'two or three . . . principal Platonic Dialogues' he knew at the time (*AV B* 12).[20] The poem's presiding symbol is the tower; moreover, in the first draft, Love (or Aengus in be-towered Ireland) had direct charge of the poem's vision and song. But, more important, the Platonic doctrine that Milton presented – as a parable on 'matrimonial love' – perfectly suited the poet's ingenious second conception of the poem. This conception, in deference to the Miltonic modification of Plato's metaphor of the charioteer and his two steeds, placed the soul in a corporeal tower before two travellers, who seem imaginative projections of the poet's primary and antithetical selves, rather as we suppose the speakers of 'Ego Dominus Tuus'. In actuality, Yeats devised a conceit similar to the one he tried to visualize for Spenser's House of Alma (see Ch. 3, section III; and plate 12). However, in this case, Milton's presentation of 'twinborn' Eros and Anteros, opposites who seek reunion in the '*homogeneal* fire' of their first state, lent the poem a philosophical dynamic that Yeats soon attributed to the fictitious authority of the *Speculum Angelorum et Hominum* (1594) by 'Giraldus'.[21]

Probably Yeats did consult his *Phaedrus*, in 1914, when interpreting the auguries of Lady Lyttelton and W. T. Horton. Their respectively spiritualistic and mystical appropriation of the myth of Phaeton, in connection with proceedings involving Miss Georgie Hyde-Lees and the poet's discourse with his sixteenth-century 'daimon', influenced almost from inception the collaborative script which gave rise to *A Vision*.[22] Horton's 'strange adventures' in 'Platonic love' with Amy Audrey Locke – commemorated in the dedication and lyric tailpiece of that book (*AV A* x, ll. 6–7, and 253, ll. 22–3 [*VP* 471]) – seems pertinent in light of George Yeats's desire to be recognized as the 'symbol' of her husband's anti-self, or the instrument by which he came to find his 'Mask'.[23] That she succeeded is implicit in his severely elliptical use of Milton's treatise. The passage in question affirms that 'Love in marriage cannot live nor subsist, unlesse it be mutual' (i.e. that dual entities like Eros and Anteros might be joined in a way that alters the intention of Plato's original); but in the next breath, shifting to an authority that Yeats himself adopted in several philosophical poems on sexual love and the 'Beatific Vision' (see *AV A* xii), Milton makes celebration of wedlock as 'saith *Salomon* in *Ecclesiastes*': 'If *Salomons* advice be not overfrolick, *Live joyfully*, saith he, *with the wife whom thou lovest, all thy dayes, for that is thy portion*,'[24] Standing by itself (as Yeats perhaps encountered it), the whole splendid passage seems less a defence of divorce than a way of envisioning ideal marriage. Presumably George Yeats caught the allusion, in spite of its obscurity for the rest of us. However, the poet could not have expected – nor wished – his public to recognize such slight personal touches.

Milton himself, in line with Chaucer, used 'author' when he meant his own poetic insight.[25] Smith[26] argues that 'Mine author' in Yeats's poem is the poet himself, whose imaginative reconstruction of the quintessential 'narrative paradigm' from multiple 'debased variants'[27] characterizes his performance both as a storyteller and as a perpetuator of Platonic tradition. Yeats's use elsewhere of the tag 'mine author sung it me' (in *E&I* 340 and, slightly altered, in *LDW* 26) seems to confirm such reasoning.[28] In a sense, his shadow truths *are* 'without father'; his texts 'impostures'; his spokesmen the mere issue of poetic licence. Hence, the Yeatsian tower poet – 'Milton's Platonist' – draws ridicule from figments of his imagination for aspiring to wisdom 'that he will never find'.

An irony of the situation, of course, is that *as* 'Milton's Platonist', the author has already achieved sufficient transcendence over his critics (self-critics, to be sure) to write the poem and attain greater knowledge than it publishes beneath his window. His is a 'lonely tower', but solitude can be ameliorated and spiritual growth achieved, as the legend of Eros–Anteros teaches, with reconciliation of the divided self. Dialogues, as Yeats read in *Plato and Platonism* (the likely reason why Pater appears in this poem), move intelligence up the ladder of the dialectical process. In Yeats's first draft, Aengus observes that man 'longs/To come into possession of himself'. The dialogue's movement, or *processus*, according to Pater (after Arnold, as Yeats understood), serves just such a purpose, since it involves 'that dynamic, or essential, dialogue of the mind with itself'.[29] Pater helped define a literary genre for Yeats, it would seem, if Milton suggested a philosophical basis for its development: 'the essence of that method, of "dialectic" in all its forms, as its very name denotes, is dialogue, the habit of seeking truth by means of question and answer, primarily with one's self'.[30]

Yeats knew the kindred myth of Eros, or Phanes – the primordial being which unites everything with itself, having risen from the elements of Chaos in the wind-egg of Night. Reference to great eggs of the Phoenix which 'turn inside out . . . without breaking the shell' (*AV A* xxiii) testifies to the poet's knowledge of such creation mythologies. Partly, this knowledge proceeds from the teachings of H. P. Blavatsky and, more particularly, the *Orpheus* of G. R. S. Mead (London: Theosophical Publishing Society, 1896), pp. 162–74.[31] In the imaginative blending, the *processus* of Robartes' 'song' in 'The Phases of the Moon' advances by a succession of aphoristic variations on the Goatherd's song in 'Shepherd and Goatherd, ll. 95–110 (*VP* 342–3). This advance by retrograde progression of the soul from grave to cradle (here in twenty-eight 'embodiments') is the song's main theme, which recalls Thomas Taylor's Orphic theology and Spenser's Neoplatonic mysticism in the Garden of Adonis section of *The Faerie Queene*:

> [The souls are] sent into the chaungeful world agayne,
> Till thither they retourn where first they grew:
> So, like a wheele, around they ronne from old to new.
> (Quoted in *Myth* 363)

Finally, Robartes' phrase 'When all the dough has been so kneaded up/That it can take what form cook Nature fancies' (*VP* 377, ll. 114–15) expresses Henry More's idea of the plastic power of the individual and world souls (see *Myth* 348–52)[32] and calls to mind Eros's supposed ability to 'fashion forms in which a divine soul could dwell' (*Myth* 284).

In sum, the adaptive complex of antecedent sources is more than usually complex in 'The Phases of the Moon'. The dyadic relationship between Milton and Blake – as the poem suggests by resorting to a distinguished nineteenth-century tradition of illustrated Miltons, from Blake's to Palmer's[33] – might not be fully appreciated yet. However, it was not Blake's Milton, the prophet, but Yeats's Milton, the politician and the man of letters (*UP1* 307), the wishful Platonist of 'Il Penseroso', whom Yeats put to use in his first perplexedly 'Platonic' poem. The poem perplexes because of the poet's relatively small store of knowledge on Platonic philosophy – knowledge then derived substantially, and largely second-hand, from Renaissance authors.[34] In preparing for the 1937 edition of *A Vision*, Yeats shows his interest in 'dialectic' by his intention to use, in 'The Great Wheel' section of the book (the section succeeding the poem), a line from Blake's *Milton* (II.i): 'There is a place where contrarie[tie]s are equally true' (Rapallo Notebook D, NLI 13,581). New eras 'must awake into life, not Blake's human form Divine', but in revision Yeats added the names of Milton and Dürer (*AV A* 213 and n.). Moreover, in the book's 1925 edition, showing off some new-found knowledge based on Denis Saurat's *Milton, Man and Thinker* (1925; YL 1847),[35] Yeats promoted the Reniassance poet in a passage abrogated by the better-informed, later edition.[36] 'Milton', he said,

> was the first English writer who made philosophical use of the obliquity of the ecliptic [i.e. Magnus Annus, or the Great Year], but it was the Sun's annual and not his precessional movement that enabled Milton in the tenth book of Paradise Lost to explain the sudden ruin of the climate when Adam was driven out of Eden. Yet he must have known of the precession for he had in his library the Byzantine historian Georgius Syncellus who comments upon it and upon the Great Year that it defines. It is only now when we realise the antiquity of man that we know how vast and how important was the conception of that Year.
> (*AV A* 149–50)

Milton's passage (*Paradise Lost*, x.651–707) might serve as an exercise of 'sonorous rhetoric', in one man's view.[37] But we must not mistake the significance that Yeats saw in it. By accretion, his errors and understanding translated into major poetry. By such means, he discovered the process and movement of longer poetry and, as he was soon to declare, his own personal symbol. From any perspective, the Miltonic crux of 'The Phases of the Moon' (1918) recurs in poems of later date. In new combinations, indeed, its features are prominent in 'Meditations in Time of Civil War' (1921–2), 'The Tower' (1925) and 'Blood and the Moon' (1927). In essence, a textual gene had been created with Milton at or near the centre of the helix.

II

At that point, Ireland suffered the violence of its war for independence and civil war. This national crisis mirrored a personal one as Yeats responded lyrically to events. In poems outside this genetic sequence, his political views by then had allowed him, paradoxically, to make qualified poetic use of the survivors of Oliver Cromwell's regime (see below). Entertaining notions of an Irish legacy for his children and his English wife, Yeats began fashioning into a symbol of identity a restored sixteenth-century tower which stood amid and endured the insult of violent times (plates 10–11). The symbol appealed because the poet associated it with ancient aristocratic values opposed to merely practical ones (signified by the more recent annexes to his house), which he thought modern and egalitarian. Like its master, Thoor Ballylee seemed to embody contradiction. Hence projected, as if symbiotically, with Yeats's thought, it proved the readiest of settings to be employed in his longer poems.

'The Tower', in particular, demonstrates the relative ease with which the poet's chief symbol could be used to lift images from the figurative landscape of the *Anima Mundi*:

> I pace upon the battlements and stare
> On the foundations of a house, or where
> Tree, like a sooty finger, starts from the earth;
> And send imagination forth
> Under the day's declining beam, and call
> Images and memories
> From ruin or from ancient trees,
> For I would ask a question of them all.
> (*VP* 409–10, ll. 17–24)

In 'Meditations in Time of Civil War', a once-opulent Irish Big House, with its English gravelled lawns 'Where slippered Contemplation finds his ease' among 'indifferent garden deities' (*VP* 418, I.30, 28), is thrown into sharp relief against the poet's 'ancient bridge, and . . . more ancient tower', his 'farmhouse . . . sheltered by [the tower] wall', and his enclosed garden seemingly drawn from romance, Spenser or Yeats's own early works: 'An acre of stony ground / Where the symbolic rose can break into flower' (*VP* 419, II.1–4). There the contemplative 'Milton's Platonist' (via Palmer's *The Lonely Tower* and Milton's 'Il Penseroso') is again in charge of the scene, imported directly from the poem of at most four years before, 'The Phases of the Moon':

> A winding stair, a chamber arched with stone,
> A grey stone fireplace with an open hearth,
> A candle and written page.
> *Il Penseroso's* Platonist toiled on
> In some like chamber, shadowing forth
> How the daemonic rage
> Imagined everything.
> Benighted travellers
> From markets and from fairs
> Have seen his midnight candle glimmering.
> (*VP* 419–20, ıı.11–20)

'Shelley's prince' has disappeared, but not from Yeats's neglect. 'Natural instinct', like the river welling up at the foot of the tower from supposed 'Shelleyan' 'subterranean caves',[38] found expression in the later poem in a stanza deleted only after the second printing:

> The river rises, and it sinks again;
> One hears the rumble of it far below
> Under its rocky hole.
> What Median, Persian, Babylonian,
> In reverie, or in vision, saw
> Symbols of the soul,
> Mind from mind has caught:
> The subterranean streams,
> Tower where a candle gleams,
> A suffering passion and a labouring thought?
> (*VP* 420, ıı.20a–j)

North rightly observes in the accepted version of the poem a dryness in Yeats's symbolism (particularly in section ıı, 'My House') because of the way it seems to echo the mockery of 'The Phases of the Moon': 'he seeks in a book or manuscript / What he shall never find'.[39] Still, the 'wry' quality that North detects (partly engineered by Yeats's later surgical removal of ll. 20a–j) is undercut by a genuine belief that sources of knowledge do exist, that wisdom *is* possible, and that one may 'exalt a lonely mind' in the conception of 'a changeless work of art', one of the poem's 'befitting emblems of adversity' (*VP* 420, II.30). The more hysterical aspects of Yeats's response to civil war is visited upon the poem in a frenzied vision entitled 'I See Phantoms of Hatred and of the Heart's Fullness and of the Coming Emptiness'. Because of this movement, the poems of 1918 ('The Phases of the Moon'), 1921–2 ('Meditations in Time of Civil War'), and 1927 ('Blood and the Moon') may be linked in an entirely unsuspected way.

Obvious enough are the conscious echoes of 'The Phases of the Moon', especially in draft. The initial iconographic focus on Yeats's Miltonic, Palmeresque inner sanctum again gives rise to supernatural forces in 'Blood and the Moon':

> Blessed be this place,
> More blessed still this tower;
> A bloody, arrogant power
> Rose out of the race
> Uttering, mastering it,
> Rose like these walls from these
> Storm-beaten cottages . . . .
> (*VP* 480, ll. 1–7)

The specific property of Yeats is generalized, analogically, with respect to two of the ancient wonders, the Pharos (a lighthouse) at Alexandria and the biblical Tower of Babel. This gesture, equivalent to the poet's invocation of Pallas Athene in the earlier poem, precedes thought that 'Shelley had his towers, thought's crowned powers' (l. 15; see *E&I* 86–7), and a proclamation reminiscent of the mythologizing which had accompanied, in 1925, Yeats's diatribe against the Catholic opposition to a bill of divorce:

> I declare this tower is my symbol; I declare
> This winding, gyring, spiring treadmill of a stair
>   is my ancestral stair;
> That Goldsmith and the Dean, Berkeley and Burke
>   have travelled there.
> (*VP* 480–1, ll. 16–18)

Not apparent is the fact that the vision of 'blood-saturated ground' before and within the tower ('Odour of blood on the ancestral stair!' – *VP* 482, l. 40) was anticipated in the first draft of 'The

Phases of the Moon'. The later poem, like the final section of 'Meditations in Time of Civil War', entertains a 'drunken frenzy for the moon' (l. 42), or a vision of general adversity:

> Seven centuries have passed . . . ,
> The blood of innocence has left no stain.
> There, on blood-saturated ground, have stood
> Soldier, assassin, executioner,
> Whether for daily pittance or in blind fear
> Or out of abstract hatred, and shed blood,
> But could not cast a single jet thereon.
> (ll. 33–9)

At variance with fact, Yeats's personal symbol is given an imaginative 700-year span, reaching back to the brink of Ireland's heroic period, as Yeats had once conceived in 1918:

> "Look at those women kneeling by the dead"
> He whispered "look at those dark or fair ~~head~~ haired girls
> ~~Till they~~
> They pluck men by there slee[ve] & pluck them on
> ~~Till blood be shed & [——] &~~ that neith[er] knew
> ~~Nor what / That cares what natu[re] rise or fall~~
> What any has wh[at?] history what king what throne
> Sat ~~in——~~
> ~~is emptied a[nd] wh[a]t throne is filled~~
> So th[a]t [the] man ~~who~~ up[on] his face & eye
> ~~They ha[d] shed their blond[?] h~~
> ~~Th~~ They had thrown the[i]r blo[nd?] hair upo[n] whom
> Their lips have breath[e]d in bitte[r] ecstasy
> Endure t[o] th[e] end.
> Till blood is shed, & yet no car[e] have th[e]y
> Wh[a]t throne is empt[i]ed or what throne is fill[e]d
> Nor any joy that the men th[e]y choose
> And play[?] with the[i]r long hair   endure
> In bitte[r] e[c]sta[s]y till the end come"
> (Aengus to Cuchulain in NLI 13,587[21], L14r)

This scene stuck in Yeats's memory even if he did not make immediate use of it in the poetry of 1918. A play of that year, however, *The Only Jealousy of Emer* (*VP1* 529–65), renders a close parallel to such images in the poem and associates the women of Aengus's vision with Fand and the Sidhe, seductresses who 'drop their hair upon' men, 'Lap them in cloudy hair or kiss their lips' (*VP1* 549, ll. 214a and 214), in order to steal men's souls. Vampire imagery pervades the play, which is about Cuchulain's fight to maintain possession of himself. 'Oil and Blood', written as a companion to 'Blood and the Moon', carries such imagery to the poems for the first time –

> under heavy loads of trampled clay
> Lie bodies of the vampires full of blood;
> Their shrouds are bloody and their lips are wet
> (*VP* 483, ll. 3–6)

– just as the poet's heroic stand-in for the last time 'strode among the dead' and 'those bird-like things' in 'Cuchulain Comforted' (*VP* 634–5).

Present sensibilities rarely fail to perceive the depravity in such imagery, but so, too, must one attempt to understand Yeats's poetry on his terms. The dead were the 'mediatorial shades' of the Daimon, one's personal opposite (*Myth* 361); their dreams the waking state of the living and vice versa (*AV A* 246). Yeats's view of the famous or 'passionate dead' (*Myth* 360) may, of course, be regarded in part as the poet's peculiarly vivid imaginative engagement with past authors who spoke to him first in their works but who later assisted him with his own ('thus mine author sung it'). On occasion, the Renaissance instructors of Yeats's maturity seemed the agents of living poets whom he assisted with laudatory introductions. His friend and ally in the first Irish government, Oliver St John Gogarty, published verse with Yeats's press which 'discovered the rhythm of Herrick and of Fletcher, something different from himself yet akin to himself',[40] and presented Yeats with an opportunity to express his late, little-known enthusiasm for the non-dramatic poetry of George Chapman.[41] Although this excitement over *The Works of George Chapman: Poems and Minor Translations* (*YL* 370) may be read in the Rapallo Notebooks and in a very late unattributed quotation in Yeats's 'A General Introduction for my Work' (*E&I* 515), it seems not to have influenced his poetry in the way the Renaissance craftsmen did whose wares he elected to imitate between July 1927 and January 1939.[42]

Surprisingly, these masters included the English interregnum poets Marvell, Cowley, and Waller. (On the last two, see above, Ch. 4, section IV, and below, section III.) Marvell's place in the pantheon is particularly unusual for the little effort that Yeats made to read him extensively. In spite of the fact that Grierson found Marvell (after Milton) 'the strongest personality', 'the most interesting personality between Donne and Dryden, and at his very best a finer poet than either', Yeats's slight acquaintance with the seventeenth-century master of paradox remained almost entirely limited to the handful of poems presented in Grierson's anthology of 1921.[43] Of Marvell's few pieces that Yeats knew by this means, the debates between body and soul made the most significant impact on the Irish poet as he laboured, between July and December 1927, to compose one of his most famous lyrics, 'A Dialogue of Self and Soul'.[44] The adaptive complex of Yeats's lyric – including both 'A Dialogue between the Soul and Body' and 'A Dialogue between the Resolved Soul and Created Pleasure', as well as 'On a Drop of Dew' and 'The Garden' – shows that Grierson's volume was indeed Yeats's primary source, having become such not long *after* the poet's initial scribblings, as unpublished evidence shows.

Yeats's first thought was to write a dialogue after the fashion of one he had recently aborted with the adaptation of Donne in 'Chosen' and 'Parting' (see Ch. 5). His synopsis in NLI 13,590(3) outlines an exchange between two speakers, 'She' and 'He', who transform into personages identified, respectively, as 'He' and 'Me'. The monologue of 'My Self' in part II of the finished poem had yet to be conceived, even though its complaint about 'folly that man does/Or must suffer, if he woos/A proud woman not kindred of his soul' (*VP* 479, ll. 62–4) was projected by a gambit about the poet's appetite for 'things . . . Emblematical of love and war' (*VP* 477, ll. 18–19; or in the synopsis, 'neve[r] enough of women –'). The stair and the court dress were there (the latter being the most troublesome image for the poet to arrest in ensuing drafts). Sato's sword, devoid of its wrappings and splendid particularity, appears just once. Promising perhaps no more than another skirmish between irreconcilable viewpoints – as between love and war, Venus and Mars, female and male – the underlying conception of Yeats's poem changed radically for the better as he embraced both speakers, understanding that the poem's proper movement was to be that of a dialogue with himself, a 'dynamic, or essential, dialogue of the mind with itself', as Pater wrote.

Still, if the dialogue between 'My Soul' and 'My Self' were an authentic debate, the author might not have arranged in part 1 for the soul to ask all of the questions and for the self to do all of the declaiming. Rather like Marvell's witty Body in 'A Dialogue between the Soul and Body' ('O who shall me deliver whole, / From bonds of this Tyrannic Soul' – ll. 11–12), Yeats's Self poses mostly rhetorical questions for his dark auditor:

> What matter if the ditches are impure?
> What matter if I live it all once more?
> . . .
> How in the name of Heaven can [man] escape
> That defiling and disfigured shape
> The mirror of malicious eyes
> Casts upon his until at last
> He thinks that shape must be his shape?
> And what's the good of an escape
> If honour find him in the wintry blast?
>   (*VP* 478–9, ll. 42–3, 50–6)

Thus, the Self's supposed 'winning' of the debate is really a matter of engineering. Body's victory in Marvell's lyric and its defeat in the companion poem, as Pleasure, occur for the same reason. On the one hand (in 'A Dialogue between the Soul and Body'), Body gets the last word; on the other (in 'A Dialogue between the Resolved Soul and Created Pleasure'), the tactical advantage is given to Soul with a chorus added at the end to make clear the winner:

> *Triumph, triumph, victorious Soul;*
> *The World has not one Pleasure more:*
> *The rest does lie beyond the Pole,*
> *And is thine everlasting Store.*
>   (ll. 75–8)

Although Yeats threw the contest in favour of sensation, he made Soul speak of the 'hidden pole' (in manuscript, the 'pole star & the silence at the pole') where 'all thought is done' (ll. 5–7). The 'basin of the mind' to which this soul refers in its last speech (equivalent to the 'heavenly bowl' in the manuscript), the destination to which souls conventionally aspire, seems empty and cold, akin to its 'darkness'. In counterpoint to such abject purity, 'My Self' exults in the impurity, the 'ignominy' of endless cycles of change 'if it be life' (l. 58). Like Ille in 'Ego Dominus Tuus' and Robartes in 'The Phases of the Moon', the self is a cast of a divided being whose divisiveness is material to the artist who would make 'spotless' emblems of day to 'set against' the soul's 'emblematical' tower of night. That cast intentionally dominates the poem.

Keane shows how Yeats's 'interactions' with tradition contradicted most of the poem's precursors, beginning with the Neoplatonic Spenser and Macrobius,[45] whose commentary on Cicero's dialogue *Somnium Scipionis* figured largely in the culmination of the poem 'Chosen' in 1926–7 (see Ch. 5, section IV). *Contemptus mundi* (or, in Yeats, 'remorse') is rejected for joyful acceptance of 'things' as they are:

> So great a sweetness flows into the breast
> We must laugh and we must sing,
> We are blest by everything,
> Everything we look upon is blest.
> ('A Dialogue of Self and Soul', ll. 69–72)

Somewhat a surprise (given the negligible attention that Keane pays to Marvell's dialogues) is the important role that Milton's *Comus* and Marvell's 'On a Drop of Dew' are supposed to have in the cluster of images related to the 'most fecund ditch' into which life is to be tossed at the end of Yeats's poem. 'While the Yeatsian Self aligns himself with the "flowering" embroidery of "Heart's purple" and "drinks his drop" ', Keane observes, noticing the shunned 'purple flow'r' in 'On a Drop of Dew',

> the Marvellian drop longs only to return to the clear heaven from which it has fallen. Yeats is also, I suspect, echoing the famous dialogue between the chaste Lady and Comus in Milton's *Maske at Ludlow*. Milton's Neoplatonic Attendant Spirit resembles the Yeatsian Soul, while the role of Self is anticipated by Comus, the advocate of the descending path. . . . Even Self's 'frog-spawn of a blind man's ditch' – though it echoes the language of Edgar as Poor Tom in *King Lear* [see III.iv.128–39] – has its thematic original in Comus's image of bountiful nature 'thronging the seas with spawn innumerable'.[46]

Keane's suspicion that Comus somehow contributed the argumentative stance to 'My Self' should not be pushed too far. Quite likely, Lear's frog-eating, 'green mantle'-drinking 'philosopher' did have something to do with Yeats's exaggerated parody of the green world strangely celebrated by palsied Body in 'A Dialogue between the Soul and Body' ('What but a Soul could have the wit / To build me up for sin so fit?' – ll. 41–2).[47] In Grierson's edition, furthermore, the poem 'On a Drop of Dew' faces Marvell's more famous lyric 'The Garden', a work Yeats seems already to have used once (by 26 September 1926) in 'Sailing to Byzantium':

> Casting the Bodies Vest aside,
> My Soul into the boughs does glide:
> There like a Bird it sits, and sings,
> Then whets, and combs its silver Wings . . .
> ('The Garden', ll. 51–4)[48]

This 'Casting . . . aside' of the body's vestment is converted in Yeats's 'Dialogue of Self and Soul' to the 'cast[ing] out' of 'remorse' and the flowing of 'sweetness . . . into the breast' with laughter and singing (ll. 68–70). (Compare the 'fullness' that 'overflows / And falls into the basin of the mind' [ll. 33–4] with life that, in the manuscripts of 'Chosen', 'flow[s] / Into one midnight[']s hollow cup . . . too full of its own sweet to spill'.) The Platonic metaphor of the mind as ocean 'where each kind / Does streight its own resemblance find' is in Marvell's poem ('The Garden', ll. 43–4) as well as in Yeats's, both as the 'ancestral night' of the resolved soul and as the primordial 'frog-spawn' of life (in 'Sailing to Byzantium', 'The salmon-falls, the mackerel-crowded seas' of 'dying generations').

III

Yeats at his last – and, as some think, his best – often exults in the celebration of generative life. The so-called 'second puberty' of the dying man became another milestone in his long, distinguished career as a poetic craftsman.[49] But he had never been one to neglect the roots and channels by which inspiration came to flower in his poetry. Hence, to the end, his achievements may be traced to a complex of images and techniques developed over time. He appropriated from himself what became his by an adaptive process which regarded his spiritual ancestors, the 'passionate dead', as virtual collaborators. Especially apparent in his last book of poetry, the posthumous *Last Poems and Plays* (1940; Wade 203), is Yeats's deliberate reaching back to the first years following his marriage – particularly to the *anni mirabiles* 1921–5. By such means, the poet forged unity out of the discrete entity of individual poems, out of the canon as a whole, and out of the mature period during which so much of that canon was defined through revision and recision.

Between April and June 1938, Yeats in many ways reached back as he forged ahead with a poem now regarded as one of his best and most amusing philosophical poems, 'News for the Delphic Oracle'.[50] The orgiastic conception of Achilles as Peleus and Thetis couple in Porphyry's Homeric Cave of the Nymphs may be traced to Taylor's edition of Porphyry's essay on book XIII of the *Odyssey* as well as to Henry More's poem 'The Oracle'.[51] By consensus, the poem translates from the pictorial medium the subject of Poussin's painting in the National Gallery of Ireland, *The Marriage of Thetis and Peleus*, and makes use of the Renaissance statue *Dead Child on a Dolphin* by Raphael.[52] The poem is informed by Yeats's substantial, but largely post-1921, reading of the Mackenna translations of Plotinus.[53] Furthermore, while it is doubtful that Comus's assault on chastity contributed directly to 'News for the Delphic Oracle' (with his profane vision of Nature 'Thronging the Seas with spawn innumerable'), Milton did play an unexpected role in the creation of the poem, despite its very crudely comic disruption of pastoral harmony:

> Down from the mountain walls
> From where Pan's cavern is
> Intolerable music falls.
> Foul goat-head, brutal arm appear,
> Belly, shoulder, bum,
> Flash fishlike; nymphs and satyrs
> Copulate in the foam.
> (*VP* 612, ll. 30–6)

This is the sensational climax of a poem which originated on the flyleaf of *The Poetical Works of John Milton*, ed. H. C. Beeching (London: Oxford University Press, 1935):[54]

Conclusion

>   A letter to the Delphic Oracle
>   ~~Ther[e]~~
>   ~~All the~~ There all
>   [—]
>   Th[e] gold[en?] peopl[e] ~~all were ther[e]~~
>   ~~And there the golden~~ peopl[e]
>
>   amid
> lay ~~Long~~ in the silver dew
>   And   There
>   ∧ ~~H[e]re~~ ∧ great waters sigh with love
>   A[n]d th[e] wind sighed to[o]
>
>   Ther[e]   leaned &
>   sat
>   Ther[e] ∧ man picker picke Neme ∧ sighed
>   By
>   ~~For~~ Ushee[n] on the gras[s]
>   A[n]d aro[u]nd th[e?] choir of love
>   Tall Pythagoras ~~ha[vin]g stre[tched] a whil[e]~~
>   ~~Th[e] salt flak[e]s on breast~~
>   came & loo[ked] about
>   Plotina[s] cam[e] & ~~stood ther[e]~~
>   Th[e] salt flak[e]s on his bre[a]st
>
>   hav[in]g
>   And ∧ stre[t]ched & yawn[e]d a whil[e]
>   Lay sigh[ing] lik[e] the rest.
>   (NLI 13,593[34])

The source of inspiration was mainly Milton's hymn 'On the Morning of Christ's Nativity', which Yeats possessed in several other editions, including the Ricketts-decorated *Early Poems* (1896; *YL* 1319) and a special Blake-illustrated edition of the hymn (1923; *YL* 1320). His attention focused on the Renaissance poet with revision of *AV A* 205–6 for *AV B*, in which Yeats accounted for Milton's 'unreality and cold rhetoric' in terms of the synthesis of form and subject matter and the 'awaken[ed] sexual desire' evident in Italian painting between 1550 and 1650:

> The two elements [of the synthesis] have fallen apart in the hymn 'On the Morning of Christ's Nativity', the one is sacred, the other profane; [Milton's] classical mythology is an artificial ornament; whereas no great Italian artist from 1450 to the sack of Rome saw any difference between them, and when difference

came, as it did with Titian, it was God and the Angels that seemed artificial. (*AV B* 295)

The idea of union between the sacred and the profane, rather than a desire to 'supersede'[55] a poet whom Yeats thought a typical 'Platonist of his time',[56] governs Yeats's seeming parodic subversion of Milton's hymn and the implicit 'joke'[57] played in Yeats's title at the expense of Milton's nineteenth stanza:

> The Oracles are dumb,
> No voice or hideous hum
>   Runs through the arched roof in words deceiving.
> *Apollo* from his shrine
> Can no more divine,
>   With hollow shriek the steep of *Delphos* leaving.
> No nightly trance, or breathed spell,
> Inspires the pale-ey'd Priest from the prophetic cell.
>   ('On the Morning of Christ Nativity', ll. 193–200)[58]

As the climax of Yeats's poem announces, the Oracles of old are not dumb; the music of the 'Angel Choir' to which Milton added his voice gives place to the Pythagorean 'choir of love' which dominated the pre-Christian, or antithetical, era of classical Greek civilization. Also mentioned in 'The Delphic Oracle upon Plotinus' (*VP* 530–1), the 'Golden Race' which the primary, Christian era retires throughout most of Milton's poem (stanzas 14–26) includes the Irish figures Oisin and Niamh (in manuscript, 'Usheen' and 'Neme'). The languid air of Yeats's polytheistic Elysium of the 'golden codgers' ('the golden people' in draft) also originated in Milton's hymn as unexpectant 'Shepherds on the Lawn' are about to be visited by 'heavenly Pan, the Virgilian Christ'.[59]

> But peaceful was the night
> Wherein the Price of light
>   His reign of peace upon earth began:
> The Winds, with wonder whist,
> Smoothly the waters kiss't,
>   Whispering new joys to the mild Ocean,
> Who now hath quite forgot to rave,
> While Birds of Calm sit brooding on the charmed wave.

> . . .
> The Shepherds on the Lawn,
> Or ere the point of dawn,
>   Sat simply chatting in a rustic row;
> Full little thought they then,
> That the mighty *Pan*
>   Was kindly come to live with them below . . .
>
>   (ll. 61–8, 85–90)⁶⁰

The specific cues which Yeats converted to use in a most un-Miltonic (as opposed to anti-Miltonic) poem make an interesting gloss, as do marked passages in 'Il Penseroso' (ll. 65–148) and *Paradise Lost* (IV.211–94) which coincidentally employ, for different purposes, both 'Universal Pan' and 'murmuring waters'.⁶¹ Such cues, none the less, must be read in a broad context.

With its 'golden people . . . long in the silver dew', Yeats's manuscript and poem are mostly Yeatsian, reminiscent of 'The Wanderings of Oisin', book III, and the 'monstrous slumbering folk' of the Island of Forgetfulness whom Oisin joins in his hundred-year dream of the Red Branch cycle. In *The Island of Statues*, Spenserian, Miltonic, and Shelleyan influences – among others – converge in Almintor's outburst of sorrow for the usurped god of Arcadia (see Ch. 3, section IV); and a derivative response to the changing of the guard in 'On the Morning of Christ's Nativity' may be found in Yeats's early unpublished manuscripts.⁶² In 1938, the poet's admixture of Irish and classical mythology, his rendering of a Platonic *Tir na nOg* in which the dead and the immortals awaken to re-create the heroic age of which they have been dreaming, was perhaps encouraged by Milton's association of Christ and Pan and by the mythologically diverse company of deities laid to rest in the Nativity hymn. In 1925 and again in 1937, Yeats suggested that the Cave of Mithras at Capri was Porphyry's Cave and that a sacred and profane union of heaven and earth might be recognized in the cave and manger of Botticelli's *Nativity*:

> Had some Florentine Platonist read to Botticelli Porphyry upon the Cave of the Nymphs? for I seem to recognise it in that curious cave, with a thatched roof over the nearer entrance to make it resemble the conventional manger, in his 'Nativity' in the National Gallery.
>
>   (*AV B* 292; see *AV A* 202–3 and footnotes in each)

Yeats's system shows that the equilibrium that this observation verifies was approximated in sixth-century Byzantium and in Italy around 1450, more than a generation before the peak of her Renaissance. Yet, if Yeats commends this respite in the violence of the gyres for 'intellectual beauty' comparable to 'that kind of bodily beauty which Castiglione called "the spoil or monument of the victory of the soul"' (AV B 292–3), his last poems betray another sympathy. We do not desire, Yeats said, 'to touch the forms of Botticelli' (AV B 293) as we do the sexually enervating forms created under the influence of the eighth gyre during the European Renaissance proper (1550 to 1650) – or during Phases 16, 17 (Yeats's personal phase), and 18. The awakening dramatized in 'News for the Delphic Oracle' is not principally sexual, however, generative or degenerative, but symbolizes the fulfilment that Yeats expected in the modern age of 'work begun in the Renaissance' – work to reunite the mind, the soul, and the body to 'the living world outside us' – a labour of 'intensity', of 'passionate personality', and of 'personal art' objectified in terms of its 'syntax'.

As ever, philosophy, voice, and technique were integral to the mastery of the poet's craft. On 20 April 1936, Yeats wrote to his friend and fellow poet Dorothy Wellesley and roughly compared what he believed to be characteristic of their poetry with what he called the 'difficult work . . . being written now'. The authors of such work, the 'new poets', he said, were

> like goldsmiths working with glass screwed into one eye, whereas we stride ahead of the crowd, its swordsmen, its jugglers, looking to right & left. 'To right and left' by which I mean that we need like Milton, Shakespeare, Shelley, vast sentiments, generalizations supported by tradition. (*LDW* 58)

This thought is perhaps not expressed as precisely as it was on later occasions. The idea that his traditional path of 'naturalness & swiftness' differed from that of most of his younger colleagues surfaced again, with greater flippancy, in the Preface to his translation (with Shree Purohit Swami) of *The Ten Principal Upanishads* (1937; *Wade* 251). Pound and Eliot, with a fictitious 'Henry Airbubble', were on one road; Yeats and the Swami were on another, availing 'to some young man seeking, like Shakespeare, Dante, Milton, vast sentiments and generalisations, the oldest philosophical compositions of the world, compositions, not writings, for they were sung long before they were written down' (p. 10).

Those 'vast sentiments and generalisations' seem interchangeable with the 'phantasmagoria' that takes possession of 'the bundle of accident and incoherence that sits down to breakfast' in the person of the poet when he would be Shakespeare, Dante, Milton, Raleigh, Byron, or Shelley (E&I 509).[63] When Yeats wrote this in 1937, in 'A General Introduction for my Work', it was his 'First Principle'. 'A wise man seeks in Self', he said, quoting from the Chandogya Upanishad, 'those that are alive and those that are dead and gets what the world cannot give.' 'Self-possessed in self-surrender', he held that the natural 'contrapuntal structure' of English rhythm combined past and present moments in the 'passionate syntax' of ordinary speech (E&I 524). Shakespeare's tragic characters conveyed 'through the metaphorical patterns of their speech' visions that they beheld as they met their doom. (Shakespearean protagonists, particularly Hamlet and Lear, abound in Yeats's last poems, among the Jacobean voices.[64]) Yeats's emotion or passion was 'committed' to the substantially Spenserian lot of 'shepherds, herdsmen, camel-drivers, learned men', and to 'Milton's or Shelley's Platonist, that tower Palmer drew' (E&I 522). The first line of *Paradise Lost* proved that poetic rhythm, loosened under the influence of 'passionate prose', was nevertheless infused with the 'ghostly' pentameter voice, the 'unconscious norm' of the street singer (E&I 524).[65]

In a series of diary entries made in April 1921, Yeats brought to a focus his thoughts on the connection between personal expression and 'passionate syntax'.[66] Of interest here is the distinction he made between Milton and Dante, religious poets who stood on the near and far sides of the Renaissance:

> We tolerate, or enjoy, an artificial syntax and a rhythm which is neither speech nor anything suggesting song because our thought is artificial. Milton began it by bringing into English literature a means of thought 'to justify the ways of God to man' which was believed to have value apart from its value as dramatization. So Dante when he is not dramatizing some lost or suffering soul gives us an emotion of personal ecstasy. His *Paradiso* is a mystic vision, an exultation. He writes it all for that ecstasy itself, not for the edification of others. Milton brought the mischief from Rome which systematized what had been natural impulse in

Greece, and he thought more of the state than he thought of Paradise. . . . it goes on to our day in Academy pictures, also popular facile beauty. (NLI 13,576)

The vision of history here is similar to that depicted in an earlier diary, published in *Estrangement*, in which classical morality is said to have passed from Milton to Arnold while becoming 'more formal and empty', more or less 'as classical forms [had] passed on from Raphael to the Academicians' (*Au* 490; see also above, Ch. 2, sections I and III). In the 1920s and again in 1937, in part because of Yeats's active role in Ireland's suit to secure the Hugh Lane pictures for Dublin's Municipal Gallery, pictures and picture galleries were much on Yeats's mind. Spenser's 'spectral' procession in the 'Mutabilitie' cantos and elsewhere and Yeats's own review of history as if he were examining a succession of pictures in a gallery converged in the observation that the English Renaissance ended up rather like one of Van Dyck's 'noble ineffectual' faces, that Titianesque 'beauty like the burning sun' had declined to 'certain recognised forms of the picturesque constantly repeated, . . . the same pose or grouping . . . passing from picture to picture' (*AV B* 295).

The presence of Spenser in the mind of Yeats in old age is conspicuous in the one poem of the Yeats canon which most acknowledges the elder: 'The Municipal Gallery Re-visited' (*VP* 601–4).[67] That the poetic 'father' of Milton exercised such influence so late in Yeats's life demonstrates how the Irish poet, although liberating neither of these Renaissance writers from the cycle of declension and renewal described in *A Vision*, still believed it possible for modern poets to profit from Spenser's example.[68] A note in Lady Gregory's hand, written sometime before her death in 1932, compared Dante and Spenser ('the greatest of Allegorical poets that have written in English') and lent its verso, between 1936 and 1938, to a purported fragment of Yeats's poem 'The Wild Old Wicked Man' (*VP* 587–90).[69] If those thoughts on Spenser and his 'allegorical predecessors' Langland, Gascoigne, and Henryson had anything to do with the coarse old beggarman of that poem, as seems doubtful, a definite connection exists in the sixth stanza of 'The Municipal Gallery Re-visited' and at other points in the unpublished manuscripts. Somewhat surprisingly, considering Yeats's infrequent (or largely unacknowledged) use of Spenser after the turn of the century, the Renaissance poet was made to

Conclusion

stand in the spotlight beside Yeats, Synge, and Lady Gregory, and even, for an instant, displaced Lady Gregory in the manuscript (i.e. at NLI 13,593[29], L9r). Indeed, just beyond the near-quotation of the preceding stanza, Spenser presides over a metaphor drawn from *The Faerie Queene* (II.xi.45–6), the allegorical wrestling-bout between Arthur/Hercules and Maleger/Antaeus:

> All that we did, all that we said or sang
> Must come from contact with the soil, from that
> Contact everything Anteaus-like grew strong.
> (*PNE* 321, ll. 42–4)

(See L7v–11r in which we witness imagination grow strong as 'fabulous' becomes 'fabled', then 'an old fable showed', and 'like Anteus [sic]' becomes 'Antaeus-like'.)

Again, the power of language rests in natural speech, the vehicle by which occult images from the *Anima Mundi* rise to expression by the mediation of intelligence most 'rooted' to the soil: 'Dream of the noble and the beggarman' (l. 47). By the poem's fifth stanza, Spenser emerges as 'Master of the common tongue' (in L8r, 7v, 9r, and 8v), although not the only English Renaissance author Yeats called to mind as he began to compose this not-always-hortatory group elegy to go with a speech read in politically mixed company before members of the Irish Academy of Letters. Spenser provided inspiration for perhaps only that portion of the poem which paid quaint tribute to Lady Gregory ('My medieval knees lack health until they bend') and Synge ('that rooted man'). The best commentary on the poem, regrettably, has been content to work almost exclusively with its pictorial stratum.[70] In effecting closure for the present study, this peculiarly synoptical elegy, rooted so in Elizabethan and mid-seventeenth-century poetic tradition, testifies that such influences were impressed on Yeats's work to the very end.

Parkinson finds in 'The Municipal Gallery Re-visited' a 'sense of quotation' akin to Eliot's 'pedantry' and criticizes the poem for merely 'certif[ying] meanings already habitual' and for 'playing upon agreements already established with the audience' (*YSC&LP*, II, 170–1). Such criticism has real merit when applied to the embarrassingly unfit 'Dedication' affixed to the poem in its first printing, *A Speech and Two Poems* (*Wade* 193; see *PNE*, poem A118). This uninspiring piece of flattery was intended as a gesture of gratitude for an endowment received from 'certain wealthy Irish Americans' and never circulated except in a rare private edition of seventy copies. The more significant poem to which it was attached, as Yeats predicted in his speech while the latter poem was still 'forming in [his] head', may fail to achieve exactly what he first set out to accomplish: to write a poem on 'Ireland not as she is displayed in guidebook or history, but, Ireland seen because of the magnificent vitality of her painters, in the glory of her passions' (p. 5).[71] At present, most Yeatsians would justifiably argue that what he in fact achieved was no less than a tribute to himself and his friends:

> come to this hallowed place
> Where my friends' portraits hang and look thereon;
> Ireland's history in their lineaments trace;
> Think where man's glory most begins and ends
> And say my glory was I had such friends.
>
> (*PNE* 321, ll. 51–5)

Certainly, the Cavalier's high regard for friendship, the Jonsonian respect for decorum, self-control, 'true-filled'-yet-magnificent lines are evident in the poem, which, as of 5 September 1937, the poet 'like[d] exceedingly' as 'perhaps the best poem I have written for some years' (*L* 897). The stanza (*ottava rima*) derived from Byron, whom Yeats thought 'masculine and passionate' like Donne – a poet with 'natural momentum in the syntax', or such 'passionate syntax' as resided beneath the surface of nearly all Elizabethan and Jacobean lyrics (*L* 709–10; see Ch. 5, section III).

Critics might stress more than they do, though, the acrimonious political atmosphere which dominates the first such stanza of the poem. Indeed, actual controversy and differences of opinion turn up in press reports of the ceremony which occasioned Yeats's speech and the anticipated poems – both the good one and the embarrassing one. Some most un-Yeatsian post-revolutionary chest-thumping over the comparative patriotism of rich businessmen (specifically, 'licensed vintners') and 'Fenians in practice' such as Mr Yeats became an issue during that officious ritual, and the toasts in particular took an argumentative turn.[72] Given this reality, it would not be too surprising if the poet made at least indirect use of a satiric sub-genre which he knew through Andrew Marvell ('The Gallery' was one of the poems Yeats studied in the

Grierson anthology *Metaphysical Lyrics*) and through Edmund Waller, of whose work he owned a copy of the *Poems* edited by G. T. Drury (London: Lawrence and Bullen, 1893; *YL1920* 289). For wit, Marvell imagined his soul 'Compos'd into one Gallery' decked with 'great *Arras*-hangings, made / Of various Faces' ('The Gallery', ll. 1–5). For compliment (and Yeats surely took notice of Waller's several Penshurst poems), Waller fancifully designed his poem 'Instructions to a Painter' to depict and so to glorify, as in a painting, the exploits of the king's navy. In bestowing agency to the painters, seemingly, Waller's miniature epic unintentionally gave rise to parody in a lively series of anti-heroic painter poems, including Marvell's lampoon on the portrait-sitting of 'our Lady State', 'The Last Instructions to a Painter'.[73]

Ut pictura poesis was a commonplace dynamic of English Renaissance writers in general, and particularly strong in the Elizabethans Spenser and Donne, as Yeats understood.[74] The initial stanza of 'The Municipal Gallery Re-visited', even in its finished state, betrays a considerable tension between the heroic and the anti-heroic. The rush of images coalesces on the infamous Roger Casement trial, on the notorious Arthur Griffith 'staring in hysterical pride' (a reprise of Yeats's satirical assault against 'Griffith and his like' in the *Playboy* epigram; see *L* 525 and Ch. 1, section IV), and on 'Kevin O'Higgins' countenance that wears / A gentle questioning look that cannot hide / A soul incapable of remorse or rest' (*PNE* 319, ll. 4–7). In manuscript, O'Higgins's eyes were set 'upon what strange horizon', 'upon what death & birth'. He is 'that guilty remorseless man' whom Yeats at first associates with a studio sitting which, later in the composition, gives place to Lady Beresford's (in L3v–5r). After interjecting allusions to two additional paintings (on L5r), the poet produces an inversion of the refrains from his two best-known political poems, 'September 1913' and 'Easter 1916' – an inversion which is more telling in draft than in the finished poem:

>   Not here, not here,
>   ~~This is not~~, I say
>   an I
>   The dead Ireland of my youth but Ireland
>   ~~In the glory of her passion~~
>   ~~As~~
>   The poets have imagined, terrible & gay –

If Yeats 'said' this – and he may not actually have done so, since many of his first thoughts for the poem were adaptations of his speech of 17 August 1937 (on L1r and 4r) – he would recall that it was undermined in public by 'Lynn Doyle' Montgomery's comment that 'a lot of "bosh" was talked about the glory of the blood spilt for Ireland' (*The Irish Independent*, 18 Aug. 1937, p. 110). Yeats, of course, more than half regretted that 'Romantic Ireland' was 'dead and gone', buried with the Fenian John O'Leary. Yet, instead of being a repudiation of 'Romantic Ireland' as 'dead Ireland of my youth', the poet's assertion in 1937 was more likely a gesture of self-parody in light of the poem's initial stream of unpleasant events and personalities (the ambush in l. 2, the Casement trial, and Griffith and O'Higgins in ll. 3–5).

Juxtaposed to Ireland's 'terrible beauty' (the oxymoronic epithet coined in 'Easter 1916'), the sight of Lady Beresford, 'Beautiful and gentle in her Venetian way', overwhelms the poet with emotion. At this point, the poem becomes more personal, more opposed to the disruptive agents and events carried in the opening series of pictures, more directed toward the 'permanent or impermanent images' which several portraits in turn represent. Their arrangement is deliberate and progressive, like a Spenserian procession. Portraits of Robert Gregory and Hugh Lane, Lady Gregory's nephew, had both been the subjects of Yeats's Renaissance adaptation before (respectively, in the two elegies to the Sidneyan hero and in the subscription poem, 'To a Wealthy Man . . .'; see Ch. 4, section IV). Lane's patronage of the Dublin Municipal Gallery itself could hardly escape notice; hence his generosity was rewarded with a title summoned from the Dedication to Shakespeare's *Sonnets*, a work that Yeats was rereading at the time (see *LDW* 123–4 and Ch. 3, section I). The '"onlie begetter" of all these' (i.e. Lane's paintings) compares with Thomas Thorpe's well-known inscription to 'Mr W. H.', 'the onlie begetter of these ensuing sonnets' (see *NCom* 400).[75] The painter's wife, Hazel Lavery, came to mind not only because Yeats was confronted by her portrait, but because of her dignity in 'living and dying' and because of her important place beside husband and family (in manuscript, 'I think of her by the head of his [Sir John Lavery's] table'). This ushers in two full stanzas devoted to Lady Gregory – to her rectitude as a model of 'Approved patterns of women or of men' and to Coole, 'where / Honour had lived so long' and where in 'childless' youth he had thought his children were to find 'Deep-rooted things' (L1v and 7r–8r). As Finneran points out,[76] the invocation of Spenser which immediately follows tips us off to one of Yeats's underlying intentions in writing the poem.

Better still, the initial scribblings in pencil (L1v–3r) hint of what the poem's rudiments consisted. The lyric was to focus on the original Abbey Theatre principals (Frank Fay got cut out), or in practice the founding directors – Yeats, Lady Gregory, and John Synge. Since the last two were dead, the poet, nearing death himself (an issue on L1r and 4r), envisioned the poem as a means of 'restoring' himself to his friends. The synopsis that he wrote for a single projected 'poem to selebrities [sic]' was divided into two movements, and only the second, as executed from 'prose notes' over a period of ten days (*L* 898), seized his imagination. Between notes on Lady Gregory and Synge, Yeats jotted carelessly the words 'on its health [probably a reference to Coole; see the fifth stanza] – I think of the phrase in Muiopotmos re lairs the fox has looked[?] out of their windows'. In the final version of the poem, this vague recollection of a homely figure of speech from Spenser's *The Ruines of Time*, ll. 216–17 ('He now is gone, the whiles the fox is crept/Into the hole, the which the badger swept') became a truncated 'No fox can foul the lair the badger swept' (*PNE* 321, l. 39). Although manuscripts show Yeats struggling with the business of documenting this allusion in the next stanza (by making it seem, at first, a quotation but simultaneously withholding the identity of his source), we may suppose that he looked no further than his own selected edition of *Poems of Spenser* (1906; *Wade* 235) – on p. 72, under the caption 'Courtiers and Great Men/The Death of the Earl of Leicester', which drew the following comment in Yeats's Introduction:

> the lamentation over the Earl of Leicester's death is more than a conventional Ode to a dead patron. . . . At the end of a long beautiful passage he [that is, Spenser] laments that unworthy men should be in the dead Earl's place, and compares them to the fox – an unclean feeder – hiding in the lair 'the badger swept'. (*E&I* 359–60)

Implicit, then, is Yeats's intention to memorialize his friends, and himself by association, so they may forgo the fate of Leicester – of being merely replaced and forgotten in the scheme of things. The impulse to make monuments or to erect tombs is recurrent in

Yeats's last phase. Perhaps his most interesting accomplishment here was to conclude, in some sense, where he began. The generally complicated nature of the adaptive complex – by which writers distort and modify the stuff of originals into new originals – is confirmed by a particularly characteristic adaptive habit: the erstwhile student and editor of Spenser must first 'own' what he will permit himself to expropriate. He alters even his most direct borrowing from the 'Master' by a curious act of compression (the reduction of two lines to one), intensifying in the process the effect of the original by turning to himself as mediator – that is, to his own words of thirty-five years before. As this study has occasionally been able to demonstrate, Yeats's characteristic approach to his craft involved an intuitive dependence on his own faculties while those channels were open to the advice of his predecessors. He grew as a poet as he profited from their example and made his own mark by 're-inventing', as Vendler claims, 'every traditional form he touched'.[77]

As manuscript evidence permits one to see, Yeats's genius was his ability to fashion in 'human words' (the crux of the last stanza, in VP 603) an artistic synthesis of form and content derived from multiple sources but rarely drawn, unadulteratedly, from books. Thus, in 'The Municipal Gallery Re-visited', English Renaissance literature and modern Irish history make an interesting union in a literally spectacular collision of 'old' convention and 'revolutionary' insight. Yeats's 'great pictured song' about Ireland, as he called it in his address to the Irish Academy, seems somehow unimaginable without his making use of an Elizabethan authority or two. Indeed, like most works examined in this study, the poem offers a veritable host of such possibilities.

Notes

CHAPTER 1 TRADITION, 'IMITATION', AND THE SYNTHESIS OF CONTENT AND FORM

1. Roger Ascham, *The Scholemaster* (London, 1570; facsimile repr. Menston, Yorks: Scholar Press, 1967) bk II, fo. 47r; also see *The Schoolmaster (1570)*, ed. Lawrence V. Ryan (Ithaca, NY: Cornell University Press, 1967) bk II, p. 117, where the Latin is translated as follows: 'Similar treatment of dissimilar matter and also dissimilar treatment of similar matter.'
2. First published by C. G. Martin, in 'W. B. Yeats: an Unpublished Letter', *Notes and Queries*, n.s. 5 (1958) 260–1. Recipient unknown.
3. Sir Philip Sidney, *Defence of Poesy*, ed. Dorothy M. Macardle (London: Macmillan, 1959) p. 3.
4. See Vivian Mercier, *The Irish Comic Tradition* (London: Oxford University Press, 1962) p. 107; and Dudley Young, *Out of Ireland: The Poetry of W. B. Yeats* (1975; repr. Dingle, Co. Kerry: Brandon, 1982), on Yeats's revival of the Gaelic bard. Young contrasts a sceptical Shakespeare, the 'touchstone of sanity for the English mind', with Yeats, who is distinguished by his faith in magic.
5. See A. Norman Jeffares and A. S. Knowland, *A Commentary on the Collected Plays of W. B. Yeats* (Stanford, Calif.: Stanford University Press, 1975) p. 43, where Lady Wilde's translation of the tale is reprinted, a version that, unlike Yeats's tragedy, reconciled Seanchan, the *Ard-File* (Chief Poet of Ireland) and Guaire, the King of the Gort Cats.
6. The publication dates do not always reflect the period during which Yeats was occupied with a particular play. For instance, *The Shadowy Waters* was composed and rewritten repeatedly in a number of manuscripts dating from 1883 to 1899, before the first printing in 1900. See Michael Sidnell, George Mayhew, and David R. Clark (eds), *Druid Craft: the Writing of 'The Shadowy Waters'* (London: Oxford University Press, 1972). Jeffares and Knowland (*Commentary on the Collected Plays*, p. 124) point out that Yeats first conceived of *The Hour Glass* in 1902 and that its source was, as with *The King's Threshold*, in Lady Wilde's *Ancient Legends, Mystic Charms, and Superstitions of Ireland*. See also Curtis Bradford's *W. B. Yeats: The Writing of 'The Player Queen'* (Dekalb: Northern Illinois University Press, 1977).
7. *Ben Jonson*, ed. C. H. Herford and Percy and Evelyn Simpson, 11 vols (Oxford: Clarendon Press, 1925–51) VIII: *The Poems, the Prose Works*, pp. 638–9.
8. The letter (in NLI 13,663) is substantially quoted by Edd W. and Aileen

219

W. Parks in their study *Thomas MacDonagh: The Man, the Patriot, the Writer* (Athens, Ga: University of Georgia Press, 1967) p. 7. Much less is provided by Johann A. Norstedt, in *Thomas MacDonagh: A Critical Biography* (Charlottesville: University Press of Virginia, 1980) pp. 31–2, and in his 'The Gift of Reputation: Yeats and MacDonagh', *Éire–Ireland* 29, no. 3 (1984) 136–7. Though Yeats's letter bears only the heading 'Nassau Hotel/Dublin/Nov. 9', speculation about the year in which it was written (1902) can be laid to rest by comparing its discussion over particulars of production with cost estimates provided by local printers in January 1902, and with a letter from Sealy, Bryers and Walker (Yeats's own first publisher, mentioned in his letter) about revised proofs of MacDonagh's book. With the others, this last letter ('22 Decb. 1902') is in NLI 10,854(1).

9. Full citations for MacDonagh's metrical studies are, in order cited above, *Thomas Campion and the Art of English Poetry* (Dublin: Hodges, Figgis, 1913) and *Literature in Ireland* (Dublin: Talbot, 1916). See also Parkinson (*YSC&LP* II, 189–94) and Hone (*WBY* 318).

10. Ironically, the young poet, scholar and political martyr lived long enough to suppress these early lyrics from his *Poetical Works* (1916). Yeats eulogized him, of course, in 'Easter 1916' and 'Sixteen Dead Men'.

11. Hone (*WBY* 450) dates the composition from 1931, not 1930, and is undoubtedly right. The occasion giving rise to the 'letter' was a search for a school for young Michael in Dublin after nearly two years' residence in Rapallo, Italy (early 1929 to late 1930).

12. Partial accounts of the genesis of this poem are given by Bradford (*YW* 5–11), by Parkinson (*YSC&LP* II, 92–113), and by Jacqueline Genet, in *William Butler Yeats: les fondements et l'évolution de la création poétique* (Villeneuve-d'Ascq: Université de Lille III, 1976) pp. 552–3 and 703.

13. That Yeats knew Milton's tractate *Of Education* is probable. His Senate speeches opposing government censorship and copyright restraints suggest familiarity with the *Areopagitica*, and his impassioned speech opposing the Catholic majority's bill on divorce makes issue of Milton's tracts on that subject. See Ch. 6, section 1; and *SS* 92, 100 and 102.

14. *Ben Jonson*, VIII, 637, 639 (in *Discoveries*). For more on Jonson's views on imitation, see Richard S. Peterson's *Imitation and Praise in the Poems of Ben Jonson* (New Haven, Conn., and London: University Press, 1981).

15. Sidney's apologia is most akin to Jonson's critical line, as was Puttenham's *The Art of English Poesy* (1589). Yeats knew Shelley's *Defence of Poetry* (1823), which is informed at several points by Sidney's treatise. See *Shelley's Poetry and Prose: Authoritative Texts, Criticism*, ed. Donald H. Reiman and Sharon B. Powers (New York: Norton, 1977) pp. 478–508. Shelley, who equated the poet of imagination with the *vates* (see p. 482), was not insensitive to the Platonic concept of imitation: 'in the motions of the dance, in the melody of the song, in the combinations of language, in the series of [men's] imitations of natural objects, . . . there is a certain order or rhythm belonging to

each of these classes of mimetic representation, from which the hearer and the spectator receive an intenser and purer pleasure than from any other' (p. 481; see also pp. 486–7). Arnold was interested in human character, too, as well as in 'human actions'; hence the argument of his Preface rests conventionally on the authority of Aristotle's *Poetics*.
16. Ascham, *The Scholemaster*, bk II, fo. 48r.
17. The album is signed but not dated. In *YL Notes*, I argue for a dating around 1881 for drafts of an unpublished poem found in this album and on the back flyleaf of Yeats's copy of Tennyson's *Locksley Hall and Other Poems* (1874; *YL* 2115). This date is suggested by watermarks on a related loose sheet in the album and by a stationer's stamp on a sheet of drawing-paper. The first poems that Yeats published – all written in the shadow of Spenser – appeared in 1885 in the *Dublin University Review*, although drafted the previous year in other exercise books. Other evidence in NLI 12,161, including pastel and ink sketches by George Russell, associates the album with Yeats's time as a student at Erasmus Smith High School, Harcourt Street, Dublin (1881–3), and at the Metropolitan School of Art, Kildare Street, Dublin (1884). The 'Inscription for a christmas card', written beneath another derivative poem, 'The Dell', appears on L2r. Though much was unused, a good many of the album's leaves have been removed, presumably destroyed.
18. The woodland meeting which the last five lines of the draft depict is not *in* Spenser. Yeats probably had in mind the alliance of the Faerie Queene (here, 'mab') and Prince Arthur which was to have formed the climax of Spenser's twelfth book. Spenser discusses his stratagem in the prefatory letter (to Raleigh) affixed to his epic. See *The Works of Edmund Spenser: A Variorum Edition*, ed. Edwin Greenlaw, Charles Osgood, and Frederick Padelford, 10 vols (Baltimore: Johns Hopkins University Press, 1932–57) I, 167–70.
19. MacDonagh, *Literature in Ireland*, p. 17.
20. In *The Life of Cowley*, Johnson wrote that 'Wit' perceives unity despite extreme differences; it is a thought-process in which 'the most heterogeneous ideas are yoked by violence together'. See Samuel Johnson, *The Lives of the English Poets*, ed. George B. Hill, 3 vols (Oxford: Clarendon Press, 1905) I, 20. The underscoring of 'Genius' in my transcription might be read as a cancellation.
21. From the earliest manuscript (NLI 13,587[20]) to the corrected typescript in the Berg Collection, New York Public Library, and every version reported in *VP*, the only change in these lines was the addition of a comma in l. 46. Yeats rather spectacularly confused his speakers in the NLI manuscript. But the message itself seems always to have been clear.
22. Here I am most indebted to Frank J. Warnke's *Versions of Baroque* (New Haven, Conn., and London: Yale University Press, 1972). However, I take exception to his view that Baroque poetry 'is more specifically form-conscious than is Renaissance poetry' (p. 20). The content-orientation of most seventeenth-century verse (outside the Spenser-

ians') is antithetical to the Elizabethan commitment to form. Since both Elizabethan and seventeenth-century styles might as easily be defined in terms of form as in terms of intellectual content, the point should be that Baroque style (particularly in Metaphysical poetry) intervened between two periods of classicism – Renaissance and Augustan – and is distinguished from each of these by its very opposition to classical style and fixed forms.
23. See Morris W. Croll, *'Attic' and Baroque Prose Style* (Princeton, NJ: Princeton University Press, 1969) p. 87.
24. George Williamson, *Seventeenth Century Contexts*, rev. edn (Chicago: University of Chicago Press, 1969) p. 124.
25. Though Chapter 4 addresses Yeats's kinship to Jonson and will have more to say about both on the epigram, it is worth noting that 'Against Unworthy Praise', a companion to 'The Fascination of What's Difficult' employs the same vocabulary (see ll. 1–3, 15–17). Other signs of Jonsonian influence in *GH* occur in 'A Drinking Song', 'The Coming of Wisdom with Time', 'On hearing that the Students of our New University have joined the Agitation against Immoral Literature', 'To a Poet . . .', and 'All Things can Tempt me'. The list fails to exhaust the possibilities.
26. My transcriptions from the Journal are reconstructions based on Donoghue's directions in *Mem* 15.
27. See, for example, *Epigrammes*, XXXIX and LXI, 'On Old Colt' and 'To Foole, or Knave'. Yeats's revision shows that he was intent on adapting Jonson's idiom: 'There is something / What is it ails our colt' rings of Jonson's wit, even though, seemingly, self-effacing here.
28. *Ben Jonson*, VI, 492.
29. Yeats would have known Jonson's account of inspiration in *Timber, or Discoveries*: 'the *Poet* must bee able by nature, and instinct, to powre out the Treasure of his minde. . . . Then it riseth higher, as by a divine Instinct, when it contemnes common, and knowne conceptions. It utters somewhat above a mortall mouth. Then it gets a loft, and flies away with his Ryder. . . . This the *Poets* understood by their *Helicon, Pegasus,* or *Parnassus* . . .' (*Ben Jonson*, VIII, 637).
30. Jeffares (*NCom* 90–1) offers two sources for Yeats's carthorse image. The more interesting one is a passage from T. Sturge Moore's *Art and Life* (1910). Moore, a good friend of Yeats's, said that Swift had 'used his Pegasus for a cart-horse', that 'its [plodding] motion betrays the mettle in which it here revels'.
31. The word is untraced in Jonson's poetry.
32. See William M. Carpenter, 'The *Green Helmet* Poems and Yeats's Myth of the Renaissance', *Modern Philology*, 67, no. 1 (1969) 54–6.
33. Lady Gregory was interested in the French Renaissance as a whole, although her interest focused on Molière, whose work she translated and adapted in *The Kiltartan Molière* (Dublin: Maunsel, 1910) and elsewhere. Synge would have passed to Yeats his own enthusiasms – Villon, Rabelais, Petrarch, and Ronsard, whose example inspired 'Epitaph / After reading Ronsard's lines from Rabelais'. See Douglas Duncan, 'Synge and Jonson (with a Parenthesis on Ronsard)',

SMD 205–18.
34. Pierre de Ronsard, *Le Second Livre des Amours*, ed. Alexandre Micha (Geneva: Librairie Droz, 1951) pp. 12–13.
35. Corinna Salvadori, *Yeats and Castiglione* (Dublin: Hodges, Figgis, 1965) pp. 19–20, has pointed out that Yeats read *The Courtier* in more than one translation. See also B. Rajan, 'Yeats and the Renaissance', *Mosaic* 5, no. 4 (1972) 114; and Carpenter, who observes that '*sprezzatura* or recklessness, "the wild will that stirs desire", [is] a quality of the Renaissance personality which Yeats connects, as Castiglione did not, with the ideal artistic personality' (*Modern Philology*, 67, no. 1, p. 53).
36. See Wayne K. Chapman, 'The Annotated *Responsibilities*: Errors in the Variorum Edition and a New Reading of the Genesis of Two Poems, "On those that hated 'The Playboy of the Western World'", 1907" and "The New Faces" ', *YA* 6 (1988) 108–33, in which much of this account appears.
37. See New York Public Library (the Research Libraries), *The Dictionary Catalog of the Henry W. and Albert A. Berg Collection of English and American Literature*, IV (1969) 487.
38. The date of this letter, which Wade has given as 'Sunday [March 8, 1909]', should in fact be 'Sunday [7 March 1909]'. A corrected typescript of this letter (NLI 18,688) gives 'Eunics' as Yeats's original spelling.
39. For discussion of Ricketts' painting in light of Yeats's poem, see J. G. P. Delaney, ' "Heirs of the Great Generation": Yeats's Friendship with Charles Ricketts and Charles Shannon', *YA* 4 (1985) 60–1.
40. This letter, in its postmarked envelope, is an uncatalogued item in the Berg Collection, which has now, through recent acquisition, most of the extant correspondence between Yeats and Lady Gregory.
41. This document is now owned by the University of Texas Libraries and is part of the Yeats collection at the Harry Ransom Humanities Research Center at Austin. See Chapman, in *YA* 6 (1988) 131 n. 14.
42. 'The Theatre' has been published by Robert O'Driscoll in 'Yeats on Personality: Three Unpublished Lectures', *YT* 16–25. This and the following quotation from this lecture are from p. 17. See also Yeats's lecture of 19 December 1913, delivered at another London location and published by O'Driscoll in 'Two lectures on the Irish Theatre by W. B. Yeats' – Robert O'Driscoll (ed.), *Theatre and Nationalism in Twentieth-Century Ireland* (Toronto: University of Toronto Press, 1971) pp. 66–88, 209–12 – where another reference to Grassi's work is made in this vein (pp. 75, 210n.).
43. The play on the opening night (22 Feb. 1910, the night after *Justice* opened) was *Feudalismo*, possibly the play Yeats mentioned in his lecture.

CHAPTER 2 PROTO-MODERN POET, 1885–1910: SUMMONING THE RENAISSANCE SPIRIT WITH ARNOLD, PATER, AND JOHN BUTLER YEATS

1. *YL* 816. See T. S. Eliot, 'The Metaphysical Poets', *Selected Prose of*

T. S. Eliot (New York: Harcourt Brace Jovanovich, 1975) pp. 59–67.
2. See F. W. Bateson, 'Contributions to a Dictionary of Critical Terms: II. *Dissociation of Sensibility*', *Essays in Criticism* (Oxford), 1 (1951) 302–12; and Frank Kermode, 'Dissociation of Sensibility', *Kenyon Review*, 19 (1957) 169–94. Kermode's article, slightly revised, appears as a chapter in *RI*.
3. *Au* 490 was drawn from Yeats's Journal (*Mem* 179), entry 83, 'March 9 [1909]'. The second quotation (*E&I* 196) is from an essay dated '1895' in *Ideas of Good and Evil* (1903).
4. Eliot, *Selected Prose*, p. 64; Kermode, *RI* 138.
5. Eliot, *Selected Prose*, p. 64.
6. George Bornstein, 'Last Romantic or Last Victorian: Yeats, Tennyson, and Browning', *YA* 1 (1982) 114. See also Dwight Eddins, *Yeats: The Nineteenth Century Matrix* (University, Ala: University of Alabama Press, 1971); W. J. McCormack, *Ascendancy and Tradition in Anglo-Irish Literary History from 1789 to 1939* (Oxford: Clarendon Press, 1985) ch. 8: 'W. B. Yeats: Two Approaches'; and, to some extent, Harold Bloom, whose *Yeats* (London: Oxford University Press, 1970) represents one extreme of Yeats criticism by insisting that Yeats's lasting accomplishment is to be found in the nineteenth-century phase of his work – a phase which Bloom sees as an extension of the earlier High Romantic period of the century. Bloom's extremism is accommodated by Eddins, who attempts to marry it to the opposing view of Louis MacNeice.
7. See Ronald Schuchard, 'Yeats, Arnold, and the Morbidity of Modernism', *YAACTS* 3 (1985) 88–106.
8. Matthew Arnold, *The Complete Prose Works of Matthew Arnold*, v: '*Culture and Anarchy*' *with* '*Friendship's Garland*' *and Some Literary Essays*, ed. R. H. Super (Ann Arbor: University of Michigan Press, 1965) pp. 172, 174.
9. Just beyond the passage quoted above in *Culture and Anarchy*, Arnold writes without much conviction, 'Apparently, too, as we said of the former defeat of Hellenism, if Hellenism was defeated, this shows that Hellenism was imperfect, and that its ascendancy at that moment would not have been for the world's good'. If Hellenism *was* defeated, he concludes, the result has been 'the beginnings of confusion', 'a certain confusion and false movement, of which we are now beginning to feel, in almost every direction, the inconvenience' (*Works*, v, 174).
10. Ibid., p. 146.
11. Ibid., p. 140.
12. Ibid., p. 144.
13. Matthew Arnold, *The Complete Prose Works of Matthew Arnold*, III: *Lectures and Essays in Criticism*, ed. R. H. Super (Ann Arbor: University of Michigan Press, 1962) 353, 361. Yeats's own copy of *The Study of Celtic Literature* (London: Smith, Elder, 1891; *YL* 55) was marked and scored from his reading, perhaps as he made his study for 'The Celtic Element in Literature', the first section of which was originally published in *Cosmopolis* in June 1898. See *Wade* 46.
14. The review, entitled simply 'Spenser', first appeared in *The Times Literary Supplement*, 5, no. 251 (2 Nov 1906) 365–6. It was later reprinted

by its author, John Bailey, in *Poets and Poetry: Being Articles Reprinted from the Literary Supplement of 'The Times'* (Oxford: Clarendon Press, 1911) pp. 45–54. Not all of the review was kept – or has remained – in Yeats's album. The concluding part, or some six column-inches, is missing.

15. Yeats and Edwin Ellis had in fact devised an Irish pedigree for William Blake based on a tenuous connection claimed by Dr Charles Carter Blake of London. The 'poet' of the *Outlook* was probably familiar with some of Yeats's work reprinted in *Ideas of Good and Evil* (London: Bullen, 1903), a volume which included two essays on Blake, the one already mentioned on Shakespeare, and 'The Celtic Element in Literature'. The Blake pieces and 'The Celtic Element in Literature' first appeared in periodicals between 1896 and 1898. Undoubtedly the critic was directly ridiculing the Yeats–Ellis theory of Blake's heredity – a theory which Yeats propounded on the first page of his Introduction to *The Poems of William Blake*, ed. W. B. Yeats (London: Lawrence and Bullen, 1893). Swinburne, whose 1866 study was slighted by Yeats and Ellis in their edition of *The Works of William Blake* (London: Quaritch, 1893), derided the pair as 'some Hibernian commentator on Blake' whose racial advantage exceeded his own since he belonged to 'a race in which reason and imagination are the possibly preferable substitutes for [Celtic] fever and fancy'. Swinburne issued this caustic remark in the 1906 reprint of *William Blake: A Critical Study*; see Hazard Adams, *Blake and Yeats: The Contrary Vision* (Ithaca, NY: Cornell University Press, 1955) p. 46.

16. See Marvel Shmiefsky, *Sense at War with Soul* (The Hague: Mouton, 1972) pp. 140–1; and Ronald Schuchard, 'The Ministrel in the Theatre: Arnold, Chaucer, and Yeats's New Spiritual Democracy', *YA* 2 (1983) 4–5. Linda Dowling, arguing in *Language and Decadence in the Victorian Fin de Siècle* (Princeton, NJ: Princeton University Press, 1986) pp. 276-7, that Yeats's oral folk orientation was set in opposition to Arnold's 'culture of scholarship', adds the linguistic crisis introduced by nineteenth-century philology to the usual ones attached by historians to the Victorian age.

17. Cf. sentence 1 in Pater's 'Coleridge' essay in *Appreciations* (1889): 'Forms of intellectual and spiritual culture sometimes exercise their subtlest and most artful charm when life is already passing from them'.

18. Schuchard, in *YA* 2 (1983) 4.

19. In 'The Grey Rock', Yeats's poetic celebration of his 'tavern comrades' ('Poets with whom I learned my trade, / Companions of the Cheshire Cheese'), Yeats almost certainly made a conscious effort to adapt the Anacreonic spirit of Ben Jonson's celebrated gatherings (i.e. those featured in Jonson's own 'An Epistle Answering to One That Asked to Be Sealed of the Tribe of Ben' and in Herrick's famous ode to his voluble master of ceremonies at 'the *Sun*, / The *Dog*, the triple *Tunne*'). However, in addition to that awareness, Yeats knew that Samuel Johnson and others had been habitués of this particular old Fleet Street chop-house.

20. The editions of Pater used in this discussion are *The Renaissance: Studies in Art and Poetry – the 1893 Text*, ed. Donald L. Hill (Berkeley, Los Angeles, and London: University of California Press, 1980); *Plato and Platonism: A Series of Lectures* (London: Macmillan, 1893; YL 1538); and *Appreciations; With an Essay on Style* (London: Macmillan, 1910; repr. Oxford: Basil Blackwell, 1967).
21. F. C. McGrath, ' "Rosa Alchemica": Pater Scrutinized and Alchemized', *Yeats/Eliot Review*, 5, no. 2 (1978) 13.
22. Pater, *The Renaissance*, p. 186.
23. See F. C. McGrath, 'Heroic Aestheticism: Yeats, Pater, and the Marriage of Ireland and England', *Irish University Review*, 8 (1978) 183–4.
24. See David J. DeLaura, *Hebrew and Hellene in Victorian England: Newman, Arnold, and Pater* (Austin and London: University of Texas Press, 1969). DeLaura compares both Victorian writers, sensitive to their contradictions.
25. Pater, *The Renaissance*, p. 190. His debt was also English, of course. DeLaura closes one discussion with the following observation: 'Aestheticism, with roots in the Romantics, Ruskin, the Pre-Raphaelites, and Swinburne, found an adequate rhetoric only in Pater: the terms were in Arnold, but where they reappear, they are "the same yet different". Arnold is a father of Aestheticism but only in an oblique and problematical way' (*Hebrew and Hellene*, p. 230).
26. Lorna Sage observes that the word 'Renaissance' meant for Yeats (before its significance was 'demoted' in *A Vision*) 'several important things: the historical period, of course, but also a timeless event which had happened many times, and might be induced to happen again; and perhaps just as important – a tone of voice, an aura of assumptions, a style' – 'Hardy, Yeats and Tradition', in Malcolm Bradley and David Palmer (eds), *Victorian Poetry*, Stratford-upon-Avon Studies 15 (London: Edward Arnold, 1972) p. 269.
27. Pater, *The Renaissance*, p. xxiv.
28. Ibid., pp. 34, 37.
29. Balachandra Rajan, 'Yeats and the Renaissance', *Mosaic*, 5, no. 4 (1972) 113. See also Marjorie Reeves and Warwick Gould, *Joachim of Fiore and the Myth of the Eternal Evangel in the Nineteenth Century* (Oxford: Clarendon Press, 1987), which, tracing through its similarly difficult subject, makes cases for Pater (pp. 166–76) and Yeats (pp. 203–71) and documents Yeats's acquaintance with *The Renaissance* in its early forms.
30. The essay is appended, with a lengthy set of 'notes' and a short article called 'Witches and Wizards and Irish Folk-lore' – each of which makes some reference to Yeats's Renaissance authorities – to Lady Gregory's *Visions* (311–36). See *YL* and *YL Notes*.
31. See *YL* 1538. Yeats's scorings often mark passages or phrasings that caught his attention. Occasionally, particularly between pp. 60–4 in the section on 'Plato and the Doctrine of Number', he seems mostly attracted to the length of Pater's sentences. Several marginally scored passages are accompanied by the comment 'long'. One such passage, on pp. 67–8, bears the emphatic remark 'style!' Such evidence reflects

the long-suspected influence of Pater's prose style on Yeats. However, his interaction with this text shows that he was not in total agreement with Pater on style or on content. On p. 6 the reader penned in the margin, 'It is part of his [the young scholar's] duty to love or hate what he reads, and *form* is all *important* to this. Pater's own strain cannot be heard with indifference.' Yeats also scored and noted his disagreement with the following statement on p. 16: 'From the *lifeless* [WBY's underscoring] background of an unprogressive world – Egypt, Syria, frozen Scythia – a world in which the unconscious social aggregate had been everything, the conscious individual, his capacity and rights, almost nothing, the Greek had stepped forth, like the young prince in the fable, to set things going.' Yeats's comment to this: 'No'. A final curiosity, misread in *YL*, is a revision of Henry Vaughan's poem 'The Retreat', quoted on p. 65 of Pater's book. To Yeats's ear and perhaps according to how he would interpret the poem, the second line of the couplet 'And when this dust falls to the urn/In that state I came return' should have been 'To that state whence I came I turn'.

32. Pater, *Plato and Platonism*, p. 61.
33. Ibid., pp. 63–4.
34. Leonard E. Nathan, *The Tragic Drama of William Butler Yeats* (New York: Columbia University Press, 1965) pp. 103–8, and 'W. B. Yeats's Experiments with an Influence', *Victorian Studies*, 6, no. 1 (1962) 66–74; McGrath, in *Irish University Review*, 8, and 'Paterian Aesthetics in Yeats's Drama', *Comparative Drama*, 13 (1979) 33–48; and Desai, *YShak* 32–4.
35. Pater, *Appreciations*, p. 190.
36. Ibid., pp. 199–200.
37. J. B. Yeats's epistolary talents were celebrated in his lifetime by two volumes printed by the Cuala Press: *Passages from the Letters of John Butler Yeats: Selected by Ezra Pound* (1917) and *Further Letters of John Butler Yeats: Selected by Lennox Robinson* (1920). W. B. Yeats officiated as general editor for his sisters' press, and the letters used in both selections were written to him. A third volume was later produced by the resurrected Cuala Press in 1972, and edited by William J. Murphy; this was called *Letters from Bedford Park*. Other relevant collections of correspondence are *CL1, L, LJBY, LTWBY, TB, The Letters of John Quinn to William Butler Yeats*, ed. Alan Himber (Ann Arbor, Mich.: University of Michigan Research Press, 1983). To complement his son's collections of memoirs and essays, we have only J. B. Yeats's *Early Memories: Some Chapters of Autobiography* (Dublin: Cuala Press, 1923), *Essays: Irish and American* (1919: repr. Freeport, NY: Books for Libraries Press, 1969), and three volumes of unpublished memoirs. So far the best accounts of the father–son relationship are in Hone's *WBY*; in William Murphy's *Prodigal Father* (Ithaca, NY, and London: Cornell University Press, 1978), and 'Father and Son: The Early Education of William Butler Yeats', *Review of English Literature* (Leeds), 8, no. 4 (1967) 75–96; in Jeffares' *YM&P*, and his 'John Butler Yeats', in A. Norman Jeffares and K. G. W. Cross (eds), *In Excited Reverie* (New York:

Macmillan, 1965); and in Ellmann's *YM&M*.
38. John Eglinton (William Kirkpatrick Magee), 'Yeats at the High School', *Erasmian* (Dublin), 30 (1939) 11; repr. in E. H. Mikhail (ed.), *W. B. Yeats: Interviews and Recollections* (London: Macmillan, 1977) I, 3. See also Murphy, in *Review of English Literature*, 8, no. 4, pp. 90–1.
39. The unpublished source is cited as '*Memoirs*, I, f. 62' by Murphy (ibid., p. 91). Cf. *Au* 23, which employs the sea-cliff trope differently, in eulogy: 'We [the Yeatses] have ideas and no passions, but by marriage with a Pollexfen we have given a tongue to the sea cliffs.'
40. Of those mentioned, only Lyster's role is unaccounted for in *Au*. As the editors observer in *UP2*, Lyster was the 'Quaker librarian', the director of the National Library of Ireland, cited in Joyce's *Ulysses*. According to Yeats (who chaired the Lyster Memorial Committee as Senator and wrote, in 1926, a brief tribute), Lyster's was a guiding hand in Yeats's first indisputably published work of 1885. See NLI 10,543; and *UP2* 307n. and 470–2. For an interesting discussion on Yeats and Dowden and the use Yeats made of the latter in his defence of Shelley against Arnold's critical stance, see Bornstein, *Y&Shel* 4–5.
41. See Jeffares, in Jeffares and Cross, *In Excited Reverie*, p. 30. In London, J. B. Yeats and three friends – Edwin Ellis, George Wilson, and the Pre-Raphaelite water-colourist J. T. Nettleship – formed their own 'Brotherhood', a group known to Rossetti.
42. Joseph Ronsley's transcription of Yeats's lecture notes (*YT* 60–81) shows that the stenographer's version, quoted above, praised Milton most. In two other versions, Yeats asserted only that the 'formal lofty moral attitude . . . was a passion in Milton' (*YT* 72) or largely copied the Journal entry (cancelled on *YT* 70), the less-than-enthusiastic endorsement published in *Estrangement* (1926).
43. J. B. Yeats, *Early Memories*, p. 37.
44. The phrase 'rockie face' appears in Jonson's 'My Picture Left in Scotland', which Yeats knew from *The Under-wood* (IX) or from *Conversations with William Drummond of Hawthornden*, where it is one of two poems quoted in full. J. R. Mulryne (in 'The "Last Poems" ', *HonGuest* 125–6) first noted Jonson's part in what is now generally regarded as a compound mask.
45. The phrase is Arnold Stein's in 'Yeats: A Study in Recklessness', *Sewanee Review*, 57 (1949) 615.
46. T. McAlindon, 'Yeats and the English Renaissance', *PMLA*, 82 (1967) 157–69.
47. In his 'Memorial to the Late T. W. Lyster' (*UP2* 471), Yeats asserted that as 'a very young man' he had read 'Elizabethan literature . . . constantly under [Lyster's] guidance' and that *The Island of Statues*, the first published work that Yeats ever acknowledged, 'owed much to [Lyster's] correction'. 'When a young man writes his first poem', Yeats observed, 'there will often be a good line followed by a bad line, and he should always go to a scholar to be advised; and MR LYSTER did that for me. I used to go to his house, and he would go over the manuscript of my play with me, and help me to correct the bad lines.'

48. Cf. Marion Witt's transcription of the manuscript in 'Yeats's "The Song of the Happy Shepherd" ', *Philological Quarterly*, 32, no. 1 (1953) 1–8. Witt's reading is generally reliable, though she misplaces the few lines drafted on fo. 69v (revisions made beside the text on fo. 70r), inserting them too early, as the 1885 printing makes clear.
49. J. B. Yeats, *Essays*, p. 18.
50. J. B. Yeats once gave his schoolboy son an assignment to write an essay on the Shakespearean motto, 'To thine own self be true . . .'. The occasion is reported in *Au* 58. Witt (in *Philological Quarterly*, 32, no. 1, p. 4) was probably the first to comment on the debt to Sidney. What I find most interesting is the censure of three lines in manuscript. If Yeats failed to perceive the problem of controlling the accidentals of these lines, Lyster, to be sure, might have suggested the amputation and transplant to spare the poet the consequences of being rhetorically bold with the Church and with Academia, an institution to which Lyster belonged.
51. See Jeffares, *NCom* 3–5. 'I-wis', a form of 'ywis' (or 'wist'), almost certainly derived from Spenser.
52. See Judith Anne Colbert, 'The Passionate Artifice: Yeats and the Later Renaissance' (unpublished dissertation, University of Western Ontario, 1978) pp. 333–9. A general reading of Yeats's companion poems is given in Frank Murphy's *Yeats's Early Poetry* (Baton Rouge: Louisiana State University Press, 1975) pp. 11–19, but without reference to Milton. Yeats's acquaintance with 'L'Allegro' is later attested to by ll. 78–80, quoted in *Mem* 78: 'more than once as I looked over to the grey wall and roof [of Lissadell] I repeated to myself Milton's lines:/["]Bossomed deep [Yeats's substitution for "high"] in tufted trees, / Where perhaps some beauty lies, / The cynosure of neighboring eyes["]'.
53. Jeffares (*NCom* 4–5) and Colbert ('Passionate Artifice', p. 336) trace 'optic glass' to Milton. Possibly Yeats, who was a young *reader* as well as a young poet in 1885, was aided by an anthology such as Leigh Hunt's popular *Imagination and Fancy; or Selections from the English Poets, Illustrative of those first Requisites of their Art; with Markings of the Best Passages* . . . (London: Smith, Elder, 1844), which is still in the National Library of Ireland. Hunt's book set in italics precisely those lines just quoted. The selections from Milton included set-pieces on Satan, 'L'Allegro', 'Il Penseroso', 'Lycidas', and excerpts from *Comus*.
54. Unpublished letter; see Jeffares, *YM&P* 167.

CHAPTER 3   YEATS AND SPENSER: FORM, PHILOSOPHY, AND PICTORIALISM, 1881–1902

1. Bornstein's *Y&Shel* tends to ignore the equal credit that Yeats almost always gave to Spenser whenever he cited Shelley and others who mattered to him at this early stage in his career. Bornstein's most recent works on the drafts of Yeats's poetry up to 1886 address this omission.

2. The term has very different meaning when employed by Frank Lentricchia, after the philosopher Charles Sanders Peirce. In *After the New Criticism* (Chicago: University of Chicago Press, 1980) p. 338, for example, it refers to the 'ephebe–precursor' relationship in the analysis of the Bloomian 'anxiety principle'. This is quite different from plain use of the word 'dyad' to represent the tendency to find in the same works of Yeats bipartite (often somewhat opposed) sources of influence.
3. Micheál Ó hAodha, 'When Was Yeats First Published?', *Irish Times*, 5 June 1965, p. 10; rpt. in *Éire–Ireland*, 2, no. 2 (1967) 67–71. Richard J. Finneran, in 'Appendix A: Poems by "Y." in *Hibernia*, 1882–83', *Editing Yeats's Poems* (London: Macmillan, 1983) pp. 121–8, finds Ó hAodha's circumstantial evidence compelling enough to reprint all eleven poems, in spite of some doubts abouts the attribution of authorship.
4. Cf. *CL1* 7, which has been adapted in one particular: cancellation of 'soul' is indicated by a line through the word rather than by angle brackets.
5. See Hone, *WBY* 45, 48–9; Jeffares, *YM&P* 23; and especially William Murphy, *Prodigal Father* (Ithaca, NY, and London: Cornell University Press, 1978) pp. 127–30. Particularly well known are Yeats's contacts with Dowden, beginning in 1884. However, their acquaintance began in late autumn 1881, following the Yeatses' move to Howth and the opening of J. B. Yeats's York Street studio in Dublin. See also Maurice Elliott, 'Yeats and the Professors', *Ariel* 3, no. 3 (1972) 5–30.
6. Cf. Murphy, *Prodigal Father*, p. 127.
7. The fifth version, or printer's copy, of *The Island of Statues* features frequent entries in another hand. These entries, usually corrections of spelling, are probably Lyster's, since at two points in the manuscript (at the end of Act I, scene i, and the end of the play) the printer is directed to send proofs to Yeats and to Lyster at their respective home addresses. In the first instance, the corrections were apparently made *only* by Lyster, according to a note entered by one signing himself 'W. Frazer'. This very interesting textual evidence may be read in *The Early Poetry*, I: *'Mosada' and 'The Island of Statues' Manuscript Materials*, ed. George Bornstein (Ithaca, NY, and London: Cornell University Press, 1987) pp. 378–438.
8. Letter of 26 Aug 1886, Edward Dowden to John Todhunter, as quoted in Murphy, *Prodigal Father*, p. 144.
9. Quoted in Edward Dowden, *Letters of Edward Dowden and his Correspondents*, ed. Elizabeth D. and Hilda M. Dowden (London: Dent; New York: Dutton, 1914) p. 108.
10. Edmund Spenser, *The Complete Works in Verse and Prose of Edmund Spenser*, ed. Alexander B. Grosart, 10 vols (London: The Spenser Society, 1882–4). Dowden contributed to vol. I (pp. 304–39) the essay 'Spenser, The Poet and Teacher', repr. in *Transcripts and Studies* (London: Paul, 1887) pp. 268–304.
11. Dowden, *Letters*, pp. 109–10.
12. See Charles Johnston, 'Yeats in the Making' and 'Personal Impressions of W. B. Yeats', repr. in E. H. Mikhail (ed.), *W. B. Yeats: Interviews*

and Recollections (London: Macmillan, 1977) I, 6–13 and 13–15. These pieces first appeared in (respectively) *Poet Lore* (Boston, Mass.) 17, no. 2 (1906) 102–12, and *Harper's Weekly* (New York), 48 (20 Feb 1904) 291. Hone (*LJBY* 52n.) states that 'W. B. Yeats wrote his first poems in 1882, just before he was seventeen.' See also Murphy, *Prodigal Father*, p. 132; and Bornstein, *Y&Shel* 13.

13. Johnston, in Mikhail, *Yeats: Interviews and Recollections*, I, 10.
14. Ibid., p. 11.
15. Only partial reconstruction is possible, based on the fragments of NLI 30,440 and 30,830, which match by subject, stanza (finally) and paper (watermark, etc.). The early poem was first noted by Ellmann (*YM&M* 28–9), who produced a silently emended version of the first stanza (from NLI 30,830) and surmised the epic to be 'on Sir Roland in Spenserian stanzas' because of direct reference in the fifth stanza: 'Sir Roland passed in singing that old stave / within the mouth of Lethe's vale profound'. George Bornstein, in 'The Making of Yeats's Spenser', *YAACTS* 2 (1984) 21–9, briefly outlines the poem, preliminary to the reconstruction due in *W. B. Yeats: The Early Poetry*, II (Ithaca, NY, and London: Cornell University Press, forthcoming).
16. Johnston, in Mikhail, *Yeats: Interviews and Recollections*, I, 11.
17. Unpublished memoirs, quoted by William Murphy in 'Father and Son: The Early Education of William Butler Yeats', *Review of English Literature* (Leeds) 8, no. 4 (1967) 92. Yeats's difficulties are conceded in *Au* 67.
18. Bornstein, *Y&Shel* 14–19.
19. A pervasive influence such as Blake's, one might add, casts shadows over both and all. Yeats's Blakean preference for symbolism over allegory, as registered in his Spenser essay (*E&I* 382), found earlier expression in his Introduction to W. T. Horton's *A Book of Images* (1898), revised for 'Symbolism in Painting' (1900; see *E&I* 146–7, and below, Ch. 3, section III). Later, in the hue of Henry More, Yeats repeated his juxtaposition of Spenser and Shelley in *Per Amica Silentia Lunae* (1917); see n. 31.
20. Patty Gurd, in *The Early Poetry of William Butler Yeats* (Lancaster, Penn.: New Era, 1916) p. 27, believes that Infamy was suggested by the 'strange procession in the enchanted persecutions of Amoret' – a procession which does seem to have fascinated Yeats (see *E&I* 382–3). In fact, *The Faerie Queene*, III.xii.25 (the last in a nineteen-stanza litany of vices in 'The maske of Cupid') concludes with the words 'Death with infamy'. Such evidence is not of the strongest sort, though Gurd's suggestion has merit since Yeats was most impressed with Spenser's devices in books II and III of *The Faerie Queene*, and seems not to have read beyond book IV until 1902.
21. Bornstein, *W. B. Yeats: The Early Poetry*, I, 12.
22. The case for Yeats's 'imitation of Shelley' seems overstated in Bornstein's *Y&Shel* 13–20 (*passim*) and particularly in Adele M. Dalsimer's 'My Chief of Men: Yeats's Juvenilia and Shelley's *Alastor*', *Éire–Ireland* 8 (1973) 71–90, where Spenser is all but 'set aside' or regarded as a mere 'peppering' of archaisms (Dalsimer's words), as though Spenser and Shelley were in competition for the upper hand in influence.

23. See *Au* 89–92. With Charles Johnston, Yeats began to investigate European magic, mystic philosophy, and Eastern religion at about this time, founding the Dublin Hermetic Society (*c.* 1885, according to Ellmann, *YM&M* 41) on the inspiration of such works as A. P. Sinnett's *The Occult World* and *Esoteric Buddhism* – discovering at least the latter in the drawing-room of Edward Dowden in the waning days of the scholar's influence upon him. Also see Ellmann (*YM&M* 59–62) on the poet's initial contact with the Theosophical Society through Johnston and Claude Wright.
24. Bornstein, *W. B. Yeats: The Early Poetry*, I, 15.
25. See ibid., p. 366.
26. Two critical studies of Yeats's quest motif (with no insight on Spenser) are Frank Murphy, *Yeats's Early Poetry* (Baton Rouge: Louisiana State University Press, 1978); and Thomas Byrd, Jr, *The Early Poetry of W. B. Yeats* (Port Washington, NY: Kennikat, 1978).
27. See *UP1* 81–104. In October and November 1886, Yeats published in the *Dublin University Review* two articles entitled 'The Poetry of Sir Samuel Ferguson'. Yeats liked Ferguson's work for what he called, quoting Spenser (*The Faerie Queene*, I.vi.2), its 'barbarous truth' (*UP1* 87). In the second article he took a swipe at Dowden, who generally underrated Ireland's contribution to English letters, Yeats felt, and had failed, as 'the most distinguished of [Ireland's] critics', to put his reputation to the defence of Ferguson's. See also William Murphy, *Prodigal Father*, p. 149; and Phillip L. Marcus, *Yeats and the Beginning of the Irish Renaissance* (Ithaca, NY, and London: Cornell University Press, 1970) pp. 104–21.
28. Geoffrey Keating, author of *Foras feasa an Éirinn* (*History of Ireland*, *c.* 1620–32), took pains to defend Ireland against the prose tracts and histories of 'Cambrensis, Spenser, Stanihurst, Hanmer, Camden, Barckly, Moryson, Davies [and] Campion . . . and every other new foreigner . . . insomuch that it is [almost] the fashion of the beetle they practice when writing on the Irish' – quoted in *Vindication of the Sources of Irish History*, ed. David Comyn for the Gaelic League (Dublin: Gill, 1898) p. 53. Yeats struck nearly the same attitude toward Spenser's *View of the Present State of Ireland* (1596). He also found Keating a valuable source of information on Irish folkways and on Druids, citing him as such in a long note to the poem 'The Secret Rose' (*VP* 812).
29. Yeats became a member of this Rosicrucian order on 7 March 1890. The rose was, of course, its central symbol. Some of his rituals, chiefly featuring root and tree imagery, may be found in NLI 13,568, with notes and other materials by Annie Horniman, Yeats, and others bearing on the scheme to establish a mystical Celtic order. Yeats once reported that he had been 'a student of the medieval mystics since 1887 and found in such authors as Valentin Andrea [from A. E. Waite's *The Real History of the Rosicrucians*, 1887] authority for [his] use of the rose' (*L* 592). This primary symbol of Yeats's nineties poetry is indeed credited with a heavy load of associations – some concrete, some most abstract – as we find in Frank Murphy's list (*Yeats's Early Poetry*, p. 33).
30. See Isabel Rivers, *Classical and Christian Ideas in English Renaissance*

Poetry (London: Allen and Unwin, 1979) p. 38. Possibly Spenser knew Hoby's translation of *The Book of the Courtier* (1561) but drew upon Ficino's translation of Plotinus while composing the 'Fowre Hymnes'.
31. Carlos Baker, in *The Echoing Green* (Princeton, NJ: Princeton University Press, 1984) pp. 163–5, discusses the intersection between Spenser's Neoplatonism in the account of the Garden of Adonis and Shelley's use of such images as star, light, and flame in 'Adonais'. Baker extends this point of intersection from Shelley to Yeats by attributing to stanza 54 of 'Adonais' Yeats's statement that 'If all our mental images . . . are forms existing in the general vehicle of *Anima Mundi* and mirrored in our particular vehicle, many crooked things are made straight' (*Myth* 352). Baker's case for 'transference' is less than obvious as presented, since Yeats worked directly from Henry More and the Cambridge Platonists in writing *Per Amica Silentia Lunae*. Yeats does mention Shelley earlier in the passage, but after leading with More. When Yeats concludes the paragraph, it is by quoting three lines from *The Faerie Queene* to illustrate how the Garden of Adonis may represent the *Anima Mundi*. Later linking More and Spenser ('who was among More's masters' – *Myth* 363), Yeats quotes an entire stanza (III.vi.33) from the Garden of Adonis passage. A page later (or twelve pages beyond the passage Baker cites) comes the overt allusion to the 'Adonais' stanza that Baker produces – overlooking a *dyadic* adaptation of both Spenser and Shelley in the presence of Henry More.
32. The annotations were made as Yeats read, in 1902 for the first time, all of Spenser's work. The edition he used was *The Works of Edmund Spenser*, ed. J. Payne Collier, 5 vols (London: Bell, 1862), apparently a gift set from Lady Gregory. These marked volumes constitute the reading-notes for his selected *Poems of Spenser* (1906) and, in some cases, for points made in his Introduction. (See *YL* 1978–1978D and *YL Notes* 1978 [for A–C].) It is not a copytext; indeed, T. C. and E. C. Jack (Edinburgh), the publisher of the Yeats edition, probably used a similar but later text for typesetting. Richard B. Davidson, in 'Yeats's Images of Spenser: A Question of Literary Influence' (unpublished dissertation, Michigan State University, 1973) pp. 103 and 107, suggests that the Yeats edition (*Wade* 235) may have been set from the Globe Edition: *The Works of Edmund Spenser*, ed. R. Morris with memoir by John W. Hales (London: Macmillan, 1869; rev. 1893 and 1897; repr. 1899 and 1902). This seems likely. Yeats's annotated text (Collier) compares with both the Morris and Hales edition and *Wade* 235. All three are close in spelling and punctuation, for Morris and Hales followed Collier in most particulars (noted in Morris's Preface). Where there are differences, these favour the Macmillan volume, probably the more available text in 1902.
33. Bornstein, in *YAACTS* 2 (1984) 25, infers that Yeats 'delighted in drawing the astrological sign of Venus . . . in the margin next to references to the goddess, star, or any other figure he could associate with Intellectual Beauty'; and one is inclined to agree that Yeats's 'marginalia simply reveal that charming side of Yeats which he so rigorously excised from his public persona' (p. 24).

34. Marsilio Ficino, *Commentary on Plato's Symposium*, ed. and intro. Sears R. Jayne (Columbia, Mo.: University of Missouri Press, 1944) p. 142.
35. The notes to Yeats's *Poems of Spenser*, pp. 265–6, are useful here because of their pedantry. On Spenser's use of Apelles' painting, an unspecified passage in Lyly's *Campaspe* (of which Yeats probably had no knowledge) is cited for comparison. On Anacreon (Spenser's 'Teian poet'), the notes refer the reader to Byron. For a classical analogy to God's light (l. 162 in Spenser's poem), a quotation from Keats is provided. And more detailed references are given for Venus in Yeats's 'Teares of the Muses' selection (e.g. to Virgil's *Aeneid* and to Ovid's *Metamorphoses* and *Elegies*).
36. See YL 1978D. Cf. 'An Hymne of Heavenly Beautie', ll. 82–4; beginning at this point and extending over the next three stanzas, this passage in Spenser was annotated by Yeats.
37. Elizabeth B. Loizeaux, *Yeats and the Visual Arts* (New Brunswick, NJ, and London: Rutgers University Press, 1986) pp. 37 and 48. Loizeaux's source for the unpublished verse is Ellmann, *YM&M* 29.
38. For illustration of the device each member of the Order studied to make for himself, see Kathleen Raine, *Yeats, the Tarot and the Golden Dawn*, rev. edn (Dublin: Dolmen Press, 1976) pp. 8–11.
39. I do not mean that Yeats or Gyles invented the rose-tree design, but that Yeats, like Gyles, fleshes out abstract rudiments received from other sources. For more on the relationship between Yeats and Gyles and their collaboration in the literary and visual arts, see Ian Fletcher, 'Poet and Designer: W. B. Yeats and Althea Gyles', *Yeats Studies*, 1 (1971) 42–79. On Yeats's symbolic use of the rose, and its sources, see Ellmann, *Identity* 63–79.
40. Several stories of the volume dramatize supposed or fictional events of local Irish history set in the Middle Ages or the seventeenth century. Yeats's treatment of history by a progression of these stories is examined by Steven Putzel, *Reconstructing Yeats* (Dublin: Gill and Macmillan, 1986). Also see *VSR*.
41. For the Hebrew names of the Sephiroth of plate 6, see Ellic Howe, *The Magicians of the Golden Dawn* (London: Routledge and Kegan Paul, 1972; New York: Weiser, 1978) p. xi. For variations on the Rosy Cross and for several interesting representations of the serpent on the Tree of Life, see Raine, *Yeats, the Tarot and the Golden Dawn*, pp. 12–22; and Allen R. Grossman, *Poetic Knowledge in the Early Yeats* (Charlottesville: University Press of Virginia, 1969) plates 3–6.
42. Edward O'Shea, *Yeats as Editor* (Dublin: Dolmen Press, 1975) p. 32.
43. See ibid., pp. 30–2; Davidson, 'Yeats's Images of Spenser', pp. 6–8, 11–12, 95ff.; and Enoch Brater, 'W. B. Yeats: Poet as Critic', *Journal of Modern Literature*, 4 (1975) 662–7.
44. See Muriel C. Bradbrook, 'Yeats and Elizabethan Love Poetry', *Dublin Magazine*, 4, no. 2 (1965) 42–3.
45. It seems clear from detail that Yeats saw John Pye's 1822 engraving of *The Temple of Jupiter Restored*, a lost painting recently recovered. The engraving and painting are reconstructions of the stately ruins in Turner's *View of the Temple of Jupiter Panellenius on the Island of Aegina*

with the Greek National Dance of the Romaika (1816; engraved by H. Dawe but not published). See Martin Butlin and Evelyn Joll (eds), *The Paintings of J. M. W. Turner*, 2 vols (New Haven, Conn.; and London: Yale University Press, 1977) I, 86–8, and II (plates), 132 and 133. The Claude was evidently a contemporary engraving of *Landscape with the Marriage of Isaac and Rebekah* (also known as *The Mill*, 1648), which the Turner Bequest places next to his own work in a corner of the National Gallery, London. The Claude is itself a rendition of another Claude, *Il Mulino* (or *The Mill*) in the Palazzo Doria at Rome. The National Gallery painting is frequently cited by Ruskin to the advantage of Turner. See, for example, *Modern Painters*, in *The Works of John Ruskin*, ed. E. T. Cook and Alexander Wedderburn, 39 vols (London: Allen; New York: Longmans, 1903–12) III, 41–4, 305, 331, 348, 436–8. Yeats follows the comparison but reverses the opinion.

46. Yeats's selections are as follows (table based on the contents list of *Wade* 235).

HAPPY AND UNHAPPY LOVE
An Hymne of Heavenly Beauty
The Muse Complains of the Poets that Sing of Light Love (*The Teares of the Muses*, ll. 385–402)
Poems in Honour of Cupid. Epigrams
Epithalamion
The Faerie Queene
  Enchanted Trees (I.ii.28–45)
  The Sad Story of Florimell and Marinell (III.iv.7–43; viii, 30–42; IV.xi.1–9, 52, 53; xii.1–35)

COURTIERS AND GREAT MEN
Good and Bad Courtiers (*Mother Hubberd's Tale*, ll. 717–844)
The Death of the Earl of Leicester (*The Ruines of Time*, ll. 27–32)
The Muse Laments there are no Great Men to Sing of (*The Teares of the Muses*, ll. 434–463)
The Muse Laments there are no more Great Poets (*The Teares of the Muses*, ll. 559–70)

EMBLEMS AND QUALITIES
The House of Despair (*The Faerie Queene*, I.ix.21–54)
The House of Richesse (*The Faerie Queene*, II.vii.3–66)
The House of Love (*The Faerie Queene*, III.xi.21–30, 47–55; xii.1–45)
The House of Friendship (*The Faerie Queene*, IV.x.3–58)
Mutabilitie (*The Faerie Queene*, VII.vi.1–55; vii.1–59)
The Wandering of the Stars (*The Faerie Queene*, v[Intro.].1–11)

GARDENS OF DELIGHT
The Islands of Phaedria and Acrasia (*The Faerie Queene*, II.v.28–34; vi.2–26; xii.1–87)
Garden of Adonis (*The Faerie Queene*, III.vi.30–48)

FAUNS AND SATYRS AND SHEPHERDS
Praise of the Shepherd's Life (*Virgil's Gnat*, ll. 113–52)
Una among the Fauns and Satyrs (*The Faerie Queene*, I.vi.7–31)
The Shepheardes Calender ('February', 'October', 'November', 'December')

47. In all likelihood, Yeats had nothing to do with the coloured illustrations for *Wade* 235. His letters show that, on the promise of £35, he had completed most of his work for the volume by 26 September 1902 and that by 2 January 1903 he had posted his Introduction to the printer (*L* 365, 380, 390–1). The project was very nearly aborted, as he informed Lady Gregory in ten days, 'owing to the delay of several authors about sending in of MSS.' (*L* 396); as a result, publication was delayed for nearly four years, the illustrations being, presumably, among the last tasks to follow typesetting of Yeats's selections.
48. Loizeaux, *Yeats and the Visual Arts*, p. 53. See also Michael North, 'The Paradox of the Mausoleum: Public Monuments and the Early Aesthetics of W. B. Yeats', *Centennial Review*, 26, no. 3 (1982) 221–38.
49. Lorizeaux, *Yeats and the Visual Arts*, p. 49.
50. See Ch. 2, n. 53, which suggests that Yeats may have known this work. Hunt's awareness of the Claudian tradition and its place in Renaissance painting is implicit when he claims, with customary hyperbole, that, if Spenser 'had not been a great poet, he would have been a great painter; [hence] . . . England would have possessed her Claude' – *Imagination and Fancy; or Selections from the English Poets* . . . (London: Smith, Elder, 1844) p. 105.
51. Ibid., pp. 106–7.
52. John B. Bender, *Spenser and Literary Pictorialism* (Princeton, NJ: Princeton University Press, 1972); Judith Dundas, *The Spider and the Bee: The Artistry of Spenser's 'Faerie Queene'* (Urbana and Chicago: University of Illinois Press, 1985).
53. See above, note 46.
54. See *The Works of Edmund Spenser: A Variorum Edition*, ed. Edwin Greenlaw, Charles Osgood, and Frederick Padelford, 10 vols (Baltimore: Johns Hopkins University Press, 1932–57) II, 472–85 (Appendix XI: 'The Twenty-Second Stanza of Canto 9'), where Digby's *Observations* is quoted in full, followed by excerpts from Upton, Dowden, and others. Also see the very different diagram and the Pythagorean account of Hopper's reconstruction of the Castle of Alma in Alastair Fowler's *Spenser and the Numbers of Time* (London: Routledge and Kegan Paul, 1964) pp. 260–88.
55. Yeats was perplexed, for instance, by *Muiopotmos*, at the close of which he jotted the following query: 'I[s?] th / ? / Is this poem aligorical – Is it mer / Earth[l]y talent again[s]t desire, reason again[s]t / instinct, calculatio[n] aga[ins]t genius or what? / WBY.'
56. Dowden, *Transcripts and Studies*, p. 300. Yeats points out in his Spenser essay how the 'Iron Man', Oliver Cromwell, came to execute recommendations set forth in Spenser's *A View of the Present State of Ireland*, from which Yeats quotes liberally to emphasize his censure.

Notes

Yeats's sympathies can be surprisingly ambiguous, however, as one discovers in an early poem partly inspired by Spenser, 'The Protestants' Leap / (Lug-na-Gall, Sligo). / The Cromwellian Speaks' (1887). See John S. Kelly, 'Aesthete among the Athletes: Yeats's Contributions to *The Gael'*, *YAACTS* 2 (1984) 75–143, esp. pp. 130–1. Yeats thought Dowden, condescendingly, a mere 'West Briton'; yet Yeats was himself Anglo-Irish by birth and temperament, despite his nationalism. This fact probably checked his impulse to reject Spenser the poet because of Spenser the politician.

CHAPTER 4 YEATS AND THE SCHOOL OF JONSON: BOOKS, MASQUES, EPIGRAMS AND ELEGIES, 1902–19

1. *L* 478–9. A. H. Bullen, Elizabethan scholar and, for a time, Yeats's chief publisher after his falling-out with Unwin, was just then printing in the *Gentleman's Magazine* the first of two unsigned instalments of 'My Thoughts and Second Thoughts' (later *Discoveries* [1907], *Wade* 72); the second instalment (*Discoveries* XI–XVII) is alluded to in this dispatch. See John S. Kelly, 'Books and Numberless Dreams: Yeats's Relations with his Early Publishers', *YS&I* 232–53.
2. Una Ellis-Fermor, *The Irish Dramatic Movement*, 2nd ed (London: Methuen, 1967) pp. 46–7. A brief account which quotes at length a leading article in *The Irish Times* (5 Aug 1904) may be found in Robert Hogan and James Kilroy, *Laying the Foundations, 1902–1904*, vol. II of *The Modern Irish Drama: A Documentary History* (Dublin: Dolmen Press, 1976).
3. In part, these are terms of the patent recorded by Joseph Holloway, on Saturday, 20 August 1904, now published in Robert Hogan and Michael J. O'Neill (eds), *Joseph Holloway's Abbey Theatre* (Carbondale and Edwardsville: Southern Illionis University Press, 1967) p. 42.
4. A short piece entitled 'Private and Confidential: Paragraphs Written in Nov., 1909' (*Wade* 244b) makes this point clear. The item, co-authored and distributed by Yeats and Lady Gregory to raise money for a new patent, has been reprinted in Lady Gregory's *Our Irish Theatre: A Chapter of Autobiography* (Gerrards Cross, Bucks: Colin Smythe, 1972) pp. 196–8. Speaking of their plans for the future theatre, the authors assert that 'the creation of a folk drama was . . . but a part of the original scheme, and now that it has been accomplished we can enlarge our activities . . .; and when we apply for a new Patent we shall hope to remove the limitation of our present one, which prevents us from performing any Elizabethan work' (pp. 197–8).
5. Yeats was familiar with at least one of the four plays in Rhys's edition, and three years before the edition came out in 1894. This was *Old Fortunatus*, cited with the masques of Ben Jonson and with Chapman's *Bussy D'Ambois* for 'poetic oratory' and 'audacious metaphors' in 'A Poetic Drama', *Providence Sunday Journal*, 26 July 1891; repr. in *LNI* 216. The only other Dekker that Yeats owned was a 1904 edition of *The Gull's Hornbook* (*YL* 502).

6. The phrase follows notice of three Elizabethans – Marlowe, Shakespeare, and Jonson. The idea was probably suggested first (though noted later) by Emerson's view of Shakespeare as 'a Master of the Revels to mankind' (*E&I* 368).
7. Yeats was sometimes mistaken. In *Samhain: 1901*, for example (*Ex* 81), he said that he thought *The Under-wood* the source of 'the only fragment that has come down to us of Shakespeare's conversation', obviously confusing Jonson's volume of poetry with *Timber; or Discoveries*, which seems to have been background reading for Yeats's Shakespeare essay since he alludes to the passage in an essay of the previous year as the 'one bull [that] is all that remains of Shakespeare's talk' (*E&I* 153). In another instance, he praises a falsely attributed or misquoted lyric – 'Beauty like sorrow dwelleth everywhere' (*E&I* 7) – which is untraced in Jonson.
8. Douglas Duncan, 'Synge and Jonson (with a parenthesis on Ronsard)', *SMD* 205–18.
9. Algernon C. Swinburne, *A Study of Ben Jonson* (London: Chatto, 1889) p. 35; John A. Symonds, *Ben Jonson* (1886; repr. London: Longmans, 1888) p. 74. It is likely that Symonds was the source of the phrase for both Yeats, who also owned a copy of Symonds's *A Short History of the Renaissance in Italy* (1893; YL 2050), and Swinburne, whose work would not have been in press before Symonds's book was out. With a note of irony, Yeats echoed Symonds's implicit disapproval of Jonson's 'cold cynicism' and 'implacability' (*Ben Jonson*, p. 72) when he observed late in life that the lack of 'marriage bells' in the end for Celia and Bonario, a reward for their innocence and virtue, 'makes us share in Jonson's cold implacability' (in *On the Boiler*, 1939; *Ex* 445). See also *L* 664–5.
10. Probably Yeats bought the Mermaid Jonson – vol. III only (YL 1028) – at about the same time as he purchased Symonds's Dekker and Heywood (YL 892). (Yeats's library holds an inscribed copy of Symonds's Webster and Tourneur, YL 2228, dated 'Oct. 9, 1888'.) Besides *The Poetaster* and *Cynthia's Revels*, the first of Jonson's satires to be read by Yeats were *Volpone*, *Epicoene*, and *The Alchemist*. These remained his favourites, if one is to judge by the frequency with which Yeats mentioned them, beginning in 1905: *L* 450, 612, 664–5; *E&I* 280; *UP2* 349, 355; *Ex* 445. Another work which he acquired and possibly read at this time was *Every Man in his Humour* (see YL 1030). An apparent allusion to it may be found in *Mem* 269–70. *Bartholomew Fair*, which Synge admired greatly, is cited in Yeats's retort to the opposition to *The Playboy of the Western World* as reported in *The Freeman's Journal*, 30 Jan 1907, 7, and is also mentioned enthusiastically in *L* 671. See S. B. Bushrui, 'Synge and Yeats', *SMD* 189–203. See also Ch. 2, section III, on Yeats and his father.
11. The full title (from the 1641 edition of Jonson's work) is *TIMBER: / OR, / DISCOVERIES; / MADE VPON MEN / AND MATTER: AS THEY / have flow'd out of his daily Read- / ings; or had their refluxe to his / peculiar Notion of the Times*. (The text is headed *Explorata: or Discoveries*). The similarity of titles was first noticed by T. McAlindon,

in 'Yeats and the English Renaissance', *PMLA*, 82 (1967) 164.
12. Bullen seems to have preferred the Elizabethans to the Jacobeans for their poetry, and in this particular resembles Dowden. However, as a publisher of dramatic works, he directed much of his resources to minor Jacobean dramatists. In addition to his edition of Marston, he produced multi-volume editions of Middleton, Peele, and Day. He did, however, publish one three-volume Marlowe and works by contemporaries such as Yeats. See Paul Morgan, 'Arthur Henry Bullen (1857–1920) and the Shakespeare Head Press', in *Frank Sidgwick's Diary* (Oxford: Basil Blackwell, 1975) pp. 69–90; and Frank C. Nelick, 'Yeats, Bullen, and the Irish Drama', *Modern Drama*, 1 (1958) 196–202.
13. Yeats is only known to have read Bacon's essay 'Of Beauty', attested by *UP2* 412 and, perhaps, *UP1* 237. Other references to Bacon – i.e. *Ex* 333 and *AV B* 296 – are general or imply familiarity with Bacon's scientific treatises. Yeats once owned a copy of G. Walter Steeves's *Francis Bacon: A Sketch of his Life, Works and Literary Friends* (1910; *YL* 1920 288), but this may have been 'weeded out', in O'Shea's words, as a 'faded enthusiasm'.
14. Drummond's book, printed by the Shakespeare Head Press in 1907, was acquired after Yeats's *Discoveries* pieces were written. Yeats's interest undoubtedly stemmed from the *Conversations*, but he would have been attracted to its matter, too, since this discourse on death and the soul is reminiscent of those works of Browne which Yeats consulted (see *Myth* 267), possibly encouraged by a reading of Pater's 'Sir Thomas Browne' (1886) in *Appreciations*. A copy of *Religio Medici, and Urn Burial* (London: Dent, 1896) is signed 'W. B. Yeats./June, 1897.' An older *Religio Medici, Urn Burial, Christian Morals, and Other Essays*, ed. J. A. Symonds (London: Scott, 1886), is much marked, apparently by its original owner, John Masefield. Another edition of the latter title (decorated by Charles Ricketts and edited by C. J. Holmes) was a gift of '13.6.1905'.
15. Yeats's use of Jusserand in *Ex* 190 is evidently based on the French scholar's article. Among the books 'weeded out' of Yeats's library (see *YL1920* 284) were three by Jusserand: *The English Novel in the Time of Shakespeare* (1901), *English Wayfaring Life in the Middle Ages* (1909), and *The Literary History of the English People* (1907). For Yeats's stock of Shakespeare, see *YL* 1875–81 and *YL1920* 288. See also Desai, *YShak* 35–6; and J. Kleinstuck, 'Yeats and Shakespeare', *W. B. Yeats, 1865–1965: Centenary Essays*, ed. D. E. S. Maxwell and S. B. Bushrui (Ibadan: Ibadan University Press, 1965) pp. 14–15, where it is suggested that Yeats strongly identified with Shakespeare. Bornstein (*Y&Shel* 218) makes the same claim for Shelley on the authority of Mrs Yeats. Yeats himself is mute on the matter, defining Shelley and Shakespeare very differently in *AV B* 140–5 and 151–4.
16. When Yeats wrote to Bullen on 21 September 1906, the first echoes of *The Poetaster* were already set down for copying. Desai (*YShak* 39) thinks that Yeats may have seen Sidney Lee's *A Life of William Shakespeare* (1898), which anticipates Yeats's opinion.
17. See *YL* 369 and the more complete report in *YL Notes* 369.

18. Francis Beaumont and John Fletcher, *The Works of Francis Beaumont and John Fletcher*, 10 vols (Cambridge: Cambridge University Press, 1905–12). The passage, according to YL, occurs on p. 50 (Act v, scene i) of vol. II: *The Elder Brother and Other Plays*, ed. Arnold Glover and A. R. Waller (n.d.). See also *E&I* 280, where Yeats speaks glowingly of Philip Carr's revival of Beaumont's *The Knight of the Burning Pestle*.
19. See Peter Ure, *Yeats and Anglo-Irish Literature*, ed. C. J. Rawson (Liverpool: Liverpool University Press, 1974) pp. 220–21.
20. See *Au* 165; and Ellmann's *ED* 9–27, which argues this thesis.
21. See Christina Hunt Mahony, 'The Influence of John Todhunter on the Plays of W. B. Yeats', in Heinz Kosok (ed.), *Studies in Anglo-Irish Literature* (Bonn: Bouvier, 1982) pp. 262–8.
22. Dowden's essay 'The English Masque' appears in his collected *Essays Modern and Elizabethan* (London: Dent, 1910) pp. 334–50. Symons's 'A New Art of the Stage' (1902, 1906), 'A Symbolist Farce' (1888), and 'Pantomime and the Poetic Drama' (1898) were reprinted in his multidisciplinary *Studies in the Seven Arts* (New York: Dutton, 1925) pp. 227–47. On Symons's acting-debut, see Ronald Schuchard, 'W. B. Yeats and the London Theatre Societies, 1901–1904', *Review of English Studies*, 29, no. 116 (1978) 434.
23. See Ernest Dowson, *The Letters of Ernest Dowson*, ed. Desmond Flower and Henry Maas (Rutherford, NJ: Fairleigh Dickinson University Press, 1967) pp. 379 and 403. Dowson's novel *A Comedy of Masks* (1893; written with Arthur Moore) also reflects Dowson's excitement over this theatrical convention.
24. See Robin Skelton, 'A Literary Theatre: A Note on English Poetic Drama in the Time of Yeats', in Robin Skelton and Ann Saddlemyer (eds), *The World of W. B. Yeats*, rev. edn (Seattle: University of Washington Press, 1967) pp. 103–10. Yeats's interest in the masque is strongly indicated in YL 560 – John Dryden, *The Poetical Works* ed. W. D. Christie, (London: Macmillan, 1908) – where Yeats cut only those pages which bear the Contents, 'The Secular Masque', and a few songs apparently in the same gathering with the latter.
25. See Clinton Vickers, 'Image into Symbol: The Evolution of the Dance in the Poetry and Drama of W. B. Yeats', *Dissertation Abstracts International*, 35 (1974) 484A (University of Massachusetts). Some seven sheets of such dialogue (in Yeats's hand) are part of NLI 13,568, 'Notes and other materials by Miss Horniman, Yeats, & others towards the establishment of a mystical Celtic order'.
26. See *E&I* 13–27, which shows that Bullen was engaged as one of Farr's coaches because he, while not tone-deaf as Yeats was, 'hate[d] all music but that of poetry' (*E&I* 20). In 1902–3, Yeats lectured extensively on the recitative technique Farr demonstrated for him. Ronald Schuchard, in 'The Minstrel in the Theatre: Arnold, Chaucer, and Yeats's New Spiritual Democracy', *YA* 2 (1983) 3–34, gives an account of some of Yeats's lecture notices in the press. Yeats reviewed Farr's production of *The Shrine of the Golden Hawk*, the 'rigorously decorative [scenic] arrangements' of which, he said, 'imitated the severe forms of Egyptian mural painting' (*UP2* 266). In 1906, this play, which Farr wrote with

Olivia Shakespear, was revived and played with Yeats's mystic allegory *The Shadowy Waters*, sponsored by the Theosophical Society (see *VP* 815). Both plays received considerable notice, as attested in NLI 12,146, fos 16–34.

27. W. B. Yeats, *Beltaine*, 2 (February 1900) 3.
28. The Yeats–Craig relationship has been fairly thoroughly investigated. See Katharine Worth, *The Irish Drama of Europe from Yeats to Beckett* (Atlantic Highlands, NJ: Humanities Press, 1978) pp. 48–53; and, on other sources, Wayne K. Chapman, 'Yeats's "Theatre of Beauty" and the Masque Tradition', *YAACTS* 7 (1990) n. 11.
29. Yeats's letter is quoted in full in Edward Gordon Craig, *Index to the Story of my Days* (New York: Viking, 1957) p. 239 (see also p. 242).
30. The text here is that of *Ben Jonson*, ed. C. H. Herford and Percy and Evelyn Simpson, 11 vols (Oxford: Clarendon Press, 1925–51) VII, 229. The convergence of Bacon and Jonson in Yeats's compliment to Robert Gregory is noted in Richard Allen Cave's *Yeats's Late Plays: 'A High Grave Dignity and Strangeness'*, British Academy Proceedings 78 (London: Oxford University Press, 1984) pp. 299–300. Similar references to Jonson's masques are in *The Masque of Blacknesse* (ll. 266–74) and *The Masque of Queenes* (ll. 15–22, 344–6, 351). Cave (*Yeats's Late Plays*, p. 301) observes that Yeats echoed Jonson again (*L* 611) when referring to the dramatic invention in his first Noh adaptation, *At the Hawk's Well*. The Bacon–Jonson convergence becomes a point of confluence given Pater's adaptation of Bacon in *Appreciations*: 'the addition of strangeness to beauty . . . constitutes the romantic character in art'.
31. *Ben Jonson*, VII, 91.
32. Ibid., VIII, 628 (l. 2128) See 'Living Emblems' (chiefly about the Jonsonian masque) in Forrest G. Robinson's *The Shape of Things Known* (Cambridge, Mass.: Harvard University Press, 1972) pp. 214–25; and Stephen Orgel, *The Jonsonian Masque* (Cambridge, Mass.: Harvard University Press, 1965) 156–8.
33. I am indebted to Christina Mahony for this information. She writes that the John Todhunter collection at Reading University includes the typescript of a masque intended for this play; she offers the following summary of the masque's conventional plot: 'Elizabeth is allied with the Virgin Mary, and a female Love disarms (or emasculates) a male Beauty, preserving virtue and the monarchy simultaneously.'
34. Christopher Innes, *Edward Gordon Craig* (Cambridge: Cambridge University Press 1983) p. 133; see also Craig, *Index to the Story of my Days*, pp. 248, 267. Schuchard (in *Review of English Studies*, 29, no. 116, p. 434) mentions that Craig, with Martin Shaw, had also penned *A Masque: The Harvest Home*, which was then forthcoming in *The Green Sheaf*, the periodical of Pamela Coleman 'Pixie' Smith.
35. Brief notices of the Masquers are given in Ann Saddlemyer's 'The Heroic Discipline of the Looking-Glass: W. B. Yeats's Search for Dramatic Design', in Skelton and Saddlemyer, *The World of W. B. Yeats*, p. 71; and Hone's *WBY* 202–3. Schuchard's study in *Review of English Studies*, 29, no. 116, pp. 430–46, chronicles the nine-month life

of the Masquers in the context of two other societies, the Literary Theatre Club and the Stage Society.
36. Schuchard, in *Review of English Studies*, 29, no. 116, p. 433; see *LTWBY* 131.
37. Quoted here as presented by Saddlemyer, in Skelton and Saddlemyer, *The World of W. B. Yeats*, p. 71.
38. Yeats as quoted by Schuchard, in *Review of English Studies*, 29, no. 116, p. 433, from unpublished materials in the Gilbert Murray Papers. By autumn 1903, Florence Farr was rehearsing choruses from Murray's translation of *The Bacchae*, as Schuchard thinks (p. 442), in anticipation of her own *The Mystery of Time: A Masque* (1905).
39. The scenario is quoted by Schuchard, in *Review of English Studies*, 29, no. 116, pp. 441–2; and by Chapman, in *YAACTS*, 7 (1990) Appendix.
40. *Ben Jonson*, VII, 239. See Allan H. Gilbert, *The Symbolic Persons in the Masques of Ben Jonson* (Durham, NC: Duke University Press, 1948) pp. 238–42.
41. Innes (*Craig*, pp. 129–31) makes this point on Craig, stressing the importance of the seventeenth-century shows of Jonson and Jones. Innes claims that the 1899 adaptation *Beauty's Awakening: A Masque of Winter and of Spring*, staged by the Art Workers' Guild in London, strongly influenced Craig.
42. On Craig's publications in the Yeats library, see Chapman, in *YAACTS*, 7 (1990) n. 23.
43. *The Mask*, I, no. 2 (1908) 3–15.
44. The praise actually began with a letter to Lady Gregory (dated 'Dec 29 [1909]' in the Berg Collection; cf. *L* 545), wherein Yeats disclosed that Craig had shown him 'an arrangement of what look like great white cubes but really are folding screens [*sic*]'. By that summer, Yeats had secured a model of Craig's invention and began devising scenes for his plays (see *UP2* 392). A notice appeared in Orage's *The New Age* (*UP2* 382); but see *UP2* 393 and *VP1* 644–5 on Craig's adaptation of the Abbey stage and on the *Hour-Glass* set he helped engineer. For Yeats's revision of *Deirdre* to accommodate Craig's scene, see *VP1* 396. Nelick (in *Modern Drama*, 1, pp. 201–2) summarizes several of Yeats's letters on the Yeats–Craig collaboration of 1910; see, too, Christine Thilliez, 'From One Theatrical Reformer to Another: W. B. Yeats's Unpublished Letters to Gordon Craig', in Patrick Rafroidi *et al.* (eds), *Aspects of the Irish Theatre* (Paris: Editions Universitaires, 1972) pp. 275–86.
45. Innes, *Craig*, p. 129.
46. See Worth, *The Irish Drama in Europe*, pp. 48–51.
47. See Elizabeth B. Loizeaux, *Yeats and the Visual Arts* (New Brunswick, NJ, and London: Rutgers University Press, 1986) p. 99; and *YT* 105–6.
48. From a typescript prospectus of 1913 at the NLI, quoted by Thilliez (in Rafroidi *et al.*, *Aspects of the Irish Theatre*, p. 284); the stated aim of the proposed theatre was to 'appeal to the sense of beauty and admit of beautiful staging'. See *YT* 105–6.
49. Edward Gordon Craig, *Craig on Theatre*, ed. J. Michael Walton (London:

Methuen, 1983) p. 155.
50. He also owned a copy of *Three Chester Whitsun Plays*, ed. Joseph Bridge (1906; YL 2135), and for a time, a book entitled *The Old English Miracle Play of Abraham and Isaac* (1905; YL 1920 286). YL 734 consists of Gascoigne's *Supposes* and *Jocasta*. YL 649, one of Rhys's 'Everyman' editions, includes *Everyman*; the Chester pageants *The Deluge* and *Abraham and Isaac*; the Wakefield *Second Shepherd's Play, The Harrowing of Hell*, and *The Miracle-Play of the Crucifixion* (from the Townley Collection); the Coventry *Nativity Play*; two Cornish mystery plays; and John Bale's *The Interlude of God's Promises*. Some of these plays are older than early Tudor, but Yeats's ownership of these texts does underline his interest in the origin of English Renaissance drama.
51. See Jeffares, *NCom* 89; and John Unterecker, *A Reader's Guide to William Butler Yeats* (New York: Farrar Straus Giroux, 1959) p. 108. See also A. C. Partridge, *The Language of Modern Poetry* (London: André Deutsch, 1976) pp. 91–5, on technical similarities between Jonson's epigrams in imitation of Horace and Yeats's poems 'The Folly of Being Comforted' (*VP* 199–200) and 'These are the Clouds' (*VP* 265).
52. On Yeats's view of the 'Faustian . . . full Renaissance Personality', see E. Engelberg, *The Vast Design* (Toronto: University of Toronto Press, 1964) pp. 178–80.
53. Jonson, Dedication to *Epigrammes*, in *Ben Jonson*, VIII, 26–7.
54. *Ben Jonson*, VIII, 609.
55. The poem appears to be in the mature hand of Yeats's middle period, recalls 'The Scholars' (c. 1914–April 1915), and is written on a sheet of folded stationery, half of which has been discarded. On the verso of this sheet, in pencil, is the name 'W. S. B. Woolhouse' and, at opposite end, is the note: 'Jan 22 old style / (Gregori[an]) / would be / 11 days later / ——in / Gregoria[n]'. Possibly little help in dating the poem.
56. *Ben Jonson*, VIII, 611.
57. This idea is expanded in Yeats's unfinished second series of *Discoveries*, written in 1908 or 1909: 'The beauty of the men of the Renaissance as we see it [in] pictures and in chronicles . . . was, like all fine things, an artifice and a toil. . . . Their generation had something present to their minds which they copied. They would imitate Christ or Caesar in their lives, or with [their] bodies some classic statue. They sought at all times the realization of something deliberately chosen . . .' – 'Discoveries: Second Series', ed. Curtis B. Bradford in *Massachusetts Review*, 5 (1964) 306.
58. From the earliest extant drafts in *Mem* 221–2 to the last official version in *VP*, the final line took seven different forms. See my discussion in 'The Annotated *Responsibilities*: Errors in the *Variorum Edition* and a New Reading of the Genesis of Two Poems, "On those that hated 'The Playboy of the Western World', 1907" and "The New Faces" ', *YA* 6 (1988) 108–33.
59. For a short summary of Jonsonian 'echoes' in these and other epigrams as noted by critics, see Judith A. Colbert, 'Masks of Ben Jonson in W. B. Yeats's *The Green Helmet* and *Responsibilities*', *Canadian Journal of Irish Studies*, 7, no. 1 (1981) 39–44.

60. *Ben Jonson*, IV, 324.
61. Ibid., VIII, 175.
62. On the revival of Jonson's reputation from the close of the nineteenth century to within twenty years of the present, see J. G. Nichols, *The Poetry of Ben Jonson* (New York: Barnes and Noble, 1969) pp. 1–55. Nichols's Appendix B (pp. 161–62), not only notices Yeats's reference to the *Poetaster* epilogue and Jonson's ode to himself, but also detects 'echoes' in four of Yeats's poems. Historical studies (not already mentioned) that Yeats owned were Grierson's *The First Half of the Seventeenth Century* (1906), Thomas Ordish's *Shakespeare's London* (1904), and A. Hamilton Thompson's *A History of English Literature* (1903). These are listed in YL 1920 (284, 286 and 289).
63. See Harold Bloom, *Yeats* (London: Oxford University Press, 1970) pp. 176, 189.
64. Untraced in Erasmus. Sixteen years later, Yeats noted in a diary (*Ex* 330) that he was preparing something ' "spiritualistic" in type which I shall publish when ready – to adapt a metaphor from Erasmus – to make myself a post for dogs and journalists to defile'. Harris (*YCP&B* 66n.) has suggested that Yeats may have confused Erasmus and Rabelais (*Gargantua*, II.xxii). A rudimentary form of Yeats's image cluster first saw print in *The Arrow*, 23 Feb 1907, where the poet defended himself and Synge's *Playboy* against 'the tyranny of cliques': 'I would indeed despise myself if for the sake of popularity . . . I were to mar the task I have set my hands to, and to cast the precious things of the soul into the trodden mire' – quoted in Robert O'Driscoll, 'Letters and Lectures of W. B. Yeats', *University Review* (Dublin), 3, no. 8 (1966) 49.
65. Pound's review of *RPP* is in *Poetry* (Chicago) 4, no. 2 (May 1914) 64–9. The Pound–Yeats relationship has been studied before and since Ellmann's chapter in *ED*. See Thomas Parkinson, 'Yeats and Pound: The Illusion of Influence', *Contemporary Literature*, 6 (1954) 256–64; K. L. Goodwin, *The Influence of Ezra Pound* (London: Oxford University Press, 1966) pp. 75–105; Thomas Rees, 'Ezra Pound and the Modernization of Yeats', *Journal of Modern Literature*, 4 (1975) 574–92; A. Walton Litz, 'Pound and Yeats: The Road to Stone Cottage', in George Bornstein (ed.), *Ezra Pound among the Poets* (Chicago: University of Chicago Press, 1985) pp. 128–48; and James Longenbach, *Stone Cottage: Pound, Yeats and Modernism* (New York and Oxford: Oxford University Press, 1988).
66. Litz, in Bornstein, *Ezra Pound among the Poets*, pp. 139–40.
67. Leonard Unger argues in 'Yeats and Milton', *South Atlantic Quarterly*, 61, no. 2 (1962) 198, that Yeats was reading *Areopagitica*.
68. Hugh Kenner, 'Some Post-Symbolist Structures', in Frank Brady *et al.* (eds), *Literary Theory and Structure* (New Haven, Conn.: Yale University Press, 1973) pp. 379–93.
69. K. P. S. Jochum, 'Yeats's Sonnets', *Modern British Literature*, 4, no. 1 (1979) 37.
70. See ch. 2, n. 31.
71. The corrected proof, bearing the handiwork of both Pound and Yeats,

is in the Woodruff Library, Emory University; a partial report of the revisions is provided in Ronald Schuchard, 'The Lady Gregory–Yeats Collection at Emory University', *YA* 3 (1985) 162. Copies, including the corrected proof and an insert slip for ll. 5–9, exist in British Library RP 1799(iv), items 3 and 4. Pound's hand stands out most in querying the spelling of 'Kyle-na-Ino', Lady Gregory's wood: '? Kyle-na-No. / its got to be No or Kno. / to scan. He pronounced it / Kyle-na-No.'

72. See Donald Davie, ' "Michael Robartes and the Dancer" ', *HonGuest* 82–5.
73. A moral objection to Yeats's attraction to the Anglo-Irish heritage of the Ascendancy is lodged by Antony Coleman in 'The Big House, Yeats, and the Irish Context', *YA* 3 (1984) 33–52. See also Breandan S. MacAodha, 'The Big House in Western Ireland: The Background to Yeats's Writing', *Gaeliana* 6 (1984) 217–23; and W. J. McCormack, *Ascendancy and Tradition in Anglo-Irish Literary History from 1789 to 1939* (Oxford: Clarendon Press, 1985) pp. 293–399. These works extend and sometimes challenge the critical consensus represented by Harris, *YCP&B*, and by Richard Gill, *Happy Rural Seat* (New Haven, Conn.: Yale University Press, 1972).
74. See William A. McClung, *The Country House in English Renaissance Poetry* (Los Angeles: University of California Press, 1977). In light of his collection of Herrick's poems (*YL* 886–9), Yeats probably knew 'A Panegyrick to Sir Lewis Pemberton' as well as Herrick's poems on country life.
75. Coleman, in *YA* 3 (1984) 34.
76. As one of his letters to Lady Gregory (*L* 379) shows, the social theory of Friedrich Nietzsche attracted Yeats's attention in 1902. Nietzsche thereafter mediated, to some extent, the way in which Yeats viewed Jonson, Castiglione, Spenser, and other writers of the Renaissance. See McAlindon, in *PMLA*, 82, pp. 157–8; and Otto Bohlmann, *Yeats and Nietzsche* (London: Macmillan; Totowa, NJ: Barnes and Noble, 1982).
77. Jeffares, *NCom* 93 (cf. l. 116 in Blake's 'King Edward the Third': 'The Eagle, that doth gaze upon the sun').
78. See Harris, *YCP&B* 62–4, for explication of the poem in this context. A detailed account of Augusta Gregory's adverse response to the poem and how it plagued Yeats between 1912 and 1922 is provided in my article 'The Annotated *Responsibilities*', in *YA* 6 (1988) 115–29. Cf. the proofs of the epilogue to *RPP*, ll. 6–8, quoted above.
79. *Ben Jonson*, VIII, 278.
80. Cf. ibid., plate facing p. 274, and pp. 275–81; also *VP* 362 ('Her Courtesy') and 365 ('Her Race').
81. *Ben Jonson*, VIII, 242–7.
82. See Ch. 3, n. 46.
83. See *The Poems of Theocritus*, ed. and tr. Anna Rist (Chapel Hill: University of North Carolina Press, 1978) pp. 23–33, 61–74.
84. Harper, *Making AV*, I, 28–9, 187–8, 201, 230–1, and 239–40. Harper shows that from 11 November 1917 to 19 March 1918 George and Yeats engaged in psychical research on matters that Yeats published

in the Goatherd's song, 'Shepherd and Goatherd', ll. 89–112. Yeats put to his entranced wife some specific questions about Robert Gregory.
85. F. A. C. Wilson, *W. B. Yeats and Tradition* (New York: Macmillan, 1958) p. 201; he quotes Thomas Taylor, *A Dissertation* (1790) p. 138.
86. These sheets may bear the only surviving draft (though fragmentary) of this poem. I cannot verify the existence of a draft called 'A dead shepherd', reported by Marion Witt in 'The Making of an Elegy: Yeats's "In Memory of Major Robert Gregory" ', *Modern Philology*, 48, no. 2 (1950) 113. It is not in the Berg Collection (New York Public Library) or the National Library of Ireland.
87. Frank Kermode has written that, at best, the pastoral form might have helped him achieve a 'monumental apathy', 'an interesting stoic coldness', but that it 'sorts ill' with the poet's new mythology (*RI* 36). Similar views are expressed by Witt, in *Modern Philology*, 48, no. 2, p. 113; and by Peter Ure in *Yeats* (Edinburgh and London: Oliver and Boyd, 1963) p. 64. Marjorie Perloff, in 'The Consolation Theme in Yeats's "In Memory of Major Robert Gregory" ', *Modern Language Quarterly* 27, no. 3 (1966) 306–22, seems to agree with those critics on 'Shepherd and Goatherd' but establishes her own view of the later elegy. Peter Sacks, in *The English Elegy* (Baltimore: Johns Hopkins University Press, 1985) pp. 265, 267, argues that Yeats was attracted to 'the remote, impersonal, and mythic aspects of the old convention' but that his 'formulaic exercise' of it defeated his effort to introduce it to new subject matter.
88. Earl Miner, *The Cavalier Mode from Jonson to Cotton* (Princeton, NJ: Princeton University Press, 1971) p. 3.
89. The numbers in the stanza outline indicate number of stresses per line. (The basic metre is iambic.) Kermode (*RI* 38–40), without benefit of the poet's notes, was the first to notice Yeats's debt to Cowley for the stanza of 'In Memory of Major Robert Gregory'. This stanza was re-employed in 'A Prayer for my Daughter' and in section II of 'The Tower'. Also, Jacqueline Genet, in *William Butler Yeats: les fondements et l'évolution de la création poétique* (Villeneuve-d'Ascq: Université de Lille III, 1976) pp. 329–30, concludes that the 'Byzantium' stanza is a variant of this. Parkinson (*YSC&LP*, II, 199–200) adds to the list 'A Dialogue of Self and Soul'. Both Genet (*William Butler Yeats*, p. 586) and Parkinson (*YSC&LP* 199) offer partial transcriptions from Yeats's white vellum notebook of 1930–3 to show that he later took notes on the first stanza of the concluding lyric in Cowley's 'Essay on Solitude' and applied the paradigm in 'The Mother of God' (*VP* 499). This is also mentioned by Bradford in *YW* 114. At the same point in the notebook (on microfilm at the State University of New York at Stony Brook, reel 21, vol. 5, p. 135) are notes that Yeats took, and apparently did not use, on the opening octave of the second untitled poem in Cowley's 'A Discourse Concerning the Government of Oliver Cromwell'. Those notes may be reduced here to the formula 5a–4a–5b–4b–4c–4c–4d–6d.
90. *Ben Jonson*, VIII, 245–6.

91. McAlindon, in *PMLA*, 82, pp. 168–9. Moreover, Harris (*YCP&B* 135n.) shows that Yeats's preparation for 'Shepherd and Goatherd' influenced the second Gregory elegy. The phrase 'a world's delight' in stanza 9 comes from 'Astrophel' (or 'The Lay of Clorinda'), the Countess of Pembroke's tribute to her departed brother. Yeats's familiarity with the other elegies on Sidney in *Colin Clout's Come Home Again* (1595) seems probable given his quotation (in *E&I* 381) of Matthew Roydon's 'An Elegie, or Friends Passion, for his Astrophill', ll. 103–6.
92. Witt (in *Modern Philology*, 48, no. 2, p. 117) reports that the stanza in manuscript was preceded by the comment, 'The following stanza was added in proof as Mrs. Gregory did not think I had said enough of Robert's courage.' I have not been able to locate this comment in the Berg Collection, though a note to this effect was made by Mrs Yeats beside stanza 8 of the poem in *YL* 2323 (unnoticed by the editor). Based on the Berg and NLI typescripts, the stanza was drafted *after* 24 May 1918 (the date given on a signed, shorter typescript), and by 14 June 1918, when Yeats wrote to Lady Gregory, 'I . . . have just finished a long poem in memory of Robert Gregory, which is among my best works' (*L* 650).
93. Graham Martin, 'The Wild Swans at Coole', *HonGuest* 72. Harris's reading of the two elegies finds 'Shepherd and Goatherd' an 'extraordinary deviation' of the Jonsonian country-house poem (*YCP&B* 125).

CHAPTER 5 YEATS, DONNE, AND THE METAPHYSICALS: POLEMICS AND LYRICS, 1896–1929

1. For example, Cleanth Brooks, *Modern Poetry and the Tradition* (Chapel Hill: University of North Carolina Press, 1939) pp. 173–202; Louis L. Martz, *The Poetry of Meditation* (New Haven, Conn.: Yale University Press, 1954) pp. 321–9; Rosemond Tuve, *Elizabethan and Metaphysical Imagery* (Chicago: University of Chicago Press, 1947); Margaret Willy, 'The Poetry of Donne: Its Interest and Influence Today', *Essays and Studies*, 7 (1954) 100–2; Frank Kermode, 'Dissociation of Sensibility', *Kenyon Review*, 19 (1957) 169–94; and Joseph E. Duncan, *The Revival of Metaphysical Poetry* (Minneapolis: University of Minnesota Press, 1959) esp. pp. 130–42.
2. Samuel Johnson, *The Lives of the English Poets*, ed. George B. Hill, 3 vols (Oxford: Clarendon Press, 1905) I, 20.
3. Edward Dowden, 'The Poetry of John Donne', *New Studies in Literature* (1895; London: Kegan Paul, 1902) p. 106. Originally read before the Elizabethan Literary Society in 1890, Dowden's essay refutes the view that Donne and the Metaphysical poets were to blame for a post-Elizabethan decline in English poetry. According to Dowden, Donne's 'delight in subtleties of thought, in over-ingenious fantasies, in far-fetched imagery, in curiosity ["not always felicitous curiosity"] of expression' was typical in his time and commonplace in Shakespeare's early history plays and comedies and in the final books of *The Faerie Queene*. Duncan (*The Revival of Metaphysical Poetry*, p. 217

n. 4) mentions Dowden as a formative influence on H. J. C. Grierson.
4. Frank J. Warnke (ed.), *John Donne: Poetry and Prose* (New York: Modern Library, 1967) p. xxvi. A full discussion is provided in Warnke's Introduction, but see too his *Versions of Baroque* (New Haven, Conn., and London: Yale University Press, 1972), and 'Metaphysical Poetry and the European Context', in Malcolm Bradbury and David Palmer (ed.), *Metaphysical Poetry* (Bloomington: Indiana University Press, 1970) pp. 261–76. Warnke equates 'mannerism' with Baroque style and views the latter's antithetical relationship to classical style in terms of a theory of flux – that is, Baroque (hence Metaphysical) poetry occurs between two periods of classicism: Renaissance and Augustan.
5. Harold Bloom, in *Yeats* (London: Oxford University Press, 1970) p. 173, equates Landor's and Jonson's 'epigrammatic strength and stoic knowingness'. Yeats himself suggests an equation when he characterizes '*Antithetical* men, . . . like Landor, [who are] violent in themselves because they hate all that impedes their personality, but are in their intellect . . . gentle' (*AV B* 84–5). Compare this description with that of Jonson (as opposed to Shakespeare) on p. 153; then see pp. 144–5 and *Myth* 328–9.
6. Bornstein (*Y&Shel* 208) equates Shelley's metaphysical literary quest with what Yeats called 'automatonism'. Bornstein quotes *Au* 326 to show that Yeats thought Donne the complementary opposite of Shelley on 'sexuality and suffering', and sees parallels between Donne's 'The Extasie' and Yeats's Crazy Jane poems. In such works, Bornstein thinks, sexuality permits both poets 'to include the realm of metaphysics and spirit without seeming "unhuman" '.
7. One of those modes, the English country-house poem, is considered by Charles Tomlinson, 'Yeats and the Practising Poet', in *HonGuest* 1–7. Marjorie Perloff adds the Coleridgean conversation poem (for a synthesis of 'public event and private experience') in 'Yeats and the Occasional Poem: "Easter 1916" ', *Papers on Language and Literature*, 4, no. 3 (1968) 308–28, but soon refines her theory by substituting the '*débat* convention' for that of the 'topographical poem': ' "Another Emblem There": Theme and Convention in Yeats's "Coole Park and Ballylee, 1931" ', *Journal of English and Germanic Philology*, 69, no. 2 (1970) 223–40. Without mentioning Donne, she makes extensive use of Marvell's interesting 'topographical debate' in 'Upon Appleton House'. Bornstein shifts the spotlight in 'Yeats and the Greater Romantic Lyric', in George Bornstein (ed.), *Romantic and Modern* (Pittsburgh: University of Pittsburgh Press, 1977) pp. 91–110, indebted to M. H. Abrams's definition of the longer Romantic lyric, a mode developed from the topographical poem through Denham and from seventeenth-century meditative poetry through poets such as Vaughan and Herbert. Donne's strong influence on Yeats, as on Eliot, is cautiously suggested by Bornstein in *Transformations of Romanticism in Yeats, Eliot, and Stevens* (Chicago: University of Chicago Press, 1976) p. 17.
8. The contested elegies are nos xxxviii–xli in Jonson's *The Underwood*

(1641). No. xxxix, now generally thought to be by Donne, was among the manuscripts collected for the 1633 edition of Donne's poems, in which it received the title 'The Expostulation'. The dispute over the authorship of these poems is summarized by J. G. Nichols in *The Poetry of Ben Jonson* (New York: Barnes and Noble, 1969) pp. 5–8. The only certainty is that *both* poets were capable of producing the poems. The issue is understandable considering the textual complexities reported in *The Poems of John Donne*, ed. Herbert J. C. Grierson, 2 vols (Oxford: Clarendon Press, 1912) II, lvi–cliii.

9. See Warwick Gould, 'The Flame of the Spirit: A Love Tribute from W. B. Yeats', *The Times Literary Supplement*, 17 July 1987, p. 770. The manuscript book is referred to by Richard Ellmann in *YM&M* 102.

10. Gould, in *The Times Literary Supplement*, 17 July 1987, p. 770.

11. See John Harwood, *Olivia Shakespear and W. B. Yeats: 'After Long Silence'* (London: Macmillan, 1989) pp. 59–82, on Yeats's affairs of the body, heart, and mind with Mrs Shakespear and her impact on WR.

12. See James Allen, 'Life as Art: Yeats and the Alchemical Quest', *Studies in the Literary Imagination*, 14, no. 1 (1981) 17–42.

13. These essays (revised from *The Speaker*, *The Academy*, and the *Daily Chronicle*) were collected in Johnson's *Post Liminium: Essays and Critical Papers*, ed. Thomas Whittemore (London: Elkin Mathews, 1911), which Yeats owned (*YL* 1022). In light of Yeats's later reconciliation of the mannerisms of Donne and Jonson, one might recall Lionel Johnson's despair in 'Mystic and Cavalier': 'Go from me: I am one of those, who fall.' Yeats alludes to this memorable first line in 'In Memory of Major Robert Gregory' (*VP* 324, ll. 19–20: ' . . . much falling he / Brooded upon sanctity').

14. Possibly the scorings in *YL* 2222 – *The Lives of Dr. John Donne, Sir Henry Wotton* . . . (London: Washbourne, 1840) – were by Yeats. O'Shea expresses some doubt, and he may be right. Still, if they *are* Yeats's, they show that he took note of Donne's self-absorbed delivery: 'a preacher in earnest; weeping sometimes for his auditory, sometimes with them; always preaching to himself, like an angel from a cloud, but in none' (p. 36). They mark a synaesthetic epithet (that Donne's 'memory smelleth like a *Field* that the Lord hath blessed' – p. xiv), an editor's note on Thomas Morton (school-fellow of 'the notorious Guy Fawkes' – p. 16), and the anonymous epitaph 'Reader! I am to let thee know, / Donne's Body only lies below; / For, could the grave his Soul comprise, / Earth would be richer than the Skies!' (p. 79).

15. Johnson, *Post Liminum*, p. 271.

16. Arthur Symons, 'John Donne', *Fortnightly Review*, 66 (1 Nov 1899) 734–45.

17. Gosse's work is subject to the implicit criticism of not being an artistic masterpiece to compare with Walton's *Life and Death of Dr Donne*, wherein 'every word is the touch of a cunning brush painting a picture'. Yet, as Symons wrote, Gosse's biography had the virtue of being 'faithful to the document' and 'make[s] no pretence to harmon-

ise a sometimes discordant existence' (*Fortnightly Review*, 66, p. 734).
18. Ibid., p. 735.
19. George Saintsbury, Introduction to the *Poems of John Donne*, ed. E. K. Chambers (London: Routledge, 1896) I, xxxiii; see also pp. xxxi–ii, for a rather perplexing apology for Donne's 'gross' faults and extravagances. Utilizing Donne's biography (i.e. from Walton's *Lives* and Saintsbury's Elizabethan history) to make inferences about the Jacobean divine's poetry, Dowden's 'The Poetry of John Donne' (*New Studies in Literature*, p. 91) likens the latter to 'twenty-five pennyweights of . . . [gold] in a ton of quartz and wash-dirt'.
20. Symons, in *Fortnightly Review*, 66, p. 744.
21. Ibid., p. 743.
22. Ibid., p. 741.
23. Ibid., p. 740.
24. Ibid., p. 742.
25. Ibid.
26. Herbert Grierson, Preface to V. K. Narayana Menon, *The Development of William Butler Yeats* (Edinburgh: Oliver and Boyd, 1942) p. xiii.
27. See, for example, Donne, *Poems*, ed. Grierson, I, 86 and 100. The contents list of *VP* shows that such titles ('His Dream', 'His Memories', 'His Wildness', 'His Confidence', 'His Bargain', etc.) occur only within the sequences 'Raymond Lully and his Wife Pernella' (1910), 'A Man Young and Old' (1928), 'A Woman Young and Old' (1929) and 'Words for Music Perhaps' (1932). Possibly by intent, the titles of those poems (above named) resemble those borne by Donne's Elegies V and XII ('His Picture' and 'His parting from her'). In an ambitious adaptive exercise of 1926 (see Ch. 5, section IV), Yeats's 'Parting' (*VP* 535–6) was inspired by Elegy XII ('Since she must go, and I must mourn, come Night'), as well as by other poems by Donne. The coincidence of Yeats's revision of titles in *WR* and evidence, in *Discoveries* and elsewhere, that Donne was beginning to exert a strong influence on Yeats in the same year, 1906, is compelling. Herrick's *Hesperides*, too (in *YL* 886–9), contains numerous prototypes of such titles. See John T. Shawcross, 'A Consideration of Title-Names in the Poetry of Donne and Yeats', *Names: Journal of the American Name Society*, 31, no. 3 (1983) 159–66.
28. As we marvel at the few sonnets and near-sonnets in Yeats's canon, it is hard to believe that such mastery came unbidden. There *was* practice, c. 1881–4, as shown by the title '(Sonnit 1)', centred at the head of L3v in NLI 12,161, evidently to be followed by a fair copy of a poem produced elsewhere. Dowden was obsessed with the form, and Yeats had Shakespeare's sonnets via Dowden's edition (*YL* 1879, presented to J. B. Yeats in 1881). He was critical of Spenser's 'many intolerably artificial sonnets' (*E&I* 362) and, typical of his reading, was acquainted with Sidney long before he came to own copies of the works themselves (*YL* 1916–17).
29. R. H. Super, 'Dining with Landor', *YAACTS*, 5 (1987) 146. Super compares Landor with Yeats; Donne, the 'companion' of Yeats and Landor in 'To a Young Beauty', receives scant attention for 'the

obvious care with which his poems are wrought' (p. 143). Part I of 'Dust Hath Closed Helen's Eye', Yeats's essay about blind Raftery and the beautiful Mary Hynes, appeared in *The Dome* (Oct 1899) before being added to the revised edition of *The Celtic Twilight* (1902; Wade 35). The quaint elegiac tone of Nashe's poem ('Beauty is but a flower/Which wrinkles will devour;/Brightness falls from the air;/Queens have died young and fair;/Dust hath closed Helen's eye') is akin to that of Yeats's early poetry (for instance, 'The Rose of the World': 'Who dreamed that beauty passes like a dream? . . . Troy passed away in one high funeral gleam'). Yeats quoted Nashe's lines in 'The Symbolism of Poetry' (1900; *E&I* 156) and did so again in his notes to Lady Gregory's *Cuchulain of Muirthemne* (1902).

30. Marlowe's role has been cited before (see Ch. 4, section III). Use of Chapman's Homer in 'A Woman Homer Sung', 'No Second Troy', 'Peace', and later poems is perhaps suggested by YL 370 and 907, with the Buckley translation of *The Iliad* (1870; YL 905) and adaptations by Bridges (YL 274) and Morris ('Scenes from the Fall of Troy', ll. 3–51, in YL 1389, p. 24).

31. See Robert O'Driscoll, 'Letters and Lectures of W. B. Yeats', *University Review* (Dublin), 3, no. 8 (1966) 33.

32. In 'Rosa Alchemica', Robartes, the chief adept, or magus, of the Order of the Alchemical Rose, speaks to the narrator: 'I have read your books, and now I see you among all these images, and I understand you better than you do yourself, for I have been with many and many dreamers at the same crossways.' Yeats applied this Cabbalistic term to the early 'Ballads and Lyrics' – rechristened 'Crossways' in *P(1895)* – and later noted similar usage in Burton's *Anatomy*. See YL 311 and the summary in YL Notes. Quite late, Yeats raided his copy of *The Anatomy of Melancholy* (London: Bell, 1912) for a long passage (1.2.1.vi) quoted in *On the Boiler* (1938; *Ex* 418–20).

33. Herbert J. C. Grierson, *The First Half of the Seventeenth Century* (New York: Scribner's, 1906) p. 153.

34. O'Driscoll (in *University Review*, 3, no. 8, p. 36) quotes Yeats's letter to Grierson of 28 June 1907, bearing the admission, 'It was my conversation with you some time ago that sent me to Italy for it started me reading Gardner's books about Ferrara, and in the end sent me to Ferrara.' The works of Edmund Garratt Gardner which Yeats read are *Dukes and Poets in Ferrara* (1904; YL 728), *The King and the Court Poets* (1906; YL 729), and *The Story of Florence* (1905; YL 1920 283).

35. See above, Chs. 1 (section I; p. 9 and n. 35) and 3 (p. 88 and n. 30).

36. Grierson, *The First Half of the Seventeenth Century*, p. 153.

37. Ibid., pp. 155–6.

38. Ibid., p. 159.

39. Donne, *Poems*, ed. Grierson, I, 258.

40. See, for example, William M. Carpenter, 'The *Green Helmet* Poems and Yeats's Myth of the Renaissance', *Modern Philology*, 67, no. 1 (1969) 53; and Patrick J. Keane, *Yeats's Interactions with Tradition* (Columbia, Mo.: University of Missouri Press, 1987) pp. 26–7.

41. Saintsbury, Introduction to Donne, *Poems*, ed. Chambers, I, xxiv.
42. According to William Drummond, Jonson claimed 'that Dones Anniversarie was profane and full of Blasphemies[;] that he told Mr. Donne, if it had been written of ye Virgin Marie it had been something/to which he answered that he described the Idea of a Woman and not as she was[;] that Done for not keeping of accent deserved hanging' – *Conversations*, 4, in *Ben Jonson: Discoveries, 1641; [and] Conversations with William Drummond of Hawthornden, 1619* (London: Bodley Head Quartos, 1922–6; repr. New York: Barnes and Noble, 1966.
43. See *Mem* 49; Gould, in *The Times Literary Supplement*, 17 July 1987, p. 770; Curtis B. Bradford, 'Yeats and Maud Gonne', *Texas Studies in Language and Literature*, 3, no. 4 (1962) 461, 463; and George Mills Harper, *Yeats's Golden Dawn* (New York: Barnes and Noble, 1974) p. 161.
44. The Donne–Herbert connection was first made by Duncan (*The Revival of Metaphysical Poetry*, pp. 135–6).
45. Yeats, 'Discoveries: Second Series', ed. Curtis B. Bradford, in *Massachusetts Review*, 5 (1964) 305; see *YL* 351. Roughly contemporary with the poems published in *GH*, the last essay of the series characteristically shows how, in Platonic terms, Hoby's translation described the perfect man. The essay also reads as a gloss to Yeats's theory of composition in 'Adam's Curse', 'Words', and other poems.
46. Donne, *Poems*, ed. Grierson, I, 53.
47. See James L. Allen, Jr., 'Yeats's Use of the Serious Pun', *Southern Review*, 1, no. 2 (1963) 153–66; and Conrad A. Balliet, 'W. B. Yeats: The Pun of a Gonne', *Modern British Literature*, 4, no. 1 (1979) 44–50. Balliet even goes so far as to place significance in the 'potential eye-rhyme of "Gonne–Donne", as well as the near rhyme of "gone-Donne" ' in 'To a Young Beauty' (p. 47). Keane (*Yeats's Interactions with Tradition*, pp. 123, 127–8) cites Yeats's spiritual–genital punning in poems of the 1930s, attributing this to Donne's influence.
48. Donne, *Poems*, ed. Grierson, I, 58–9, 62–3.
49. Ibid., p. 95.
50. Maud Gonne MacBride, *A Servant of the Queen* (Dublin: Golden Eagle, 1950) pp. 329–30.
51. Saintsbury, Introduction to Donne, *Poems*, ed. Chambers, I, xxxii.
52. Donne, *Poems*, ed. Grierson, pp. 7, 10, 11–12.
53. The origin of Yeats's metaphor of the sieve is uncertain. Helena (in *All's Well that Ends Well*, I.iii.198–200) uses it to show Shakespeare's emblematic use of the *vas* or *frustra*: 'I know I love in vain, strive against hope;/Yet in this captious and intenible sieve/I still pour in the waters of my love.' Much closer to Yeats's sexual word-play are the First Witch's lines in *Macbeth*, I.iii.8–10: 'But in a sieve I'll thither sail,/And, like a rat without a tail,/I'll do, I'll do, and I'll do.'
54. Examples are from *Mem* 143. See Bradford, *YW* 44–6. Yeats's expropriation of Donne's pun must have been fairly conscious, as was Landor's in the prose dialogue Yeats read in *Imaginary Conversations* (*YL* 1081, vol. IV), in imitative lyrics presented as if written by Donne

in 'meridian heat of youth and genius': 'She was so beautiful, had God but died/For her, and none beside, . . . with bright zeal, the buoyant Sun/Cried thro' his worlds well done!' (p. 171; see Duncan, *The Revival of Metaphysical Poetry*, p. 39).
55. See YL 2210, A. E. Waite's *Lives of Alchemystical Philosophers* (London: George Redway, 1888) p. 107. Taking delight in 'seeing and contemplating *the admirable works of Nature within the vessels* . . .', Flamel cites how on three occasions (made trebly emphatic by repetition) he had 'done it', succeeded in changing base mercury to gold with the aid of Perrenelle.
56. Donne, *Poems*, ed. Grierson, II, xxxi (Introduction).
57. Ibid., I, 187–8.
58. Ibid., II, xxxiv; see also pp. xxii–xxiii, xlv, 37–9.
59. See Duncan, *The Revival of Metaphysical Poetry*, p. 136.
60. Donne, *Poems*, ed. Grierson, I, xlv.
61. Ibid., p. xlvi.
62. Ibid., p. xxxiv.
63. Drawing its title from Dante's *Vita Nuova* (see Jeffares, *NCom* 166), Yeats first published 'Ego Dominus Tuus' in *Poetry* (Chicago) in October 1917, the month of his marriage, although the poem had been completed two years before, in December 1915 (as shown by *Myth* 324 and the Berg Collection typescript 'The Anti-Self').
64. Austin Clarke, 'Poet and Artist', *The Observer*, 5 Feb 1939, p. 8. Attributing to Yeats 'an astute awareness of literary fashions, that kept the poet from sinking into a groove', Clarke recalled, 'when I met Yeats many years ago . . . in the Seven Woods of Coole, he was engrossed in the study of Donne and the Jacobeans, and could speak of nothing else.' Clarke probably met Yeats around 1916.
65. Though complete by February 1916, the book was delayed for various reasons.
66. Yeats's acquaintance with *The Republic* (courtesy of Lionel Johnson, 1893) and other Platonic dialogues (through Stephen Gwynn) would be an exception. Her first-hand knowledge of Plotinus, save for the sixth treatise of the First Ennead, came with the acquisition of a complete set of Mackenna's translations some time after the early 1920s.
67. Duncan, *The Revival of Metaphysical Poetry*, p. 132.
68. Yeats was a great reader of Landor's works. He owned a complete set of the *Imaginary Conversations*, a two-volume *Poems, Dialogues in Verse, and Epigrams* (all annotated), and other titles (YL 1080–4). See n. 54. Yet Landor alone could not have provided the model for such Yeatsian dialogues as 'Solomon to Sheba', 'Michael Robartes and the Dancer', 'Solomon and the Witch', and 'An Image from a Past Life'. Laurence Perrine, in 'Yeats and Landor: "To a Young Beauty" ', *Notes and Queries*, 19, no. 9 (1972) 330, argues that the closing lines of Yeats's poem ('And I may dine at journey's end/With Landor and with Donne' – *VP* 336) were suggested by the dialogue 'Archdeacon Hare and Walter Landor' in *Imaginary Conversations*, though perhaps Yeats only recalled the closing allusion in Osman Edwards' essay on

Verhaeren in *The Savoy*, 2, no. 7 (Nov 1896), a memorable number for carrying two of Yeats's poems and his story 'The Tables of the Law'.
69. Donne, *Poems*, ed. Grierson, I, xiv (Introduction).
70. Yeats's attachment to Henry More argues how he might have regarded Thomas Vaughan's hermetic writings. More and Vaughan were jealous rivals who quarrelled in their works. Morever, Vaughan was satirized in Samuel Butler's 'Character of an Hermetic Philosopher' and in *Hudibras*, which Yeats read in *YL* 317. In the British Museum, Yeats possibly read Waite's 1888 edition of *The Magical Works of Thomas Vaughan*, of which the *Magica Adamica* and *Coelum Terrae* touch on Flamel and Lully. The Theosophical Publishing Society also made available, in 1896, an edition of Vaughan's *Euphrates or The Waters of the East* (1655), with commentary by Florence Farr. Yeats owned a copy of it (*YL* 1563).
71. *YL 1920* 282 and 284 testify to similar lapses with respect to Crashaw (whose works Yeats sold) and Herbert (whose works were thinned) some time after the early 1920s.
72. See Ch. 2, no. 31.
73. Vaughan's transfiguring-effect on 'Sailing to Byzantium' and 'Byzantium' is suggested in Stallworthy's *Between the Lines: Yeats's Poetry in the Making* (Oxford: Clarendon Press, 1963) pp. 108–9 and 130. In manuscript, Yeats used overtly alchemical diction and modified the image 'birds of Hades' to 'cocks of Hades', as in Vaughan's 'Cock Crowing', so introducing the 'old Resurrection symbol' of the cock crowing at sunrise. In 'George Herbert and Yeats's "Sailing to Byzantium" ', *Four Decades of Poetry, 1890–1930*, 1, no. 1 (1976) 51–3, Ronald E. McFarland, drawing upon the often 'misleading' transcription of Curtis Bradford (see Stallworthy, *Between the Lines*, p. 102) makes a less-than-convincing case that Herbert's 'Love (II)' is the inspiration for 'Byzantium', particularly the third stanza. Duncan, in *The Revival of Metaphysical Poetry*, p. 141, regards the Byzantium poems as Metaphysical wit, in which 'intellectual subtlety' and 'erudition dance lightly together'.
74. See Harper, *Making AV*, I, 90, 205, and II, 42, 94, 97, 143, 419, 427; also *Au* 248. According to Clarke (*The Observer*, 5 Feb 1939, p. 8) Yeats once recommended Herbert to him because of the religious poet's 'austerity'. See Keane, *Yeats's Interactions with Tradition*, p. 126.
75. See Balachandra Rajan, *W. B. Yeats* (London: Hutchinson, 1969) p. 110.
76. Johnson, *Lives of the English Poets*, I, 19.
77. Donne, *Poems*, ed. Grierson, II, xiv (Introduction).
78. Gregory's 'body thought', rendered in an image of self-mastery and a gesture of *sprezzatura*, seems the point of stanza VIII: 'He rode the race without a bit[,]/And yet his mind outran the horses' feet.' See Duncan, *The Revival of Metaphysical Poetry*, p. 136; and Keane, *Yeats's Interactions with Tradition*, p. 219. Along with the other echoes in stanza XI, Keane would have one hear Dryden's 'all Mankind's Epitome' (from *Absalom and Achitophel*), but Yeats's copy of Dryden's

Poetical Works (YL 560) argues against this (see Ch. 4, n. 24). Consider the verses from 'The Feaver' and 'The Sunne Rising' quoted in Ch. 5, section II, in light of Marlowe's 'Infinite riches in a little room' (*The Jew of Malta*, 1.i.37) and Donne's 'The Canonization': 'We'll build in sonnets pretty roomes. . . . Who did the whole worlds soule contract . . . (So made such mirrors, and such spies, / That they did all to you epitomize)' (ll. 32, 40, 42–4, in *Poems*, ed. Grierson, I, 15). Cf. Yeats: 'Some burn damp faggots, others may consume / The entire combustible world in one small room . . . Soldier, scholar, horseman, he, / As 'twere all life's epitome' (*VP* 327, ll. 81–2, 86–7).

79. Stanza I of Yeats's poem, entitled 'Her Courtesy', is remarkably like Jonson's third movement, 'The Picture of her Body', evoking a mental picture similar to the actual one Jonson described, which is now in the Dulwich Picture Gallery and reproduced in *Ben Jonson*, ed. C. H. Herford and Percy and Evelyn Simpson, 11 vols (Oxford: Clarendon Press, 1925–51), VII, facing p. 274. Lady Digby's face ('all light rose there') and Mabel Beardsley's ('rouge on the pallor of her face') are not, however, as similar as are the inner vitality Donne portrayed in 'The Second Anniversary', ll. 241–6 (*Poems*, ed. Grierson, I, 258) and Yeats's Donnean paradox-infused perspective: 'her eyes are laughter-lit, / Her speech a wicked tale that we may vie with her, / Matching our broken-hearted wit against her wit' (*VP* 362, ll. 5–7).

80. This paper, 'Lord Byron: Arnold and Swinburne', was delivered at the British Academy in 1920, according to Grierson in *The Background of English Literature*, 2nd edn (London: Chatto, 1934) p. vii.

81. O'Driscoll, in *University Review*, 3, no. 8, p. 38.

82. Henry King may be a case in point, a poet whose work was represented by three lyrics but whose *Poems* (YL 1062) Yeats owned three years later.

83. See Balachandra Rajan, 'The Poetry of Confrontation: Yeats and the Dialogue Poem', in Joseph Ronsley (ed.), *Myth and Reality in Irish Literature* (Waterloo, Ont.: Wilfrid Laurier University Press, 1977) pp. 117–28.

84. Grierson argued that 'to call these poets the "school of Donne" or "metaphysical" poets may easily mislead if one takes either phrase in too full a sense'. The reason for this has to do with what Grierson (and, I believe, Yeats) saw as Donne's anomalous relation to the other so-called Metaphysical poets: 'It is not only that [the other poets] show little of Donne's subtlety of mind', Grierson wrote, ' . . . but they want . . . the complexity of mood, the range of personal feeling which lends such fullness of life to Donne's strange and troubled poetry – Introduction to *Metaphysical Lyrics and Poems of the Seventeenth Century, Donne to Butler* (Oxford: Clarendon Press, 1921) p. xxx.

85. Ibid., pp. xxii, xxviii.

86. Grierson, *The Background of English Literature*, pp. 78, 79, 86.

87. For a list of these poems, see Jacqueline Genet, *William Butler Yeats: les fondements et l'évolution de la création poétique* (Villeneuve-d'Ascq: Universite de Lille III, 1976) pp. 585–6. Her discussion of Yeats's

experiments with the octave is supplemented by Robert Beum, *The Poetic Art of William Butler Yeats* (New York: Ungar, 1969) pp. 120–31.
88. Donne, *Poems*, ed. Grierson, I, 5.
89. On Browning's poem and Yeats's verse epistle, see Daniel Harris, 'The "Figured Page": Dramatic Epistle in Browning and Yeats', *YA* 1 (1982). Harris finds Yeats's verse after 1918 'studded with echoes of Browning' – echoes which join the rather more obvious reverberations of Donne and Jonson in *Responsibilities and Other Poems* (London: Macmillan, 1916) p. 185. Oil and lamp, candle-wick and taper-wick imagery are rife in Browning as they are not in the Renaissance authors Yeats read at the time – Herbert, Marvell, Vaughan, Milton, Crashaw. Indeed, a passage in 'Tertium Quid' (*The Ring and the Book*, IV) illustrates how well Browning's conceit may have combined with Donne's to suggest the self-consuming metaphor of Yeats's 'The Living Beauty'. Browning's monologue gives a cynical view of Pietro and Violante, who 'love themselves, / Spend their own oil in feeding their own lamp / That their own faces may grow bright thereby. / They get to fifty and over: how's the lamp? / Full the depth o' the wick . . .' (ll. 72–6).
90. Stephen Parrish, 'A New Solomon and Sheba Poem', *YA* 6 (1988) 211–13.
91. Northrop Frye, 'The Top of the Tower: A Study of the Imagery of Yeats', in Patrick J. Keane (ed.), *William Butler Yeats* (New York: McGraw-Hill, 1973) 126; see *LDW* 51–2 and 82.
92. In manuscript (see NLI 13,588[4]), '& wick' is careted in, an indication that Yeats was copying from another sheet.
93. See above, n. 73.
94. Donne, *Poems*, ed. Grierson, I, 28.
95. David R. Clark, *Yeats at Songs and Choruses* (Amherst: University of Massachusetts Press, 1983) pp. 28–9. Clark connects Jane's so-called 'black day', the day she lost her virginity to Jack the Journeyman, with the lyrics 'Black out; Heaven blazing into the head' and 'the sun's / Under eclipse and the day blotted out' from 'Lapis Lazuli' and 'The Tower' (*VP* 566, l. 19; and 414, ll. 119–20). Each case has its analogue in the passage quoted from *Au* at the outset of this chapter.
96. Keane, *Yeats's Interactions with Tradition*, p. 129.
97. O'Driscoll, in *University Review*, 3, no. 8, pp. 39–40.
98. See Marjorie Perloff, ' "Heart Mysteries": The Later Love Lyrics of W. B. Yeats,' *Contemporary Literature*, 10 (1969) 266–83. Perloff opines that Yeats's 'personal experience in love', expressed in the self-dramatizing poems of 1917–34, was the 'opposite' of Donne's: 'Despite the fact that Yeats, like Donne, makes much of the fusion of body and soul in the achievement of true love, of Unity of Being, there is none of Donne's sense of joyous conquest in Yeats, for whom "one little roome" never becomes "an every where", and who can never tell his sweetheart that "reverend love" has made them "one another's hermitage" ' (p. 268).
99. John Somer, 'Unaging Monuments: A Study of W. B. Yeats' Poetry

Sequence, "A Man Young and Old" ', *Ball State University Forum*, 12, no. 4 (1971) 32.
100. 'Imagining . . . That another mouthful / And his beating heart would burst' recalls the divinatory meanings of the Ace of Cups, as listed in A. E. Waite's *The Pictorial Key to the Tarot* (London: Rider, 1911) p. 224: 'House of the true heart, joy, content, abode, nourishment, abundance, fertility.' To Waite, who stressed the Tarot signification, Bayley's elliptical association of the eucharistic emblem with the ciborium seemed strained (p. 10). The issue may have brought Yeats to Bayley. The tale is in *The Book of the Thousand Nights and One Night*, tr. from the French of J. C. Mardrus by E. Powys Mathers, 16 vols (London: Casanova Society, 1923) II, 32–44; see p. 35 for Yeats's lyric source. My thanks to Warwick Gould for the citation. Yeats owned the four-volume edition (*YL* 251) printed the same year.
101. In NLI 13,589(24), the last six lines are cancelled and replaced by four lines very like the version which has come down to us in *VP*.
102. Mrs Yeats told the same story to Lennox Robinson, similarly withholding the boy's real name (HM 51868, *c*. 1926, in the Huntington Library, San Marino, Calif.) though she took care to write it in her record copy of *The Collected Poems*, p. 308 (*YL* 2323, unreported).
103. See Parkinson (*YSC&LP* II, 64–5), who also silently punctuates the entry preceding the 'Father and Child' draft, which is otherwise comparable to the transcription above. Duncan (*The Revival of Metaphysical Poetry*, p. 136) first connected Herbert's poem with l. 1 of Yeats's ('She hears me strike the board and say'); also, Duncan recognized similarities of technique and imagery between Yeats's poem 'Veronica's Napkin' (*c*. 1929) and Herbert's 'Sunday': 'Veronica's napkin is the "Tent-pole of Eden; the tent's drapery". Herbert's "Sundaies the pillars are, / On which heav'ns palace arched lies", and his "Content" depicts a soul as draped from the world's tent-poles' (ibid.).
104. Keane, *Yeats's Interactions with Tradition*, p. 125.
105. Ibid., p. 127.
106. Stallworthy, *Between the Lines*, pp. 136–63.
107. Except for 'a few poems' added to the Crazy Jane sequence in 1933, most of these poems were drafted at around the same time. As Yeats observed in the 'Notes' to *Wade* 169 and 171, '*A Woman Young and Old* was written before the publication of *The Tower* but left out for some reason I cannot recall' (*VP* 831).
108. See Genet, *William Butler Yeats*, pp. 705–8, 710, 709 (in that order) for a verso-to-recto view (in Rapallo Notebook C, L52v–55r) of 'Love's Loneliness' and 'His Bargain'. Unfortunately, leaves unrepresented (L48v–52r) illustrate the proximity of 'Her Dream' and its inseparable relationship to the other two poems.
109. Duncan, *The Revival of Metaphysical Poetry*, p. 135.
110. A similar incendiary image from Jonson occurs in 'In Memory of Eva Gore-Booth and Con Markiewicz' (*VP* 476; dated 'October 1927'): 'Arise and bid me strike a match / And strike another till time catch' (ll. 26–7). Cf. Jonson's 'Meddle with your match, / And the strong lines, that so the time doe catch' (*The Under-wood*, XLIII.71–8). See

Keane, *Yeats's Interactions with Tradition*, p. 297.
111. Details on manuscripts related to 'Parting' and 'Chosen' are in Stallworthy, *Between the Lines*, pp. 135–63. Stallworthy ignores the obvious Donne factor, despite notices in F. A. C. Wilson, *W. B. Yeats and Tradition* (New York: Macmillan, 1958) pp. 205–11; John Unterecker, *A Reader's Guide to William Butler Yeats* (New York: Farrar Straus Giroux, 1959) pp. 237–8; and Giorgio Melchiori, *The Whole Mystery of Art* (London: Routledge and Kegan Paul, 1960) pp. 179–85.
112. Donne, *Poems*, ed. Grierson, I, 101. See Duncan, *The Revival of Metaphysical Poetry*, p. 135; Stallworthy, *Between the Lines*, p. 143.
113. Donne, *Poems*, ed. Grierson, I, 23. See Grierson's note in II, 22–3.
114. Ibid., I, 100–1.
115. See Ch. 2, n. 44.
116. Duncan, *The Revival of Metaphysical Poetry*, p. 135.
117. According to Mrs Yeats's note on 'Parting' in YL 2323, the date of composition was August 1926. Given the discrepancy between this date and Yeats's boast to Grierson, in February, that he had already completed his adaptation of Donne, the later date might actually represent the approximate point at which the dialogue 'Morning' gave up one (if not two) of its four parts to become a separate poem.
118. Wilson, *Yeats and Tradition*, p. 206.
119. Melchiori, *The Whole Mystery of Art*, p. 181.
120. Keane, *Yeats's Interactions with Tradition*, p. 130.
121. In Stallworthy, *Between the Lines*, p. 139.
122. See ibid., p. 159, on L14r.
123. See Melchiori, *The Whole Mystery of Art*, pp. 181–2.
124. Ibid., p. 182.
125. See Wilson, *Yeats and Tradition*, p. 210.
126. Stallworthy, *Between the Lines*, p. 161.

CHAPTER 6 CONCLUSION: THE RAPPROCHEMENT WITH MILTON AND SPENSER, 1918–39

1. See Ch. 3, n. 46.
2. Ellmann and Litz both show that Yeats responded to Pound's call 'to get rid of Miltonic generalizations', by which the Irish poet understood 'modern [or Renaissance] abstractions' as opposed to 'medieval naturalness', or 'the definite and the concrete'. See Ellmann, *ED* 66; and A. Walton Litz, 'Pound and Yeats: The Road to Stone Cottage', in George Bornstein (ed.), *Ezra Pound among the Poets* (Chicago: University of Chicago Press, 1985) p. 139. Quoting one of Pound's letters to Dorothy Shakespear, Litz reveals how Pound had just spent a miserable holiday at Milton's cottage ('Beastly dark low-ceilinged hole') before joining Yeats at Stone Cottage in 1913, preaching, as he did to another writer in twenty years, a sermon on the poisoned 'dogbiscuit of Milton's rhetoric' – K. L. Goodwin, *The Influence of Ezra Pound* (London: Oxford University Press, 1966) pp. 59–60. Eliot's

Notes 259

famous review of Grierson's *Metaphysical Lyrics* (1921) placed Milton just beyond the Renaissance. Eliot's shifting on Milton may be read in his essays 'Milton I' (1936) and 'Milton II' (1947) in *Selected Prose of T. S. Eliot* (New York: Harcourt Brace Jovanovich, 1975). See Kermode, *RI* 139–41, 146–7.

3. Yeats, 'Discoveries: Second Series', ed. Curtis B. Bradford, in *Massachusetts Review*, 5 (1964) 299.
4. Graham Hough's *The Mystery Religion of W. B. Yeats* (Brighton: Harvester, 1984) begins by crediting Denis Saurat's *Literature and Occult Tradition* as the first really significant consideration of Cabbalistic and hermetic (or 'heterodox, non-Christian' – p. 2) traditions in the works of Renaissance Christian poets such as Spenser and Milton. Hough seems on the right track, but more important to Yeats, in fact, as the Yeats library now indicates, were Saurat's *Blake and Modern Thought* (1929; YL 1846) and *Milton, Man and Thinker* (1925; YL 1847).
5. See W. J. McCormack, 'Yeats and a New Tradition', *The Crane Bag Book of Irish Studies (1977–1981)* (Dublin: Blackwater Press, 1982) pp. 362–72; see also *UP1* 351–3 and 360–4. McCormack describes the circle of Yeats's movement from rejection of Swift and Berkeley in the 1880s and 1890s to something more than full acceptance by the close of the First World War. McCormack cites Yeats's political quarrel with Edward Dowden over rural consciousness in emergent Irish nationalism. Fuller discussion of Yeats's gradual reversal may be read in Torchiana's *Y&GI*, esp. pp. 3–35.
6. Yeats, in an elegiac mood, often recalled Sidney, as he did in 1910 after the death of Synge. In tribute, 'J. M. Synge and the Ireland of his Time' (*E&I* 323) reprinted ll. 3–6 from song VII of *Astrophel and Stella* (YL 1917) to support the view that Synge had failed to articulate a 'definite philosophy' only because he was a 'pure artist'. Hone asserts that Yeats trained for this essay, in May 1910, by 'reading a little of Milton's prose every morning before he began to work' (*WBY* 252).
7. Harper, *Making AV* II, 30 and 421n. Two, of four, Robartes–Aherne manuscripts contain lines from the poem. Because of this, and also because the poem was not originally conceived around either one of these characters, as one may read in NLI 13,587(21), the poem may have preceded the prose dialogues.
8. See *AV B* 19–20; *YL* 1586–7A and 1589–95A; also *YL* 1080–4 (much annotated), Landor's *Imaginary Conversations* and verse dialogues. On 1 December 1916, Yeats told Alexandra Schepeler that he was reading Landor while composing a letter to his 'daimon', Leo Africanus (HM 28379, in the Huntington Library, San Marino, Calif.).
9. Many of Yeats's queries for his spirit 'communicators' were about how specific people related to the system which evolved in this way. Some of these people were cited as examples of the twenty-eight incarnations in *A Vision*. Milton, as Harper shows (*Making AV* II, 42, 93, 170), originally stood with Horace, Dr Johnson, Flaubert, and Napoleon in Phase 21, a slot finally occupied by Shaw, Wells, and George Moore.
10. The ensuing account of 'The Phases of the Moon' manuscripts,

together with a complete transcription of the surprising early version, appears also in Wayne K. Chapman, 'The Miltonic Crux of "The Phases of the Moon" ', *YA* 8 (1990).

11. The frontispiece to *LT* is not the illustration Yeats would have encountered in Palmer's book. The picture differs somewhat in content and substantially in form, being the reversal of Palmer's illustration in *The Shorter Poems of John Milton*. Although Yeats may have known this other engraving, since he was an expert on Palmer, as he was on the illustrators Blake and Calvert – see *YL* 333–4, 1320–1, 2202–3, and *YA* 4 (1986) 286 – this is not the picture that brought him to Milton's text. For that illustration, see plate 9.

12. In John Milton, *Complete Poems and Major Prose*, ed. Merritt Y. Hughes (Indianapolis: Odyssey, 1957) p. 74.

13. Conceivably, 'Yo[un]g A[t]henean light' could be my misreading for 'Yo[un]g A[t]hanase['s] light' in L4r. Yet the next draft clearly produces 'Yo[u]ng Athena's light again, an image / . . . T̶h̶a̶t̶ ̶S̶h̶e̶l̶l̶e̶y̶ ̶p̶i̶c̶t̶u̶r̶e̶d̶ ̶t̶h̶e̶r̶[̶e̶]̶ ̶f̶r̶o̶m̶ ̶t̶[̶h̶e̶]̶ ̶t̶o̶w̶e̶r̶ / From . . . that far tower where Milton['s] plato[n]ist. . . .' No doubt, Athene appears because she is the goddess of wisdom. Her transfer to l. 45 in *VP* ('Athene takes Achilles by the hair') receives comment in *AV A* 215. In *NCom* 174, Jeffares' speculations about the influence of 'Il Penseroso' on Shelley's 'Prince Athanase, A Fragment' (1817) seem apt given the complex Yeats discloses at the outset of his poem. Nevertheless, the emphasis on Shelley seems misplaced in light of additional evidence and in light of Shelley's poem itself, which features no tower at all, but a *soul* which had 'wedded Wisdom . . . clothed in which he sate / Apart from men, *as in* a lonely tower' (ll. 31–3, emphasis added). In his first revision, Yeats associated 'Shelleyan' 'subterranean caves', the source of the river's 'bubling up [*sic*]', with the well 'of natural insti[n]cts' – a passage excised from the poem before completion.

14. See Ch. 2, n. 31.

15. Kathleen Raine, in *Yeats the Initiate* (Mountrath, Co. Laois: Dolmen Press; London: Allen and Unwin, 1986) 235–44. We might recall similarities between Blake's twenty-seven churches of the time-world ('Mundane egg') in *Milton* and Yeats's twenty-eight phases of existence in *A Vision*. For more on such parallels, see Raine's 'From Blake to *A Vision*' (*Yeats the Initiate*, pp. 106–76).

16. *The Complete Poetry and Prose of William Blake*, ed. David V. Erdman (Berkeley Calif.: University of California Press, 1982) p. 730. Certainly, the Romantic poet and artist must not be far in the background, for Yeats knew well Blake's *Milton* and Blake's illustrations for Milton's works. See *YL* 206 and 1320–1. What is more, Yeats made considerable use of Blake's system in the 1925 edition of *A Vision*.

17. Stan Smith, 'Porphyry's Cup: Yeats, Forgetfulness and the Narrative Order', *YA* 5 (1987) 38; Warwick Gould, ' "A Lesson for the Circumspect": W. B. Yeats's Two Versions of *A Vision* and *The Arabian Nights*', in Peter L. Caracciolo (ed.), in *The 'Arabian Nights' in English Literature* (London: Macmillan, 1988) pp. 245–6, 254 and 277.

18. See Harper, *Making AV* i, 54, 97; and *AV A* (Notes) 10, on how the

'28 mansions' got into the automatic script and the poem, having been marked in Chaucer and typed out by Mrs Yeats. The text she used (hence the one followed here) was *The Complete Works of Geoffrey Chaucer*, ed. Walter W. Skeat, 6 vols (Oxford: Clarendon Press, 1894) IV, 493–4 (*Canterbury Tales*, F. 1117–25, 1129–34). Cf. YL 376–8.
19. The text presented here is from the *Complete Prose Works of John Milton*, ed. Douglas Bush et al., 8 vols (New Haven, Conn., and London: Yale University Press, 1953–82) II, 254–6, The Richard Garnett edition, *Prose of Milton* (London: Walter Scott, 1894; see YL 1920 286), is the probable source of Yeats's quotation. But possibly his attention was first drawn to this passage by the editor's preface (I, xvi) in *The Prose Works of John Milton*, ed. J. A. St John, 5 vols (London: Bohn's Library, 1848–54), where it is prominently featured (quoted in full from III, 194–5) as 'a grand dithyrambic digression'.
20. The *Phaedrus* he may have consulted is in vol. I of a five-volume set of Plato, *The Dialogues*, tr. B. Jowett (1875; YL 1586). The set originally belonged to Yeats's school friend Stephen Gwynn, and it is impossible to say when Yeats came by it. The only notes and markings in vol. I belong to Gwynn (in *Phaedo*). The closest thing in the Jowett *Phaedrus* to Milton's metaphor the 'Towr of . . . Apogaeum' is a 'steep' incline 'to the top of the vault of heaven' up which the procession of the gods 'march in their appointed order' (p. 453). See Donald T. Torchiana, 'Yeats and Plato', *Modern British Literature*, 4, no. 1 (1979) 5–16.
21. Yeats's fiction was, as Raine recently observes, 'a kind of scholarship in reverse' ('Giraldus', *Yeats the Initiate*, p. 410). She argues that his fictional author was a composite of a number of historical sources centring upon the sixteenth-century Neoplatonist and courtier, L. G. Gyraldus of Ferrara, rather than the twelfth-century Giraldus Cambrensis and other candidates proposed by Yeats scholars. She cites Robartes' story in *AV A* xvii (told second-hand by Aherne), which associates Gyraldus with Dr John Dee (see YL 501) and the alchemist Edward Kelley. Travel literature such as Charles M. Doughty's *Wanderings in Arabia* (see YL 538–9), mentioned by Raine, found an avid reader in Yeats, who believed he had discovered his antithetical self during various spiritualist events and in *A Geographical Historie of Africa* (1600; YL 1106) by John Leo or 'Leo Africanus'.
22. See George M. Harper, *W. B. Yeats and W. T. Horton* (Atlantic Highlands, NJ: Humanities Press, 1980) pp. 35, 58–63. See also his *Making AV*, I, 10–15, 22, and II, 277–8, 344–5, 398.
23. See again Harper, *Making AV* I, 121–2, and II, 316–17, on the impact of the Platonic Horton–Locke liaison on Yeats and George; and especially Harper's interpretation of Mrs Yeats's 'symbolic' role as read from the script (II, 292) and of the tower as 'symbol of conjugal union' (I, 245). See also my review 'From Platonic Metaphor to Yeatsian Scripture', *Cauda Pavonis: Studies in Hermeticism*, 8, no. 1 (1989) 11–13.
24. Milton, *Complete Prose*, II, 256.
25. See ibid., n. 9.
26. Smith, *YA* 5 (1987) 39.
27. Ibid., p. 19.

28. Yeats's two other uses of the quotation, dating from 1910 and 1935, respectively, are discussed in Smith, *YA* 5 (1987) 40–1.
29. Walter Pater, *Plato and Platonism* (London: Macmillan, 1893; *YL* 1538) pp. 166–7. Pater's phrase 'the dialogue of the mind with itself' was drawn from Arnold's 1853 Preface to his *Poems*. The passage, on Arnold's withdrawal of *Empedocles on Etna*, specifically came to mind when Yeats referred to it, in 1936, in *OBMV* xxxiv.
30. Pater, *Plato and Platonism*, p. 161.
31. See Giorgio Melchiori, *The Whole Mystery of Art* (London: Routledge and Kegan Paul, 1960) pp. 165ff. *YL 1920* 286 reports as missing a copy of Mead's book (1891 edn). In fact, an annotated 1896 edition is in Yeats's library; see my 'Notes on the Yeats Library, 1904 and 1989', *YA* 8 (1990).
32. Following Yeats's discussion on the pages I cite, Yeats anticipated his cook–dough metaphor of 1918 with a similar sculptor–clay metaphor, which concluded his work of mid-1917. Being 'in the place where the Daimon [or the anti-self] is', he writes: 'I am full of uncertainty, not knowing when I am the finger, when the clay' (*Myth* 366). Yeats cites More in *Per Amica*, the essays and notes of *Visions*, and *E&I* 412–18.
33. Yeats's personal copies of Milton's poems included two illustrated by Blake, *On the Morning of Christ's Nativity* (*YL* 1320) and *Paradise Lost* (*YL* 1321). He apparently disposed of a second copy of the latter – see *YA* 4 (1986) 286 – and surely knew Blake's illustrations for *Comus*, 'L'Allegro' and 'Il Penseroso'. To the end of his life Yeats remained interested in the masque as a literary form, and so it is not surprising to hear the Old Man in *The Death of Cuchulain* revile the modern audience and praise 'those who listened to the first performance of Milton's *Comus*' (*VP1* 1051). The passage is interesting as it emerged from draft. See Phillip L. Marcus, (ed.), *The Death of Cuchulain Manuscript Materials* (Ithaca, NY: Cornell University Press, 1982) pp. 27–9, 128–9, 169; and *UP2* 489, which quotes lines from *Comus*.
34. See Rosemary Puglia Ritvo, 'A Vision B: The Plotinian Metaphysical Basis', *Review of English Studies*, 26 (1975) 34–46.
35. Denis Saurat, *Milton, Man and Thinker* (London: Jonathan Cape, 1925) p. 254.
36. In Saurat's *Milton, Man and Thinker*, Yeats would have read with great sympathy how 'the "Puritan" Milton and "Swedenborgian" Blake belonged to the same school' (p. v). This thesis was explored in a later work Yeats read, Saurat's *Blake and Modern Thought* (1929; *YL* 1846, much annotated). In the earlier study, Saurat presented Yeats with a Milton steeped in the Cabbala and viewed in light of such hermeticists as Robert Fludd.
37. Roland Blenner-Hassett, 'Yeats' Use of Chaucer', *Anglia*, 72, no. 4 (1954) 457.
38. Discarded imagery from the drafts of 'The Phases of the Moon'; see above, n. 13.
39. Michael North, 'Symbolism and Obscurity in *Meditations in Time of Civil War*', *Critical Quarterly*, 19, no. 1 (1977) 7. His sense of sarcasm or disillusionment in the poem compares with Stan Smith's in 'Writing

a Will: Yeats's Ancestral Voices in ' "The Tower" and "Meditations in Time of Civil War" ', *Irish University Review*, 13, no. 1 (1983) 25. Smith reads these poems as interior dialogues with the texts they imitate or parody.

40. W. B. Yeats, Preface to Oliver St John Gogarty's *An Offering of Swans* (Dublin: Cuala Press, 1923), second unnumbered page. Although Yeats preferred seventeenth-century poets at this time, he continued to read the Elizabethans. One finds circumstantial evidence of this in his library, in volumes such as Michael Drayton's *Nimphidia, the Court of Fayrie* (Stratford-upon-Avon: Shakespeare Head Press, 1921), or YL 546.

41. In his Preface to Gogarty's *Wild Apples* (Dublin: Cuala Press, 1930), Yeats noted the author's penchant for carelessness but also his ability to produce 'a sense of hardship borne and chosen out of pride and joy. Some Elizabethans had that indeed, though Chapman alone constantly, and after that nobody – until Landor; and after that nobody except when some great Romantic forgot, perhaps under the influence of the Classics, his self-forgetting emotion, and wrote out of character' (pp. iii–iv).

42. In Rapallo Notebook D (NLI 13,581), Yeats noted his thought of replacing with lines from Chapman's *Ovid's Banquet of Sense* Keats's *Endymion* (IV.263–7) in *AV B* 107. This would have been the following five lines from Chapman for the same number from Keats, suggesting that *AV B* had more or less acquired its present shape in Part 3 of 'The Great Wheel' and that the note was later overlooked: 'O that as intellects themselves transite,/To each intelligible quality,/My life might pass into my love's conceit,/Thus to be form'd in words, her tunes, and breath,/And with her kisses sing itself to death' (YL 370, p. 25). Yeats found these lines above a footnote, which he also copied as best he could: 'The philosopher saith, *Intellectus in ipsa intellegibilia transit*, upon which is grounded this invention, that in the same manner his life might pass into his mistress's conceit; intending his intellectual life or soul; which by this analogy should be *Intellectus*, and her conceit, *Intelligibilis*.' Not far ahead of this, in *Hymnus in Noctem* (VII.255–6), Yeats found two lines he felt worth slipping into the Introduction to the aborted Scribner edition of his poems: 'Fall, Hercules, from heaven, in tempest hurl'd, / And cleanse this beastly stable of the world.' A draft of Yeats's Preface to *Wild Apples* is on the next page in Rapallo D.

43. Herbert H. J. Grierson (ed.), Introduction to *Metaphysical Lyrics and Poems of the Seventeenth Century, Donne to Butler* (Oxford: Clarendon Press, 1921; YL 816) p. xxxvii. The volume contains the following poems by Marvell: 'To his Coy Mistress', 'The Gallery', 'The Fair Singer', 'The Definition of Love', 'The Picture of Little *T. C.* in a Prospect of Flowers', 'A Dialogue between the Resolved Soul and Created Pleasure', 'The Coronet', 'A Dialogue between the Soul and Body', 'On a Drop of Dew', and 'The Garden'. Melchiori (*The Whole Mystery of Art*, p. 275) suggests that Yeats's 'The Song of the Happy Shepherd' (*VP* 67, ll. 45–54) echoes Marvell's Civil War poem 'The

Nymph Complaining for the Death of her Faun'. Yeats also alluded to Marvell's 'An Horatian Ode upon Cromwell's Return from Ireland' in *E&I* 255.

44. The dates are Mrs Yeats's, entered next to the title in YL 2323. The terminus ('December 1927') is given in two dated typescripts jumbled in NLI 13,590(3). Harris, *YCP&B* 203, and Balachandra Rajan, 'The Poetry of Confrontation: Yeats and the Dialogue Poem', in Joseph Ronsley (ed.), *Myth and Reality in Irish Literature* (Waterloo, Ont.: Wilfrid Laurier University Press, 1977) pp. 123–4, connect the dialogues of Yeats and Marvell. Rajan associates Marvell's dialogues with Jacapone da Todi's *Dialogue of the Body with the Soul*, although Yeats was probably unaware of it.

45. Keane's analogy between Spenser's sickle of Time in the *Faerie Queene*'s Garden of Adonis and Sato's sword in Yeats's poem seems a little gratuitous but worthwhile to the extent that the Spenserian model of *contemptus mundi* defines its Yeatsian complement by inverse relation – Patrick J. Keane, *Yeats's Interactions with Tradition* (Columbia, Mo.: University of Missouri Press, 1987) p. 143.

46. Ibid., p. 146; the *Comus* quotation is from l. 713, in Milton, *Complete Poems and Major Prose*, p. 106. Omitted from this account is Keane's unlikely theory that Comus's wand and cup provided suggestion, as 'phallic and vaginal equivalents', for Yeats's Japanese sword and sheath. It is clear that the latter properties were real and didn't need suggesting.

47. Edgar's feigned madness and Self's gesture of madness in monologue are similar. Poor Tom steals Shakespeare's scene and closes it with lines establishing a probable mnemonic link between Edgar and the Yeatsian persona: 'Child Rowland to the dark tower came . . .' (*King Lear*, III.iv.181–3).

48. First noted by Frederick Gwynn in 'Yeats's Byzantium and its Sources', *Philosophical Quarterly*, 32 (1953) 21. Gwynn may also be credited with establishing a connection between Shakespeare's *King Lear* and Yeats's Byzantium poems. It is this *complex* that Yeats brings to his famous dialogue. Melchiori found convincing Gwynn's argument about the Marvell connection and includes discussion of 'The Garden' in his second excursus, 'The Enchanted Garden' (*The Whole Mystery of Art*, pp. 274–5). Henn, who missed the contact in his first edition of *LT*, picked it up in his Byzantium chapter in the second edition (1965). Thomas Whitaker, in *Swan and Shadow* (Chapel Hill: University of North Carolina Press, 1964) p. 100, cites Marvell's 'The Garden' beside Spenser's Garden of Adonis in the context of Yeats's 'Fragments' (1926): 'Locke sank into a swoon; / The Garden died . . .'.

49. See Richard Ellmann, 'Yeats's Second Puberty', *New York Review of Books*, 32, no. 8 (9 May 1985) 10, 12, 14–16, and 18.

50. As Jeffares notes (*NCom* 417), the exact date of 'News for the Delphic Oracle' is uncertain. He claims, however, that 'The Statues' was written in April 1938, although Bradford and Ellmann give June/April– June 1938 as the approximate date of composition. The draft materials of 'News . . . ' (in NLI 13,593[34]) bear a fragment of 'The Statues' on

a sheet marked 'D'. These stray lines from one poem-in-process, with those of another, suggests that the two poems were written at about the same time. See Keane, *Yeats's Interactions with Tradition*, p. 119; Harold Bloom, *Yeats* (London: Oxford University Press, 1970) p. 445; and Daniel Albright, *The Myth against Myth* (London: Oxford University Press, 1972) pp. 121–2.

51. Subtitled 'A Paraphrastical Interpretation of the answer of Apollo, when he was consulted by Amelius whither Plotinus soul went when he departed this life'; see Robert Snukal, *High Talk* (Cambridge: Cambridge University Press, 1973) pp. 35–8, 240–65. More's poem is in the *Philosophical Poems* (YL 1379). Yeats acquired the 1931 edition after receiving Hayward's Donne, *Complete Poetry and Selected Prose* (YL 530; George Yeats to her husband, 1930) and Edith Sitwell's anthology *The Pleasures of Poetry . . . Milton and The Augustan Age* (1930; YL 1933).

52. See Henn, *LT* facing pp. 228, 235, 343; and Raine, *Yeats the Initiate*, pp. 286–94.

53. See F. A. C. Wilson, *W. B. Yeats and Tradition* (New York: Macmillan, 1958) pp. 213, 215–23; and Bloom (*Yeats*, pp. 445–8), who emphasizes nineteenth-century influences such as Shelley and Browning. Although Yeats owned a copy of Mackenna's translation of the sixth treatise of the First Ennead (1908; YL 1594), the poet came by most of his Plotinus by marriage. By signature and date, two or three such volumes belonged to Mrs Yeats before her marriage. Vols II–V of the Mackenna translation were probably acquired as they came out, in 1921, 1924, 1926 and 1930 (see YL 1589–95A). Yeats had every confidence in George's Latin scholarship, as he wrote (NLI 21,749, c. 1918) to his old mentor, the librarian T. W. Lyster, requesting that she be allowed to consult Larminie's manuscript translation of Johannes Scotus Erigina.

54. This valuable book is in the Richard Ellmann Collection, Department of Special Collections, McFarlin Library, University of Tulsa. Ellmann received it from Mrs Yeats. A photographic positive exists at the National Library of Ireland, in NLI 13,593(34). See Albright, *The Myth against Myth*, p. 121; and Leonard Unger, 'Yeats and Milton', *South Atlantic Quarterly*, 61, no. 2 (1962) 209n. Neither scholar actually saw the draft, which amounts to more than 'the first few lines' of the poem, since it rehearses the entire initial stanza.

55. Keane; *Yeats's Interactions with Tradition*, p. 120.

56. In notes to Lady Gregory's *Visions* (347), Yeats quotes *Paradise Lost*, I.423–31 in support of his claim that 'Milton writes like any Platonist of his time' and that the Renaissance poet, like Wordsworth (see *AV B* 236 for similar use of the Romantic poet's *The White Doe of Rylestone*), believed that spirits could change shape at will. Again, Yeats's late regard for Milton is influenced by Blake, by Saurat's works on both Blake and Milton, by the Platonists, and by Yeats's own heterodox theology.

57. Albright, *The Myth against Myth*, p. 122.

58. Milton, *Complete Poems and Major Prose*, p. 48.

59. Albright, *The Myth against Myth*, p. 122.
60. Milton, *Complete Poems and Major Prose*, pp. 44–5.
61. Stuck in at pp. 26–7 and 252–3, a Dublin tram ticket and a leaf mark these passages in the Beeching Milton. The first, opposite lines accompanying Palmer's *The Lonely Tower* (ll. 85–7), concerns the sylvan covert of Milton's Platonist, with 'Waters murmuring / With such consort as they keep, / Entice the dewy-feather'd Sleep' (ll. 144–6). The second offers Satan's first view of Eden, with its bowers, groves, lawns, 'umbrageous Grots and Caves / Of coole recess' – its 'murmuring waters . . . disperst . . . while Universal *Pan* / Knit with the *Graces* . . . in dance / Led in th' Eternal Spring' and Adam and Eve in 'naked Majestie' (ll. 248–90).
62. Yeats's early rejection of Milton's Christianized Pan may be read in drafts of a poem entitled 'Pan' (NLI 12,161) and rehearsed in *The Works of Alfred Tennyson* (YL 2115, facing half-title page). See *YL Notes*.
63. The poet would become something 'complete', an 'idea'. If Shakespeare was absorbed by 'characters' he read in the English histories or in 'traditional romance', Dante and Milton were possessed by 'mythologies' (in manuscript, 'Christian mythologies'). See Edward Callan, *Yeats on Yeats*, New Yeats Papers 20 (Dublin: Dolmen Press, 1981) pp. 38–9.
64. The poems 'Lapis Lazuli', 'An Acre of Grass', 'The Old Stone Cross', 'The Municipal Gallery Re-visited', and 'The Statues' come to mind. Such use of Shakespeare is well known; but see Desai, *YShak* 18–24; and Laurence Perrine, 'Yeats and Shakespeare: "The Old Stone Cross" ', *Modern British Literature*, 3, no. 2 (1978) 159–60.
65. The poet's demonstration argues against his professed ignorance of prosody (see *E&I* xi). His ear for speech-rhythm was keenly sensitive, and his judgement weighed much upon such complex issues as the shifting nature of syllable stress as commanded by voice or inflection. The opening line of *Paradise Lost*, for example, he believed could be sung in iambic pentameter or, 'crossed with another emphasis, that of passionate prose', read as tetrameter. See Adelyn Dougherty, ' "Traditional Metres" and "Passionate Syntax" in the Verse of William Butler Yeats', *Language and Style*, 14, no. 3 (1981) 216–17. The example derived from a passage Yeats once summoned from memory to eject a bad spirit (see *Au* 104).
66. Found in NLI 13,576, much of this series has been quoted by Parkinson in *YSC&LP* II, 184–6. A complete but undiplomatic transcription is available in Richard Fallis's mistitled article 'Language and Rhythm in Poetry: A Previously Unpublished Essay by W. B. Yeats', *Shenandoah*, 26, no. 4 (1975) 77–9. Both Parkinson and Fallis represent the series of entries as an unfinished essay. These relatively short themes are interspersed among work for *A Vision* and poems such as 'Father and Child' and 'Among School Children'; possibly Yeats never regarded them as more than 'think pieces' dated separately 'April 7', 'April 24', and 'April 26' (1921).
67. In matters of text and title, this study follows *PNE*. The differences between the *VP* and *PNE* texts of 'The Municipal Gallery Re-visited'

are discussed in Finneran's book *Editing Yeats's Poems* (London: Macmillan, 1983) pp. 58–63. The text I choose restores the authority of the typescript in NLI 13,593(29). The typescript generally resembles the one produced in *New Poems* (Dublin: Cuala Press, 1938), the only collection bearing the poem that Yeats lived to see. All manuscript materials referred to here and below are given in the appendix of my article ' "That is from a master": The Writing of Yeats's "The Municipal Gallery Re-visited" ', *YA* 9 (1991).

68. I have in mind Kermode's plea (*RI* 165) that Spenser and especially Milton needed liberating from the oppression of 'Symbolist assumptions' translated into 'the Symbolist historical doctrine of dissociation of sensibility'. I think Yeats's late and early uses of both poets support Kermode and help distinguish Yeats from Modernists like Pound and Eliot.

69. Lady Gregory's note bearing the fragment attributed to Yeats's poem constitutes NLI 21,874.

70. Arland Ussher's pamphlet *Yeats at the Municipal Gallery* (Dublin: Dolmen Press, 1959) is still among the most useful of introductions to the poem's many pictorial inspirations. Elizabeth W. Bergman (Loizeaux) discusses the elegy in light of Yeats's other picture poems in 'Yeats's Gallery', *Colby Library Quarterly*, 15 (1979) 127–36; and T. R. Henn, who was disappointed by the poem, has discussed Yeats's pictorialism without it in 'Yeats and the Picture Galleries', *Southern Review*, 1, no. 1 (1965) 57–75. More useful from a literary standpoint are Helen Vendler's treatment of the poem as a 'group-elegy' in 'Four Elegies', *YS&I* 216–31; and Arra M. Garab's exposition in 'Times of Glory: Yeats's "The Municipal Gallery Revisited" ', in Jon Stallworthy (ed.), *Yeats's Last Poems: A Casebook* (London: Macmillan, 1968) pp. 182–93.

71. The 'guidebook' referred to here (and the 'Text book or guide book' mentioned in manuscript, on L4r) is evidently *[The Dublin] Municipal Gallery of Modern Art and Civil Museum* (Dublin: Browne and Nolan, 1933), which the Curator, John C. Reynolds, gave the poet. Yeats's two complimentary copies (*YL* 571 and 571a) were inscribed, separately, on 1 July and 30 December 1933.

72. See 'New Demand for Art Treasures / Government to Press British for Lane Pictures. / Action by Late King George V.', *The Irish Independent*, 18 Aug 1937, p. 10.

73. Many poems of this type, by some of 'the greatest wits of the age', are collected in *Poems on Affairs of State: From the Time of Oliver Cromwell, to the Abdication of K. James the Second* . . . 5th edn, 4 vols (London: no publisher, 1703–4). See Warren L. Chernaik, *The Poetry of Limitation: A Study of Edmund Waller* (New Haven, Conn., and London: Yale University Press, 1968) pp. 187–93.

74. Rosemond Tuve, *Elizabethan and Metaphysical Imagery* (Chicago: University of Chicago Press, 1947) pp. 50–60.

75. Curiously, a copy of Gogarty's *Selected Poems* (New York: Macmillan, 1933; *YL* 756) was inscribed by the author 'To W. B. / the onlie begetter . . .'. So Yeats's renewed reading of the *Sonnets* in 1937 would not

have brought the phrase to his attention for the first time. He may have seen T. W. Lyster's review 'Dowden's Shakespeare's Sonnets', *Hibernia*, 1 Apr 1882, p. 52a, which specifically addressed the matter of Thorpe's dedication and appeared at a time when he was fully under the influence of both the reviewer and his subject, Edward Dowden.
76. Finneran, *Editing Yeats's Poems*, p. 62.
77. Vendler, in *VS&I* 216.

Select Bibliography

BOOKS ANNOTATED BY YEATS

Burton, Robert, *The Anatomy of Melancholy*, ed. the Revd. A. R. Shilleto, 3 vols, Bohn's Libraries (London: G. Bell, 1912). Property of Anne B. Yeats [YL 311].

Chapman, George, *The Works of George Chapman*, I: *Plays*, ed. Richard Herne Shepherd (London: Chatto and Windus, 1889). Property of Anne B. Yeats [YL 369].

——, *The Works of George Chapman*, II: *Poems and Minor Translations*, intro. Algernon Charles Swinburne (London: Chatto and Windus, 1904). Property of Anne B. Yeats [YL 370].

Cudworth, R[alph], *The True Intellectual System of the Universe. The first part* . . . (London: Richard Royston, 1678). Property of Anne B. Yeats [YL 435].

Glanvil, Joseph, *Sadducismus Triumphatus* . . . , 4th edn, tr. with additions by Dr Horneck (London: printed for A. Bettesworth and J. Batley . . . ; W. Mears, and J. Hooke, 1726). Property of Anne B. Yeats [YL 750].

Herbert, Edward, *The Autobiography of Edward, Lord Herbert of Cherbury*, 2nd edn, intro. Sidney Lee (London: George Routledge, [1906]). Property of Anne B. Yeats [YL 878].

MacDonagh, Thomas, *Literature in Ireland* . . . (Dublin: Talbot Press, 1916). Property of Anne B. Yeats [YL 1180].

——, *Thomas Campion and the Art of English Poetry* (Dublin: Hodges, Figgis, 1913). Property of Anne B. Yeats [YL 1182].

Milton, John, *The Poetical Works of John Milton*, ed. H. C. Beeching (London: Oxford University Press, 1935). Richard Ellmann Collection, Department of Special Collections, McFarlin Library, University of Tulsa.

More, Dr Henry, *A Collection of Several Philosophical Writings*, 2nd ed (London: William Morden, 1662). Property of Anne B. Yeats [YL 1377].

Pater, Walter, *Plato and Platonism* (London: Macmillan, 1893). Property of Anne B. Yeats [YL 1538].

Spenser, Edmund, *The Works of Edmund Spenser*, ed. J. Payne Collier, 5 vols (London: Bell and Daldy, 1852). Property of Anne B. Yeats [YL 1978–1978D].

Tennyson, Alfred, *The Works of Alfred Tennyson*, Cabinet Edition, III: *Locksley Hall and Other Poems* (London: Henry S. King, 1874). Property of Anne B. Yeats [YL 2115].

Walton, Izaak, *The Lives of Dr. John Donne, Sir Henry Wotton, Mr. Richard Hooker, Mr. George Herbert, and Dr. Robert Sanderson* (London: Henry Washbourne, 1840). Property of Anne B. Yeats [YL 2222].

YEATS, PUBLISHED PRIMARY WORKS

Gregory, Isabella Augusta, *Visions and Beliefs in the West of Ireland*, with two essays and notes by W. B. Yeats (1920; Gerrards Cross, Bucks: Colin Smythe, 1979).
Horton, W. T., with W. B. Yeats, *A Book of Images Drawn by W. T. Horton and Introduced by W. B. Yeats* (London: Unicorn, 1898).
Yeats, W. B., *Autobiographies* (London: Macmillan, 1955).
——, *The Celtic Twilight* (London: Bullen, 1902).
——, *The Collected Letters of W. B. Yeats*, I: *1865–1892*, ed. John Kelly and Eric Domville (Oxford: Clarendon Press, 1985).
——, *The Collected Poems* (London: Macmillan, 1933).
——, *The Countess Kathleen and Various Legends and Lyrics* (London: Unwin, 1892).
——, *A Critical Edition of Yeats's 'A Vision' (1925)*, ed. George M. Harper and Walter K. Hood (London: Macmillan, 1978).
——, *The Death of Cuchulain Manuscript Materials, Including the Author's Final Text*, ed. Phillip L. Marcus (Ithaca, NY, and London: Cornell University Press, 1982).
——, 'Discoveries: Second Series', ed. Curtis B. Bradford, in *Massachusetts Review*, 5 (1964) 297–306.
——, *Essays and Introductions* (London and New York: Macmillan, 1961).
——, *Explorations* (London: Macmillan, 1962; New York: Macmillan, 1963).
——, 'From One Theatrical Reformer to Another: W. B. Yeats's Unpublished Letters to Gordon Craig', in Patrick Rafroidi, Raymonde Popot, and William Parker (eds), *Aspects of the Irish Theatre* (Paris: Editions Universitaires, 1972) pp. 275–86.
——, *The Green Helmet and Other Poems* (Dundrum; Cuala Press, 1910).
——, *The Green Helmet and Other Poems* (London: Macmillan, 1912).
——, *Ideas of Good and Evil* (London: Bullen, 1903).
——, *In the Seven Woods* (Dundrum: Cuala Press, 1903).
——, 'Language and Rhythm in Poetry: A Previously Unpublished Essay by W. B. Yeats', ed. Richard Fallis, in *Shenandoah*, 26, no. 4 (1975) 77–81.
——, *Last Poems and Plays* (London: Macmillan, 1940).
——, *Last Poems and Two Plays* (Dublin: Cuala Press, 1939).
——, 'Letters and Lectures of W. B. Yeats', ed. Robert O'Driscoll, in *University Review* (Dublin), 3, no. 8 (1966) 29–55.
——, *The Letters of W. B. Yeats*, ed. Allan Wade (London: Rupert Hart-Davis, 1954).
——, *Letters on Poetry from W. B. Yeats to Dorothy Wellesley*, intro. Kathleen Raine (London and New York: Oxford University Press, 1964).
——, *Letters to the New Island*, ed. Horace Reynolds (Cambridge, Mass.: Harvard University Press, 1934).
——, *Memoirs: Autobiography—First Draft[;] and Journal*, ed. Denis Donoghue (London: Macmillan, 1972; New York: Macmillan, 1973).
——, *Michael Robartes and the Dancer* (Dundrum: Cuala Press, 1920).
——, *Mythologies* (London and New York: Macmillan, 1959).
——, *New Poems* (Dublin: Cuala Press, 1938).

Select Bibliography

——, *Nine Poems* (London: Shorter, 1918).
——, *On the Boiler* (Dublin: Cuala Press, 1938).
——, *Per Amica Silentia Lunae* (London: Macmillan, 1918).
——, *Plays for an Irish Theatre*, with designs by Gordon Craig (London and Stratford-upon-Avon: Bullen, 1911).
——, *Poems* (London: Unwin, 1895).
——, *Poems, 1899–1905* (London: Bullen, 1906).
——, *The Poems: A New Edition*, ed. Richard J. Finneran (London: Macmillan, 1984).
——, *The Poetical Works*, vol. I: *Lyrical Poems* (New York and London: Macmillan, 1906).
——, *Responsibilities and Other Poems* (London: Macmillan, 1916).
——, *Responsibilities: Poems and a Play* (Dundrum: Cuala Press, 1914).
——, *Reveries over Childhood and Youth* (London: Macmillan, 1916).
——, *The Secret Rose: Stories by W. B. Yeats: A Variorum Edition*, ed. Phillip L. Marcus, Warwick Gould, Michael J. Sidnell (Ithaca, NY: Cornell University Press, 1981).
——, *The Senate Speeches*, ed. Donald R. Pearce (Bloomington: Indiana University Press, 1960).
——, 'Some New Letters from Yeats to Lady Gregory', ed. Donald T. Torchiana and Glenn O'Malley, in *Review of English Literature*, 4, no. 3 (1963) 9–47.
——, *A Speech and Two Poems* (Dublin: Sign of the Three Candles, 1937).
——, *The Tower* (London: Macmillan, 1928).
——, 'Two Lectures on the Irish Theatre by W. B. Yeats', in Robert O'Driscoll (ed.), *Theatre and Nationalism in Twentieth Century Ireland* (Toronto: University of Toronto Press, 1971) pp. 66–88.
——, *Uncollected Prose by W. B. Yeats*, I, ed. John P. Frayne (London: Macmillan, 1970; New York: Columbia University Press, 1970).
——, *Uncollected Prose by W. B. Yeats*, II, ed. John P. Frayne and Colton Johnson (London: Macmillan, 1975; New York: Columbia University Press, 1976).
——, *The Variorum Edition of the Poems of W. B. Yeats*, ed. Peter Allt and Russell K. Alspach (New York and London: Macmillan, 1957).
——, *The Variorum Edition of the Plays of W. B. Yeats*, ed. Russell K. Alspach (London and New York: Macmillan, 1966).
——, *A Vision* (New York: Macmillan, 1961).
——, 'W. B. Yeats: An Unpublished Letter', ed. C. G. Martin, in *Notes and Queries*, n.s., 5 (1958) 260–1.
——, *W. B. Yeats: The Early Poetry*, I: *'Mosada' and 'The Island of Statues' Manuscript Materials*, ed. George Bornstein (Ithaca, NY: Cornell University Press, 1987).
——, *W. B. Yeats: The Writing of 'The Player Queen'*, ed. Curtis Bradford (Dekalb: Northern Illinois University Press, 1977).
——, *The Wanderings of Oisin and Other Poems* (London: Kegan Paul, 1889).
——, *The Wild Swans at Coole* (London: Macmillan, 1919).
——, *The Wind Among the Reeds* (London: Elkin Mathews, 1899).
——, *The Winding Stair* (New York: Fountain Press, 1929).
——, *The Winding Stair* (London: Macmillan, 1933).

——, 'Yeats on Personality: Three Unpublished Lectures', in Robert O'Driscoll and Lorna Reynolds (eds), *Yeats and the Theatre* (Toronto and London: Macmillan, 1975) pp. 4–59.

——, (ed.), *Beltaine*, 2 (Feb 1900).

——, (ed.), *The Oxford Book of Modern Verse, 1892–1935* (Oxford: Clarendon Press, 1936).

Yeats, W. B., and Lady Gregory, 'Private and Confidential: Paragraphs Written in Nov., 1909' (Wade 244b), repr. in Lady Gregory, *Our Irish Theatre: A Chapter of Autobiography* (Gerrards Cross, Bucks: Colin Smythe, 1972).

Yeats, W. B., Lady Gregory and J. M. Synge, *Theatre Business: The Correspondence of the First Abbey Theatre Directors: William Butler Yeats, Lady Gregory and J. M. Synge*, ed. Ann Saddlemyer (University Park and London: Pennsylvania State University Press, 1982).

Yeats, W. B., and Lionel Johnson, *Poetry and Ireland: Essays by W. B. Yeats and Lionel Johnson* (Dundrum: Cuala Press, 1908).

Yeats, W. B., and Shree Purohit Swami (ed. and tr.), *The Ten Principal Upanishads* (London: Faber, 1937).

YEATS, PRIMARY WORKS IN TYPESCRIPT/MANUSCRIPT

BERG COLLECTION, NEW YORK PUBLIC LIBRARY: LADY GREGORY PAPERS

'Ego Dominus Tuus', ts. with ms. corrections.
'In Memory of Major Robert Gregory', 3 ts. copies of the poem.
'On Those that hated "The Playboy of the Western World"', 1907', ms.
'Opening Ceremony for The Masquers', ts. (carbon).

HARRY RANSOM HUMANITIES RESEARCH CENTER, UNIVERSITY OF TEXAS AT AUSTIN

'On Those that hated "The Playboy of the Western World"', 1907', ms.

YEATS COLLECTION, SPECIAL COLLECTIONS, WOODRUFF LIBRARY, EMORY UNIVERSITY

Revised proof sheet of 'While I, from that reed-throated whisperer' and insert slip for ll. 6–8. [Copies in the British Library (London), RP 1799.]

NATIONAL LIBRARY OF IRELAND, DUBLIN: YEATS PAPERS

MS. 3,726. An aphorism, beside 1886 draft of 'The Wanderings of Oisin'. Also (on fos 69r–71v), a draft of 'The Song of the Happy Shepherd'.

MS. 10,543. Letters, clippings, lists, and publicity regarding subscriptions collected by the Lyster Memorial Committee, chaired by Yeats.

MS. 12,145. Album of news-clippings, 1897–1904.

MS. 12,146. Album of news-clippings, 1904–1909.

MS. 12,161. Album of miscellaneous juvenilia, c. 1881–3. Drafts of 'Inscription of a christmas card' and 'Pan' (among those cited).

MS. 13,568. Notes, etc., by Miss Annie Horniman, Yeats, and others towards the establishment of a mystical Celtic order.

MS. 13,575. Notes and drafts in a hardbacked notebook and three folders for Lady Gregory's *Visions and Beliefs* and Yeats's essay 'Swedenborg, Mediums, and the Desolate Places'.

MS. 13,576. Diary notebook dated 7 April, 1921. Among notes for *A Vision*, the 'subject' and draft of 'Father and Child' and a fragmentary essay on 'passionate syntax'.

MS. 13,580. Rapallo Notebook C. Contains Diary of Thought, notes for *A Vision*, and holograph poems for *The Winding Stair* and 'Words for Music Perhaps'.

MS. 13,581. Rapallo Notebook D. Notes and thoughts for *A Vision*, draft Preface for Oliver Gogarty's *Wild Apples*, and, *inter alia*, holograph poems for *The Winding Stair*.

MS. 13,583. Among miscellaneous and unsorted materials, draft 'Notes' for the 1933 *Collected Poems*.

MS. 13,587(4). 'The Living Beauty', bearing on verso a fragmentary version of a poem about Solomon and Sheba.

MS. 13,587(6). Rejected ending to 'Shepherd and Goatherd'.

MS. 13,587(20). 'Ego Dominus Tuus'.

MS. 13,587(21). 'The Phases of the Moon' with leaf from 'The Living Beauty'.

MS. 13,588(4). 'Solomon and the Witch'.

MS. 13,589(1)–(32). Drafts of poems for *The Tower*.

MS. 13,589(24)–(25). 'The Empty Cup'.

MS. 13,589(31). Notebook containing 'Parting' and 'Chosen', as parts of an aborted poem entitled 'Morning'.

MS. 13,590(3). 'A Dialogue of Self and Soul'.

MS. 13,590–2. Drafts of poems for *The Winding Stair*, in 60 folders.

MS. 13,593(29). 'The Municipal Gallery Re-visited'.

MS. 13,593(34). 'News for the Delphic Oracle'.

MS. 13,663. Holograph letter. W. B. Yeats to Thomas MacDonagh, 9 Nov [1902]. (Date is established by comparing with letter from Sealy, Bryers and Walker, Dublin, to MacDonagh, 22 Dec 1902, in MS. 10,854[1] of the Thomas MacDonagh Papers.)

MS. 18,688. Corrected ts. letter. W. B. Yeats to Lady Gregory, 7 Mar 1909. Cf. *L* 525.

MS. 21,749. Holograph letter. W. B. Yeats to T. W. Lyster, *c*. 1918.

MS. 21,867–8. 'In Memory of Major Robert Gregory'.

MS. 21,874. Holograph fragment, possibly early draft of 'Wild Old Wicked Man', on verso of which appears Lady Gregory's comments (apparently part of a letter to Yeats) on Spenser and allegorical poets.

MS. 30,440. Juvenilia stanzas, 'Sansloy – sansfoy – sansjoy'. Three versions: in nonce stanza of seven lines, *rime royal* and Spenserian stanzas.

MS. 30,450. Fragments from 'The Sad Shepherd'.

MS. 30,469. Fragments from 'The Sad Shepherd'.

MS. 30,510. Unpublished epigram, 'Art without imitation'.

MS. 30,830. Fragments from an epic in Spenserian stanzas.

Index

Abbey Theatre 22–7, 100, 103, 114–15, 118–19, 217, 242
Abrams, M. H. 248
Adams, Hazard 225
adaptation *see* imitation
adaptive complex xii, 12, 25, 48, 50, 67, 69, 77, 91, 103, 109, 111, 119, 129, 133, 145, 151, 154, 170, 188, 195, 202, 205–6, 218, 264
Aestheticism 33, 40–1, 43, 50–1, 56–8, 226
Albright, Daniel 265–6
Agrippa von Nettesheim, Heinrich Cornelius 165
Alfarabi (Muhammad ibn Muhammad) 148
allegory 5, 82–4, 92–3, 95, 97–100, 133, 231
Allen, James Lovic 249, 252
Anacreon 91, 225, 234
Andreae, Johann Valentin 232
Anima Mundi 69, 197, 213, 233
anti-self *see* mask
Apelles of Ephesus
 Aphrodite Anadyomene 91, 234
Arabian Nights 175–6, 257, 261
archetypal woman *see* woman, the idea of
Ardilaun, Lord 124, 130
Aristotle
 Poetics 221
Arnold, Matthew xiii, 9, 31, 33, 34–41, 43–4, 48–52 *passim*, 168, 194, 212, 221, 224–6, 228, 255, 262
Ascham, Roger 1, 5, 10
 The Scholemaster 1, 9, 219, 221
Avicenna 148

Bacon, Francis 18, 105, 119, 187, 242
 De Augmentis 18
 Essays 107, 115, 239

Bailey, John 38–9, 49, 224–5
Baker, Carlos 233
Bale, John
 The Interlude of God's Promises 243
Balliet, Conrad 252
Barckly (untraced) 232
Basilius Valentinus 148
Bateson, F. W. 32, 224
Bayley, Harold 175, 257
Beardsley, Aubrey 96, 112
Beardsley, Mabel 132, 167, 255
Beaumont, Francis
 The Elder Brother 109, 240
 King and No King 121, 156–7
 Knight of the Burning Pestle 240
 The Maid's Tragedy 79–80
Beaumont, John 165
Bedford, Lucy, Countess of 162, 167
Beeching, H. C. 206, 266
Bender, John B. 97, 236
Benson, F. R. 113
Beresford, Lady Charles 215–16
Berkeley, George 187, 199, 259
Blake, Charles Carter 225
Blake, William 7, 19, 40, 41, 50, 52, 53, 60, 66, 69, 97, 129, 145–6, 150–1, 188, 192, 195–6, 207, 225, 231, 245, 259–60, 262, 265
Blavatsky, H. P. 165, 195
Blenner-Hassett, Roland 262
Bloom, Harold 224, 230, 244, 248, 265
Boehme, Jacob 146, 165
Bonaparte, Napoleon 260
Bornstein, George 34, 76, 79, 100, 224, 228–32, 233, 239, 248–9
Botticelli, Sandro 209–10
Bradbrook, Muriel C. 234
Bradford, Curtis 16, 219, 220, 243, 246, 252, 254, 259, 265
Brater, Enoch 234
Breton, Nicholas 134, 166

Index

Bridges, Robert 116, 251
Brooks, Cleanth 247
Browne, Sir Thomas 6, 165, 239
  Christian Morals 239
  Religio Medici 107, 148, 239
  Urn Burial 107, 148, 239
Browne, William, of Tavistock 134, 166
Browning, Robert 33, 54–5, 167, 171, 256, 265
Buckley, Theodore 133, 251
Bullen, A. H. 102, 104, 106–9, 237–40
Bunyan, John 97
  Pilgrim's Progress 92
Burke, Edmund 187, 199
Burleigh, Lord 186
Burns, Robert 7, 167–8
Burton, Robert 11, 151
  The Anatomy of Melancholy 251
Bushrui, S. B. 239
Butler, Samuel 167–8
  Hudibras 254
Butlin, Martin 235
Byrd, Thomas, Jr 232
Byron, George Gordon 25, 55, 111, 167–9, 178, 211, 214, 234, 255

Calderón de la Barca, Pedro 149
Callan, Edward 266
Calvert, Edward 97, 260
Camden, William 232
Campion, Edmund 232
Carew, Thomas 128
Carlyle, Thomas 37
Carpenter, William 23, 222, 252
Carr, Philip 240
Casement, Roger 215–16
Castiglione, Baldassare 9, 153–6, 160, 210
  The Courtier (tr. Thomas Hoby) 9, 24, 61, 88, 155, 223, 233, 252
Cavalier poets *see under individual names*
Cave, Richard Allen 241
Chambers, E. K. 148–9
Chapman, George 100, 102, 109, 151, 201, 251, 263
  Bussy D'Ambois 112, 238
  Hero and Leander 121
  Hymnus in Noctem 263
  Ovid's Banquet of Sense 263
  Revenge of Bussy D'Ambois 109
Chapman, Wayne K. 221, 223, 241–3, 245, 260, 261–2, 267
character *see* personality
Charles I, King 106
Chaucer, Geoffrey 6, 192, 194, 262–4
Chernaik, Warren L. 268
Cheshire Cheese, The 42, 225
Child, Francis James 98
Christ, Jesus 50, 83, 90, 93, 207–9, 243, 266
Cicero 204
Clarendon, Edward [Hyde] Earl of 102, 105
  History of the Civil Wars in England 105
  The Life of Edward, Earl of Clarendon 105
Clark, David R. xii, 173, 219, 256
Clarke, Austin 164, 253
Claude Lorrain 96–7, 235, 236, plate 4
Colbert, Judith Anne 229, 244
Coleman, Antony 129, 245
Coleridge, Samuel Taylor 41, 55, 225
Collier, J. Payne (quoted) 98
  his edition of Spenser 233
Comte, Auguste 34, 52
conceits and icons
  a coal 155
  cup 174–7
  eagle 129–32, 245
  lamp 191
  match 258
  mirror 108, 117–18, 123, 144, 242
  painting 122–4, 131–2
  sieve 159–60, 252
  taper ('wick and oil') 170–1, 173, 175, 191, 256
  tower 188–201, 260–1, 263, 266, plates 9–12
  wages and wagers 171–2

Congreve, William 22–3, 28, 110, 116
Cotton, Charles 128
country-house poem 127–41 *passim*, 245–7
courtly (Platonic) love 88–93, 146–60, 193–4
  see also Neoplationism
Cowley, Abraham 137–8, 143, 185, 202, 246–7
  'A Discourse Concerning the Government of Oliver Cromwell' 247
  'Essay on Solitude' 246
  'Ode on the Death of Mr William Harvey' 137, 246
Cowper, William 167
Craig, Edith 116
Craig, Edward Gordon 28, 113–16, 118–20, 241–3
Crane, Walter 112, 116
Crashaw, Richard 148, 166, 254, 256
  'A Hymn to Saint Teresa' 166
Croll, Morris W. 222
Cromwell, Oliver 35, 59, 197, 236–7
Cronin, Mary 70
Cudworth, Ralph 45, 146, 165

daimon 50, 191, 193, 201, 262
Dalsimer, Adele M. 231
Daniel, Samuel 9
Dante Aligheri 97, 164–7, 210–12, 253, 266
Darwin, Charles 53, 72
Davidson, C. 133
Davidson, John 112
Davidson, Richard B. 233–4
Davie, Donald 245
Davies, John 232
Day, John 239
Dee, John 261
Dekker, Thomas 102, 109, 238
  The Gull's Hornbook 238
  Old Fortunatus 112, 238
  Satiromastix 238
Delaney, G. P. 26, 223
DeLaura, David 226

De Quincey, Thomas 161
Denham, John 248
Desai, Rupin 47, 227, 240, 266
dialogue poems 152, 157, 164, 166–7, 171–84 *passim*, 187–96, 202–5, 253–4, 260–4
Digby, Kenelm 98, 236
Digby, (Lady) Venetia 132, 167, 255
'dissociation of sensibility' 32–3, 224
Donne, John xi, xiii, 18, 24, 33, 69, 137, 141–84 *passim*, 202, 214–15, 247–58, 265
  collections: 'Elegies' 146, 161; 'Holy Sonnets' 161; 'Letters to Severall Personages' 161; 'Of the Progresse of the Soule' 153, 161; 'Satyres' 161; 'Songs and Sonets' 146, 161
  individual poems: 'Aire and Angels' 183; 'An Anatomie of the World' 183; 'The Apparition' 163; 'Breake of day' 179; 'The Canonization' 167, 170, 191, 255; 'The Dreame' 157; 'The Expostulation' 172; 'The Extasie' 147, 156–7, 163, 172, 248; 'A Feaver' 155, 167, 255; 'The Funerall' 157, 178; 'The good-morrow' 158, 182–3; 'His parting from her' 179–80; 'His Picture' 250; 'Loves Alchemie' 147; 'A nocturnall upon S. Lucies day' 162, 169, 180–3; 'The Relique' 157, 178–9; 'The Second Anniversary' 153, 257; 'The Sunne Rising' 159, 167, 182–3, 255; 'Twicknam Garden' 173; 'The undertaking' 158
Dougherty, Adelyn 266
Doughty, Charles, M. 261
Dowden, Edward 47–8, 52–3, 70–2, 87, 99, 106, 112, 144, 151,

Index

Dowden, Edward – *continued* 228, 230–2, 236–7, 239–40, 247–8, 250, 259, 268
Dowling, Linda 225
Dowson, Ernest 56, 112, 240
Drayton, Michael 263
  Nimphidia, the Court of Fayrie 263
Drummond, William 105, 252
  A Cypress Grove 107, 239
Drury, Elizabeth 154, 167, 170
Drury, G. T. 215
Dryden, John 33, 143–4, 149, 167, 185, 202
  Absalom and Achitophel 255
  'The Secular Masque' 240
Dublin Municipal Gallery 212–18 *passim*, 267
Dulac, Edmund 119
Dumas, Alexandre 8
Duncan, Douglas 106, 222, 238
Duncan, Joseph 178, 247, 253–5, 257–8
Dundas, Judith 97, 236
Dürer, Albrecht 196
dyad xii, 69, 77, 91, 96, 107, 144, 233

Eddins, Dwight 224
Edwards, Osman 254
Eglinton, John *see* Magee, William K.
elegy 73–4, 127–41, 145, 212–18, 245–7, 267
Eliot, T. S. 1, 32–3, 143, 186, 210, 213, 223–4, 249, 259
Elizabeth I, Queen 36, 54, 241
Elizabethan English 2, 6, 11–12, 18, 33–4, 38, 39, 54–6, 78–9
Elizabethan stage 103, 110–11, 113–15, 118–20
Elizabethan Stage Society 103, 113
Elliott, Ebenezer 71–2
Elliott, Maurice 230
Ellis, Edwin 41, 52, 53, 146, 225, 228
Ellis-Fermor, Una 237
Ellmann, Richard 52, 126, 228, 231–2, 234, 240, 244, 249, 258, 265

Elyot, John 9
Emerson, Ralph Waldo 238
Emery, Mrs Edward *see* Farr, Florence
Engelberg, Edward 243
English press 27–8, 38–40, 48–9
epic 72–8, 215
epigram 13–15, 16–17, 18–22, 25–8, 121–7, 129–30, 145, 222, 243–5
Erasmus, Desiderius 9, 126, 244
Esterling, Edward 98
Euripides 116
Evans, Edward 108

Fallis, Richard 266–7
Farr, Florence 111–12, 116, 241–2, 254
Fay, Frank 217
Fenollosa, Ernest 120
Fenollosa, Mrs Ernest 110
Ferguson, Samuel 87, 232
Ficino, Marsilio 88, 90, 233–4
fili 3, 219
  see also vates
Finneran, Richard J. 217, 230, 267–8
Flamel, Nicolas (and wife, Perrenelle) 148, 154, 157, 167
Flaubert, Gustave 261
Fletcher, Ian 234
Fletcher, John 201
  The Elder Brother 109, 240
  The Faithful Shepherdess 111
  King and No King 121, 156–7
  The Maid's Tragedy 79–80
  Two Noble Kinsmen 121
Fletcher, Phineas 166
Fludd, Robert 262
Fowler, Alastair 236
Frazer, W. 230
Frederick, Duke of Urbino 153
Freeman's Journal 125, 238
Frye, Northrop 172–3, 256

Galsworthy, John 27–9
Garab, Arra M. 268
Gardner, Garratt 251
Garnett, Richard 261
Gascoigne, George 212
  Supposes and *Jocasta* 121

Genet, Jacqueline 220, 247, 256–7
Georgius Syncellus 196
Gill, Richard 245
Giraldus Cambrensis 232, 261
Glanvil, Joseph 45, 146, 165
Goethe, J. W. von 7, 55
Gogarty, Oliver St John 201, 263, 268
Golden Dawn 87–94 *passim*, 112, 146, 157–8, 233–4
Goldoni, Carlo 103
Goldsmith, Oliver 55, 103, 187, 199
Gonne, Iseult 162, 170
Gonne, Maud 53, 131, 146–7, 151–2, 154–60, 162–3, 170, 252
Goodwin, K. L. 244, 259
Gosse, Edmund 71, 149, 250
Gould, Warwick 192, 226, 249, 252, 257, 261
Gourmont, Rémy de 32
Grassi, Giovanni 26–9, 223
Grattan, Henry 187
Gregory, (Lady) Augusta 8, 22, 23–4, 26–7, 47, 66, 103, 115, 125–6, 128–41 *passim*, 152, 155, 165, 213, 216–17, 223, 226, 237, 242, 245–6, 251, 265, 268
Gregory, Margaret 133, 247
Gregory, Robert 78, 130–41 *passim*, 216, 241, 246–7
Grey de Wilton, Arthur Lord 99
Grierson, Herbert J. C. 15, 32, 150–4, 160–4, 166–9, 174, 202, 205, 215, 244, 248–50, 251–59, 263
Griffith, Arthur 26, 215–16
Grosart, Alexander B. 71, 230
Grossman, Allen R. 234
Gurd, Patty 231
Gwynn, Frederick 264
Gwynn, Stephen 253, 261
Gyles, Althea 94, 234, plate 7
Gyraldus of Ferrara, L. G. 261

Hallam, Arthur Henry 40, 56
Hanmer, Meredith 232
Harper, George 134, 170, 246, 252, 254, 259–61

Harris, Daniel 141, 244–5, 247, 256, 264
Harun al-Rasid 171, 176
Harwood, John 249
Hayward, John 265
Hebraism and Hellenism 34–6, 43, 45, 224
Helen 121, 151, 154, 157
Henley, William Ernest 2, 53
Henn, T. R. 163, 167, 179, 265–7
Henryson, Robert 212
Herbert, Auberon E. W. M. 52
Herbert, Edward, Lord Herbert of Cherbury
  The Autobiography 151, 161
Herbert, George 148, 151, 161, 166–7, 248, 252, 254–6
  'The Collar' 176–8, 257
  'Love II' 254
  'Sunday' 257
  'Virtue' 155
Herrick, Robert 110, 128, 147, 149, 161, 166, 201, 225, 245
  Hesperides 137, 250
  Noble Numbers 137
  'A Panegyrick to Sir Lewis Pemberton' 245
history 4–5, 32, 33, 34–6, 38–9, 41, 43–7, 48–9, 58–60, 105–6, 110, 120, 131, 153, 185–7, 207–12, 267
Hobbes, Thomas 187
Hoby, Thomas *see* Castiglione, Baldassare
Hogan, Robert 237
Holloway, Joseph 237
Homer 8, 121, 157, 251
Hone, Joseph 8, 116, 127, 220, 230–1, 242, 259
Hooker, Richard 148
Horace 5, 109, 126, 243, 260
Horniman, Annie 232, 240
Horton, W. T. 92–3, 193, 231, 261, plates 1a–2a
Hough, Graham 259–60
Howe, Ellic 234
Hugo, Victor 43
humour *see* wit
Hunt, Leigh 97, 229, 236

Huxley, Thomas Henry 52, 105
Hyde, Douglas 124
Hyde-Lees, Georgie *see* Yeats, George

imitation (or adaptation) xi, xii, 1, 5–11, 15, 18–19, 23–4, 28, 30–3, 50, 55–6, 66, 68, 70, 72, 77–8, 91, 101, 103–4, 110–13, 116–18, 120, 122–7, 141–5, 154, 179–84, 212–18, 232
  copying (perjorative) 7–8, 9, 10, 15, 40–1
  Platonic 'idea' 3, 10, 91, 115, 131; mimesis 47, 56, 58–9, 61, 91, 117, 122–4, 156–7, 159, 220
  prescriptive 5–7, 10–11, 29–30, 50, 57, 58–9, 91
  see also style, mask, personality, *and* simulacrum .
influence xi–xiii, 5, 12, 18–19, 28, 32, 51–2, 56, 57, 61, 65–6, 76–8, 148, 158, 162, 174, 184, 209, 232
  see also imitation *and* mediation
Innes, Christopher 241–2
'Intellectual Beauty' 68, 89–92, 94, 99, 233
Irish Academy of Letters 213–16, 218
Irish Independent, The 216, 267
Irish language and literature 3–8, 16, 29–30, 54–5, 56, 103, 165, 187
Irish literary revival 3–4, 7, 44, 53, 103, 110, 114, 131, 166
Irish Literary Theatre 112
Irish National Theatre Society 103

Jacapone da Todi 265
James I, King 106, 153
Japanese theatre 110–11, 114
  Noh 110, 118, 120, 241
Jeffares, A. Norman 64, 93, 157, 216, 219, 222, 227, 228, 229, 230, 243, 245, 260, 265
Jochum, K. P. S. 127, 245

Johannes Scotus Erigina 265
Johnson, Lionel 42, 56, 139, 148, 166, 249, 253
Johnson, Samuel 17, 143–4, 167, 221, 225, 247, 260
Johnston, Charles 72–3, 231–2
Joll, Evelyn 235
Jones, Inigo 114, 119
Jonson, Ben xi, xiii, 5–6, 18–28 *passim*, 42, 61, 69, 100, 102–42, 144–5, 147, 153–5, 167, 169, 172, 180, 219, 220, 222, 225, 237–49, 256
  Collections, plays, prose: *The Alchemist* 238; *Conversations with William Drummond* 105, 107, 248, 253; *Cynthia's Revels* 104, 107–8, 115, 117, 239; *Discoveries* 5, 9, 106–7, 115, 122, 153, 222, 238; *Epicoene* 109, 238; *Epigrams* 21, 121–3, 127, 222, 243; *The Forrest* 127, 179; *Hymenaei* 115, 117; *Masque of Blacknesse* 241; *Masque of Queenes* 241; *The New Inn* 21, 105; *The Poetaster* 102, 104, 108–10, 125–6, 238, 240, 244; *The Sad Shepherd* 79, 82, 106, 111; *The Under-wood* 22, 125, 127, 138, 167, 228, 238, 249, 258; *Volpone* 106, 112, 119, 179, 238
  individual poems: the Cary–Morison ode 132, 138–40; 'An Epistle Answering to One . . .' 110, 225; 'Euphemé 132, 167, 247, 255; 'A Fit of Rime against Rime' 22; 'My Picture Left in Scotland' 228; 'Ode *to himselfe*' 21, 125; 'Song. To Celia' 179; 'To Old-End Gatherer' 122–3; 'To Penshurst' 127; 'To Provle the Plagiary' 122
Jowett, B. 261
Joyce, James 228
Jusserand, J. J. 108, 239

Keane, Patrick J. 177–8, 180, 204, 252, 255, 256–58, 264–5
Keating, Geoffrey 87, 232
  Foras feasa an Éirinn 232
  Vindication of the Sources of Irish History 232
Keats, John 53, 55, 79, 97, 100, 164–5, 186, 234
Kelley, Edward 261
Kelly, John S. 237
Kenner, Hugh 244
Kermode, Frank 32, 137, 224, 246–7, 259, 267
Kilroy, James 237
King, Henry 255
King, Jessie M. 96, 236, plates 2b–3b
Kirk, Robert 165
Kleinstuck, J. 239
Knowland, A. S. 219
Kyd, Thomas
  Spanish Tragedy 121

Landor, Walter Savage 144, 151, 165–7, 188, 248, 251, 253–4, 259, 263
Lane, Hugh 212, 216
Langland, William 97, 212
Larminie, William 94, 265
Lavery, Hazel 216
Lavery, Sir John 216
Lawrence, D. H. 2
Lee, Sidney 240
Leicester, Earl of 133, 217, 235
Lentricchia, Frank 230
Leo, John (Leo Africanus) 259, 261
  A Geographical Historie of Africa 261
Lewis, C. Day 1
Litz, A. Walton 244, 258
Locke, Amy Audrey 193, 261
Locke, John 105, 187, 264
Loizeaux (Bergman), Elizabeth 92, 97, 234, 236, 242, 267
Longenbach, James 244
Lully, Raymond 148, 154
Lyly, John
  Campaspe 234

Lyster, T. W. 53, 61, 70–1, 79, 106, 228–9, 230, 265, 268
Lyttelton, (Lady) Edith 193

MacAodha, Breandan S. 245
Macaulay, Thomas 7
MacBride, John 154
MacDonagh, Thomas 5–6, 16, 219–20
Mackenna, Stephen 206, 253, 265
Macrobius 181, 183, 204
Magee, William K. 53, 228
magic 5, 38–9, 40–1, 44–7, 53, 77, 84, 88, 219, 234, 259–66 *passim*
  spiritual alchemy 32, 44, 146–60 *passim*, 249, 253, 261–3
Mahony, Christina Hunt 240–1
Mallarmé, Stéphane 149
Malory, Thomas 39
Mangan, Clarence 7
Marcus, Phillip 232, 262
Marionette, The (Florence) 118
Marlowe, Christopher 151, 168, 238, 239, 251
  Doctor Faustus 116, 121, 244
  Hero and Leander 100, 121
  The Jew of Malta 255
Marston, John 102, 104, 109, 239
  Antonio and Mellida 104
  The Dutch Cortezan 104
  Histriomastix 104
Martin, C. G. 219
Martin, Graham 140, 247
Martin Marprelate pamphlets 38
Martyn, Edward 112–13
Martz, Louis 163, 247
Marvell, Andrew 128, 202, 214–15, 256, 263–4
  'The Coronet' 264
  'The Definition of Love' 263
  'A Dialogue between the Resolved Soul and Created Pleasure' 168, 202–4, 264
  'A Dialogue between the Soul and Body' 168, 202–3, 205, 264
  'A Drop of Dew' 202, 204–5, 264
  'The Fair Singer' 263–4
  'The Gallery' 214–15, 263

Marvell, Andrew – *continued*
  'The Garden' 202, 205, 264
  'An Horatian Ode upon Cromwell's Return from Ireland' 264
  'The Last Instructions to a Painter' 215
  'The Nymph Complaining . . .' 264
  'The Picture of Little T. C. . . .' 263–4
  'Upon Appleton House' 248
Masefield, John 121, 148, 239
mask 2, 3, 25, 30, 55, 57–8, 59–61, 65, 66, 108, 110–11, 118, 193
  see also personality
Mask, The (Florence) 113, 118, 242
masque 102, 105–6, 110–18, 120, 238, 240–3
Masquer's Society, The 116–18, 242
Massinger, Philip 106
Mathers, MacGregor 192
Mayhew, George 219
McAlindon, T. 61, 138, 228, 245, 247
McClung, William A. 245
McCormack, W. J. 224, 245, 259
McFarland, Ronald E. 254
McGrath, F. C. 42, 47, 226, 227
Mead, G. R. S. 195
mediation xi, xii, 27–8, 32, 34–41, 41–51, 51–8, 66, 77–8, 107, 218
Medici, Lorenzo de' 44
Melchiori, Giorgio 180–1, 183, 258, 262, 264
Mercier, Vivian 219
Metaphysical poets *see under individual names*
metre 1–2, 11–15 *passim*, 66, 71–8, 123, 131, 138, 211, 246–7, 267–8; *see also* stanzas
Middleton, Thomas 239
Mill, John Stuart 52
Milton, John xi, xiii, 8–9, 31–3, 56, 59, 61, 64–6, 69, 127, 168, 184, 186–96, 199, 202, 206, 210—12, 228, 229, 256, 258–67

  poetry: 'Arcades' 64; *Comus* 204–6, 229, 262, 264; 'Il Penseroso' 64, 191, 195, 198, 209, 229, 262, 266; 'L'Allegro' 64, 229, 262; 'Lycidas' 85, 229; 'On the Morning of Christ's Nativity' 207–9, 262; *Paradise Lost* 64–5, 196, 209, 262, 265–6; tr. Psalm 5, 64
  prose: *Areopagitica* 130, 220, 244; *The Doctrine and Discipline of Divorce* 187, 192–4, 261; *Of Education* 220
'Miltonic rhetoric' 66, 109, 127, 186–7, 196, 207, 258–9
'Milton's Platonist' xiii, 191, 194–5, 197–8, 211, 261–4, 266, plate 9
Miner, Earl 137, 246
Mirandola, Pico della 45
modernism 1–2, 30–4, 53, 57–8, 65–6, 267
Molière (Jean-Baptiste Poquelin) 103, 119, 223
Montaigne, Michel de 107
Montgomery, 'Lynn Doyle' 216
Moore, George 113, 124–6, 260
Moore, T. Sturge 116, 222
moralities, interludes, pageants 118, 121, 243
More, Ann 167
More, Henry 45, 133, 146, 148, 165–6, 188, 195, 231, 233, 254
  'The Oracle' 206, 265
  Philosophical Poems 166, 265
  'Psychozoia' 166
Morgan, Paul 239
Morienus 148
Morley, Henry 112
Morris, William 7, 77, 251
Morton, Thomas 249
Moryson, Fynes 232
Mulcaster, Richard 9
Mulryne, J. R. 228
Murphy, Frank 229, 232
Murphy, William 227–8, 230–2
Murray, Gilbert 116, 242

Nashe, Thomas
  'Adieu, farewell Earth's Bliss' 151, 251–2
Nathan, Leonard E. 47, 227
Nelick, Frank C. 239, 242
Neoplatonism 4, 45, 84, 87–94, 133, 156, 180–1, 188, 193, 195, 204, 233
Nettleship, J. T. 228
Newman, John Henry 34
Newton, Isaac 187
Nichols, J. G. 244, 249
Nietzsche, Friedrich 245
Norstedt, Johann A. 220
North, Michael 198, 236, 263

O'Driscoll, Robert 57, 223, 244, 251, 256
O'Grady, Standish 87, 94
Ó hAodha, Micheál 69, 230
O'Higgins, Kevin 215–16
O'Leary, John 39, 53, 216
O'Neill, Michael J. 237
Ordish, Thomas 243
Orgel, Stephen 241
O'Shea, Edward 95, 234, 239, 249
Outlook, The 39–40, 225
Ovid 234

Pall Mall Gazette 48–9
Palmer, Samuel 97, 133, 188–9, 195, 198–9, 211, 261–2, 266, plate 9
Parkinson, Thomas 177, 213, 220, 244, 246, 257, 266
Parks, Aileen W. 219–20
Parks, Edd W. 219–20
Parrish, Stephen 256
Partridge, A. C. 243
'passionate syntax' 2, 8, 16, 24, 55–6, 210–11, 214, 266
Pater, Walter xiii, 33, 39, 41–52, 57, 60, 106, 115, 119, 127, 146, 149, 151, 188, 191, 194–5, 202, 225–7, 239, 241, 262
Peele, George 239
Peirce, Charles Sanders 230
Pembroke, Mary, Countess of
  'The Lay of Clorinda' 247

pensées 106–7, 131
Perloff, Marjorie 246, 248, 256–7
Perrine, Lawrence 253–4, 266
personality 10–12, 18, 28–30, 32, 42, 44–9 *passim*, 100, 104, 108–11, 152, 202, 243, 248
  character 29, 52, 54–5, 100, 110, 263
  'passionate personality' 21, 52, 56–8, 60–1, 100–11 *passim*, 210
  Renaissance spirit 11–12, 28, 35, 43–7, 50, 100, 105, 107, 111, 152–3, 243
  will 54–7, 57–8, 100
  see also style
Peterson, Richard S. 220
Petrarca, Francesco 69, 150, 223
pictorialism 73, 75–6, 87–101, 114–15, 122–3, 129–32, 140, 185–201, 206–18, 233–7, 260–2, 266–8
Plato and Platonism xi, xiii, 3, 8, 10, 18, 32, 35, 42, 45–7, 58–9, 61, 84, 87–94, 130–6, 143, 146, 148, 152–4, 156, 159, 164–6, 171–2, 188–98, 204–10, 220–1, 226–7, 233, 253–4, 259–68
Platonists, Cambridge 45, 133, 146, 148, 165–6, 188, 195, 231, 233, 253, 265
Plotinus 206, 233, 255, 262, 261
Plutarch 30
Poe, Edgar 74
Poel, William 113
Poems on Affairs of State 267
poetic drama 103, 110–120, 237–43
  see also masque *and* 'Theatre of Beauty'
poietes 5, 103
  see also vates
Pollexfen, George 139
Pope, Alexander 23, 128, 167
Porphyry 206, 209
Pound, Ezra 1–2, 32, 34, 110, 120, 125–7, 186, 210, 227, 244, 258–9, 267
Poussin, Nicolas 206
primum mobile 45, 62–3, 65

procession *see* Spenserian procession
Purcell, Henry 113
Puritanism 35–6, 38–9, 95, 99, 105–6, 186–7, 236–7, 262
Purohit Swami, Shree 210
Puttenham, George
  The Art of English Poesy 220
Putzel, Steven 234
Pye, John 234, plate 5
Pythagoras 3, 18, 45–6, 207–8, 236

Rabelais, Francis 222, 244
Raine, Kathleen 234, 260–1, 265
Rajan, Balachandra 223, 229, 254–5, 264
Raleigh, Sir Walter 211
Raphael (Raffaello Sanzio) 41, 206, 212
Rees, Thomas 244
Reeves, Marjorie 226
Reformation, The 35, 54
region *see* Hunt, Leigh
Renaissance 7, 11, 28–30, 33–6, 43, 45, 50, 56, 59, 60–1, 105, 110–11, 124, 153, 186–7, 210
  English 2–12 *passim*, 24, 30, 32–3, 35–6, 44–51, 54–60 *passim*, 70, 75, 100–1, 106, 111, 114, 120, 124, 144, 186, 212
  Italian 9, 24, 41–5, 50, 61, 114, 120, 124, 127, 130, 153, 207, 209–11, 238, 251
'Renaissance man' 28, 32, 44–51, 57–8, 59, 107, 111, 124, 133, 243
reverie 13, 60–3
  see also 'tragic joy' and *sprezzatura*
Reynolds, John C. 267
Rhymers' Club poets 28–30, 41–3, 45, 50–1, 54, 56–7, 104–6, 110, 112, 146, 166
Rhys, Ernest 104, 106, 237, 243
Ricketts, Charles 26–8, 119, 121, 137, 207, 223, 239
Ritvo, Rosemary Puglia 262
Rivers, Isabel 232–3
Robinson, Forrest G. 241
Robinson, Lennox 227, 257

'Rocky Face' 59, 228
Romaunt emblems 175
Ronsard, Pierre 19, 23–4, 222–3
Ronsley, Joseph 228, 264
Rosicrucianism *see* Golden Dawn
Rossetti, Dante Gabriel 8, 60, 151, 228
Roydon, Matthew
  'An Elegy, or Friends Passion for his Astrophill' 247
Ruskin, John 34, 60, 226, 235
Russell, George (AE) 11, 124, 167, 221
Rutland, Elizabeth, Countess of 179

Sacks, Peter 246
Saddlemyer, Ann 242
Sage, Lorna 226
Sainte-Beuve, Charles Augustin 60
St John, J. A. 261
St John of the Cross 149
Saintsbury, George 149, 154, 158, 160, 250, 252
Salvadori, Corinna 223
Sanderson, Robert 148
Saurat, Denis 196, 259, 262
Savoy, The 112, 254
Schepeler, Alexandra 259
Schmiefsky, Marvel 225
Schuchard, Ronald 224, 225, 240–2, 245
Scott, Walter 7
Selden, John
  Table Talk 107
Seneca 56
sententiae 17–18, 107
Sephiroth 93–4, 234, plates 6 and 7
Shakespear, Dorothy 258
Shakespear, Olivia 146–7, 154, 175–6, 178, 241, 249
Shakespeare, William 3, 7–8, 24, 27–8, 36, 44, 47–50, 52–5, 58–61, 63, 66, 69, 71, 81–2, 100, 102–3, 105, 107–10, 113–14, 118–20, 124, 127, 139, 144, 150, 210–11, 219, 229, 238–40, 244, 248, 266

Shakespeare, William – *continued*
  All's Well that Ends Well 252
  As You Like It 81–2
  Hamlet 119–21
  King Lear 204–5, 264
  Macbeth 252
  Richard III 129
  Romeo and Juliet 179
  'The Phoenix and the Turtle' 172–3
  Sonnets 216, 250, 268
  Timon of Athens 30
Shakespearean personae 27, 48–50, 58–60, 81–2, 204–5, 211, 264
Shannon, Charles 26, 223
Shaw, George Bernard 25, 260
Shaw, Martin 241
Shawcross, John T. 250
Sheba *see* Solomon
Sheil, Richard 80
Shelley, Percy Bysshe 4, 9, 12, 14, 53–5, 68–9, 71, 74, 76–81, 87–93, 96, 99–100, 107–8, 111, 133, 144–51, 167, 186, 188, 191, 198–9, 209–11, 220, 228–9, 230, 233, 239, 248, 260, 265
Sheridan, Richard Brinsley 103
Sicilians, The *see* Grassi, Giovanni
Sidnell, Michael 219
Sidney, Sir Philip 3, 9, 63, 98, 132–3, 137–8, 140, 150, 188, 216, 229, 250, 259
  Arcadia 134
  Astrophel and Stella 259
  Defence of Poesy 219, 220
simulacrum 103, 116–17, 120, 122–4, 126–7, 141
Sinnett, A. P. 232
Sitwell, Edith 1, 265
Skeat, Walter W. 261
Skelton, Robin 240
Smith, Pamela Coleman 116, 241
Smith, Stan 192, 194, 260, 262–3
Snukal, Robert 265
Solomon 50, 169, 171–3, 194
Somer, John 174, 257
Southey, Robert 168
Speaker, The 48, 113

Spencer, Herbert 52
Spenser, Edmund xiii, 6, 7, 12–14, 37–9, 49, 61, 64, 68–101, 104–8, 111, 132–8, 141, 144, 150, 184–8, 197, 204, 209, 211–18, 221, 229–37, 259, 264, 268
  gardens, isles, roses 83–7, 97, 100, 188, 195, 233, 264
  House of Temperance (Alma) 98–9, 188, 193, 236, plate 12
  works: *Amoretti* 69, 250; 'Astrophel' 78, 132–7, 187–8; *Daphnaida* 75; *Epithalamion* 96, 235; *Fowre Hymnes* 75, 88–91, 130, 234–5; *The Faerie Queene* 14, 73, 76–100 *passim*, 186, 188, 195, 213, 221, 231–7 *passim*, 264; *Mother Hubberd's Tale* 235; *Muiopotmos* 217, 236; 'Mutabilitie' cantos 185, 212; *The Ruines of Time* 75, 133, 217, 235; *The Shepheardes Calender* 78, 81, 85, 95–6, 134, 236; *Teares of the Muses* 234–5; *View of the Present State of Ireland* 232, 236; *Virgil's Gnat* 236
Spenserian procession (allegorical) 95–7, 99, 185–6, 212–18
  see also allegory
Spenserians, the 18, 134, 166, 221–2
sprezzatura 24–5, 29, 60, 223, 254
Stallworthy, Jon 178–9, 254, 258
Stanihurst, Richard 232
stanzas 16, 19–21, 69–78
  ballad 13, 73–4
  Cowleyan 137–40, 246–7
  ottava rima 9, 168–9, 173, 214, 256
  rime royal 74–5
  septet 73–4
  sonnet 24, 69, 72, 108, 125–7, 150
  Spenserian 72, 76–8, 92, 98–9
Steeves, G. Walter 239
Stein, Arnold 228

strangeness in beauty 114–15, 119–20, 121, 153, 241
style
  Baroque 17–18, 107, 144, 150, 221–2, 249
  development and practice xiii, 2, 4–5, 7, 10–30 *passim*, 32, 34, 51–67 *passim*, 72–8, 110–20 (dramatic), 121–7 (epigrammatic), 128–41 (elegiac), 142–83 (poetic idiom), 191
  Elizabethan 11–12, 17–18, 70, 221–2
  marriage of matter and manner 2, 4–5, 10–13, 16, 18, 23, 71, 110–11, 127, 132–45, 149–50, 169
  personality 11, 12, 18, 28–30, 60, 100
  voice 2–3, 5, 7, 11–15, 20–1, 23–4, 39, 54–7, 61, 66, 78–9, 100–1, 103–4, 100, 142, 151–2, 210–18 *passim*
Suckling, John 137
Super, R. H. 251
Surrey, Henry Howard, Earl of 150
Swedenborg, Emanuel 165, 262
Swift, Jonathan 167, 187, 199, 222, 259
Swinburne, Algernon Charles 60, 106, 125, 139, 151, 168, 225, 226, 238, 255
Symbolist poetic 33, 41–2, 43, 50–1, 149, 231, 267
Symonds, John Addington 106, 125, 139, 238–9
Symons, Arthur 42, 106, 112, 116, 148–50, 153, 160, 240, 250
Synge, John 22, 23, 25, 29, 55, 106, 139, 213, 217, 222, 259

Tarot 175–6, 192, 257
Taylor, Thomas 134, 188, 195, 206, 246
Tennyson, Alfred 33, 37, 40, 56, 60, 221, 266
Thilliez, Christine 242

'Theatre of Beauty' 110, 114–16, 118–20, 240–3
Theocritus 134, 187–8, 246
'thinking of the body' 14, 123, 153–4, 156, 162–3, 170, 255
Thompson, A. Hamilton 244
Thoor Ballylee castle 188, 197–200 *passim*, plates 10–11
Thorpe, Thomas 216, 268
Times, The (London) 27–8, 38–9, 49, 224–5
Tintoretto (Jacopo Robusti) 124
Titian (Tiziano Vecellio) 208, 212
Todhunter, John 111–12, 115–16, 230, 240–1
Tomlinson, Charles 248
Torchiana, Donald T. 187, 259, 261
Tourneur, Cyril 238
tradition 1–8 *passim*, 16–17, 31–2, 106–7, 118, 127, 130, 164, 187, 194, 204, 210–13, 218
  pastoral 3–4, 61–5, 76, 82–4, 97, 99, 128–41 *passim*, 207–10, 246, 259–62, 265–6
  see also history
'tragic joy' 50, 59–61, 63
  see also reverie, sprezzatura
Turner, J. M. W. 96–7, 234–5, plate 5
Turner, W. J. 1–2
Tutin, J. R. 166
Tuve, Rosemond 247, 268
Tynan, Katharine 85

Ungar, Leonard 244, 265
United Ireland 166
'unity of being' 32–3, 43–4, 51, 53, 143, 150, 256
Unterecker, John 243, 258
Upton, John 98, 236
Ure, Peter 109, 240, 246
Ussher, Arland 267

Van Dyck, Anthony 212
vates 3, 5, 220
  see also fili and *poietes*
Vaughan, Henry 148, 166–7, 173, 249, 256
  'Cock Crowing' 254
  'The Retreate' 167, 227

Vaughan, Thomas 166
    Coelum Terrae 254
    Euphrates or The Waters of the East 254
    Magica Adamica 254
Vendler, Helen 267–8
verse epistles 145, 161
Vickers, Clinton 240
Villon, Francois 166, 222
Virgil 97, 102, 109, 133, 136, 138, 187–8, 208, 234

Wagner, Richard 114
Waite, A. E. 148, 154, 232, 253–4, 257
Waller, Edmund 128, 137, 202, 215, 267
    'Instructions to a Painter' 215
    Penshurst poems 215
Walton, Izaak 148, 161
    The Compleat Angler 148
    Lives 148, 249–50
war of the theatres 24, 102–5
Ward, Adolphus 148
Ward, Richard 166
Warnke, Frank J. 144, 221–2, 248
Webster, John 238
Wellesley, Dorothy 210
Wells, H. G. 260
Whitaker, Thomas 264
Wilde, (Lady) Jane 219
Wilde, Oscar 111
Williamson, George 18, 222
Willy, Margaret 247
Wilson, F. A. C. 134, 180–1, 246, 258, 265
Wilson, George 228
wit 22–3, 29, 110, 143–4, 161–4, 172, 176, 215, 255
Wither, George 134, 166
Witt, Marion 229, 246–7
woman, the idea of 147, 150–4, 156–7, 172–3, 176–8, 252
Wordsworth, William 31, 54, 55, 56, 265
Worth, Katharine 241–2
Wotton, Henry 148, 161
Wright, Claude 232
Wyatt, Thomas 150

Yeats, Anne 176–7
Yeats, George 134, 164, 167, 169, 176–7, 188, 193–4, 197, 239, 257–8, 261, 264–5
Yeats, John Butler xiii, 47, 51–8, 61, 63, 65–6, 71, 84, 88, 106, 227–230, 238, 250
Yeats, William Butler
    general: antagonistic to science 53, 61, 63, 65, 105, 122–4, 144; anti-materialism 29–30, 34–8, 59, 105, 124; aptitude for science 53, 61, 63, 72, 77, 92; aristocratic values 2, 3–4, 24–5, 36–7, 60–1, 120, 125–41 *passim*; beginnings as a poet 13–15, 17, 51–4, 61–5, 68–87 *passim*; contradiction and dialectic 5, 31, 32–69 *passim*, 88, 104, 110, 120, 127, 131, 142–5, 147, 150, 162–4, 169, 194–6; early mentors 47, 51–8, 61, 63, 66–7, 70–2, 82–3; manliness 11–12, 17–18, 29–30, 50, 57, 90, 92–4, 107–8, 142–3, 150, 152, 214; originality 1–3, 5, 7, 12–13, 24, 38, 49, 71, 103, 124, 218; philosophy in poetry 2–5, 32–3, 42–7 *passim*, 51, 71, 78–87, 145–8, 153, 164–7, 187–8; post-1900 change in style 4, 5, 11–12, 16–25 *passim*, 58–9, 68, 142, 151–2; racial ideology and nationalism 37–41, 53, 95, 261; Victorian affinities and antipathies 33–58 *passim*, 129
    plays: *At the Hawk's Well* 110, 241; *The Countess Cathleen* 113; *The Death of Cuchulain* 262; *Deirdre* 242; *Four Plays for Dancers* 118; *The Golden Helmet* 121; *The Green Helmet: An Heroic Farce* 121; *The Hour-Glass* 4, 118, 120–1, 219, 242; *The Island of Statues* 64, 69, 71, 76, 79–

Yeats, William Butler – *continued*
    plays – *continued*
        87, 97, 111, 209, 229; *the King's Threshold* 3, 4, 116, 219; *Mosada* 111; *On Baile's Strand* 118; *The Only Jealousy of Emer* 200–1; *The Player Queen* 4, 5, 118–19, 121; *Plays for an Irish Theatre* 113–14; *The Shadowy Waters* 4, 128, 219, 241
    published poetry – collections: *The Collected Poems* 257; *The Countess Kathleen and Various Legends and Lyrics* 41, 68, 87; *The Green Helmet and Other Poems* 19, 129, 131, 137, 141, 145, 147, 151, 154, 162, 222, 252; *In the Seven Woods* 121, 128; *Last Poems and Plays* 206; *New Poems* 180, 267; *Nine Poems* 164; *Poems* (1895) 63, 87; *Poems, 1899–1905* 152; *The Poetical Works* (1906) 146, 150; *Responsibilities* 154, 162, 243–5; *The Tower* 141, 147, 174, 178, 257; *The Wanderings of Oisin and Other Poems* 4, 41, 63, 85; *The Wild Swans at Coole* 134, 164, 166; *The Wind Among the Reeds* 146–8, 150, 154, 249–50; *The Winding Stair* 141, 147, 167, 174, 178, 181
    published poetry – groups and sequences: 'Crossways' 251; 'A Man Young and Old' 174–6, 178, 250, 257; 'Momentary Thoughts' 129, 131, 141, 145, 155; 'Raymond Lully and his Wife Pernella' 131, 141, 145, 151, 154, 157, 250; 'The Rose' 68, 87, 92–3; 'A Woman Young and Old' 174, 176–84, 250, 257; 'Words for Music Perhaps' 173, 178, 250
    published poetry – individual poems: 'An Acre of Grass' 266; 'Adam's Curse' 152, 172, 252; 'Against Unworthy Praise' 121, 155, 222; 'All Souls' Night' 175; 'All Things can Tempt me' 222; 'Among School Children' 8, 169, 267; 'An Appointment' 124; 'At the Abbey Theatre' 23–4, 26, 34, 124; 'At Galway Races' 137, 140; 'Blood and the Moon' 196, 199–201; 'Byzantium' 163, 167, 254, 264; 'The Choice' 173–4; 'Chosen' 179–84, 202, 204, 258; 'The Circus Animals' Desertion' 169; 'The Cold Heaven' 162–4, 170; 'The Coming of Wisdom with Time' 222; 'Coole Park, 1929' 127, 131, 169; 'Consolation' 178; 'Coole Park and Ballylee, 1931' 127, 131, 169, 173; 'Crazy Jane and Jack the Journeyman' 178; 'Crazy Jane on the Day of Judgement' 173, 256; 'Cuchulain Comforted' 201; 'The Delphic Oracle upon Plotinus' 208; 'Dedication' 213–14; 'A Dialogue of Self and Soul' 168, 202–5; 'A Drinking Song' 222; 'Easter 1916' 215–16, 220; 'Ego Dominus Tuus' 5, 17, 164–5, 193, 204, 221, 253; 'The Empty Cup' 174–6, 182, 257; 'Fallen Majesty' 162–3; 'The Fascination of What's Difficult' 18–24, 26, 121, 222; 'Father and Child' 176–8, 257, 266–7; 'A First Confession' 178, 181; 'The Folly of Being Comforted' 243; 'Fragments' 264; 'Friends' 162–3; 'A Friend's Illness' 21, 155; 'From

Yeats, William Butler – *continued*
published poetry – individual – *continued*
"Oedipus at Colonus"' 176; 'The Gift of Harun Al-Rashid' 171; 'The Grey Rock' 137, 225; 'The Gyres' 60, 169, 180, 228; 'The Harp of Aengus' 188; 'He wishes his Beloved were dead' 147, 151; 'Her Dream' 178–9, 257; 'Her Vision in the Wood' 169; 'His Bargain' 178–9, 250, 257; 'His Confidence' 250; 'His Dream' 157, 250; 'His Memories' 250; 'His Wildness' 250; 'I walked the seven woods of Coole' 128; 'An Image from a Past Life' 253; 'In Memory of Eva Gore-Booth and Con Markiewicz' 258; 'In Memory of Major Robert Gregory' 132, 136–41, 167, 216, 246, 249, 255; 'King and No King' 121, 156–7; 'The Lake Isle of Innisfree' 16, 87; 'Lapis Lazuli' 59, 256, 266; 'Leda and the Swan' 121; 'The Living Beauty' 170–1, 173, 175–6, 256; 'Long-legged Fly' 121; 'The Lover tells of the Rose in his Heart' 147; 'Love's Loneliness' 178, 257; 'The Man who Dreamed of Faeryland' 87; 'Meditations in Time of Civil War' 169, 196–200, 263; 'A Memory of Youth' 162; 'Michael Robartes and the Dancer' 172–3, 253; 'The Moods' 16; 'The Mother of God' 246; 'The Mountain Tomb' 162; 'The Municipal Gallery Revisited' 169, 186, 212–18, 266–8; 'The New Faces' 131, 245; 'News for the Delphic Oracle' 206–10, 265–6; 'Nineteen Hundred and Nineteen' 168; 'No Second Troy' 121, 157–8, 251; 'Oil and Blood' 201; 'The Old Stone Cross' 266; 'On hearing that the Students . . .' 124, 222; 'On those that hated "The Playboy of the Western World", 1907' 25–8, 124, 215, 223; 'On Woman' 172; 'Parting' 179–84, 202, 250, 258; 'Paudeen' 37, 124; 'Peace' 121, 157, 251; 'The Phases of the Moon' xiii, 99, 134, 188–96, 198–200, 204, 259–63; 'The Players ask for a Blessing . . .' 112; 'The Poet pleads with the Elemental Powers' 147; A Poet to his Beloved' 16; 'A Prayer for my Daughter' 127, 246; 'The Protestant's Leap . . . A Cromwellian Speaks' 237; 'Reconciliation' 156, 176; 'The Rose of the World' 251; 'The Sad Shepherd' 63, 64; 'Sailing to Byzantium' 167, 169, 205, 254, 264; 'The Scholars' 9–10, 243; 'The Second Coming' 106, 127, 139; 'The Secret Rose' 94, 232; 'The Seeker' 76, 79, 94; 'September 1913' 215–16; 'Shepherd and Goatherd' 99, 132–8, 140–1, 187, 195, 216, 246–7; 'Sixteen Dead Men' 221; 'Solomon and the Witch' 172–3, 253; 'Solomon to Sheba' 171, 253; 'A Song' 170; 'Song of the Happy Shepherd' 61–5, 229, 264; 'The Statues' 266; 'The Stolen Child' 87; 'That the Night Come' 162; 'These are the Clouds' 137, 140, 243; 'Time and the Witch Vivien' 71, 111; 'To a

Yeats, William Butler – *continued*
published poetry – individual – *continued*
Child Dancing in the Wind' 162; 'To a Friend whose Work has come to Nothing' 124, 126; 'To a Poet . . .' 124, 222, 243; 'To an Isle in the Water' 87; 'To a Wealthy Man . . .' 37, 124, 130, 216; 'To a Young Beauty' 144, 166, 170, 251, 253; 'To a Young Girl' 170; 'The Tower' 127, 196–7, 246, 256, 263; 'Two Years Later' 162; 'Under the Moon' 188–9; 'Under the Round Tower' 170; 'Upon a Dying Lady' 132, 167, 255; 'Upon a House shaken by the Land Agitation' 21, 128–30; 'Veronica's Napkin' 178, 257; 'The Wanderings of Oisin' 16–17; 'When Helen Lived' 121, 162; 'When You are Old' 23; 'While I, from that reed-throated whisperer' 124–7; 'The White Birds' 87; 'The Wild Old Wicked Man' 212; 'A Woman Homer Sung' 121, 157, 251; 'Words' 158–60, 252
published prose – books and journals: *Autobiographies* 16, 30, 31, 40–1, 42, 51, 64, 66, 68, 70, 77, 79, 94, 100, 104–5, 108, 117, 142, 144, 149, 187, 212, 224, 228, 229, 240, 248, 256, 266; *Beltaine* 112–13, 241; *The Celtic Twilight* 251; *Collected Works* (VIII) 107; *Discoveries* (I and II) 28, 51, 102, 106–9, 117, 123–4, 131, 153–4, 156, 160, 237–9, 243, 250, 252, 259; *Estrangement* 212, 228; *Ideas of Good and Evil* 48, 224, 225; *Letters to the New Island* 44, 106, 109, 111–12, 238; *Memoirs* 19–24, 25–6, 30, 50, 56, 66, 108, 125–6, 128, 147, 157–9, 222, 224, 228, 229, 238, 252–3; *On the Boiler* 238, 251; *Pages from a Diary* . . . 2, 239; *Per Amica Silentia Lunae* 5, 108, 133, 139, 143–4, 164–5, 195, 201, 231, 233, 248, 253, 262; *Poetry and Ireland* 148; *Reveries over Childhood and Youth* 51; *Samhain* 7–8, 25, 103, 106, 113, 115, 120, 238, 239; *The Secret Rose* 93–4, 148, 151, 234, plate 7; *Senate Speeches* 187, 220; *Uncollected Prose* 56, 71–2, 79, 103, 106, 113–15, 120, 148, 187, 195, 228, 232, 239, 241–2; *A Vision* 3, 45–1, 55–6, 68, 108, 144, 149–50, 165, 167, 172, 178, 185–7, 193–6, 201, 207–10, 212, 239, 260–3, 265
published prose – individual essays, etc.: 'At Stratford-on-Avon' 36, 44, 47–50; 'The Body of the Father Christian Rosencrux' 31, 44, 224; 'The Celtic Element in Literature' 40, 224, 225; 'Certain Noble Plays of Japan' 120; 'The Controversy over *The Playboy* . . .' 119; 'Dust Hath Closed Helen's Eye' 251; 'Edmund Spenser' 11–12, 37–8, 41, 47, 49, 77–8, 86, 95–101, 121, 133, 185–7, 217, 238; 'A General Introduction for my Work' 2–3, 7, 12, 16, 24, 66, 106, 130, 201, 211; 'I Became an Author' 72; 'Introduction' to *A Book of Images* 93; 'J. M. Synge and the Ireland of his Time' 8, 55, 194, 261; 'Literature and the Living Voice' 151–3; 'My Friend's Book' 262; 'A

Yeats, William Butler – *continued*
published prose – individual – *continued*
People's Theatre' 8, 110; 'The Philosophy of Shelley's Poetry' 12, 199; 'A Poetic Drama' 238; 'Poetry and Tradition' 28, 57, 60–1, 264; 'Rosa Alchemica' 42, 112, 117, 148, 195, 239, 251; 'Speaking to the Psaltery' 116, 240; 'Swedenborg, Mediums, and the Desolate Places' 45, 165, 262; 'Symbolism in Painting' 92; 'The Symbolism of Poetry' 44, 57, 239, 251; 'The Theatre of Beauty' 113–14; 'The Tragic Theatre' 113, 119; 'The Well of the Saints' 7; 'What Is "Popular Poetry"?' 7, 106, 238; 'Witches and Wizards and Irish Folk-lore' 165, 226, 262
published works – editions: *The Oxford Book of Modern Verse* 1, 264; *Poems of Spenser* 37, 48, 49, 77, 91, 95–101, 103, 105–6, 129–30, 133, 185, 217, 233–6; *The Poems of William Blake* (1893) 41, 225; *Ten Principal Upanishads* 210–11; *The Works of William Blake* (with Edwin Ellis) 41, 225
unpublished works: 'Art without imitation' 122–3, 243; 'Contemporary Irish Theatre' 29; 'The Dell' 221; 'The Flame of the Spirit' 146; 'A flower has blossomed . . .' 70; 'Friends of My Youth' 29–30, 56–7, 110; 'Inscription for a christmas card' 13–15, 221; 'Morning' 179–84, 258; 'Opening Ceremony for The Masquers' 117–18; 'Pan' 266; 'Sansloy – sansfoy – sansjoy' 73–6; 'The Theatre' 28, 29, 223; 'When two its end o'er rippened july nears' 73–9, 92; untitled aphorism 17; untitled Solomon and Sheba poem 171–2
correspondence 1, 11, 26, 48, 54, 56, 66, 70, 72, 86, 102–3, 107, 109, 112–13, 116, 119, 133, 140, 143, 160, 162, 169, 175–6, 181, 187–8, 194, 210, 214–17, 230, 236, 237–8, 241–2; unpublished 6, 219, 223, 229, 242
Young, Dudley 219